W9-DDO-369

14.95
SoP

Abortion and Catholicism

"Abortion and Catholicism"

The American Debate

Edited by
Patricia Beattie Jung
and
Thomas A. Shannon

HQ 767.3
.A252

(seab)

CROSSROAD • NEW YORK

The United Library
Garrett-Evangelical/Seabury-Western Seminaries
2121 Sheridan Road
Evanston, IL 60201

1988

The Crossroad Publishing Company
370 Lexington Avenue, New York, N.Y. 10017
Copyright © 1988 by Patricia Beattie Jung and Thomas A. Shannon
All rights reserved. No part of this book may be reproduced,
stored in a retrieval system, or transmitted, in any form
or by any means, electronic, mechanical, photocopying,
recording or otherwise, without the written permission of
The Crossroad Publishing Company.

Printed in the United States of America

Library of Congress Cataloging-in-Publication Data

Abortion and Catholicism : the American debate / edited by Patricia
Beattie Jung and Thomas A. Shannon.
   p. cm.
   Bibliography: p.
   ISBN 0-8245-0884-X
   1. Abortion—Religious aspects—Catholic Church. 2. Abortion—
Political aspects—United States. 3. Abortion—United States—
Public opinion. 4. Public opinion—United States. I. Jung,
Patricia Beattie. II. Shannon, Thomas A. (Thomas Anthony), 1940–

HQ767.3.A25 1988
241'.6976—dc19
                                    88-362
                                    CIP

Contents

Part II Abortion: The Political Debate

Part III Abortion: The Ecclesial Debate

Introduction

A heated debate over abortion has been raging in the United States for well over a decade. The 1973 *Roe v. Wade* Supreme Court decision resulted in the removal of restrictive policies on abortion in the vast majority of states and a total decriminalization of abortion in all states. Reactions against this liberalization and the strategies employed by its opponents are detailed in various articles in this collection.

Today the debate is entering a phase of heightened intensity. Many are calling for a constitutional amendment prohibiting abortion, restrictions on federal funds for abortion and abortion counseling, and the restructuring of the Supreme Court as a means of repealing *Roe v. Wade.* Many others are just as determined not to permit any change in the status quo.

One major issue in the debate over abortion is the sheer volume of abortions performed in this country annually. For about ten years the number has hovered around 1.5 million per year. Another issue is the large number of abortions obtained by teenagers.[1] The huge quantity of abortions performed annually have brought many people into the antiabortion camp or made them more sympathetic to that perspective.

The 1984 presidential election campaign gave the abortion debate an additional level of intensity. Many felt, for example, that abortion was *the* issue of the campaign. Frequently one's position on abortion became the litmus test of acceptability for many other issues. Indeed, some argued that if candidates did not vote "the right way" on abortion, then they would not be supported at all. Finally, many prochoice Catholic candidates in various elections found themselves directly or indirectly attacked by members of the Catholic community. These elements gave the campaign a particularly bitter dimension.

During this same election campaign, Catholics for Free Choice, an organization based in Washington, D.C., placed a full-page advertisement in the *New York Times* signed by more than one hundred Catholics. They claimed that there is no univocal position on abortion in the Catholic Church. Almost immediately the Vatican responded with a demand that the religious and clerical signers of the ad formally retract their signatures and publicly affirm the official Catholic position on abortion. Irrespective of whether more clarity or confusion about the debate was triggered by this ad, clearly some American Catholics were willing to make a previously in-house argument privy to the general public.

The debate about abortion crosses religious, moral, political, ideological, and

1

regional lines. No individual group or organization in the country is immune from at least some aspects of the debate. The Catholic Church is no exception. Catholics are among those who procure abortions and who support its availability for others. While these activities are less widely practiced among Catholics than by the population as a whole, they do not conform to magisterial teaching.[2] This discrepancy may in part reflect a gap between principle and practice. Christians have never claimed they could perfectly embody all that they should. Even in the apostolic church many found the Spirit to be willing but the flesh weak. However, it would be a mistake to reduce all dissent among Catholics to moral weakness. Many practicing Catholics do not adhere to all of the church's moral teachings because in good conscience they do not agree with them. There is within the Catholic Church a genuine debate about abortion and we have collected in this volume essays representative of that debate in the United States.

CLARIFICATION OF PERSPECTIVES

In this anthology, we have collected numerous articles which we think best articulate the various perspectives on abortion constitutive of the Catholic debate. We recognize that our selection of articles implicitly validates the abortion debate. In fact, we think it is extremely important to present, confront, and evaluate the various components of this debate.

First, it is clear to us that few, if any, abortions will be prevented simply because the practice has been prohibited by an ecclesial authority. The days of blind obedience to and unexamined conformity with the moral teachings of the Catholic Church seem to have passed. Even though such a situation may be accompanied by confusion and error, moral maturation should not be stunted because we wish to avoid the pain of moral adulthood. Second, Catholics in fact obtain abortions and that fact needs to be examined and evaluated. Third, some arguments in favor of abortion have at least a *prima facie* validity for many people. The merits of these dissenting arguments need to be evaluated. Moral consensus cannot be imposed upon disputants. It must be forged by the faithful through thoughtful discussion and prayerful reflection. Fourth, women religious and Catholic lay women are speaking up on the abortion question, expressing both prolife and prochoice positions. As their full membership in the church is recognized, room must be made for their distinctive perspectives. Finally, the entire Roman Catholic perspective on matters of sexual morality is being challenged and the resolution on this dispute will have a profound impact on the abortion question.

From our perspective, then, it is important to provide participants in this debate with a full spectrum of viewpoints on abortion so that discussion can be conducted in a responsible manner. The articles selected focus on various aspects of this debate and we have provided the reader with a wide range of perspectives on key issues. We think it is important not only to provide the traditional or magisterial position on abortion but also critiques of it, articulations of it from different perspectives, and essays that raise concerns not directly addressed by the mainline tradition. Within this context we hope that the key moral and religious perspectives on abortion will receive a thorough examination.

CONTROVERSIAL ISSUES

While all dimensions of the abortion debate are controversial, some are more so than others. The following issues are in need of special examination.

Whether abortion can be debated at all by Catholics is perhaps the most controversial of all issues. Many, within and without the magisterium, consider abortion to be a closed topic. The magisterial teaching is clear, it is repeated frequently, and it has a long tradition associated with it. Thus for many the matter is settled and cannot be debated. Despite this, some Catholics in fact have raised questions about both the method used to resolve the problem and the quality of the arguments which support the teaching. While the antiabortion tradition is a long one, there are many Catholics who believe dimensions of it need reformulation. More radically, some Catholics simply reject the traditional teaching altogether.

The fact is that there is a debate on abortion within the Catholic Church. To continue to deny its presence will be counterproductive. Such communal arguments are buried only at great cost to the strength and vitality of its individual members. To say this is not *a priori* to validate abortion or legitimate its practice. It is simply a common-sense position that recognizes that to deny the debate will only prolong its presence and intensify the harm that it has already engendered.

The status of the fetus is another highly controversial topic. While none of the authors we present take the radical position that the fetus is a piece of tissue to be disposed of as one wishes, some reject the position that it has the absolute, inviolable value affirmed by the magisterium. Some of the articles here illustrate how various scholars approach the fetus and evaluate its status.

Even if some consensus on the status of the fetus is achieved, debate continues about what levels of protection and nurturance it ought to have. The issues here are whose rights take precedence and what may legitimately be required of mothers during pregnancy. How these are to be resolved is a matter of great controversy both within and without the Catholic Church.

Finally, public-policy perspectives on abortion raise many controversial issues regarding the relation of ethics and law, religion and government, church and state, and the appropriateness and feasibility of various public policies. The issue of the "seamless garment ethic" is one way to address many of these topics, but not all have found this approach helpful. However, the "seamless garment ethic" has opened up fruitful areas of discussion within the Catholic Church as well as engendering claims that this formulation detracts from the emphasis that should be placed on abortion.

While not exhaustive, these disputed areas provide a thematic unity for many of the articles in this book. While some focus more on one aspect of the debate than others, all the articles in some fashion touch on all aspects of the debate.

ESTABLISHING PARAMETERS FOR THE DEBATE

We think the articles we have selected are representative of the basic lines of the abortion debate within the Roman Catholic Church. However, some lines of argumentation are not represented. Perspectives from the radical right and left, for example, are omitted, as well as purely ideological or authoritarian pronouncements. What we seek to present is the middle ground of the abortion debate, where and on what basis positions differ, and what premises might be held in common by authors who differ nonetheless with respect to their conclusions. Our basic point is that on both sides of the debate it is possible to develop reasonable arguments based on commonly held principles. Thus we focus on the middle ground—where the arguments are both more responsible, more complex, and often not that far apart.

The debate has caused tremendous distress and raised difficulties for many individuals, both publicly and privately. Yet until this issue is faced and resolved on grounds other than authoritative pronouncements that many find unconvincing, the problem will remain and so will the debate. The articles presented, then, make a first step at structuring the debate and establishing some parameters for it.

HOW THIS BOOK IS ORGANIZED

We have divided this anthology into three parts, focusing in each one on a major aspect of the debate: moral, political, and ecclesial.

The Moral Debate

We have chosen the teaching of the magisterium as the starting point for our section. While on the one hand the position of the magisterium is clear—all direct abortions are prohibited—aspects of that teaching are debated. Thus we begin with defenses of that perspective.

Other perspectives on and articulations of that teaching follow, especially those that focus on the moral status of fetal life. Certainly one's position on abortion is significantly shaped by one's view of the fetus. Additionally, we think it is most critical to hear the voices of women on this topic. They, after all, are the ones who become pregnant, carry the pregnancy, and, in most cultures, bear primary responsibility for child rearing. Thus women have a high level of responsibility in all dimensions of the reproductive process and coincident with this responsibility have a privileged voice in this matter and a special claim on the formation of our communal conscience.

The Political Debate

The public policy debate is critical because it touches on the problem of the establishment of rights and their social implementation and protection. Thus the question of what public services, if any, ought be available to women facing problematic pregnancies is a matter of critical debate. Additionally there is the problem of how a Catholic politician should articulate his or her beliefs on abortion and then relate them to public policy, whether established or newly proposed.

The Ecclesial Debate

Two aspects of the current abortion debate are somewhat unique to the Catholic context. Within the church there is considerable discussion about the relationship of this prohibition to other moral teachings regarding life issues. The concern is for moral consistency or integrity. Also unique to the Catholic context is the assessment of abortion as part of a broader debate in Catholicism about the role and authority of the magisterium, the relation of the theologian to the magisterium, and the nature and legitimacy of dissent within the church. Thus while the specific topic under consideration is abortion, that discussion is going on in a wider context and may in fact serve as the occasion for debating other issues. In part 3 we attend to two of these broader issues as they relate to abortion.

CONCLUSION

Why We Do Not Want to Do This Book

To sign one's name to anything on abortion leaves one open to the possibility of all sorts of vilification. And to accept the idea of the validity of a debate on abortion, at least by implication, is clearly to ask for trouble. Files have been started on individuals for less than the simple task of editing a book. Censorship is having an unfortunate revival and is casting a rather chilling pall over both writing and publishing. Younger teacher-scholars are legitimately concerned about how the content of their teaching and publishing will influence their candidacy for tenure at Catholic colleges and universities.

We have been personally involved in various debates on the abortion question, and those situations have not been particularly pleasant. We realize that by editing this book we are opening ourselves to a variety of labels and allegations. The prospect of having our names identified with this topic does not *prima facie* appear to be too pleasant. We have even decided not to dedicate this book to any person or group because of problems this may cause.

Why We Are Doing This Book

Yet there is a debate on abortion within the Catholic Church. One can wish it were not there, one can pretend that it is not there, and one can command it to go away. But it hasn't and probably won't go away. The dispute over abortion and its practice by Catholics is real and goes deep within the Catholic community.

We are convinced that only open, honest, and respectful dialogue will bring the Catholic community to some resolution of this problem. Thus we present this book as a first step in the initiation of such a dialogue. We assume the dialogue will be vigorous and spirited—as it should be. But we hope that the discussion can be carried forward in a manner that is respectful of the consciences and persons of all its participants.

NOTES

1. Elise F. Jones and others, "Teenage Pregnancy in Developed Countries: Determinants and Policy Implications," *Family Planning Perspectives* 17 (Mar./Apr. 1985) 53ff.

2. For a presentation of some statistical data on Catholics and abortion, confer F. S. Jaffee, B. L. Lindheim, and P. R. Lee, *Abortion Politics: Private Morality and Public Policy* (New York: McGraw Hill, 1981) 105ff.; also D. Grangerg and B. W. Grangerg, "Abortion Planning Perspectives, 1965–1980: Trends and Determinants," *Family Planning Perspectives* 12 (Sept./Oct. 1980) 250.

Part I

Abortion:
The Moral Debate

Chapter 1

Perspectives on Church Teaching

This first chapter situates the debate by presenting an overview of the magisterial position together with discussions of various aspects of it. We selected testimony by Roach and Cooke because it situates the teaching historically, discusses its personal and social applications, and takes the teaching into a political context by arguing for a constitutional amendment. Thus the testimony gives a point of reference for the ensuing debate on the traditional teaching and situates well the political aspects of the debate.

In his essay, O'Donnell briefly summarizes the traditional Catholic view that a human person is (or, at least, probably is) present from the moment of conception. This essay sets in bold relief a central feature of the debate. Donceel's article reviews what he calls a "minority Catholic position" according to which a human person is not yet present in the very early stages of pregnancy. The parameters of the debate about fetal life are outlined by these two articles. Within this framework, the Tauer essay explores in great detail the moral implications of probabilism as an appropriate methodology for resolving some of the uncertainties about the status of early embryonic life that are generated by contemporary reproductive biology. In the Cahill essay, the tendency of political liberalism to circumvent the question of the status of prenatal life is examined, along with the tendency of modern dualism to ignore the significance of corporeality in the resolution of this question.

Testimony in Support of the Hatch Amendment

Archbishop John R. Roach and Cardinal Terence Cooke

The National Conference of Catholic Bishops has testified before congressional subcommittees on two previous occasions on the subject of abortion and the need for a human life amendment: March 7, 1974, before the subcommittee on constitutional amendments of the Senate Committee on the Judiciary; and March 24, 1976, before the subcommittee on civil and constitutional rights of the House Committee on the Judiciary.

Neither in 1974 nor in 1976 was any version of a human life amendment reported out of committee and voted on by Congress. As a result this issue has not been brought before the state legislatures for their own determination. It is our fervent hope that this subcommittee and this Congress will show their respect for the democratic process by making it possible for the elected representatives of the American people to consider such a constitutional amendment.

In our previous testimony we have commented on a great many aspects of the abortion debate.

In 1974, we presented a wealth of evidence on the humanity and dignity of the unborn child. We pointed to the American legal tradition which recognizes the inherent right to life of all human beings and noted that until the Supreme Court stripped virtually all legal protection from the unborn child the life of that child was seen as deserving of legal protection. We noted the virtually absolute character of the right to abortion created by the court, which gave the unborn child no recourse or appeal under the law. The conclusion reached in that testimony was:

> After much consideration and study, we have come to the conclusion that the only feasible way to reverse the decision of the court and to provide some constitutional base for the legal protection of the unborn child is by amending the Constitution. Moreover, this is a legal option consistent with the democratic process. It reflects the commitment to human rights that must be at the heart of all human law, international as well as national, and because human life is such an eminent value, the effort to pass an amendment is a moral imperative of the highest order.

On March 24 of this year the NCCB Administrative Committee voted unanimously to reaffirm this 1974 statement.

In 1976 our testimony concentrated on reactions to the Supreme Court's abortion decisions and on the early effects those decisions had on law and society. By that time many distinguished legal scholars, representing a wide variety of views on abortion itself, had criticized the 1973 decisions as having little or no basis in the Constitution or in American legal history. Preliminary statistics suggested that legalization did increase the number of abortions performed by making abortion more easily available and more socially acceptable. This situation produced its own threats to women's lives and health while failing to put an end to illegal abortions.

The abortion mentality was already helping to erode some physicians' respect for human life in other spheres, most noticeably in the treatment of handicapped newborns who could be classified as falling below someone's standard of "meaningful humanhood." At that time we condemned as patronizing and sometimes punitive the attitude that "abortion is good enough for the poor," as well as the general tendency to see the quick and violent "solution" of abortion as the answer to a variety of social ills which have their own appropriate and infinitely more humane solutions.

We renewed our criticism of the abortion decisions themselves, observing that they had created a "new legalism . . . destructive of the human spirit." The Supreme Court had imposed this "new legalism" by replacing the facts about the beginnings of human life with new legal fictions and by failing even to recognize many of the individual and social values at stake in public policy decisions on abortion. By isolating the pregnant woman in her "right of privacy," the court had done a disservice both to her and to her child, cutting them off from the familial and societal bonds which can support and encourage life-affirming attitudes.

We responded to the claim that laws restricting abortion constitute an establishment of religion or a denial of religious freedom, pointing out that the idea of abortion as an affirmative good is a novelty created by the Supreme Court and not one maintained by any major religious denomination. While noting the complexity of the abortion issue and agreeing that it has moral and religious dimensions, we reasserted our conviction that legal protection for the unborn child can be based on a respect for human dignity and fundamental human rights commonly held by people of good will regardless of their religious affiliation.

Without repeating our 1974 and 1976 testimony in detail, we wish to take this opportunity to reaffirm our continued adamant opposition to the current public policy on abortion and our conviction that a constitutional amendment is necessary to correct this unjust and destructive policy. During the past five years there have been a number of developments which strengthen the case on behalf of an amendment. In addition, the arguments put forth to defend legalized abortion have changed in some ways, requiring new responses. These recent developments will be noted during the course of this testimony, which will address four important aspects of the abortion controversy:

First, the central issue of the human dignity of the unborn child, with special emphasis on the complementary roles which scientific evidence and ethical insight can play in appreciating this dignity.

Second, a review of Western and specifically American legal traditions on human rights and the protection of unborn human life, with comments on the ways in which the reasoning of the Supreme Court's abortion decisions distorted and weakened those traditions.

Third, the legal and social effects of *Roe v. Wade* upon American life.

Fourth, the issue of the relationship between law and morality as it applies to the abortion issue.

THE HUMAN DIGNITY OF
THE UNBORN CHILD

In 1974 and 1976, we cited a wealth of scientific literature to show that individuated human life begins at conception—that is, that a unique human individual comes into existence when male sperm and female ovum successfully unite, and that all subsequent stages of development are simply phases in the continuous process of maturation into an adult human being. No new evidence has been found to contradict this simple fact and a great deal of evidence has accumulated to confirm it. The testimony presented on this matter before the Senate subcommittee on separation of powers April 23 of this year [1981] presents a small sample of the evidence available. The federal government itself officially acknowledges the biological facts on this point. A 1979 publication of the Department of Health and Human Services reports:

> Life is a constantly evolving process that begins with conception and continues until death. Movement through time necessitates change and therefore is synonymous with life itself; the opposite state is stasis and death. . . . With the passage of time, the human organism grows from a single cell to a fully developed adult. . . . Life begins when a male sperm unites with a female egg. The new life created by this union starts as a single cell. . . . In relation to the total life span of the individual, the early developmental years are short and serve as the foundation for the remainder of one's life span. The needs of a child in the support of this growth and development begin before birth and continue throughout the growth years until maturity is reached.[1]

The development of new biological techniques has served to underscore the fact that a new human life begins at conception.

Despite the lack of a moral and legal consensus on the advisability of human *in vitro* fertilization experiments, there is consensus on one point: Baby Louise Brown, born in England in 1978, attracted so much publicity because her life as an individual began in a laboratory rather than in her mother's fallopian tubes. There is little point in claiming that this new life is a part of the mother's body when it is technically possible to transfer the developing embryo into another woman's body and may soon be possible to bring a child to maturity using an "artificial womb." It is clear that from the moment of fertilization there exists a new individual who requires nothing but a hospitable environment in which to direct its own growth and development.

Perhaps even more interesting than the strictly scientific evidence on the life of the unborn child, however, is the newfound status of the unborn child in medical practice. In 1974, when Dr. Bernard Nathanson first publicly admitted his "increasing certainty" that he had "presided over sixty thousand deaths" as director of the world's largest abortion clinic, he did not attribute his new attitude to newly discovered scientific evidence that life begins at conception, for he knew that such evidence had existed for more than a century. Rather the unborn child's humanity had been brought home to him in a new way by his experience as the director of a new perinatology unit at St. Luke's Hospital Center in Manhattan. Here, Dr. Nathanson was able to study the child in the womb for extended periods of time, to chart his or her development, to locate and correct medical problems—in short, to treat the child as a patient and thus to realize that the child in the womb is as much a member of the human community as is a newborn infant or a mature adult. Based on his medical experience and his own thoroughly secular medical ethic, Dr. Nathanson has now concluded that legal protection should be restored to the unborn child.[2]

Dr. Nathanson's medical experiences have now been duplicated many times over. The new specialties of fetology and perinatology have advanced at a tremendous rate. Amniocentesis, fetoscopy and high-resolution sonography allow us to observe the development of the unborn child and the onset of possible medical problems long before birth. The prescribing of drugs and nutritional programs for children still in the womb is becoming commonplace, and the specialty of prenatal surgery is coming into its own.[3]

Such recent medical developments add an important human dimension to what might otherwise seem like rather abstract scientific evidence on the beginnings of human life. As Dr. John C. Fletcher noted in an editorial in the *Journal of the American Medical Association*, physicians are now being confronted in new ways with the inescapable reality of the unborn child as a human patient in need of care and support.[4] Our developing prenatal technologies are stripping away the veil of ignorance which some would like to maintain with regard to the humanity of this child, forcing physicians and society as a whole to appreciate the continuity between life before and after birth.

Unless our society wants to be blind to the point where it can ignore the increasingly obvious status of the unborn child as a member of the human family, it must come to grips with the fact that the abortion debate is not over "when life begins." Rather the core of the issue concerns the intrinsic dignity and value of life already in existence. We are faced with a moment of decision which cannot be avoided: We must decide whether every human being in need of medical care will be approached with instinctive concern or with the detached eye of the technician who is equally ready to cure or to kill in accordance with the whim of family or society.

The temptation to evade this all-important decision is pressing. To face the decision honestly is to admit that acceptance of abortion is a violation of the physician's most sacred vow in all circumstances "to help or at least to do no harm." Some have therefore tried to claim that science has nothing to say about the point when a human being's life begins because such terms as "human life" and "human being" have only a religious or metaphysical rather than a scientific meaning. They attempt to dissolve the ethical dilemma of abortion by redefining the word "human" in terms of various functional abilities which make human beings worthy of respect and protection. Having concluded, then, on the basis of their own value systems that life before birth is either valueless or of less value than the social benefits of legal abortion, they reason backward from this conclusion to deny that prenatal life is "fully human."[5]

This evasion is not a new phenomenon by any means, for it was described in 1970 by the journal *California Medicine:*

> The reverence of each and every human life has been a keystone of Western medicine and is the ethic which has caused physicians to try to preserve, protect, repair, prolong and enhance every human life.
>
> Since the old ethic has not yet been fully displaced, it has been necessary to separate the idea of abortion from the idea of killing, which continues to be socially abhorrent. The result has been a curious avoidance of the scientific fact, which everyone really knows, that human life begins at conception and is continuous, whether intra- or extra-uterine, until death. The very considerable semantic gymnastics which are required to rationalize abortion as anything but taking a human life would be ludicrous if they were not often put forth under socially impeccable auspices. It is suggested that this schizophrenic sort of subterfuge is necessary because, while a new ethic is being accepted, the old one has not yet been rejected.[6]

We take some consolation in the fact that the "new ethic" for medicine has apparently still not caught on completely since "semantic gymnastics" are still necessary; but we can only regret the confusion created when such tactics are used to avoid facing the facts.

Such attempts to deny the humanity of the unborn betray the lack of understanding of the social and moral dilemma confronting our society. We do not claim that unborn children have all the physical and social abilities proper to adults, any more than we would claim that newborn children possess all such physical and social abilities. We do claim that each human individual comes into existence at conception, and that all subsequent stages of growth and development in which such abilities are acquired are just that—stages of growth and development in the life cycle of an individual already in existence.

Each abortion destroys the life of an individual human being at an early stage in his or her development. Recognition of these facts does not automatically settle the moral and legal issue of abortion, but it does focus attention directly on the fundamental question involved: Will we treat human life as having inherent dignity and worth or will we treat it in accordance with a sliding scale of value in which the right to life is a privilege granted only to those with certain functional abilities?

As spiritual leaders and representatives of an ethical tradition concerned with this question for centuries, we can give only one response to it. That response was succinctly summed up by the assembled Catholic bishops of the world at the Second Vatican Council when they ranked abortion, murder and infanticide as "offenses against life itself" and declared that such offenses "debase the perpetrators more than the victims and militate against the honor of the creator."[7] Our witness on this point is rooted in a commitment to the sanctity of life which reaches to every level of our convictions as Christians, as believers in God the Creator and as human beings.

As Christians we look to the Gospel of Jesus Christ as our norm for faith and action. In Jesus we see that God has a special concern for the most lowly and despised human beings, and we see that each human being has infinite worth as a brother or sister of Jesus who is called to eternal life with God. Jesus is presented to us in the Gospels as the paradigm of human dignity who calls to our consciences with the challenge: "As you did it to one of the least of these my brethren, you did it to me" (Mt. 25:40). At the same time we are forced to admit that in comparison with this perfect example of humanity each of us is a very imperfect specimen indeed; and we therefore deny that we or any human being can sit in judgment upon another and proclaim him or her to be "not fully human."

The New Testament parable of the Good Samaritan teaches us that no Christian can sit back and ask "Who is my neighbor?" in an attempt to define limits to his or her obligations with respect to others. Rather, each one of us has, in the words of the Second Vatican Council, "an inescapable duty to make ourselves the neighbors of every man no matter who he is."[8] This duty moves us not only to condemn abortion as the killing of our neighbor, but also to reach out to the pregnant woman with assistance and support both for her and for her child, offering life-giving alternatives to abortion and seeking the help of private agencies and of government in responding to this human need.

Finally, the Gospel calls us to a mission of forgiveness and reconciliation with regard to the woman who has had an abortion. Christ teaches us that the Father's mercy is always available and without limit. It is our duty to witness to this mercy toward all.

As heirs to the Judeo-Christian spiritual and ethical tradition which recognizes one Creator as Lord of all, we proclaim with Pope John Paul II that "all human life—from the moment of conception and through all subsequent stages—is sacred, because human life is created in the image and likeness of God."[9] God is not the Lord only of some lives or of some stages of life, but as the author of life itself, he is intimately concerned with the life of every human being from its very beginning.

The ethical tradition common to all Christians has always recognized this, condemning abortion at every stage despite occasional philosophical speculations concerning the time of "ensoulment."[10] Our Protestant brethren in particular have argued that speculations about "ensoulment" or "personhood" do not change the character of abortion as the destruction of a nascent human life called into existence by God.[11] We share the conviction that the deliberate destruction of innocent human life is the violation of God's commandment and the usurpation by man of divine authority over life and death. We believe that no human person has dominion over life and death, and therefore that no human individual or government has the right or the authority to dispense with unborn human life as it pleases.

Finally, as human beings committed to the common good of our society and the promotion of justice in the human community, we reject abortion as the killing of one who shares in our common humanity. Because the unborn child is undeniably a fellow human being, he or she deserves the same respect and the same protection as any other member of the human family. Simple human justice demands this much, as does the Golden Rule that calls on all human beings to treat others as they would have themselves treated. From a purely human viewpoint, therefore, the promotion of abortion is the prelude to the disintegration of all human dignity. It is the promotion of a selective justice in which only the powerful can survive.

At every level of our convictions—as Christians, as religious leaders and as concerned human beings—we believe the Supreme Court's abortion decisions constitute an egregious offense against human dignity. We do not suggest that every aspect of our religious convictions on this point can or should be represented in the law. But we defend our right to speak on matters of public policy precisely as religious leaders concerned with the moral and spiritual welfare of our society. We maintain that no human authority can arrogate to itself the power to classify some human lives as devoid of value, because no human authority gives human life its value. Any law which directly violates the divine law and the inherent rights of human beings, as the Supreme Court's decisions have done in this case, is itself unworthy of human respect.

WESTERN TRADITIONS ON HUMAN RIGHTS
AND THE UNBORN CHILD

Having stated our conviction that the protection of the unborn child is a demand which our common humanity makes upon us, we also wish to emphasize that this conviction is in complete harmony with our commitment as American citizens to the defense of fundamental human rights. On this point it is important to remember both the United States' traditional commitment to inherent human rights in general and its legislative record with respect to the protection of unborn human life.

At the root of Western jurisprudence and especially of American law is the conviction that governments must act according to certain commonly held moral principles and respect certain inherent rights if their laws are to be considered valid. This conviction is not restricted to one particular religious denomination or to one particular theory concerning "natural law," but is Western civilization's alternative to arbitrary, unjust or totalitarian government.

It was in recognition of government's responsibilities to a higher law that the founders of our nation claimed the right to revolt against what they considered an unjust system of colonial law. This recognition is also what justifies America's criticism of violations of human rights by certain foreign governments. Without adherence to the idea of a higher law, all such condemnation of injustice is meaningless, because there is no independent standard by which the most abhorrent practices and policies of a legally constituted authority can be considered as either just or unjust.

If human rights are grounded in human dignity, then they cannot be freely bestowed and removed by government. Instead they call out to be recognized because they exist prior to any particular government. Laws which violate or ignore these rights therefore do not truly remove them, but instead render themselves invalid.

The articulation of such rights has been the intent of some of our most revered national and international documents. The right to life is proclaimed as the most fundamental of all rights and is recognized as existing equally in all human beings regardless of their condition.

Our Declaration of Independence recognizes the right to life as inherent and inalienable from the first moment of each human being's existence when it proclaims that "all men are created equal" with respect to this right. The Fifth Amendment to our Constitution states that no person shall be deprived of life or liberty without due process of law. The Thirteenth and Fourteenth amendments attempt to strengthen the protection of human life and to assure that no class of human beings will ever again be deprived of legal protection in the United States.

The United Nations International Covenant on Civil and Political Rights provides that "every human being has the inherent right to life" and implicitly recognizes the rights of the unborn child by rejecting the use of the death penalty upon pregnant women. The U.N. Declaration of the Rights of the Child is more explicit, stating that "the child, by reason of his physical and mental immaturity, needs special safeguards and care, including appropriate legal protection, before as well as after birth." Here the mental and physical immaturity of the unborn, so often used as arguments in favor of abortion in the current American debate, are seen precisely as reasons for providing especially strong protection to the unborn because of their helplessness and greater need for the care of others. The American Convention on Human Rights, proposed by the Organization of American States in 1969, provided: "Every person has the right to have his life respected. This right shall be protected by law and, in general, from the moment of conception. No one shall be arbitrarily deprived of his life."[12]

The presumption in favor of legal protection for the unborn child created by this human rights tradition is a strong one. Since the unborn child is now recognized more clearly than ever before as a member of the human race in science and medicine, such a tradition calls on legislators to protect the right to life of the unborn child as they protect the rights of other human beings. Indeed the only sure means of avoiding such a conclusion is to deny that membership in the human race is sufficient reason in and of itself for being considered worthy of legal protection and thus ultimately to deny that the idea of inherent human rights is relevant to the law. This denial should be familiar to those who recall the history of the degrading institution of slavery in America and the constitutional remedies which were necessary in order to put an end to it. The same denial can be found more recently in Nazi Germany's ideal of the absolute sovereignty of the state over the individual and in the concept of "life devoid of value" by which it gave official sanction to a program for eliminating those considered medically or socially undesirable.[13]

Beginning in 1972, this denial has also played a role in federal court decisions dealing with abortion in the United States. In that year the highest court in the state of New York admitted that the unborn were "human" and "unquestionably alive," but ruled that there was no obligation to protect them because "it is not true that the legal order corresponds to the natural order." In dissent, Judge Adrian Burke focused directly upon this questionable disjunction between fact and law, citing the Declaration of Independence to argue that human beings are created with inherent rights. These rights, claimed Judge Burke, could not simply be overruled by the state in the name of whatever happens to pass for enlightened social policy at any particular time.[14] But in January 1973, the U.S. Supreme Court accepted the approach suggested by the majority opinion in this case, handing down the first in a series of rulings in which the concept of the inherent dignity of all human beings has been denied its proper role in the law.

Many have failed to notice this feature of the 1973 abortion decisions, because they think that the Supreme Court merely found itself unable to determine which of several views on the beginnings of human life is correct. In fact the court said that it "need not resolve the difficult question of when life begins," and implied that it could reasonably ignore the claims of the Texas state legislature that life begins at conception, because the question of whether someone was actually a living member of the human race was not determinative of legal status as a person.[15] This position was made more explicit by a federal judge in Rhode Island later in 1973, when he cited the Supreme Court's decisions as the basis for his ruling that the existence of human life at conception is "irrelevant" to the question of public policy on abortion.[16]

The result of such decisions has been the creation of a new area of law in which the natural and legal orders are separated with a thoroughness hitherto unknown in the United States, with the possible exception of early American law dealing with slavery. This is the "new legalism" which we discussed in our 1976 testimony. While claiming to promote the freedom of physicians to practice good medicine, the Supreme Court substituted legal fictions such as "meaningful life" in place of the medical facts about abortion and unborn life.

In its 1973 ruling in *Roe v. Wade,* the Supreme Court attempted to show that this approach to the unborn child has some basis in American legal history. American legislators, it claimed, granted little or no protection to the unborn child prior to the nineteenth century, and they never considered themselves as obliged to acknowledge a particular set of biological facts concerning the beginnings of life. But after eight years of research and reflection, American legal scholars and historians are still finding previously undiscovered ways in which the court's historical argument on this score is faulty.[17]

In part, the court's historical statements in *Roe v. Wade* can now be seen as relying on incomplete information. For instance, its claim that there were no civil statutes against abortion until the nineteenth century ignored laws of the fifteenth through eighteenth centuries regulating midwifery, in which abortions performed for any reason were prohibited.[18] More often, the court's historical arguments involved an apparent misunderstanding of the way in which the law in each historical period has interacted with contemporaneous scientific knowledge and medical realities. Thus it mentioned that abortion was considered a crime only after "quickening" for some centuries, but it failed to appreciate that this subjective sensation on the part of the pregnant woman was given undue importance because of the primitive state of medical technology at that time.[19]

The court discussed medieval speculations concerning "delayed animation," grossly misrepresented them as having been Catholic "dogma" until the nineteenth century, failed to note that the church's moral teaching always condemned abortion at every stage and seemed oblivious of the fact that the philosophical speculations in question were based partly on Aristotelian biological ideas now totally obsolete.[20]

Similarly the court noted the role of the American Medical Association in enacting new abortion laws in the nineteenth century, but simply juxtaposed its statements with the AMA's proabortion statements of the 1960s instead of looking carefully at the reasons behind those statements.[21] In 1859, when the AMA urged American legislatures to enact much stricter laws against abortion, it based its stance specifically on scientific evidence that human life begins at conception. In 1871, the AMA could quote with approval from *Archbold's Criminal Practice and Pleadings*:

> It was generally supposed that the foetus becomes animated at the period of quickening; but this idea is exploded. Physiology considers the foetus as much a living being immediately after conception as at any other time before delivery, and its future progress but as the development and increase of those constituent principles which it then received. It considers quickening as a mere adventitious event, and looks upon life as entirely consistent with the most profound foetal repose and consequent inaction. Long before quickening takes place, motion, the pulsation of the heart and other signs of vitality, have been distinctly perceived, and, according to approved authority, the foetus enjoys life long before the sensation of quickening is felt by the mother. Indeed, no other doctrine appears to be consonant with reason or physiology but that which admits the embryo to possess vitality from the very moment of conception.[22]

This position has never been contradicted by more recent AMA statements; instead, its statement of fact has been subordinated to a subjective view of social progress which has little to do with the AMA's scientific competence. A recognition of developing medical knowledge is also behind the Catholic Church's decision in the nineteenth century to treat all abortions from conception on as equally serious crimes against human life in the context of canon law.[23]

In other words, the history of Western law on abortion had demonstrated a clear trend toward greater and greater protection for the unborn child, based on the perceived need for such legislation and on the developing medical knowledge at a given point in time concerning life's beginnings. The Supreme Court's documentation in *Roe v. Wade* juxtaposed differing laws on the matter from different historical periods and argued that these differences create an irreducible pluralism which the court cannot resolve—as though it were forced to give equal attention, for example, to modern medical knowledge and ancient Stoic philosophy.[24]

Roe v. Wade's treatment of constitutional "personhood" is another example of its inadequate reflection on this entire issue. The court simply went through the Constitution with a concordance and concluded that most uses of the term "person" therein (with regard to voting, eligibility for presidential office, etc.) have only "postnatal application."[25] Almost all of the examples noted by the court, in fact, apply only to adults. Yet the Fourteenth Amendment proclaims that all persons who are either born or naturalized in the United States are citizens of the United States. No court has used this wording to argue that new immigrants who are not yet naturalized are "nonpersons" who can be killed with impunity—rather it is assumed that immigrants are "persons" with an inherent right to life long before assuming the special rights and responsibilities of American citizens. The Supreme Court interpreted this clause in the opposite sense in the case of those not yet born, as though the absence of full-fledged citizenship automatically meant the absence of any inalienable human rights.

This interpretation is imposed upon the Fourteenth Amendment from without, ignoring evidence that the amendment was intended to prevent any class of human beings from being denied the rights of persons. It is clear from the legislative history of the Fourteenth Amendment that the word "person" was not intended to distinguish between members of the human race who had rights and those who did not—on the contrary, words such as "man," "human being" and "member of the human race" were all used in congressional debate by the framers of this amendment as common-sense synonyms for the term "person."[26]

The status of the unborn child in relation to laws on abortion was not explicitly discussed during the debate; but when the AMA urged new abortion laws in 1859 and 1871 to protect the unborn child from conception on in all but the most extreme cases, the same state and federal legislators who ratified the Fourteenth Amendment responded promptly in recognition of their solemn responsibility to protect human life.[27] The protection of unborn life was seen as being in harmony with the basic purpose of the Fourteenth Amendment, which was, in the words of one of its Senate supporters, to "establish . . . equality before the law, and . . . give to the humblest, the poorest, the most despised of the race the same rights and the same protection before the law as it gives to the most powerful, the most wealthy, or the most haughty."[28] It is this principle of the innate equality of all members of the human race which the Supreme Court denied in the case of the unborn child, reversing the obvious trend toward protection of all human life found in American law prior to the "liberalization" of some state abortion laws in the late 1960s.

The implications of *Roe v. Wade*'s principles for the legal status of human beings who are handicapped or dependent on others, or those who in any way fall below the standard of what some court or legislature may consider "meaningful life," reach far beyond the abortion issue itself. To appreciate these implications is to realize that the abortion debate is not between science and religion, or between moralism and pluralism or between two different interpretations of scientific data. The debate is between the conviction that all human beings are inherently equal in rights and dignity, and the idea that the inherent dignity of membership in the human race should be considered irrelevant to the law.

Some who agree with the Supreme Court's abortion decisions argue that legal protection should be accorded only to those who can articulate and justify their needs in the public forum; others propose a sliding scale of rights corresponding to the possession of certain mental or physical abilities; still others eschew such considerations, arguing simply that legal abortion is necessary for the efficient pursuit of social goods and liberties and that this is sufficient reason for its acceptance. But these positions all have two things in common: They require us to reject the idea that all human beings have inherent value and inherent rights by reason of a commonly shared humanity, and they can easily be applied to the killing of other classes of human beings in addition to the unborn.

We have recognized for years that the arguments by which the Supreme Court devalued unborn life have the potential for undermining the idea of inherent human rights with regard to those already born. In its 1974 Declaration on Abortion, the Roman Catholic Church's Sacred Congregation for the Doctrine of the Faith stated that an unequivocal defense of the right to life of human beings must be grounded in the conviction that this right exists prior to any state's recognition of it, indeed that it must exist as soon as life itself comes into existence. To argue that the right to life rests instead on official legal recognition by the state or that it exists only upon arrival at some particular stage or condition of life which the state is willing to regard as socially valuable or "meaningful," is to deny that there is such a thing as an inherent right to life at all.[29] The logical conclusion of the principles used by the Supreme Court to legalize abortion is that our own fundamental rights are held only as privileges bestowed upon us by the state. Thus when Pope John Paul II said last year [1980] that there is a "patent contradiction" in the attempt to reconcile abortion with the furthering of human dignity, his words held special significance for the situation in the United States, in which the very principles used to justify abortion involve a denial of our traditional commitment to the natural rights of mankind.

With Pope John Paul we hold that "the right to life is the most fundamental right of the human being, a personal right that obliges from the very beginning," and that the attempt to deny this right with respect to the unborn child is an attack upon the fundamental rights of all of us.[30]

THE LEGAL AND SOCIAL EFFECTS
OF ROE V. WADE

When *Roe v. Wade* and *Doe v. Bolton* were handed down by the Supreme Court in 1973, the public policy they created with regard to abortion was hailed by some Americans as an example of progressive social policy. Abortion advocates predicted that a variety of social benefits would soon follow. Safe and legal abortion would make unsafe "back alley" abortions a thing of the past; infant and maternal mortality rates would plummet; every child who was allowed to be born would be a "wanted" child, and so the abuse and neglect of children would become less of a problem; teen-age childbearing and illegitimate children would become less of a burden upon society; etc.

Eight years later we see no sign that the brave new world predicted in 1973 has materialized. Nor is there any reason to expect that a few more years of the same policy will eventually bear the promised fruit. Some of the more obvious failures of the current policy are as follows.

1. Initial predictions that the annual number of abortions would level out within a few years have proved overly optimistic. The estimated number of abortions performed last year is 1.5 million, and groups such as Planned Parenthood still point to a great unmet abortion "need" in many parts of the country.[31] At this point it seems clear that the "need" or "demand" for abortion is very flexible, growing every year as the current legal situation allows the "supply" to be openly and aggressively marketed to American women. As permissive attitudes toward abortion take hold, increasingly frivolous reasons are considered sufficient justification for abortion. Some genetic counselors who perform amniocentesis for the purpose of detecting genetic defects prenatally have complained about the growing number of women who wish to use amniocentesis simply to determine the sex of an unborn child, so that an abortion can be obtained if the child is not of the "right" sex.[32]

2. Despite the annual increase in the number of legal abortions, women continue to die every year from illegal abortions—that is, from abortions performed by nonphysicians. In addition, the huge number of legal abortions adds its own annual casualties to the maternal mortality statistics. It may be that the full story of this tragedy has not yet been told, since some findings suggest that the number of maternal deaths from legal abortion is underreported.[33] Although the number of abortion-related maternal deaths has decreased since 1973, the rate of decrease is not significantly different from the annual rate at which it has dropped since 1942 due to general advances in obstetrical medicine.[34]

In 1978 the noted obstetrician Denis Cavanaugh remarked that "there has been no major impact on the number of women dying in the United States since liberalized abortion was introduced," and indeed that "there has been less improvement in maternal mortality in the 1973–1975 period than in any other period since 1965. This suggests that approximately one million fetuses are being sacrificed each year with no evidence that it is contributing significantly to the reduction of maternal deaths in this country."[35] Since 1975 the annual number of abortion-related maternal deaths has leveled off, with the exception of 1977 when there was an increase in abortion-related maternal deaths; some legal abortions still result in the mother's death, and illegal abortions continue to be performed.[36]

From the outset we have rejected the very premise on which this argument in favor of legalized abortion was based: Even if legalization did result indirectly in some preservation of life, it would be morally reprehensible to authorize the direct destruction of life in order to achieve this goal.[37] But it is now clear that this policy fails even when seen in its own callous and pragmatic terms. At this point the only way to reduce significantly the number of maternal deaths may be to restrict the actual number of abortions as much as possible, while offering comprehensive programs of care and support to women with problem pregnancies.

3. The claim that legalized abortion reduces the infant mortality rate rests on questionable reasoning. If one kills a child before birth, then obviously he or she will never appear in the official infant mortality statistics, but this can hardly be declared a social benefit. In any case, states which have shown remarkable reductions in infant mortality during the past few years have generally attributed their success to the development of better medical care for pregnant women and their children and not to abortion.[38] Some cities which have the highest abortion rates in the country, such as the District of Columbia, also have infant mortality rates which are a national scandal.[39] There may well be a cause-and-effect relationship at work here. The most reliable recent studies indicate that women who have had two or more abortions have a much higher chance than other women of having premature births in future pregnancies. In places like the District of Columbia, where a large percentage of the abortions are obtained by women who have already had at least one previous abortion, the premature birth rate, which is a major cause of high infant mortality, may be aggravated by the high abortion rate.[40]

4. The slogan of "every child a wanted child" seems empty in the face of a national epidemic of child abuse and neglect. Some psychologists have suggested that here too there may be a cause-and-effect relationship at work. Abortion may help to break down the protective instinct of mother for child which begins to form early in pregnancy. Once weakened, it tends to affect the behavior of the mother toward the other children.[41] Whatever the truth may be with respect to this particular claim, it is clear that the ideology represented by "every child a wanted child" is destructive rather than supportive of the family as a haven for the acceptance and nurturing of life.[42] When a child is seen primarily as the projection of parents' self-serving desires and needs rather than as a unique individual with intrinsic worth, the stage is set for parental disappointment and even uncontrollable anger whenever this child does not quite measure up to parents' plans or expectations. No clear link has been shown between an initially unplanned or "unwanted" pregnancy and the later "unwantedness" of the child after birth; in fact, almost every pregnant woman has ambivalent feelings about her pregnancy at one stage or another, and this is generally recognized as a perfectly normal event of pregnancy. Many of the children who end up being abused or neglected after birth are initially "wanted" and planned children who later have fallen short of their parents' standards of perfection.[43]

5. At one time it was thought by abortion advocates that legalized abortion would enable physicians to practice medicine with greater freedom from external legal restrictions, and that this would help the medical profession to devote itself more singlemindedly to the care of human beings already born. Instead, the erosion of respect for life which is promoted by a policy of abortion on demand has spread to areas of medical practice dealing with the handicapped and the terminally ill. The Hippocratic oath is as opposed to infanticide and euthanasia as it is to abortion; but this oath is now seen as "an inadequate guide" for physicians, according to a recent weekly magazine, because "modern doctors, many of whom swore to uphold its principles when they graduated from medical school, now violate it every day."[44]

Physicians' professional and ethical opposition to practices such as infanticide for handicapped newborns and "assisted suicide" for the terminally ill thus becomes increasingly difficult to maintain.[45] A profound shift in the professional ethics of the physician can therefore be detected, in which the Hippocratic axiom "To help or at least to do no harm" is in danger of being replaced by the physician's role as technician, using his expertise either to kill or to cure as is demanded of him. As some physicians cease to consider themselves as involved in a sacred calling devoted to the nurturing of life, others have warned that such a trend may help to undermine public trust and respect for the medical profession as a whole.

According to an editorial by Dr. Seymour Glick in a recent issue of the *New England Journal of Medicine,* the most fundamental reason for modern medicine's growing crisis of respectability is its failure to stand up "for the sanctity of life and for the dignity of human beings" in an increasingly secularized society. "Our societies must come to grips with this problem," Dr. Glick concludes, "because the problem transcends medicine; it threatens the very fabric of Western societal structure and its future."[46]

6. Attempts to stem the tide of what is sometimes called the teen-age pregnancy "epidemic" have been going on for many years. In 1963 Planned Parenthood pamphlets warned teen-agers that abortion "kills the life of a baby after it has begun" and recommended contraception as a way of ensuring that one need never face the prospect of abortion.[47]

When this approach did not have the desired effect, Planned Parenthood and other groups turned to abortion as a backup to "contraceptive failure." The "epidemic" has continued, to the extent that Planned Parenthood, Inc., refers to it as "the problem that hasn't gone away."[48] Yet the response of Planned Parenthood and other groups has been to claim that more of the same approach will lower the teen-age pregnancy rate, if only the government will help them to push contraception and abortion more aggressively and on a wider scale.[49] Some abortion advocates have called for mandatory abortion for teen-age girls under a certain age as a way to solve this problem.[50] Yet this approach seems doomed to failure even if it is allowed to become coercive, because it ignores the realities of teen-age pregnancy and childbearing as human problems.

Some teen-age girls look to pregnancy, either consciously or unconsciously, as a welcome relief from a difficult or unloving home environment. Teen-agers in general have little of the self-discipline required for consistent contraceptive practice because of their romanticized attitudes toward the "spontaneity" of sex; and this lack of self-discipline is further encouraged by the offer of abortion as a quick and easy "backup" solution.[51] Researchers are beginning to notice that many of the problems once seen as results of teen-age childbearing, such as low economic and educational achievement, may actually be factors in the social situation which contributed to the likelihood of pregnancy.[52] In short, the use of abortion as a solution to problems such as teen-age pregnancy seems certain to fail even in its own pragmatic terms because it is based on a myopic view of the problem. Alternative solutions which are more complex but more respectful of human life and human dignity offer more promise in helping to solve this difficult problem.

While failing to solve the social problems once cited as justifications for the legalization of abortion, the Supreme Court's abortion decisions have created new problems in a number of legal areas. As the principles of these decisions have begun to work their way into American jurisprudence, they have provided ample evidence to support the claim that *Roe v. Wade* and its progeny constitute a threat to the rights and dignity of all Americans. Again, only some of the most obvious examples of this can be listed here.

1. The Supreme Court's dichotomy between human beings and "persons in the whole sense," and its innovations in referring to independent or "meaningful" life as the only life deserving of legal protection, have begun to affect court rulings dealing with the rights of those already born. In a 1979 abortion case the Supreme Court ruled that a child born alive during an abortion who may be capable of surviving with medical help has no legal right to that help, because the recognition of such a right would have a "chilling effect" on the woman's right to have a late-term abortion.[53] In 1980 a New York state court cited *Roe v. Wade* to claim that terminally ill comatose patients have "in the true sense, no life" for the state to protect. This court argued that "the state's interest in preservation of the life of the fetus would appear greater than any possible interest the state may have in maintaining continued life of a terminally ill comatose patient . . . [whose] claim to personhood is certainly no greater than that of a fetus."[54] Recent court cases concerned with the right of handicapped children to medical treatment and with the new concept of "wrongful life" suggest that the 1973 abortion decisions pose a threat to all human beings who are especially helpless and dependent on others.[55]

2. As we noted above, the practice of abortion and its concomitant ideology of the "wanted child" constitute a threat to the family as a life-nurturing institution. The destructive effects of abortion on the family have been multiplied by the way in which the family is explicitly treated in recent court rulings on abortion. In *Planned Parenthood of Central Missouri v. Danforth*, for instance, the Supreme Court ruled that a father's rights and responsibilities with respect to his unborn child are his only by delegation of the state, instead of being grounded in the natural relationships of parenthood and the family.[56] Even in rulings which have sustained relatively weak legislation dealing with parental consent for abortions performed on minors, the courts have insisted that a court rather than parents shall have the final say as to whether an abortion will be performed, and perhaps even the final say as to whether parents will be notified at all.[57]

The federal courts have thereby attacked that institution which the United Nations has called "the natural and fundamental unit of society . . . entitled to protection by society and the state."[58] In rulings such as these the family is seen primarily as a grouping of separate individuals or as the delegated agent of the state. In treating family structures merely as restrictions upon the rights of private individuals, the Supreme Court has ignored the family's vital role in promoting these rights. For most of us the family is that training ground where we are first educated to the very idea of inherent human dignity and rights, because it gives us our first experience of being accepted and loved simply because we are and not because we have earned acceptance through our own achievements. By intruding upon familial prerogatives and substituting their own values for the values of the family unit, courts weaken the ability of parents to provide this kind of community for their children; and when the values of the courts are themselves questionable with regard to the principle of inherent human rights, the result can only be a weakening of society's overall commitment to human dignity.

3. Some court cases dealing with abortion have provided an opportunity for attacks on the rights of individuals and groups who disagree with the current public policy on abortion. Although "conscience clauses" protecting health care personnel and privately owned hospitals have been enacted by state and federal legislatures, these clauses have been difficult to enforce.[59] Even rulings which uphold the principle of the conscience clause have noted that the consciences of employees need not be respected if this could cause "undue hardship" to the employer wishing to provide elective abortions.[60] There have also been attempts to force church-affiliated institutions to violate the moral convictions of their sponsors by making them provide abortion services.[61]

4. In some cases courts have played an intrusive role by actually making life-and-death decisions on behalf of private individuals. This has been made possible by *Roe v. Wade*'s ruling that the constitutional "right to privacy" can overrule any interest the state may have in preserving life that is not "meaningful." For

instance, the right of a patient to refuse unwanted medical treatment has traditionally been seen as a common-law right to be exercised within the familial
and doctor-patient relationship whenever possible. But some courts have begun
to treat this area of law in terms of a constitutional right to privacy which is so
personal and individual a right that it cannot be limited or exercised within those
relationships, but must be adjudicated by the court itself. In cases where a patient
is not competent to exercise this right on his or her own behalf, courts have
attempted to make the decision by their own "substituted judgment."[62] These
cases have provided an opportunity to treat all private decision-making processes
in such situations as mere delegations of a power which properly belongs to the
court itself.[63]

This judicial trend has even been applied back to the abortion issue itself,
allowing courts to order abortions for mentally retarded or incompetent women
and to demand that state legislatures provide public funding for elective abortions.[64] The general idea at work in all these cases is that, since the right to
privacy is a constitutional right to be defined by the state and federal courts, the
courts have broad powers to facilitate the exercise of that right and even to exercise
it on behalf of others. By a curious twist of reasoning, a "right to privacy" originally
formulated as an alleged defense of individualism has become a very public entity
indeed and one which can be used to ignore the dignity of human individuals
in the implementation of courts' value judgments on life and death. While proabortion groups continue to lobby against any constitutional amendment on abortion as a threat to individual freedom, we see a clear threat to freedom in this
abuse of judicial power with regard to decisions concerning life and death.

When the decisions of the Supreme Court imposed an abortion policy on this
country in 1973, many thought this marked the end of the public controversy
over legalized abortion. The court treated abortion simply as a medical procedure
and as a matter of individual privacy, and by doing so seemed to have removed
the issue from the public arena.

Eight years later, it is not possible realistically to hold such a view. While
some maintain that abortion is now a private matter between a woman and her
physician, the social and legal trends noted above indicate that the Supreme
Court's decisions have had far-reaching effects on American society. This has
happened, we believe, primarily because the court was tragically mistaken in
thinking that abortion affects only a woman and her physician. Every abortion
also involves the unborn child as an innocent third party. Every abortion involves
the father of the child and in many cases abortion has profound effects on friends,
parents and other members of the family. Every abortion also involves the future
of the society in which it takes place, for it involves moral, psychological and
emotional factors which play an important role in making up the character of
that society. By ignoring the public dimension of the practice of abortion and

failing to recognize it as the fundamental social problem that it is, we place ourselves among its passive victims.

In the United States this public dimension has been magnified by the Supreme Court's classification of abortion as a virtually absolute constitutional right and by its direct attack on the most fundamental of all rights, the right to life itself. The potential for destructiveness inherent in such action is almost unimaginable, for it reaches to the very roots of our legal system and turns its most basic principles upside down. The right to life is replaced by the right to kill, and the very concept of inherent rights is replaced by the concept of privileges bestowed by the state upon those it considers worthy of recognition.

We do not pretend to have all the solutions to the problems which abortion has been purported to solve. Indeed, the idea that there was one quick and easy solution to these problems has been at the root of some very misguided support for our current public policy on abortion. But we do know that abortion, in addition to being a moral evil, has failed to solve society's problems and has itself become a legal and social disaster, the consequences of which will be felt for many years to come. By reversing the current policy, we will clear the way to enable us to work together to promote the common good of all who live in our country. Without such a reversal we fear that our society's commitment to that common good can only erode further.

THE ISSUE OF LAW AND MORALITY

The national debate on the relationship between law and morality has become closely associated with the debate on abortion in recent years. Some groups that support legalized abortion have claimed that any law protecting the unborn child would be an imposition of a particular morality on a pluralistic society; and some have even claimed that it would impose specifically Roman Catholic religious beliefs on this society, thereby violating the nonestablishment clause of the First Amendment. We wish to conclude our testimony with some remarks on these charges.

Our response remains fundamentally the same as in 1974, when we gave the following testimony before the U.S. Senate subcommittee on constitutional amendments:

> We wish to make it clear we are not seeking to impose the Catholic moral teaching regarding abortion on the country. In our tradition moral teaching bases its claim on faith in a transcendent God and the pursuit of virtue and moral perfection. In fact, moral teaching may frequently call for more than civil law can dictate, but a just civil law cannot be opposed to moral teaching based on God's

law. We do not ask the law to take up our responsibility of teaching morality, i.e., that abortion is morally wrong. However, we do ask the government and the law to be faithful to its own principle—that the right to life is an inalienable right given to everyone by the Creator. . . .

We appear here today in fulfillment of our considered responsibility to speak in behalf of human rights. The right to life—which finds resonance in the moral and legal tradition—is a principle we share with the society and the one that impels us to take an active role in the democratic process directed toward its clear and unequivocal articulation.[65]

Since our testimony in 1976, several developments have helped to underscore the exact nature of the Catholic Church's moral concern in this area and the extent to which the abortion issue reaches beyond the bounds of any particular religion's moral teaching.

First of all, the increasingly visible involvement of other religious groups in the public debate on abortion has vividly demonstrated that this is not just a "Catholic issue." The news media have directed their attention primarily to new conservative political groups led by evangelical Protestants who were previously silent on most public policy issues. In addition, however, the governing bodies of denominations such as the Lutheran Church–Missouri Synod and the Southern Baptist Convention have approved resolutions in support of a human life amendment during the last two years and other churches which had made statements in support of permissive abortion after 1973 have begun to qualify their stance.[66]

Second, the fact that a convincing case can be made against abortion on wholly secular grounds has become increasingly obvious. This case has been ably defended by many respected scholars in the realm of political philosophy and constitutional law.[67] The author of *Aborting America,* Dr. Bernard Nathanson, has articulated his opposition to abortion in terms consistent with his own nonreligious humanistic convictions. All one needs in order to support laws against abortion, he notes, is a recognition of some simple biological facts and a commitment to the Golden Rule which has been taught in every civilized society.[68] Secular groups of every conceivable social and political background have enriched the public debate with the variety of their perspectives on this issue.[69]

Finally, the U.S. Supreme Court itself, in ruling upon the constitutionality of restrictions on the public funding of abortion, has reiterated the traditional judicial principle that a law with a "secular legislative purpose" does not violate the establishment clause of the First Amendment simply because it "happens to coincide or harmonize with the tenets of some or all religions." Noting that "laws prohibiting larceny" are not unconstitutional establishments of religion despite the fact that "the Judeo-Christian religions oppose stealing," the court concluded that a funding restriction on abortion is "as much a reflection of 'traditionalist' values toward abortion, as it is an embodiment of the views of any particular religion."[70]

The Supreme Court's argument clearly can be applied to legislation restricting abortion in general. To its own statement on the matter we wish only to add that the word "traditionalist" is no more appropriate as a description of the Catholic Church's position on abortion than it is as a description of our position on stealing. As we have emphasized throughout this testimony, our position on abortion is perfectly consistent with modern scientific knowledge and the most progressive features of American policy on human rights in general. We do not support legal protection for the unborn child because it is "traditional" to do so, but because we totally reject the idea that social "progress" lies in a retreat from the legal and ethical principles which have given the United States its reputation as a defender of the weak against the strong.

Proabortion groups have also claimed that opposition to abortion is a minority view and that we are seeking to "impose" this view on the majority of the citizens of the United States. This charge is false on two counts. First of all, every major public opinion poll taken in the last eight years has shown that most Americans are opposed to legalized abortion on demand. About half of those polled would like to see abortion made illegal except for certain rare circumstances; the other half is about equally divided between those who favor abortion on demand and those who either oppose all abortion or would make an exception only to prevent the death of the mother.[71] Two-thirds of the people of our country think that abortion is morally wrong, and almost three-fourths seem to realize that the victim of even a first-trimester abortion is a living human being.

Contrary to a rather popular stereotype, women are more opposed to legalized abortion than men are, and Americans who are poor or who are members of racial minorities are more opposed to abortion than the white and affluent.[72] The most recent analysis of public opinion on abortion by Judith Blake, who has researched this question since before the Supreme Court's 1973 decisions, indicates that popular support for the full extent of the Supreme Court's actions in this area is even more precarious than the above figures would seem to suggest. Her findings show that Americans who have "moderate" or ambivalent attitudes toward legalized abortion actually lean more toward the consistent antiabortion position than toward the consistent proabortion position.[73] These figures do not even begin to address the point that the group whose rights are in question, that of unborn children, is totally without a voice of its own and therefore deserves the special concern of legislators who are sworn to defend the rights of minorities against the power of the majority.

Second, there is no effort afoot to "impose" a law on our country from the outside, but only a drive to return this issue to the American people's elected representatives. The legalization of abortion on demand was "imposed" on this country in 1973 by seven justices of the U.S. Supreme Court. In attempting to correct this unfair decision by constitutional amendment as provided for by our Constitution, we display our commitment to American democratic principles.

There are also some who admit that the majority view is against abortion on demand, but who defend its legalization on the basis of American "pluralism." Because no view of abortion will ever claim the minds and hearts of all Americans, they argue, we must continue to leave the abortion decision up to each individual woman. There are several important flaws in this argument as well.

1. This "prochoice" argument would invalidate almost all civil rights legislation if it were applied consistently. In fact the same argument was used to defend slavery in the nineteenth century. Slave owners claimed that individuals or states that wished not to engage in the practice of slavery need not do so, but that they should respect the conscientious decisions of others in this controversial matter. President Abraham Lincoln's response was to point out that the law of the United States if it accepted such a situation, would in fact be taking the proslavery side by acting as though there were nothing wrong with slavery. The same response must be made today to the "prochoice" rationale for legalized abortion.[74] To withdraw all legal protection from the unborn child in the name of "pluralism" is to say in practice that this child is not deserving of any public attention and his or her life is to be left to the whim of the mother. It means forgetting that we are dealing not with a purely "private" decision but with one which determines the fate of a defenseless and innocent party. As we have argued elsewhere in this testimony, the current legal situation with regard to abortion also has a number of devastating effects on government and society which call for a public response.

2. The "prochoice" argument in one sense does not go far enough in its defense of pluralism. If pluralism means anything in American society, it means that we must defend the rights and freedoms of every class of human beings, regardless of age, race, sex or condition. A law which allows the killing of any class of human beings is therefore fundamentally antipluralistic and "antichoice," for it allows those human beings to be deprived of any possibility of making their own choices and expressing their own opinions in the future. A pluralism which respects only those who are currently powerful and articulate enough to put their own beliefs into practice to the detriment of others is not in our opinion a genuine or complete pluralism.

3. The argument also ignores another important factor in what we have come to know as American pluralism. This factor was fully recognized by that great defender of religious freedom, John Courtney Murray, when he wrote his classic work titled *We Hold These Truths:*

> One idea, rooted in the American tradition, has seemed to me to be central, and therefore it has been recurrent. Every proposition, if it is to be argued, supposes an epistemology of some sort. The epistemology of the American Proposition was, I think, made clear by the Declaration of Independence in the famous phrase: "We hold these truths to be self-evident. . . ."
> For the pragmatist there are, properly speaking, no truths; there are only results. But the American Proposition rests on the more traditional conviction that there

are truths; that they can be known; that they must be held; for, if they are not held, assented to, consented to, worked into the texture of institutions, there can be no hope of founding a true City, in which men may dwell in dignity, peace, unity, justice, well-being, freedom."[75]

Without this commitment to the grounding of law in an objective order of inherent rights, there is no pluralistic America; instead, there is a plurality of Americas, each committed to its own peculiar viewpoint concerning human rights. We see this destructive form of pluralism at work in the arguments of those who consider the beginning of human life as merely a matter of private opinion. Once one rejects the idea that human rights should be based on simple existence as a member of the human race, one is faced with an irreducible and chaotic pluralism of arbitrary opinions as to the beginnings of "personhood," "meaningful life" or "fully human" life. In this climate, as we have seen, the "personhood" of human beings already born becomes a matter of debate as well, since their membership in the human race is not sufficient reason for being granted the rights or privileges of legal "persons."[76] This will be a special threat to human beings such as handicapped infants or terminally ill patients, whose right to life is already being compromised by our legal system. We cannot allow this trend toward the elimination of the weak and defenseless to be pushed forward under the banner of American "pluralism" or "freedom of choice," any more than we would allow a reinstitution of slavery under this banner. Some human choices are fundamentally destructive of the rights and dignity of other human beings and therefore should be forbidden by law.

In calling for legal protection for the unborn child, we have no intention of asking the government to take over our own task of teaching moral principles and forming consciences. But the law does have a teaching function, exercised through legislation which forbids or discourages specific actions deemed to be destructive of the common good. In deciding whether abortion should be considered as among such actions, legislators inevitably make judgments as to the moral principles which will be reflected in the law. To some extent, the question before our legislatures is not whether they will "legislate morality"—it is whether the morality reflected in the law will be one which respects all human life or one which legitimates the destruction of particularly inconvenient and dependent human lives. In this controversy, to refuse to legislate is to allow the Supreme Court by its decisions to legislate the latter form of morality.

CONCLUSION

During this testimony we have touched upon many elements in the complex issue of legalized abortion. We have reaffirmed the relevance of fundamental moral principles to the debate on this issue, while pointing out the undeniable basis which our moral position has in modern biological and medical fact. We have explained the way in which our position is in harmony with the most respected principles of international and American law, as well as the ways in which the Supreme Court's abortion decisions rest upon an unjust denial of those principles. We have delineated what we see as some of the most devastating social and legal consequences of these decisions, emphasizing the point that their reversal should be an important and immediate priority for those who are committed to promoting the good of our society. Finally, we have discussed the controversial question of law and morality as it bears on this particular issue and responded to charges that our commitment to legal protection for the unborn child is inconsistent with a commitment to American freedom and pluralism. Our final remarks will deal with the specific legislative response which we think should be made to the situation we have described.

Our own comprehensive response to the Supreme Court's abortion decisions can be found in the Pastoral Plan for Pro-Life Activities, approved by the National Conference of Catholic Bishops November 20, 1975, which we presented as part of our testimony before the House subcommittee on civil and constitutional rights in 1976. This response is three-pronged, including efforts in the spheres of education and pastoral care as well as in that of public policy. Within the area of legislation and public policy, we proposed a prolife legislative program with the following elements:

a) Passage of a constitutional amendment providing protection for the unborn child to the maximum degree possible.

b) Passage of federal and state laws and adoption of administrative policies that will restrict the practice of abortion as much as possible.

c) Continual research into and refinement and precise interpretation of *Roe* and *Doe* and subsequent court decisions.

d) Support for legislation that provides alternatives to abortion.

Although we have been active in all these areas, we have restated a number of times during the past eight years that our highest legislative priority is the passage of a constitutional amendment that will reverse the Supreme Court's abortion decisions and restore legal protection to the unborn. Today we again reaffirm our commitment to such an amendment.

We have generally refrained from endorsing a specific amendment before the Congress however. Instead we have suggested certain guidelines that we believe should be taken into account in formulating an amendment which gives a constitutional base for the protection of unborn human life. These guidelines state that a constitutional amendment should do four things:

1. Establish that the unborn child is a person under the law in terms of the Constitution from conception on.

2. The Constitution should express a commitment to the preservation of life to the maximum degree possible. The protection resulting therefrom should be universal.

3. The proposed amendment should give the states the power to enact enabling legislation and to provide for ancillary matters such as record keeping, etc.

4. The right to life is described in the Declaration of Independence as "inalienable" and as a right with which all men are endowed by the Creator. The amendment should restore the basic constitutional protection for this human right to the unborn child.

Now, as in 1976, considerable controversy has raged concerning the relative merits of various proposals for an amendment. In our 1976 testimony we recognized that not every proposal was equally consonant with all of our suggested guidelines; while arguing against a pure "states' rights" amendment as an ineffective measure for giving uniform protection to the unborn in the various states, we also recognized that some proposals granting legislative authority to Congress and the states to protect unborn human life were a significant improvement on the "states' rights" approach. Similarly, September 22 of this year we expressed great interest in the new "human life federalism amendment" recently proposed by Sen. Hatch (R-Utah), which expressly overturns the right to abortion created by the Supreme Court in 1973 and gives concurrent power to Congress and the states to restrict and prohibit abortion.

As moral leaders we claim no special competence at legislative draftsmanship, and so we do not claim the expertise to comment at length on the advisability and effectiveness of specific formulations. Our own guidelines have always been offered as contributions to a dialogue in which the members of Congress were considered as the appropriate agents for the actual drafting of an amendment to be presented to the state legislatures.

We take note of the fact that some recent testimony before this subcommittee indicates a possibility that the establishment of constitutional "personhood" may not be necessary at the present time for restoring effective legal protection to unborn children, and indeed that it could fail through judicial interpretation to provide effective protection. We expect that the members of the subcommittee will take expert testimony of this sort into account, and also that they will consider the political possibilities for ratification of the various proposals which confront them. Our own fundamental commitment, as stated in our 1975 pastoral plan, is to an amendment which will actually provide the maximum degree of protection for unborn human life that is possible.

Our appearance here today is an expression of our commitment to the American democratic process. We believe that this process was short-circuited in 1973, when the decisions of the Supreme Court overturned the abortion laws of every state in the union in its singleminded drive to promote its own policy on abortion.

We urge our elected representatives in Congress to redress this injustice as soon as possible by restoring to our legal system the power to protect human life at every stage of its existence.

NOTES

1. "The Status of Children, Youth and Families 1979," U.S. Department of Health and Human Services, DHHS Publication No. (OHDS) 80-30274, pp. 29–30.

2. Bernard N. Nathanson, M.D., with Richard N. Ostling, *Aborting America* (Doubleday, 1979). See especially chaps. 16, 20, and 26.

3. Among the recent reports on such progress: "Successful Operation Is Performed on Fetus," *Washington Star*, July 27, 1981; "The Tiniest Patients: Surgery before Birth," *San Francisco Examiner*, May 26–27, 1981; "Life of Baby Is Apparently Saved by Doses of Vitamin Before Birth," *New York Times*, May 15, 1981; R. W. Smithells et al., "Possible Prevention of Neural-Tube Defects by Periconceptional Vitamin Supplementation," *Lancet*, Feb. 16, 1980, pp. 339–40; Jason C. Birnholz, M.D., and Frederick D. Frigoletto, M.D., "Antenatal Treatment of Hydrocephalus," *New England Journal of Medicine*, Apr. 23, 1981, pp. 1021–23.

4. John C. Fletcher, Ph.D., "The Fetus as Patient: Ethical Issues," *Journal of the American Medical Association*, Aug. 14, 1981, pp. 772–73.

5. This line of argument was proposed by Leon Rosenberg of Yale University in his April 24 testimony before the subcommittee on separation of powers of the Senate Committee on the Judiciary. His approach has been embraced by Dr. George Ryan of the American College of Obstetricians and Gynecologists, whose remarks on the matter were given wide public circulation by syndicated Ann Landers columns for Sept. 7–8 of this year [1981].

6. Editorial: "A New Ethic for Law and Society," *California Medicine*, Sept. 1970, p. 68.

7. *Gaudium et spes*, no. 27.

8. *Ibid*.

9. Pope John Paul II, Homily at the Washington Mall, Oct. 7, 1979, in *Origins*, Oct. 18, 1979.

10. Sacred Congregation for the Doctrine of the Faith, *Declaration on Abortion* (U.S. Catholic Conference, 1975), nos. 6–7 (pp. 3–4).

11. See the references to Calvin, Thielicke, Barth, Bonhoeffer, etc., in John T. Noonan, Jr., *A Private Choice: Abortion in America in the Seventies* (Free Press, 1979), pp. 59–61.

12. See Dennis Horan et al., "The Legal Case for the Unborn Child," in *Abortion and Social Justice*, ed. Thomas W. Hilgers and Dennis J. Horan (Sheed and Ward, 1972), pp. 133–34.

13. See Noonan, *A Private Choice*, pp. 13–14, on the dichotomy between human beings and persons. On the concept of "life devoid of value" and the Nazi euthanasia program:

Robert A. Graham, S.J., "The 'Right to Kill' in the Third Reich: Prelude to Genocide," *Catholic Historical Review*, Jan. 1976, pp. 56–76; William Brennan, *Medical Holocausts*, vol. 1, *Exterminative Medicine in Nazi Germany and Contemporary America* (Nordland Publishing International, 1980), chap. 3; Leo Alexander, M.D., "Medical Science under Dictatorship," *New England Journal of Medicine*, July 14, 1979, pp. 39–47.

14. See *A Private Choice*, pp. 16–17.

15. *Roe v. Wade*, 410 U.S. 113 at 159 (1973).

16. *Doe v. Israel*, 358 F. Supp. 1197 (D.R.I., 1973). See *A Private Choice*, pp. 17–18.

17. In our 1976 testimony we cited criticisms of the abortion decisions by John Hart Ely, Alexander Bickel, Robert Byrn, and Archibald Cox. In his new book, *Democracy and Distrust: A Theory of Judicial Review* (Harvard University Press, 1981), Professor Ely has restated his judgment that even a fairly "activist" viewpoint on judicial review fails to provide any warrant in the Constitution for *Roe v. Wade*. Liberal columnist Michael Kinsley recently voiced a growing consensus when he referred to the abortion decisions as "the one really indefensible case of judicial overreaching" in recent years (*New Republic*, Oct. '18, 1980, p. 15). On the Supreme Court's historical arguments, see Joseph P. Witherspoon, "Impact of the Abortion Decision upon the Father's Role," *Jurist*, 1975, pp. 41–47; *idem*, Testimony before the Senate subcommittee on separation of powers, June 10, 1981; Victor G. Rosenblum, Testimony before the Senate subcommittee on separation of powers, June 1, 1981. Professor Rosenblum's testimony has been reprinted by Americans United for Life as Number 11 of AUL Studies in Law and Medicine.

Recognition of the fact that the abortion decisions had no firm grounding in legal history began with the dissenting opinions of justices on the court itself. Referring to the majority opinion as "an exercise of raw judicial power," Justice White declared that "I find nothing in the language or history of the Constitution to support the court's judgment." Justice Rehnquist joined in the dissent and added his own, in which he noted that the court's imposing of specific limits on the states for each trimester of pregnancy "partakes more of judicial legislation than it does of a determination of the intent of the drafters of the 14th Amendment." See *Roe v. Wade* at 174; *Doe v. Bolton*, 410 U.S. 179 at 221–22 (1973).

18. *Roe v. Wade* at 136. See Dennis J. Horan and Thomas J. Marzen, "Abortion and Midwifery: A Footnote in Legal History," in *New Perspectives on Human Abortion*, ed. Thomas W. Hilgers et al. (University Publications of America, 1981), pp. 199–204.

19. *Roe v. Wade* at 138.

20. *Idem*, at 160–61. Philosophical speculation concerning "delayed ensoulment" have never been part of Catholic dogma. For a brief historical survey of the church's position, see John T. Noonan, Jr., "An Almost Absolute Value in History," in *The Morality of Abortion: Legal and Historical Perspectives*, ed. Noonan (Harvard University Press, 1970), pp. 1–59. The most complete study on the history of Catholic thought on this subject up to 1950 can be found in John Connery, S.J., *Abortion: The Development of the Roman Catholic Perspective* (Loyola University Press, 1977). Also see *Declaration on Abortion*, no. 7 (pp. 3–4).

21. *Roe v. Wade* at 141–42.

22. D. A. O'Donnell and W. L. Atlee, "Report on Criminal Abortion," *Transactions of the American Medical Association* 22 (1971),), p. 250. A review of the AMA abortion statements of 1859 and 1871 can be found in Brennan, *Medical Holocausts*, pp. 25–34.

23. The "treatment" in question, it should be noted, concerns only ecclesiastical penalties in canon law. The moral teaching of the church, as we have already noted above, has condemned abortion at every stage as a form of grave wrongdoing from the earliest years of the Christian era. The fiction that the church has changed its moral judgment of early abortions arises in part from a failure to understand the distinction between moral doctrine and canon law.

24. *Roe v. Wade* at 160.

25. *Idem*, at 157.

26. See Witherspoon materials cited in note 17.

27. See Witherspoon, "Impact of the Abortion Decisions," pp. 42–45; James C. Mohr, *Abortion in America: The Origins and Evolution of National Policy 1800–1900* (Oxford University Press, 1978). Mohr notes on p. 200: "The anti-abortion policies sustained in the United States through the first two-thirds of the twentieth century had their formal legislative origins, for the most part, in the wave of tough laws passed in the wake of the doctors' crusade and the public response their campaign evoked."

28. Speech of Sen. Jacob Howard of Michigan, *Congressional Globe*, 39th Congress 1st Session (May 23, 1866), p. 2766. Cited in Witherspoon, "Impact of the Abortion Decisions," p. 47.

29. See *Declaration on Abortion*, nos. 10–14 (pp. 5–7).

30. Pope John Paul II, Homily in Plaza del Campo, Siena, Sept. 14, 1980, cited in *L'Osservatore Romano* (English ed.), Sept. 22, 1980.

31. In 1978 researchers affiliated with the Alan Guttmacher Institute estimated that 1.3 million abortions had been performed in 1977 but that 550,000 women "in need" of abortions had been unable to obtain them ("Abortion in the United States, 1976–1977," *Family Planning Perspectives*, Sept./Oct. 1978, p. 271). But early this year [1981] the same researchers reported that "although 1.5 million women obtained abortions in 1979, an estimated 641,000 in need were unable to do so, largely because of the problems of geographical and financial inaccessibility" ("Abortion in the United States, 1978–1979," *Family Planning Perspectives*, Jan./Feb. 1981, p. 6). According to the *Washington Post*, Oct. 21, 1981, the current issue of *Family Planning Perspectives* reports that the women in "need" of an abortion would number about 450,000 even if every woman in the U.S. used the most effective but most dangerous contraceptive devices.

32. See Lynne McTaggart, "The Breakthrough That Backfired," *New York Sunday News Magazine*, Feb. 8, 1981.

33. See Hadley Arkes, *The Philosopher in the City: The Moral Dimension of Urban Politics* (Princeton University Press, 1981), p. 437. Arkes observes that when investigative reporters from the *Chicago Sun Times* began to uncover abuses at several legal abortion clinics in Chicago, the investigators brought in reports of twelve deaths that were attributable to four abortion clinics in their sample. Those deaths, which were uncovered in only four clinics, amounted to nearly half of the deaths that were reported officially for abortion in the nation as a whole. And if, as we suspect, the experience in Chicago can find a modest replication in New York, Detroit, Los Angeles, and other cities, the total deaths due to legal abortion may now exceed the number of deaths that were thought to occur each year as a result of illegal abortions.

34. See *Documentation on Abortion and the Right to Life*, vol. 2 (Testimony of U.S. Catholic Conference before the House subcommittee on civil and Constitutional rights, Mar. 24, 1976) (U.S. Catholic Conference, 1976), p. 10.

35. Denis Cavanaugh, letter in *American Journal of Obstetrics and Gynecology*, Feb. 1, 1978.

36. "Abortion-Related Mortality—United States, 1977," *Morbidity and Mortality Weekly Report* (Center for Disease Control, U.S. Dept. of Health and Human Services), July 6, 1979, pp. 301–4.

37. See *Declaration on Abortion*, nos. 19–20 (pp. 8–9).

38. "Several States Showing Significant Decreases in Infant Mortality," *Ob.-Gyn. News*, Jan. 15, 1981. The remarkable advances reported here for the states of South Dakota, Florida, and Alabama are attributed to better prenatal medical and nutritional care, educational programs for pregnant women, and the development of regionalized care networks.

39. The District of Columbia has a higher abortion rate than any state in the union, estimated at 173.4 per 1000 women aged fifteen to forty-four in 1978. This is more than six times the national average. See "Abortion in the United States, 1978–1979," pp. 10–11. The mayor of the District of Columbia has called its high infant mortality rate its "number one health problem." See "City Infant Mortality Rate Rises," *Washington Post*, June 17, 1981.

40. See Levin et al., "Association of Induced Abortion with Subsequent Pregnancy Loss," *Journal of the American Medical Association*, June 27, 1980, pp. 2495–99. Thirty-four percent of the women who obtained abortion in the District of Columbia in 1978 had obtained one or more previous abortions. This is the highest repeat abortion rate in the country, the national average being 29 percent. *Abortion Surveillance: Annual Summary 1978* (Center for Disease Control, U.S. Dept. of Health and Human Services, 1979), p. 4.

41. Philip G. Ney, M.D., "Infant Abortion and Child Abuse: Cause and Effect," *The Psychological Aspects of Abortion*, ed. David Mall and Walter Watts, M.D. (University Publications of America, 1979), pp. 25–38.

42. See "The Impact of Abortion" (Intervention by Cardinal Terence Cooke of New York at the 1980 Synod of Bishops), *Origins*, Oct. 16, 1980, pp. 283–85.

43. Our most eminent national authority on the problem of child abuse had already emphasized this eight years ago and predicted that the aborting of the "unwanted child" would fail to solve the problem. See Vincent J. Fontana, M.D., *Somewhere a Child Is Crying* (Macmillan, 1973), pp. 239–43.

44. Matt Clark et al., "When Doctors Play God," *Newsweek*, Aug. 31, 1981, p. 48.

45. In our 1976 testimony we noted the scandal caused by reports that handicapped newborns had been deprived of life-saving surgery at some hospitals simply because they were mentally retarded. Now newspapers report that physicians at some intensive-care nurseries have actually been giving lethal drug overdoses to such newborns. See Diane Brozek, "Let My Baby Die," *Pittsburgh Press*, June 29, 1981. The candor with which physicians are willing to discuss the advisability of voluntary euthanasia or "assisted suicide" seems to be increasing. See Dan Cryer, "Suicide and Euthanasia: Christian Barnard Tackles Controversial Subjects," *Boston Globe*, Apr. 16, 1981; editorial, "Overdose—Will Psychiatrist Please See?" *Lancet*, Jan. 24, 1981.

46. Seymour M. Glick, "Humanistic Medicine in a Modern Age," *New England Journal of Medicine*, Apr. 23, 1981, pp. 1036–38.

47. "Plan Your Children for Health and Happiness," Planned Parenthood Federation of America pamphlet, 1963.

48. Alan Guttmacher Institute, *Teenage Pregnancy: The Problem That Hasn't Gone Away* (New York, 1981).

49. See the articles on government funding of family planning services in the May–June 1981 issue of *Family Planning Perspectives,* and articles on government funding of abortion in the May–June 1980 issue, as well as the conclusions of *Teenage Pregnancy: The Problem That Hasn't Gone Away.*

50. At the fourth annual meeting of the National Abortion Federation, May 28–30, 1980, at the Hyatt Regency Hotel in Washington, D.C., a talk by Jane Hodgson included the rhetorical question: "Does freedom of choice really apply to the very young? Should we sit quietly by and allow our 12-year-olds, and our 11-year-olds, possibly 10-year-olds, to make a choice which is far more harmful to her, to society and to the ensuing generation? Shouldn't we . . . mandate against continuing pregnancy in the very young, say, those less than 14 years?" Her proposal was later endorsed by another speaker, Lonnie Meyers, who claimed that "it's time we had the guts to say that 14 is too young to have a baby." See Andrew Scholberg, "The Abortionists and Planned Parenthood: Familiar Bedfellows," *International Review of Natural Family Planning,* Winter 1980, p. 299.

51. See Sister Paula Vandegaer, SSS, *Teenagers and Sexuality* (NCCB Committee for Pro-Life Activities, 1981); "Abortion and Teenage Pregnancy," in *Respect Life!* (NCCB Committee for Pro-Life Activities, 1977–78), pp. 16–21.

52. See "Teens, Parents, Officials Don't Agree on Impact of Teen Motherhood," *Family Planning Perspectives,* Mar.–Apr. 1981, pp. 81–82; Jeanne Marecek and Eugenie Flaherty, "Correlates of Teenagers' Contraceptive Use" (Study presented at the American Psychological Association convention, September 1980). The Marecek-Flaherty study was announced in *Ob.-Gyn. News,* Jan. 1, 1981.

53. *Colautti v. Franklin,* 439 U.S. 379 (1979). The court's finding puzzled many observers, who thought that *Roe v. Wade* had placed severe restrictions on abortions performed after the point of "viability"; but even in 1973 the court had ruled that a postviability abortion could be performed for "health" reasons, and had interpreted "health" so broadly that temporary financial or emotional distress was sufficiently serious justification for an abortion in the final stages of pregnancy. In their *Philadelphia Inquirer* article "Abortion: The Dreaded Complication" (Aug. 2, 1981), Liz Jeffries and Rick Edmonds report that the problem of dealing with a child born alive during an abortion now arises hundreds of times a year in the U.S.

54. *In re Eichner,* AD 2d, 637E, Mar. 28, 1980 (Supreme Court: Appellate Division Second Department) at 43.

55. "Wrongful life" suits are predicated on the idea that a handicapped child's very existence is a "wrong" for which monetary damages can be assessed. In its 1980 ruling in *Curlender v. Bio-Science Laboratories,* the California Supreme Court suggested that a handicapped child should be able to sue her own parents for not having aborted her. In the same state, however, the courts denied the right of Phillip Becker, a child with Down's syndrome, to have surgery which could save his life but which is opposed by his parents. The parents had argued that they do not wish Phillip to outlive them because of the quality of life of which he would be capable. The Supreme Court has refused to hear an appeal from this decision (*Bothman v. Warren B.,* No. 79-698; denial of cert. Mar. 31, 1980). Another family has tried to gain temporary custody of Phillip in order to allow him the medical care he needs, but his condition may already have advanced too far for the surgery to be of help. See George F. Will, "A Trip Toward Death," *Newsweek,* Aug. 31, 1981, p. 72; Peter J. Riga, "Phillip Becker: Another Milestone," *America,* July 12, 1980, pp. 8–9.

56. 428 U.S. 52 at 69 (1976).

57. The most important cases dealing with this question are *Bellotti v. Baird,* 443 U.S. 622 (1979), and *H.L. v. Matheson,* 101 S. Ct. 1164 (1981). See the analysis by Noonan, *A Private Choice,* pp. 90–95.

58. U.N. Declaration on Human Rights, cited by Cardinal Terence Cooke in "The Impact of Abortion," p. 284.

59. See the analysis by Noonan, *A Private Choice,* pp. 83–86. This problem was mentioned by the Sacred Congregation for the Doctrine of the Faith in 1974, when it declared inadmissible a situation in which doctors or nurses would have to choose between the law of God and their professional situation: *Declaration on Abortion,* no. 22 (p. 9).

60. This principle has recently been affirmed in *Kenny v. Ambulatory Center of Miami,* 400 So. 2d 1262 (Fla. Ct. App. 1981). Here it was implied that the need to rearrange schedules substantially in order to respect a nurse's refusal to cooperate in abortions might have been considered as "undue hardship." The lower court had ruled against the nurse without seeing evidence of any hardships of this kind.

61. The NCCB has filed suit against federal guidelines which could force certain employers, including the U.S. Catholic Conference, to provide abortion benefits through employees' health insurance plans and fringe benefit programs: *NCCB v. Bell,* U.S. District Court for the District of Columbia (Filed 1980). For comments on the threat to First Amendment rights involved in such guidelines, see George F. Will, " 'Trivializing' Abortion," *Washington Post,* Aug. 19, 1979.

62. Paul Ramsey has discussed this aspect of the *Eichner* case in his article "Two-Step Fantastic: The Continuing Case of Brother Fox," *Theological Studies,* Mar. 1981, pp. 122–34. Other cases of this sort include: *Superintendent of Belchertown State School v. Saikewicz,* 373 Mass. 728 (1977); *In re Earl Spring,* No. F-2030, Mass., May 13, 1980. In its ruling *In re Grady* (Feb. 18, 1981), the New Jersey Supreme Court cited the famed Karen Quinlan case to uphold a right to sterilization as an exercise of the constitutional right to privacy. The court suggested that this right can override the state's interest in preserving a patient's life, and that only the courts can exercise such a right on behalf of a mentally incompetent patient.

63. In the *Spring* case, the lower courts (probate and appeals) had ordered that Spring's attending physician, along with his wife and son, should make the decision as to whether life-prolonging treatment would be continued. The state supreme court overruled these decisions, claiming that "we disapprove shifting of the ultimate decision-making responsibility away from the duly established courts of proper jurisdiction." The court argued that it would be forsaking its own responsibilities if it tried "to delegate its resolution to some private person or group."

64. Both *Saikewicz* and *Spring* were cited as precedents by the Massachusetts Supreme Court Feb. 17, 1981, when it ruled that the state of Massachusetts is required to subsidize elective abortions with public funds (*Moe v. Secretary of Administration and Finance*). Interpreted through these cases, the state constitution was said to provide more stringent requirements for actively supporting the pregnant woman's right to an abortion than are found in the U.S. Constitution. Similar chains of reasoning have been used by courts in California and Pennsylvania to mandate public funding of abortion in those states.

Court involvement in ordering abortions for mentally incompetent patients seems to be increasing. Justice Warren Burger recently refused to block an abortion ordered by the court-appointed guardian of a woman in a semicatatonic state, despite the fact that no evidence had been presented on a medical need for the abortion. The woman in question had been fully competent earlier in her pregnancy and had not sought an abortion (see "Justice Refuses to Bar Abortion for Sick Woman," *NC News Service,* Mar. 19, 1981). In California, a court-appointed conservator almost succeeded in ordering an abortion for an unwilling 38-year-old mental patient, although all three of her sisters were adamantly opposed to the abortion and were all willing to adopt the child even if born with congenital defects. Superior Court Judge Bob Krug denied the petition for an abortion on the basis of medical risks involved in performing a second-trimester abortion, without denying that the conservator had the right to petition the court for an abortion against the wishes of the patient and her family (see Mary Sanchez, "Petition to Do Abortion on Mental Patient Denied," *NC News Service,* Mar. 26, 1981).

65. *Documentation on the Right to Life and Abortion,* vol. 1 (Testimony of USCC before the Senate subcommittee on constitutional amendments, Mar. 7, 1974) (U.S. Catholic Conference, 1974), pp. 2–3.

66. At its 1979 national convention, the Lutheran Church–Missouri Synod approved a resolution which condemns abortion, urges its members to help secure legal protection for the defenseless unborn child, and supports efforts to enact a human life amendment to the U.S. Constitution. The American Lutheran Church, which issued a statement in support of legalized abortion in 1974, approved a statement of judgment and conviction at its 1980 national convention which rejects "the practice in which abortion is used for personally convenient or selfish reasons," recognizes that "an induced abortion ends a unique human life," and "deplores the alarming increase of induced abortions since the 1973 Supreme Court decisions." See the newsletter of Lutherans for Life, Dec. 1980 and Feb. 1981. The Southern Baptist Convention, the nation's largest Protestant body with 13.4 million members, approved a condemnation of abortion at its 1980 annual meeting which includes a call for a human life amendment banning abortion "except to save the life of the mother" (*NC News Service,* June 13, 1980).

67. In addition to the works cited elsewhere in this testimony by Noonan, Witherspoon, Rosenblum, etc., see Joseph M. Boyle, "That the Fetus Should Be Considered a Legal Person," *American Journal of Jurisprudence,* 1979, pp. 59–71; chapters on legal, social, and philosophical aspects of abortion in Hilgers et al., eds., *New Perspectives on Human Abortion.*

68. Nathanson, *Aborting America,* chap. 23.

69. Groups such as Democrats for Life, Libertarians for Life, Feminists for Life, and Pro-Lifers for Survival (a group opposed to abortion and nuclear arms) have helped to belie the stereotype that opposition to abortion is only a "conservative" phenomenon. See Mary Meehan's brief survey of some of these groups in "The Other Right to Lifers," *America,* Jan. 18, 1980.

70. *McRae v. Harris,* 100 S. Ct. 2671 at 2689 (1980).

71. This has been the consistent finding of four Gallup Polls taken over the last six years. See "Views on Abortion Show Little Change," *Washington Post,* Aug. 27, 1980.

72. The most recent ABC News–*Washington Post* poll on abortion (Survey 34, aired June 8, 1981) shows 50 percent of men and only 42 percent of women favoring the goals of the "prochoice" movement; 36 percent of women favored unrestricted abortion, compared with 45 percent of men. Nearly a third of the people strongly opposing legalized abortion make under $12,000 a year, with only 10 percent making $30,000 or more, and nearly one-quarter are black, whereas more than a quarter of those favoring legalized abortion

make $30,000 a year or more. Similar results were obtained by the Connecticut Mutual Life Insurance Company when it conducted a survey on American values in the '80s: 65 percent of all Americans considered abortion as morally wrong, but opposition was stronger among women, racial minorities, and the poor. The ABC News–*Washington Post* poll showed 71 percent support for the idea that "a fetus becomes a human being" either at conception or at some point in the first trimester; only 11 percent of those polled thought that one "becomes a human being" at birth.

73. Judith Blake and Jorge H. del Pinal, "Negativism, Equivocation, and Wobbly Assent: Public 'Support' for the Pro-choice Platform on Abortion," *Demography*, Aug. 1981, pp. 309–20.

74. See John T. Noonan, Jr., "Abortion in Our Culture" (NCCB Committee for Pro-Life Activities, 1980).

75. John Courtney Murray, *We Hold These Truths* (Sheed and Ward, 1960), pp. viii–ix.

76. This has already been suggested by the testimony given by Dr. Leon Rosenberg before the Senate subcommittee on separation of powers earlier this year (see note 5). "Some say that life begins at conception," noted Dr. Rosenberg, "but others say that life begins when brain function appears, or when the heart beats, or when a recognizable human form exists in miniature, or when the fetus can survive outside the uterus, or when brain development is completed at two years of age." Any of these would be equally valid points for beginning to protect life, he claimed. Presumably, under the last-mentioned of these standards, some mentally retarded human beings would never become "persons" at all.

A Traditional Catholic's View

Thomas J. O'Donnell

I will try to clarify two aspects of the traditional Catholic view on abortion: firstly, what the doctrine of the church has been and is now, and secondly, the components of the doctrine which have been most frequently misinterpreted or misunderstood.

As the nascent Christian church emerged from Galilee and Judea and began to carry the good news of the gospel into the heart of the Roman Empire, it immediately encountered certain mores which were inconsistent with the meaning of the message. It is not surprising that the new evangel—that men should know and love the one eternal God as Father and love each other as true brothers— might find some practices of pagan culture quite inconsistent with this new law of love; for this Christian love was to be, above all, a well-ordered and enlightened love. One of the very first of these moral problems encountered by the early church was the Roman disregard for the life of the unborn child. This disregard was reflected not only in the classical literature of Rome (as in both Juvenal and Ovid), but even in the Roman law condemning abortion, which did so with an eye more to the damage done to the expectant father than to the unborn infant.

Thus the first-century Christian *Didache* condemned abortion, as did several classic second-century Christian writings. This condemnation was picked up by Tertullian and Cyprian, among others, in the third century and was canonized by the Council of Elvira around the year 300 and by the Council of Ancyra. So it was that at the dawn of the Christian era one of the earliest moral imperatives to take form was against abortion because, as many of these writers phrased it, abortion of the human fetus was murder of the innocent.

It is true that to describe the destruction of the unborn child as the murder of the innocent is not a very euphemistic turn of phrase, but that is the way the theologians put it then—and that is the way it stands in Catholic doctrine, even 2today. This is, and always has been, the teaching of the Catholic Church, reiterated in our own time by each of the twentieth-century popes and by the recent Second Vatican Council. Even the gentle John XXIII wrote regarding abortion: "Human life is sacred—all men must recognize that fact. From its very inception it reveals the creating hand of God. Those who violate His laws not only offend the divine majesty and degrade themselves and humanity, they also sap the vitality

44

of the political community of which they are members" (*Mater et Magistra*, May 15, 1961), and the Second Vatican Council, in 1965, reunderlined the fact that in Catholic doctrine "abortion and infanticide are unspeakable crimes."

There are, however, three important modifications of this theme which have emerged throughout the long history of the church and are no less pertinent today. While they do not change the basic doctrine of the church on abortion, we must consider them briefly lest they be totally misunderstood. The first is the history of the theological speculation on abortion, the second is the variation in canonical discipline as distinct from moral doctrine, and the third is the extension of the moral malice of abortion even to the moment of conception.

Before turning our attention to these, however, we would do well to make some comment on the yet unanswered question: "When do the products of human conception become human?" or "At what stage of its development is the embryo, or fetus, a human being?"

Hippocrates, Aristotle, and Galen all struggled with the problem of the moment of specifically human animation, as did Tertullian and Apollinaris, Basil and Gregory of Nyssa, Jerome and Augustine, and Thomas Aquinas. The most common theory, that the conceptus passed through a vegetative and animal stage, finally becoming human about the fortieth day in the case of males and about the eightieth day in the case of females, is by no means bizarre against the background of the scientific method of the times. Men have generally concluded that things are probably what they appear to be. To the naked eye, a conceptus in its early stages does look like a sea anemone, and by the time an embryo is observable it looks almost like any animal embryo. At about forty days the phallic tubercule makes the embryo look more like a human male than a female, and the external genitalia of the female are not clearly discernible to the naked eye until about the eightieth day. With the theory accepted medically, it is not surprising that some contemporary theologians thought they saw confirmatory references in Leviticus (12:2–5), where the purification period of the parturient similarly varies according to the sex of the child.

While the moment of new human life still evades any known investigative process, it is interesting to note that the same scientific method of observation, aided today by modern microscopy, indicates chromosomal patterns in the nuclei of the earliest stages of cell division as specifically human and indeed already personally individualized, thus seeming to support the likelihood that from the moment of conception John is John, and not George.

The bearing which these considerations have had, and still have, on the doctrine of the Catholic Church will become more explicit as we proceed.

I have already referred to three modifications of the basic doctrine on abortion—the first being the history of theological speculation on the subject. My report on the basic doctrine as the constant teaching of the church over her long history does not mean to imply that the theologians have never speculated on the subject, nor sought to defend the licitness of abortion under some extreme circumstances. Some have held that very early abortion was permissible under the delayed animation theory when this theory was a commonly accepted medical premise. Some few have even sought to defend late abortion under the principle of the unjust aggressor, or as the lesser of two evils, or as a necessity for baptizing the fetus, or even under the presumed willingness of the unborn child to sacrifice its right to life in favor of the safety of its mother. But all of these theories have been shown to be erroneous and deficient, and in the history of Catholic thinking they were never accepted by the church as Catholic doctrine.

The second modification to which I have referred is the variation in canonical discipline as distinct from moral doctrine. The canonical discipline of the church, imposing ecclesiastical penalties for certain public crimes, is not a moral code and only a lack of scholarship would interpret it as such. When the canon law prescribes an ecclesiastical penalty for a certain crime, or certain modalities of a crime, there is no implication that other modalities of the same crime, or similar crimes which are not mentioned in the law, are morally acceptable or even any less morally reprehensible. The fact that even at this moment contemporary canonical legislation inflicts the penalty of excommunication on those who "procure abortion," but not on those who perform embryotomy, in no way implies an approval of the latter form of infanticide, or even suggests a different degree of moral malice in the two acts. Nor is this type of legalism, though ecclesiastical, inappropriate within the context of external penal law. To view this type of canonical legislation as identified with, or even suggesting, a nuance of moral doctrine is to misunderstand completely the distinction between the two entities. This matter merits particular stress because some contemporary writers, insufficiently familiar with the structure of the church, have obviously mistaken changes in canonical legislation for doctrinal variations in the matter of abortion.

The third modification to which I have referred is the extension of the moral malice of abortion even to the moment of conception. This is a point of utmost importance for the clear and correct understanding of the Catholic position. At this juncture we should note that, although in some early instances there was a certain community of principle viewed as interrelating the questions of contraception and abortion, in the light of modern embryology this is no longer the case. Abortion is a question completely distinct from, and indeed unrelated to, the notion of contraception. The still unanswered question of the moment of ensoulment figures very large in this picture. If, for example, it could be conclusively shown that prior to the second trimester the fetus is not even probably a human being, the whole question of the morality of abortion in the first trimester would be a distinct problem in Catholic theology today.

You will recall that the Catholic Church identifies the wrongness of abortion in the destruction of innocent human life. Quite obviously, then, if it were possible to verify the moment of ensoulment as later than the moment of conception, an abortion prior to ensoulment would not be the destruction of an innocent human life.

But since it is at least quite *probable* that ensoulment does coincide with the very earliest stages of embryonic life, the only practical working premise, from a moral viewpoint, is to treat the human conceptus as if the moment of a new and distinct human life were certainly the moment of conception. Since a new and distinct human life may very likely be present from that moment, directly to destroy the products of human conception, even at a very early stage of development, is at least very likely the destruction of an innocent human life.

One who does even this has already discarded from his moral code the inviolability of human life and the human person and falls far short of that regard for the dignity and rights of the individual which is basic to the entire Judeo-Christian theology and tradition. Such an action is identified with the moral malice of murder since it implies a willingness to take a human life.

As early as the fourth century, Basil pointed out the same analysis of the malice of abortion and wrote, regarding the fetus, that "any fine distinction as to its being completely formed or unformed is not admissible among us," and referred to those who procure abortion as "murderers."

In this essay I have reviewed the constant teaching of the Catholic Church on abortion as the murder of the innocent. I have made some comment on the theories of ensoulment in relation to this doctrine, and I have commented briefly on three distinct facets of the doctrine which are frequently misunderstood. I have not, indeed, commented on the reasons why the Catholic Church views the direct destruction of innocent human life as morally wrong. If some explanation of this moral stance is in order, suffice it to say that the Catholic Church recognizes the echo of sound Catholic doctrine in those immortal words of the American Declaration of Independence so basic to our American way of life: "We hold these truths to be self-evident, that all men are created equal, that they are endowed by their Creator with certain unalienable Rights"—and that among these is the right to life.

A Liberal Catholic's View

Joseph F. Donceel

I fully agree with the basic Catholic principle that we are never allowed to kill an innocent human being. Therefore, if there is a real human being from the moment of conception, abortion would have to be considered immoral at any stage of pregnancy. The majority Catholic opinion holds nowadays that there is indeed a real human being from the first moment of conception, or, at least, that we cannot be certain that such is not the case. But there is also a minority Catholic opinion, which has good standing in the church, which was the opinion of her greatest theologian, Thomas Aquinas,[1] and which is now slowly regaining favor among Catholic thinkers. This minority opinion holds that there is certainly no human being during the early stages of pregnancy. I would like to show you briefly why Thomas held this position, how it was given up by his successors on account of erroneous scientific theories, and how, even after these theories had been given up, the Catholic Church did not return to her traditional view because of a philosophy which was at variance with her official doctrine of the nature of man.

Traditional Catholic philosophy holds that what makes an organism a human being is the spiritual soul and that this soul starts to exist at the moment of its "infusion" into the body. When is the human soul infused into the body? Nowadays the majority of Catholic thinkers would not hesitate to answer: at the moment of conception. This is known as the *theory of immediate animation*. However, during long centuries Catholic philosophy and theology held that the human soul was infused into the body only when the latter began to show a human shape or outline and possessed the basic human organs. Before this time, the embryo is alive, but in the way in which a plant or an animal is alive. It possesses, as the traditional terminology puts it, a vegetative or an animal soul, not yet a human soul. In more modern terms we might say that it has reached the physiological or the psychological, not yet the spiritual level of existence. It is not yet a human person; it is evolving, within the womb, toward hominization. This is the *theory of mediate or delayed animation*.

Why did Thomas and the great medieval thinkers favor this theory? Because they held the doctrine of hylomorphism, according to which the human soul is the substantial form of man, while the human body is the result of the union of this soul with materiality, with undetermined cosmic stuff, with what was then known as prime matter. Hylomorphism holds that the human soul is to the body somewhat as the shape of a statue is to the actual statue. The shape of a statue cannot exist before the statue exists. It is not something which the sculptor first makes and subsequently introduces into a block of marble. It can exist only in the completed statue. Hylomorphism holds that, in the same way, the human soul can exist only in a real human body.

Although Thomas knew nothing about chromosomes, genes, DNA, or the code of life, he knew that whatever was growing in the mother's womb was not yet, early in pregnancy, a real human body. Therefore he held that it could not be animated by a human soul, any more than a square block of marble can possess a human shape. The medieval thinkers knew very well that this growing organism would develop into a human body, that virtually, potentially, it was a human body. But they did not admit that an actual human soul could exist in a virtual human body. The Catholic Church, which had officially adopted the hylomorphic conception of human nature at the Council of Vienne, in 1312, was so strongly convinced of this position that, for centuries, her law forbade the faithful to baptize any premature birth which did not show at least some human shape or outline.

Under the influence of erroneous scientific reports, however, Catholic thinkers gave up this traditional doctrine. In the early seventeenth century, as a result of a combination of poor microscopes and lively imaginations, some physicians saw in embryos which were only a few days old a tiny human being, a homunculus, with microscopic head, legs, and arms.[2] This view of the fetus implied the *pre-formation theory*, which held that organic development simply consists of the gradual increase in size of organs and structures which are fully present from the very start. If there really were from the beginning a human body, be it ever so small, there might also from the start exist a human soul. Even a microscopic statue must have a shape. Granted the preformation theory, immediate animation was compatible with the hylomorphic conception of man.

The theory of preformation was eventually replaced by the *theory of epigenesis*, which maintains that the organism, far from being microscopically preformed from the start, develops its organs through a complex process of growth, cleavage, differentiation, and organization.

Why did the Christian thinkers not return to the delayed animation theory, which seems to be demanded by their hylomorphic theory of man? The main reason seems to have been the influence of Cartesian dualism. For Descartes, both man's soul and his body are each a complete substance. The soul is a thinking substance, the body an extended substance. This is no longer hylomorphism. To express it in nontechnical language, this is no longer a "shape in the statue" conception, but rather a "ghost in the machine" conception of the human soul. A full-fledged ghost can manage very well with a microscopic machine. If the soul is no longer the formal cause, the constitutive idea of the body, it might well become its efficient cause, that which produces the ovum's development from the start. Instead of being the idea incarnated in the body, it has turned into the architect and the builder of the body. Just as the architect exists before the first stone of the building is laid, so there can be a real human soul from the first moment of conception, before the emergence of a real human body.[3]

This way of explaining embryogeny is not absurd. The Cartesian outlook, although quite unfashionable nowadays, has been held by many great thinkers. This kind of philosophy calls for immediate animation, which is clearly in conflict with the hylomorphic doctrine of man, solemnly endorsed by the Catholic Church at the Council of Vienne.

There have been other influences which explain the shift in Catholic opinion. One of them may have been the long-standing opposition of the church to the idea of evolution. Thomas admitted some kind of evolution of the embryo and the fetus in the mother's womb. How could the church admit this evolution in the womb and reject it in the race? Since the Catholic Church has finally come around to admitting the evolution of the human body, it might also be willing to return to Thomas's idea of evolution in the womb.[4]

Moreover, once we give up the idea of immediate animation, we can no longer say when the human soul is infused, when the embryo or the fetus becomes a human person. That is why those who want to play it absolutely safe claim that the human soul is present from the moment of conception. They seem to take it for granted that, since we do not know when the human soul is present, we neither can know for sure when it is not yet present. This assumption is false. Let us consider another case, where we do not know when a certain factor is present, while knowing very well when it is not yet present. Nobody can tell with certitude when a child is capable of performing his first free moral choice, but all of us are quite certain that, during the first months or years of his life, a human baby is not yet a free moral agent. Likewise, I do not know when the human soul is infused, when the embryo becomes human. But I feel certain that there is no human soul, hence no human person, during the first few weeks of pregnancy, as long as the embryo remains in the vegetative stage of its development.

Some people make much of the following objection to my position. They say that from the very first the fertilized ovum possesses forty-six human chromosomes, all the human genes, its code of life—that it is a human embryo. This is undeniable. But it does not make it a human person. When a heart is transplanted, it is kept alive, for a short while, outside of the donor. It is a living being, a human heart, with the human chromosomes and genes. But it is not a human being; it is not a person.

The objection may be pressed. Not only does the fertilized human ovum possess the human chromosomes; unlike the heart, it will, if circumstances are normal, develop into a human being. It is virtually a human being. I admit this, but it does not affect my position. The fertilized human ovum, the early embryo, is virtually a human body, not actually. Correctly understood, the hylomorphic conception of human nature, the official Catholic doctrine, cannot admit the presence of an actual human soul in a virtual human body. Let me use a comparison again. A deflated rubber ball is virtually round; when inflated, it can assume no other shape than the spherical shape. Yet it does not actually possess any roundness or sphericity. In the same way, the early embryo does not actually possess a human soul; it is not a human person.

Experimental embryology tells us that every single cell of the early embryo, of the morula, is virtually a human body. It does not follow that each of these cells possesses a human soul. When embryologists carefully separate the cells of a morula in lower organisms, each one of these cells may develop into a complete organism. Starting with the pioneering attempts of Hans Driesch, such an experiment has been performed on many animal species. We do not see why it might not eventually succeed with the human embryo. As a matter of fact, nature frequently performs it on human ova. Identical twins derive from one ovum fertilized by one spermatozoon. This ovum splits into two at an early stage of pregnancy and gives rise to two human beings. In this case the defenders of immediate animation must admit that one person may be divided into two persons. This is a metaphysical impossibility.

Throughout my exposition I have taken for granted the hylomorphic conception of human nature. This is in line with the purpose of my essay, which is not only to present a liberal Catholic's view of fetal animation, but also to show that this view seems to be the only one which agrees with the official Catholic conception of human nature. In other words, I submit that Catholics should give up the immediate animation theory, because it implies a Cartesian, dualistic conception of man, which conflicts with the doctrine endorsed by the Council of Vienne.

In conclusion I would like to say a few words about the standing of hylomorphism among contemporary philosophers. Very few non-Catholic philosophers hold the doctrine of hylomorphism today. Even among Catholics it has fallen into disrepute, although personally I cannot see how one may avoid dualism without this theory or some theory which resembles it. Hylomorphism is radically opposed to dualism, to the doctrine which considers both the soul and the body as complete substances. Contemporary philosophy, as a rule, is also strongly opposed to this kind of dualism. In this sense, negatively, the doctrine I have defended continues to live; it is stronger than ever, although it may be known by other names.

Both linguistic analysis, the leading philosophy in the English-speaking countries, and existential phenomenology, which tends to dominate the field elsewhere, reject any form of Cartesian dualism.[5] Gilbert Ryle, a leading British analyst, has strongly attacked what he calls "the dogma of the ghost in the machine."

And Maurice Merleau-Ponty, possibly France's greatest phenomenologist, defended a doctrine which looks very much like an updated form of hylomorphism. For him there are three kinds of behavior: the syncretic, the amovable, and the symbolic. We might perhaps put it more simply and speak of three levels in man: the level of reflex activity and of instincts, the level of learning, and the level of symbolic thinking. Or again, the physiological, the psychic, and the spiritual level. Each lower level stands to the next higher one in the same relation as data stand to their meaning, as materiality stands to the idea embodied in it. The data are not data if they do not possess some meaning, and there can be no meaning which is not embedded in some data. Each higher level presupposes the lower one; there can be no mind before the organism is ready to carry one and no spirit before the mind is capable of receiving it. I submit that this clearly implies delayed animation.

In my opinion there is a great amount of agreement between the contemporary antidualistic trend of philosophy and the hylomorphic conception of man. It is wise therefore to return to this conception or, at least, to accept the conclusions which follow from it. One of these conclusions is that the embryo is certainly not a human person during the early stages of pregnancy, and that, consequently, it is not immoral to terminate pregnancy during this time, provided there are serious reasons for such an intervention.

Let me insist on this restriction: the opinion which I have defended may lead to abuses, to abortions performed under flimsy pretexts. I would be among the first to deplore and condemn such abuses. Although a prehuman embryo cannot demand from us the absolute respect which we owe to the human person, it deserves a very great consideration, because it is a living being, endowed with a human finality, on its way to hominization. Therefore it seems to me that only very serious reasons should allow us to terminate its existence. Excesses will unavoidably occur, but they should not induce us to overlook the instances where sufficiently serious reasons exist for performing an abortion during the early stages of pregnancy.

NOTES

1. See *Summa contra Gentiles*, II, 88–89; *De Potentia*, q. 3, art. 9–12; *Summa Theologica*, I, q. 118, art. 1–3.
2. See H. de Dorlodot, "A Vindication of the Mediate Animation Theory," in *Theology and Evolution*, ed. E. C. Messenger (London, 1949) 273–83.
3. The anonymous author of an article in Latin, "De Animatione Foetus" (*Nouvelle Revue Théologique* 11 [1897] 163–86, 268–89), quotes a certain Michael Alberti Germaniat Medicus, who wrote in 1725: "quod a primis conceptionis initiis anima rationalis in foetu

adsit, eo quod sine anima alla conceptio fieri nequeat, quae tanquam artifex et architecta sui corporis praesto est; a qua deinde actus formationis dependet" ("that the rational soul is present in the fetus from the first beginnings of conception, because the conception cannot take place without this soul, which is there *like the maker and the architect of its body;* hence the act of formation depends on it") (my italics). This sounds like pure Cartesianism.

4. "For the evolutionistic way of thinking it is more probable that hominization occurs not at the moment of conception, but at a later time of embryonic development," writes J. Feiner in the most recent comprehensive treatise of dogmatic theology, *Mysterium Fidei*, ed. J. Feiner and M. Löhrer (Einsiedeln, 1967) II:581.

5. Among the few exceptions we must mention J.-P. Sartre, whose dualism constitutes one of the weakest and most controversial aspects of his philosophy.

The Tradition of Probabilism and the Moral Status of the Early Embryo

Carol A. Tauer

Within the past few decades, a number of Catholic theologians have raised questions about the moral status of the human zygote and early embryo. Richard McCormick describes the embryo during the first two weeks as "nascent human life" but does not consider it an "individual human life" until later;[1] Charles Curran concurs, stating that "truly human life" comes into being two to three weeks after fertilization;[2] Albert Di Ianni proposes that the bodily continuity of a human existence begins only several weeks after conception;[3] and Karl Rahner asserts that during the first few weeks the existence of a human subject is seriously doubtful.[4] Such speculations have arisen within the context of an authoritative church teaching: the Catholic Church, in its official magisterium, asserts that human life must be given equal protection at all stages from fertilization through adulthood.[5]

In raising questions about this authoritative teaching, theologians rely on three types of material. They examine the history of Catholic teaching on prenatal life, a tradition which is somewhat less uniform than is often recognized. They investigate the implications of philosophical theories of human nature, especially the Thomistic anthropology which is traditional in the church and believed to be most consistent with its doctrinal position. And they study the relevance of the biological facts uncovered by contemporary scientific research, some of which appear to raise problems for the church's current position. Theologians have found good reasons for calling present church teaching into question, and hence appear to be justified in their speculations.

While the teaching of the magisterium is also supported by a variety of types of evidence (biological, philosophical, and theological), its position finally appears to rest on one line of argument. This argument, which is actually the crucial point in the magisterial presentation, has been largely ignored by theologians who have offered dissenting opinions. For it does not depend either on biological information or on metaphysical theories. Rather, it is based on a theory of practical decision-making which was developed within Catholic moral theology. This theory, which provides methods for attaining practical certainty in the face of moral doubt, has a long history within the Catholic tradition. Its application is evident in official Catholic Church teaching on abortion, and in the latest document on abortion issued by the Roman magisterium it plays a central role.[6]

The speculations of Catholic theologians do not appear to address directly this argument of the magisterium, and thus it might seem that their questioning of the official teaching is unwarranted. However, in my analysis of the magisterial position within its historical context, I shall argue that the magisterial argument inaccurately interprets and applies the traditional methods for resolving moral doubt. While the traditional systems do have pertinence for the case under consideration, the official documents present an incorrect interpretation of their application to the problem of early prenatal life. Since this inadequacy is present in the magisterial argument, the conclusion of that argument is called into question. Hence theologians are justified in dissenting from the full weight of that conclusion, which is the current official teaching of the church.

QUESTIONS RAISED BY CONTEMPORARY THEOLOGIANS ABOUT THE STATUS OF EARLY PRENATAL LIFE

The discoveries of reproductive biology have had significance for Catholic theologians like Rahner, Häring, McCormick, and Curran. It is primarily these discoveries which have led them to question whether an individual human life is present during the first two or three weeks after fertilization. The biological facts which they cite are summarized in a comprehensive review article by James J. Diamond.[7] Diamond claims that, in the light of the biological evidence, "hominization" cannot possibly be said to occur before fourteen to twenty-two days after conception. According to Diamond, the change in life form which takes place between fourteen and twenty-two days is a radical and categorical one.[8]

Three aspects of this change have been regarded as both biologically significant and morally relevant. The first is the capacity for twinning and recombination, a capacity which is lost after differentiation occurs. Laboratory experimentation with animal embryos shows that the early cell mass can be teased into two halves, each of which will develop into a separate and normal embryo and adult, much as in the process of natural twinning. Conversely, if two individual embryonic cell masses are conjoined at an early stage, only one embryo and adult will result.[9] While laboratory experimentation would not be appropriate in the case of human embryos, both twinning and recombination occur naturally in the human case. André Hellegers cites knowledge of at least six human "chimeras" whose genetic karyotype of XX-XY indicates that each is the product of the fusion of a male with a female embryo.[10]

The possibility of twinning and recombination is viewed as highly significant by many theologians. Curran, for example, invokes this phenomenon to support his view that truly human life is not present until two to three weeks after conception:

> My own particular opinion is that human life is not present until individuality is established. In this context we are talking about individual human life, but irreversible and differentiated individuality is not present from the time of fecundation. The single fertilized cell undergoes cell division, but in the process twinning may occur until the fourteenth day. This indicates that individual human life is not definitely established before this time. Likewise in man there is also some evidence for recombination. . . . Thus I would argue that individuated human life is not present before this time.[11]

The stage of individuation has been seen as a morally relevant marker because it appears that only individuals can be wrongfully killed or otherwise injured. A being that is not yet fixed as an individual does not seem to have claims on us. It certainly cannot be a person or a self, as selves neither split nor fuse.[12] In other terms, such a being cannot have a human soul, if one accepts the metaphysical notion of the soul as an indestructible, indivisible supposit. For if two early embryos were to fuse, and if each had a soul before fusion, then what would become of the extra soul? Souls (like selves) cannot fuse, nor can they be destroyed; neither can a soul split if one embryo divides into two or more.

The second aspect of biological change which is taken to be significant is the change from a cellular form of human life to a form which begins to display the differentiation characteristic of the human organism, not merely human cells which lack the structure of a human organic whole.[13]

Di Ianni is impressed by this data, suggesting that "at the earliest stages we are dealing with not the presence of a human body but with the *formation* of a human body."[14] Philip Devine believes that at this period we are involved with "bits of human biological material which are neither human organisms, nor parts of human organisms, but things which are becoming human organisms."[15]

The unusual character of the zygote and early embryo leads Devine to say that this stage of development presents us with a conceptual anomaly which is bound to produce, if not a category mistake, at least conceptual discomfort.[16] It is this discomfort which leads McCormick to refer to the stage only as "nascent human life,"[17] and which motivates Häring to propose a special sort of status for the early embryo:

> Between the fertilization . . . and implantation and final individualization of the embryo there is a gray area. To disturb or to interrupt the life process during this phase is, in my eyes, not an indifferent matter. But it seems to me that it does

not have the same gravity or malice as the abortion of an individualized embryo, that is, of the embryo after successful implantation or specifically at a time when twinning is no longer possible.[18]

A third fact sometimes viewed as morally significant is the large proportion of embryos lost before and during the process of implantation. Estimates of this loss vary widely, and better studies need to be done, but 56 percent appears to be a reasonable approximation.[19] Rahner cites the high percentage of embryo loss as a basis for raising questions: "Will [today's moral theologian] be able to accept that 50 percent of all 'human beings'—real human beings with 'immortal' souls and an eternal destiny—will never get beyond this first stage of human existence?"[20]

Besides the theologians who have questioned the official church teaching largely on scientific grounds, there are many who have investigated the bearing of philosophical anthropology on the issue of human prenatal life. These theologians approach the matter from various perspectives, some being strongly influenced by existentialism, phenomenology, and other contemporary schools of thought, while others study the implications of traditional approaches, particularly that of Thomism.

Joseph Donceel is a foremost representative of the latter group. In his view the hylomorphic theory of human nature proposed by Aquinas requires that the body-soul composite form one human substance. In such a theory the human soul is the life principle and substantial form of matter, or of a body, which is also at a human level of development. The human soul, which is a rational soul, can only exist in a highly organized body, probably one which already possesses the basic structures of the human cerebral cortex.[21] Donceel is adamant on the inconsistency of hylomorphism, which is the anthropology given official approval by the church, with the church's apparent moral teachings: "Hylomorphism cannot admit that the fertilized ovum, the morula, the blastocyst, the early embryo, is animated by an intellectual human soul. . . . Even God cannot put a human soul into a rock, a plant, or a lower animal, any more than he can make the contour of a circle square."[22] Thus theologians appear to find good reasons, both biological and philosophical, for questioning official church teaching on the treatment of early prenatal human life.

TEACHING OF THE MAGISTERIUM
ON PRENATAL LIFE

Catholic Church teaching on prenatal life, while generally consistent over the centuries, has undergone subtle changes which have significance in the current debate. From the earliest days of the Christian community abortion was condemned.[23] Also from the earliest centuries, however, a distinction was made between the unformed and the formed fetus, a distinction stemming from the Septuagint translation of Exodus 21:22.[24] Both St. Jerome and St. Augustine, for example, taught that abortion is not homicide until the scattered elements are formed into a body.[25]

A parallel line of discussion, that of the process of ensoulment, gradually came to be assimilated to the concept of the formed fetus. In early Christian times three theories of the origin of the human soul were debated. Traducianism claimed that the human soul was generated along with the body at conception. The theory of preexistence took the Platonic view that the soul had a premundane existence and joined the body at or after conception. Creationism held that the soul was created at some moment *ex nihilo* and then infused by God into the developing embryo. Various versions of the creationist view located the time of infusion from conception (the Pythagoreans) to birth (the Stoics).[26]

In his canonical collection (ca. 1140), Gratian adopted the creationist theory and also asserted that the soul is not infused until the fetus is formed. From that time until 1869, canon law distinguished between the unensouled and the ensouled fetus in its treatment of the gravity of abortion and the penalties to be imposed.[27] The creationist theory received additional support from Aquinas, who found it compatible with the Aristotelian view of biology which he integrated into his theological writings: "The embryo has at the beginning only a sensitive soul. This disappears and a soul more perfect succeeds to it at once sensitive and in-tellectual. . . . Since [the intellectual soul] is an immaterial substance, it cannot be caused through generation, but only through creation by God."[28] It has always been accepted Catholic teaching that the presence of the human soul conferred human status. As its departure marked the death of the human being, so its assumption into the body marked the beginning of the life of the human being. After the definitive influence of Gratian and Aquinas, the creationist version of the origin of the soul also became part of Catholic doctrine. It was reiterated at the Council of Trent,[29] described by Pope Pius XII as *fides catholica*,[30] and taken for granted in catechisms studied by the faithful.[31]

Since the presence of the soul conferred human status, the time at which the soul was infused by God was a time of great moral significance. Though there has been disagreement through the centuries about when this time is, its sig-nificance for Catholic moral teaching has never been seriously questioned. After the infusion of the soul, abortion is homicidal, whereas before that time it could be characterized as contraceptive.[32]

When the distinction between the ensouled and the unensouled fetus was re-moved from canon law (1869), the Catholic Church seemed to be stating dog-matically that the soul is infused at the earliest possible time, that is, at fertil-ization. It is often assumed that this is the church's teaching, an assumption which is reinforced by moral pronouncements of the magisterium. For example, Vatican II stated: "From the moment of its conception life must be guarded with the greatest care,"[33] a directive which is reiterated verbatim by the American bishops in the regulations for Catholic health facilities. In case they might be misunderstood, the bishops add: "An abortion, . . . in its moral context, includes the interval between conception and implantation of the embryo."[34]

It must be noted, however, that these statements are moral judgments, not metaphysical or ontological assertions. The commission of Vatican II which developed the statement on prenatal life avoided defining abortion, since it did not consider itself, or the church, the competent body for deciding the moment after which a full human being is present. It intended to make a moral point "without touching upon the moment of animation" or ensoulment.[35]

Similarly, the most recent statement of the Catholic Church's official teaching on prenatal life explicitly recognizes philosophical uncertainty about the beginning of an individual human life. Hence it acknowledges the legitimacy of the ontological speculations cited earlier: "This declaration expressly leaves aside the question of the moment when the spiritual soul is infused. There is not a unanimous tradition on this point and authors are as yet in disagreement."[36] In this document, titled *Declaration on Abortion*, the Sacred Congregation for the Doctrine of the Faith seems to welcome continuing philosophical discussion as to the moment of infusion of the soul, and hence the beginning of human life. But at the same time it takes a moral position which does not appear to permit debate on the morally appropriate treatment of early embryonic life: "From a moral point of view this is certain: even if a doubt existed concerning whether the fruit of conception is already a human person, it is objectively a grave sin to dare to risk murder."[37] Thus the Congregation, while welcoming metaphysical or ontological inquiry, gives notice to theologians that the moral issue is essentially closed.

RELATIONSHIP OF QUESTIONING THEOLOGIANS TO MAGISTERIAL TEACHING

If the theologians who are debating the status of early prenatal life are focused solely on the metaphysical or ontological aspects of the question, then their discussion is completely within the spirit of the *Declaration on Abortion*. If their investigation of biological facts, and the relationship of these facts to metaphysical theories, is intended to establish that a particular stage of development is the time of ensoulment, then their studies are encouraged by the *Declaration*. However, unless and until there is certainty about the moment of ensoulment, the *Declaration* clearly does not encourage speculation about the moral permissibility of various courses of action. It explicitly states that as long as there is doubt, one may not risk taking a possibly human life.

In the writings of the authors previously cited, there is evidence that they do propose moral implications which may be drawn from their ontological arguments.

These implications relate to two types of situations: the question of abortion, and the issue of research in *in vitro* fertilization and other technologies involving early prenatal life.

Häring, in speaking of the (ontologically) gray area between conception and final individualization, infers that interrupting the life process at this period does not have the same gravity as an abortion after successful implantation of the embryo. In fact, he considers this distinction to be "an even more evident qualitative difference" than the difference between preventing conception and preventing the implantation of the early embryo.[38] Diamond specifically links the issue of homicide to what he calls hominization. It is only after an individual human organism is present, that is, after fourteen to twenty-two days of development, that the question of homicide arises. In Diamond's view, a destruction of the cell mass before differentiation begins cannot even constitute a risk of killing a human being.[39] Donceel, convinced by his philosophical arguments that the embryo is not ensouled at conception, believes that termination of early embryonic life would be permissible for very grave reasons. He notes that abortion becomes the "unspeakable crime" mentioned by Vatican II only when it is really infanticide, which cannot be held of early abortions.[40] Thomas Wassmer argues that, in the light of the Thomistic anthropology, early abortion in rare cases, such as rape, incest, and a predictably defective infant, could be justified.[41]

Theologians have drawn similar inferences regarding the morality of research involving early prenatal life. Curran's views on individualization led him to recommend to the Ethics Advisory Board of the Department of Health, Education, and Welfare that embryos of less than two weeks' gestation could ethically be utilized in basic research.[42] McCormick, a member of that board, hesitated to draw such a broad conclusion; but he did join the board in approving a policy which would allow this research if it were directed to, or were a corollary of, research aimed at establishing the safety and efficacy of *in vitro* fertilization with embryo transfer (a method for achieving pregnancy with certain types of infertility).[43] Rahner states a position which appears to be directly at odds with the stand asserted by the Sacred Congregation when he says: "Given a serious positive doubt about the human quality of the experimental material, the reasons in favour of experimenting might carry more weight . . . than the uncertain rights of a human being whose very existence is in doubt."[44]

When Di Ianni asks that theologians and philosophers "draw a safe line at some point well before the end of the sixth week,"[45] he too speaks directly counter to the Congregation. For the Congregation has already drawn a safe line, at the time of fertilization. According to its argument, the only safe line is the one that is the safest.

Have the theologians cited ignored this claim? While engaging in legitimate ontological speculation, they do appear to propose moral positions which are contrary to the teaching of the *Declaration*.

PERMISSIBILITY OF DISSENT FROM AUTHORITATIVE CHURCH TEACHING

Undoubtedly the theologians who have raised questions about the moral treatment of early prenatal life are aware that they are questioning an authoritative teaching of the Catholic Church. Many of them have written on the issue of the permissibility of dissent from an official moral teaching of the magisterium. While a large proportion of these discussions arose within the controversy about contraception, the discussions are general enough to apply to other moral issues.

As recently as Vatican II, the Constitution on the Church (*Lumen gentium*) in its well-known section no. 25 required "religious submission of will and *of mind*" towards a noninfallible but authoritative statement by the magisterium.[46] Rahner has commented extensively on this section, observing that its demand for an accepting silence on the part of theologians leaves many questions unanswered.[47] He sees two problems. The first is that the church has erred at times in its moral teachings in the past, and corrections of such errors cannot be made unless theologians raise objections. The ten cardinals who compose the Sacred Congregation for the Doctrine of the Faith have no special training in theology beyond their seminary days and cannot be expected to understand all aspects of the questions they are considering.

The second issue is the actual response of church authority to worldwide dissent on *Humanae vitae*. Rahner believes that the nature of this response supports his claim that *Lumen gentium* (and documents which make similar statements) is inadequate:

> If . . . the statements of *Lumen gentium* . . . on this matter were valid without qualification, then the world-wide dissent of Catholic moral theologians against *Humanae vitae* would be a massive and global assault on the authority of the magisterium. But the fact that the magisterium tolerates this assault shows that the norm of *Lumen gentium* . . . does not express in sufficiently nuanced form a legitimate praxis of the relationship between the magisterium and theologians.[48]

Häring notes that Vatican II did address the right to dissent in other of its documents. He speaks of dissent as a prophetic ministry within the church, one needed to prevent "ossification of doctrines" and "temptations of ideologies." In his view, a "common dedication to truth is possible only if there is freedom of inquiry and freedom to speak out even in dissent from official documents." Failure to do this early enough has often resulted in unfortunate errors and setbacks in the past.[49]

In a survey article McCormick cites Rahner, André Naud, and Avery Dulles to support his own position.[50] For Naud, doubt and search have a necessary role, and bishops and theologians must speak freely on controversial questions, both before and after Roman declarations.[51] Dulles fears that moral theology is currently being stifled by magisterial declarations, much as scriptural investigation was during the nineteenth century.[52] (Note the explicit appeal to authority in the conclusion of *Humanae vitae.*[53])

McCormick writes elsewhere of his fears that a literal interpretation of *Lumen gentium* could endanger theology as a profession and as a charism in the church; for that document contains "no references to modifying official formulations, extending them into new circumstances, adapting them to new culture, . . . a key creative task of theology as a discipline."[54]

Curran believes that the church's own understanding of the status of its authoritative but noninfallible teaching permits dissent. Not only have errors been made in the past, but in principle "in specific moral judgments on complex matters one cannot hope to attain a degree of certitude that excludes the possibility of error."[55] Such errors cannot be corrected unless dissent is permitted and even encouraged.

In a highly analytical article on the status of moral truths, Gerard Hughes argues that even moral truths propounded as irreformable by the church's magisterium must in principle be inadequate. These truths are timeless only in the sense that "At no future time can it turn out that what was infallibly taught *was* false."[56] In order to prove his claim of inadequacy, Hughes stipulates that each possible moral judgment be expressed in what he calls normal form: "A is right (wrong, permissible, etc.)," where A is a nonmoral description of a type of action, and the moral judgment is entirely contained in the predicate. Now there is no way to give a "timeless" description A of any type of action (e.g., artificial contraception), hence the subject in the normal form of any moral judgment will have to be continually changed. But then two formulations of the same moral judgment, one more adequate to a contemporary development than another, will yield contradictory results in practice in at least one case. Thus the less adequate formulation will require change in its actual content, and according to Hughes, "Irreformability in morals cannot . . . mean that the moral predicate which is deemed appropriate to some action A (say, that it is right, or wrong, or permissible) can never be altered."[57] While Hughes does not say so, it appears clear that greater adequacy in the formulation of moral judgments can only be obtained if these judgments may be discussed—whether or not they have been presented by the magisterium as irreformable.

Thus there appear to be sound arguments supporting the legitimacy of dissent from authoritative moral teachings, not only the noninfallible pronouncements but even those which are reputedly irreformable. These arguments have been put forward and supported by many of the theologians who raise questions about the moral treatment of early prenatal life and who see in these arguments a justification for their speculations.

MAGISTERIAL ARGUMENT AS APPLICATION OF TRADITIONAL METHODS FOR RESOLVING MORAL DOUBT

The Certainty of the Magisterial Conclusion

While dissent on authoritative moral teaching may be legitimate, it is curious that theologians who dissent from the official position on the treatment of early embryonic life do not seem to address the crucial point in the magisterial argument. The *Declaration on Abortion* attaches great importance to the moment of ensoulment, acknowledges that we are uncertain as to this moment, but then goes on to a *certain* moral conclusion. According to the *Declaration*, ensoulment "is a philosophical problem from which our moral affirmation remains independent. . . . It suffices that this presence of the soul be probable (and one can never prove the contrary) in order that the taking of life involve accepting the risk of killing a man, not only waiting for, but already in possession of his soul."[58] And according to the *Declaration*, taking such a risk is gravely sinful: "From a moral point of view this is certain: even if a doubt existed whether the fruit of conception is already a human person, it is objectively a grave sin to dare to risk murder."[59] In its argument, the Sacred Congregation follows the traditional view of Catholic moral theology that one may never act when in doubt. According to Häring, "Practical doubt is equivalent to a verdict of conscience forbidding the act until the doubt has been cleared up practically," that is, until there is no positive argument favoring the opposing position.[60] For if one acted in doubt, one would be expressing a willingness to perform an act that could be wrong. As Häring notes, this position requiring certainty has been held and taught by all teachers in the church from St. Paul on.[61]

Many of the contemporary theologians who raise doubts about the nature of early embryonic life suggest that these doubts might allow some leeway in terms of what actions are morally permissible. But if one may never act when in doubt, then the Sacred Congregation appears to be correct in categorically forbidding any harmful interventions toward early prenatal life.

Resolution of Doubt by Probabilistic Methods

However, there is another aspect of the Catholic tradition on handling doubts that must be considered. It is not always possible to resolve one's doubts directly, particularly in a situation of conflicting moral obligations, and so Catholic moral theology developed methods for arriving at what it called indirect certainty. In order to reach indirect certainty, one could invoke general principles such as "A doubtful law does not bind," principles which were considered to be *certain* moral principles. One could be certain of not being obligated by a doubtful law, and thus could act with the assurance of not sinning. For the proper application of such principles, there had to be some degree of probability that the application of the law truly was in doubt; and various systems for the moral evaluation of this probability were proposed.

In its use of the terms "doubt," "certain," and "probable," the Sacred Congregation suggests that its moral argument has roots in this portion of historical Catholic moral theology. In order to assess the Congregation's argument, it is necessary to review this theological tradition.

In the Catholic moral tradition the word "probable" is used with a broad denotation. An opinion is termed probable if one "has good and solid reasons for thinking that a certain line of action is morally correct." The characterization applies even if one "is aware at the same time that there are better, sounder, and more cogent reasons for thinking that it is not."[62] Thus, conceptually, the term "probable" may refer to a fairly small probability. The Sacred Congregation espouses this usage in saying "It suffices that this presence of the soul be probable (and one can never prove the contrary)."[63]

While "probable" as a term may refer to small probabilities, it would be foolhardy to assert that one would be acting morally on the basis of a small probability that one's opinion is correct. Prudence dictates that one have a certain level of assurance that one's position is sound before applying the maxim "A doubtful law does not bind." The tradition includes extensive discussion and debate as to what degree of assurance or probability is needed to enable one to act with impunity.

Within this debate various schools of thought emerged and gradually acquired the status of alternative systems for moral decision-making. Each of these systems considers the question of when one is at liberty with regard to a possible law, that is, when one is under no obligation to observe the law. The following are the positions of the systems which have had most influence:[64]

Probabiliorism: It is wrong to act on an opinion which favours liberty, unless the opinion is more probable than that which is in favour of the obligation.

Equiprobabilism: [When] conflicting opinions in regard to the existence of a law are equally or nearly equally probable, one may follow the opinion in favour of liberty, but when the opinion in favour of a law is certainly more probable than the contrary, it is unlawful to follow the less probable opinion in favour of liberty.

Probabilism: If there exists a really probable opinion in favour of liberty, . . . although the opinion in favour of the law is more probable, I may use the former opinion and disregard the latter.

None of the systems cited represents the official teaching of the Catholic Church. They are among the "several systems [which have been] permitted to be taught in the Church, and each system is held and defended by able theologians."[65] Since St. Alphonsus Liguori developed the system of equiprobabilism to mediate between the more extreme systems of probabiliorism and probabilism, this system seems to have had privileged status among theologians, a status enhanced when Alphonsus was declared a doctor of the church and patron of confessors and moralists.[66] In his discussion of systems for resolving doubt, Häring, for example, clearly supports a form of equiprobabilism.[67] However, in pastoral counseling, especially in the confessional, probabilism has been highly favored because of its sensitivity to individual conscience. Philip Kaufman believes that this stance is demanded of the conscientious confessor,[68] and even Häring appears to approve probabilism in the pastoral setting when he says: "In the tribunal of penance the confessor is never permitted to refuse absolution to any penitent who holds and follows an opinion proposed by prudent and learned moralists, even though the confessor himself looks upon it as false."[69] In making the strong statements contained in the *Declaration on Abortion,* members of the Sacred Congregation do not indicate the system to which they subscribe. They seem to say that no matter how probable it is that the zygote or early embryo is not yet a human person, if there is any probability that it is, then destroying it is a grave sin. For note the clause "it suffices that this presence of the soul be probable (and one can never prove the contrary)," recalling the historical use of "probable" to refer to small probabilities. In fact, the assertion suggests that in principle one could never find reasons strong enough to counter the possibility that the soul might be present at these early stages. The Sacred Congregation's conclusion appears to be based on a criterion more stringent than those of any of the systems previously described. At first glance it appears that the writers have adopted rigorism, a system which holds that "it is not allowed to follow even the most probable opinion for liberty."[70] According to this system, if there is even a slight probability that a law may be binding, then one is obligated to observe the law. However, rigorism has been condemned by the Catholic Church as a system to guide decision-making, specifically by Pope Alexander VIII in 1690, when he rejected the proposition "It is not lawful to follow a probable opinion, even if it is the most probable among probable opinions."[71]

Doubt about the Status of Prenatal Life Interpreted as a Doubt of Fact

In examining the tradition more closely, though, one finds that the Sacred Congregation has not subscribed to rigorism; for the tradition of Catholic moral theology makes a distinction between a doubt of law and a doubt of fact. Francis

Connell, in the *New Catholic Encyclopedia,* defined these terms as follows: "A doubt of law . . . is concerned with the existence or scope of a certain law. . . . A doubt of fact . . . is concerned with the performance or nonperformance of some particular act relating to the fulfillment or nonfulfillment of the law. . . ."[72] According to many moral theologians, systems like probabilism and equiprobabilism may be applied only to a doubt of law, when it is the doubtful existence or scope of a law that is in conflict with liberty.[73] Other theologians change the maxim cited earlier, "A doubtful law does not bind," to "A doubtful obligation does not bind," and allow at least some doubts of fact to be resolved by probabilistic systems.[74] But even when some doubts of fact are included, those which involve questions of human life and justice are not; in these situations, what moralists call the safer course must be followed, not the course favoring liberty. Possible harm to another person or possible infringement of his or her rights are viewed as risks which cannot be chosen on the basis that there is some (perhaps substantial) probability that the harm or wrong will not occur; for in these cases there is a law of either justice or charity which with certainty forbids one to bring about the harmful results and thus forbids one to risk bringing them about.[75] In Henry Davis's words, "Every man has a right that I should not take the risk of injuring or killing him."[76]

In applying the decision-making methods of Catholic moral theology to the problem of the uncertain ontological and moral status of the human zygote and embryo, the principle just developed seems to be pertinent. Moralists of that tradition appear to agree that one may never resolve a factual doubt which endangers the life of a human being by using a probabilistic method of decision-making. Typical examples presented to illustrate this point are: a hunter is not certain whether the movement in the bushes is that of an animal or a human being; a druggist has reason to think that one of a number of similar bottles on the shelf actually contains poison. In these cases, the hunter may not shoot and the druggist may not dispense the preparations.[77] The typical examples cited are situations which do demand caution; it seems that an ethicist of any tradition or viewpoint would require that the doubts in these cases be resolved before the hunter or druggist be at liberty to act.

Thus it does not seem justifiable to charge the Sacred Congregation with following rigorism. Rather, the Congregation mandates that the safer course be followed in a situation which resembles the cases just described. In these cases a doubt of fact exists and human life is at risk. Such examples have traditionally been used to illustrate the principle that one *must* at times choose the safer alternative. It appears that the Congregation is following this principle in requiring that the safer alternative be chosen relative to the treatment of early prenatal life. The Congregation appears to regard the existing doubt as a doubt of fact where human life is endangered.

RESPONSE OF QUESTIONING THEOLOGIANS TO MAGISTERIAL METHOD OF RESOLVING DOUBT

While the *Declaration on Abortion* apparently makes a legitimate application of the principles of Catholic moral theology for achieving certainty, this argument with its certain conclusion ("From a moral point of view this is certain: even if a doubt existed . . ., it is objectively a grave sin . . ."[78]) has been largely ignored by the theologians who question its teaching.

Both McCormick and Curran discuss probabilism,[79] with Curran stating that a thorough study of its application to early embryonic life is needed. McCormick makes use of probabilism in balancing the sufficiency of the doubt about the status of the early embryo against the tragic consequences which result from a rape situation. However, neither of these authors directly addresses the argument proposed by the Sacred Congregation. In his *Medical Ethics* Häring utilizes his theoretical work on probabilistic methods and often speaks of the probability of a particular opinion, even referring to the degree of certainty or probability possessed by a teaching of the magisterium.[80] While some of these references relate to prenatal life, none of them touches on the actual method of argumentation used by the Sacred Congregation. (Though the *Declaration on Abortion* was issued after Häring's book, its approach reflected the standard teaching and did not offer anything new or surprising. Furthermore, in an article published two years after the *Declaration,* Häring questioned the authoritative moral teaching on prenatal life without even adverting to the fact that that teaching is based on an application of traditional methods for resolving doubt.[81])

Kaufman quotes Häring's formulation of the limitation on applying probabilistic methods to doubts of fact, "If the life of our neighbor is liable to be imperiled by actions of ours, we must choose the safest course of action so as to avoid this evil effect,"[82] and draws from it what would appear to be a valid conclusion: probable opinions justifying abortion on demand, therefore, cannot be followed.[83] Almost none of the theologians who present probable opinions on prenatal life, even if limited to the earliest weeks after fertilization, attempt to show why Häring's formulation may not apply.

The Jesuit theologian Thomas Wassmer, who espouses a Thomistic theory of delayed infusion of the soul, is an exception to the general avoidance of the crucial point in the magisterial argument. Wassmer considers the use of probabilistic methods for determining the appropriate moral treatment of early prenatal life, and addresses the argument of the *Declaration* seven years before its publication.[84] He asks whether it really is the case that one may *never* use probabilistic methods to resolve a factual doubt if human life might be endangered. Finding evidence in the tradition that this is not the case, Wassmer suggests that there are times when one may not be required to follow the safer course.

Wassmer's evidence consists of counterexamples designed to show that Catholic moralists have traditionally permitted liberty in some situations of factual doubt about human life. These instances are cases where other possible evils are weighed against the risk of destruction of a human life, and where the risk taken is actually quite small. Wassmer's first example appears medically absurd, but it can be seen to serve his purpose:

> Moralists will allow a woman to use a douche after rape as late as 10 hours after the assault on the grounds that conception has been known to take place within that length of time. . . . The safer course would be to consider that impregnation and conception took place at the earliest possible time after the assault, or even during the assault.[85]

Now a douche suggests a vaginal douche, which might affect sperm that were present but would never interact with a fertilized egg. However, earlier moralists did discuss the use of an intrauterine douche which might also flow into the Fallopian tubes. This douche supposedly was to kill sperm that were present and could be used (from the moral point of view) for the period of time which was estimated as the time needed for fertilization to be completed. Up to that time it was likely that no fertilized egg was present to be affected by the douche. Of course, for medical reasons, intrauterine douche would never be recommended or even discussed today; but the example is one in which traditional moralists allowed one to act despite a factual doubt about the presence of what they presumably considered a human life, i.e., a fertilized egg.

Wassmer's second example involves a terminally-ill patient. If "there is no [*sic*] probability of a return to rational consciousness," then most traditional Catholic moralists would allow extraordinary means of life support to be terminated, resulting in the patient's death. Since Wassmer interprets this case as one where there is a doubt of fact regarding return to rational consciousness, he must mean there is "almost no probability" that this will happen.[86] The theologians cited take the position that the grave burden of indefinitely supporting an unconscious life justifies the termination of treatment; presumably these theologians would not require absolute certainty in the medical prognosis regarding the return to consciousness. The remote possibility that consciousness could return presents a factual doubt, and terminating treatment is not the safer course. Thus it appears that moral theologians do not require one always to follow the safer course simply because human life is at stake.

Wassmer uses these examples because he wants to compare them with the situation in which he is interested, abortion in early pregnancy. Along with the Sacred Congregation, Wassmer holds that the ensoulment of the embryo confers personhood. Without ensoulment the life which is present is not that of a human being. But according to Wassmer, and other questioning theologians, it is doubtful that the early embryo is ensouled. Even though this uncertainty is a factual doubt in a case where human life is at stake, Wassmer argues, it may not be obligatory to take the safer course and forbid all abortions. The examples used for comparison suggest that other evils which are imminent (e.g., damage to the mother's health, the birth of a predictably defective infant, trauma resulting from a pregnancy due to rape) may allow one to take a less safe course or to have an early abortion despite factual doubt about the embryo's possessing a soul.[87]

The Sacred Congregation takes an opposite position on the morality of such abortions, claiming that even though the presence of the soul is uncertain, one may never take the risk of destroying the life of a human being. While the Congregation does not discuss doubts of fact versus doubts of law, by its rigorous application of the moral tradition on doubt it indicates that it also considers the doubt in question to be a doubt of fact. Since the rigorist position on doubts of law has been condemned, the Congregation could hardly be adopting that position.

IS THE UNCERTAINTY ABOUT ENSOULMENT A FACTUAL DOUBT?

The Assumption That the Doubt Is Factual

As shown in the preceding section, the only theological criticism which directly addresses the application of the probabilistic tradition in the *Declaration* does so by questioning the absoluteness of that tradition. Wassmer's argument maintains that there are times when probabilism has been, and thus may be, applied to doubts of fact even if human life could be at risk. Thus, according to Wassmer, the conclusion of the Congregation is not by any means a certain one, as it is claimed to be.

Wassmer does agree with the Congregation, however, on a crucial assumption: the question of whether the zygote or early embryo possesses a human soul is a factual matter. It is this assumption which I wish to question, arguing that it is neither conceptually plausible nor consistent with the Catholic moral tradition on systems for handling doubt. Now if the moral decision to be made hinged on a doubt of law rather than a doubt of fact, then, according to the tradition, probabilistic methods could be applied, and the stringent position of the *Declaration* would not be warranted by the arguments presented.[88] And if the argument in the *Declaration* is not sound, then the theologians who question some of its conclusions are justified in offering alternative formulations of our duty towards early prenatal human life. They may even be obligated to present such alternatives, especially in relation to conflict situations where other important human values are endangered.

Concept of the Factual

In contemporary philosophy the word "fact" is customarily defined either as
a state of affairs in the world or as a true proposition about a state of affairs in
the world. While philosophers may be interested in debate as to which conceptualization is preferable, such issues are irrelevant to our discussion. However,
the debate does assume a point which is pertinent: the states of affairs in question
obtain within our spatiotemporal world and the truth of a factual proposition is
verifiable, in principle at least, by empirical methods. Frederick Suppe, a noted
philosopher of science, thus presents a standard definition of "fact" when he says:
facts are what empirically true propositions state or assert about the world.[89]

Suppe's definition restricts facts to states of affairs which are empirically observable within the spatiotemporal world. In this conceptualization facts are the
result of the ordinary observation of physical entities and events in everyday life,
or else the product of scientific observation and study of these phenomena. Attempts to extend the notion of "fact" beyond this domain appear to lead to
conceptual confusions. For example, when Raphael Demos, a philosopher of religion, holds that religion as well as science has its facts, he has to recognize
that it has a different definition of "fact."[90] Just what this definition is, is not
clear; but certainly it does not include empirical verifiability. John Hick, another
philosopher of religion, attempts to include some religious or philosophical beliefs
in the category of the factual by claiming that they *are* empirically verifiable. In
his essay on the immortality of the human soul, he claims that this issue is a
factual one because it will be verifiable after death.[91] But that understanding of
empirical, hence of factual, appears to be a highly idiosyncratic one.

In his article "Is the Fetus a Person?" Albert Di Ianni calls the status of the
fetus a "human fact," a type of fact which supposedly can be inferred from a
combination of empirical facts and value judgments.[92] This sort of fact does not
describe a state of affairs at all, but rather is a proposition which is taken to be
true because it follows from empirical facts when seen in the light of particular
value commitments or assumptions. Di Ianni holds that a statement such as "The
fetus at eight weeks is a person" belongs to the category of human facts, because
its truth depends not only on empirical data but also on the relative weight given
to the values involved. If one attaches a greater value to human life itself than
to privacy and autonomy, then one will choose to recognize the statement as
true; if one's value priorities are the reverse, then one will not. The *truth* of the
given statement thus depends at least partly on the values one wishes to support.[93]

Category of the Theoretical

In order to avoid such conceptual muddles, which arise from dividing propositions into the two classes of factual and evaluative, a third category, that of

"theory," is helpful. A theory is a body of concepts and propositions which attempts to provide an adequate explanation for what is empirically observed. While a theoretical proposition is descriptive, it goes beyond the empirical as it fulfills its explanatory function. Many of the propositions of natural science are theoretical in nature; they are devised and tested as causal explanations of empirical regularities. Analyses of theory in the scientific context suggest that metaphysical and often religious propositions belong in this category, since they too are devised as explanations for phenomena that are observed.[94]

Surely the assertions of Plato about the existence of the Forms and the nature of the human soul are properly characterized as theoretical rather than factual statements. Such a characterization does not detract from the possible truth of these assertions, but rather suggests that the method of establishing this truth is different from that used in the case of factual (or empirical) statements. Similarly, assertions in Christian theology about the mode and time of ensoulment during the human gestational process appear to partake of the character of theory rather than of fact. The facts of biology may lend themselves better to one theory than another, but they do not prove any theory. The most that can be said is that some theories appear to be incompatible with the biological facts.

Coherence of the Congregation's Argument

The Sacred Congregation is concerned about the time at which the human embryo becomes ensouled, and from its utilization of the moral tradition on handling doubts of fact, it indicates that it regards the time of ensoulment as a factual matter. Yet it explicitly states: "It is not up to the biological sciences to make a definitive judgment on questions which are properly philosophical . . ., such as the moment when a human person is constituted. . . ."[95] Furthermore, the Congregation clearly asserts that there is no way that this time can be established by methods available to us within our spatiotemporal world, saying: "It suffices that this presence of the soul be probable (*and one can never prove the contrary*)."[96] Thus the Congregation seems to recognize that the time of ensoulment is really *not* a factual matter, since *in principle* it cannot be ascertained.

Consistency with the Traditional Understanding of Doubts of Fact

At first glance it might appear that a resolution of this apparent contradiction is easily achieved. While contemporary philosophical analysis may wisely suggest distinguishing facts (as empirical) from theories (as explanatory or metaphysical), Catholic moralists have had no intention of making this distinction. When they speak of doubts of fact, they mean to include doubts about theoretical as well as empirical assertions. Thus the Congregation is true to the tradition in treating the irresolvable doubt concerning the time of ensoulment as a doubt of fact.

Now it is true that Catholic moralists of the past did not attempt to define a fact, believing that the concept was easily understood. So, in order to infer their intentions, it is necessary to examine the examples which they used as illustrations. Consider first the four examples cited earlier in this article. The issues involved are all factual in the precise contemporary sense; for in principle one can determine by empirical methods whether the thing in the bushes is a human being or an animal, whether a bottle contains poison or not, whether there is a fertilized ovum present in the Fallopian tube, and (by simply waiting) whether a person will recover from coma or illness. Other frequently cited examples also involve states of affairs that are empirically verifiable: whether liquid to be used for baptism is true water, whether the revolver chamber selected before one fires in "Russian roulette" contains the cartridge, whether a liquid to be used for saying Mass is truly grape wine, whether an accused person is guilty of the alleged crime (a fact that must be proven beyond a reasonable doubt before a conviction is justified).[97] In no source could even one example be found which involves doubt on a point of metaphysical theory.

The only evidence available to us for judging the meaning of "fact" intended by Catholic moralists is their examples. Since these examples all appear to involve empirically verifiable states of affairs, it thus is consistent with the tradition to claim that the doubt about the time of ensoulment of the human embryo is not a doubt of fact.

Possibility That Safer Course Must Always Be Followed If Human Life Is at Risk

Another resolution of the Congregation's apparent contradiction is possible. Perhaps no doubt, not even a doubt of law, may be resolved by probabilistic methods if human life or some other basic human right is at stake. It may be that moral theologians of the Catholic tradition have simply neglected to point this out, while at the same time adhering to the restriction.

Reference to several striking controversial issues should be sufficient to respond to that proposal. Historically, probabilistic methods have not only been used by theologians but have been recognized by the church's magisterium as a legitimate way of handling doubts of law in some cases where the right to life or another basic human right is involved. Two of these types of cases present situations in which we now believe that an opinion favoring liberty is clearly incorrect. The first is the castration of boys for the purpose of preserving high-pitched voices for religious choirs. A probable opinion permitting this practice was supported by the fact that thirty-two popes over a period of three hundred years accepted the use of *castrati* in the Sistine Choir.[98] A second situation is the acceptance of slavery. Affirmations by popes from Martin I in 650 through the instruction of the Holy Office in 1866, which reaffirmed the moral justification for certain types of slavery, rested on probable opinions. Actually, slavery was taught to be *certainly* justified; the application of probabilism lay in the opinions as to the sorts of slavery that were acceptable (e.g., enslavement of the offspring of non-celibate clerics, enforced in 655; and permanent enslavement of Saracens and other "pagans," permitted during the Crusades).[99]

In a textbook of moral theology once widely used in Catholic schools and colleges, Edwin Healy cites the use of probabilism made by the church's magisterium as the best evidence for its validity.[100] The ways in which the church has consistently applied this method thus provide a standard for its authentic application. Castration and slavery offer examples of situations where probabilism was utilized over a long period of time. There are additional examples which show that the church has consistently relied on probable opinions in order to determine the scope and application of the natural and divine law against killing. In making judgments about the morality of capital punishment and the extent to which one may kill or disable in self-defense, the church invokes theological opinions which have only a certain probability. In difficult life-and-death situations which arise in medical ethics, such as the termination of extraordinary means of treatment and the specification of those means, again probable opinions are cited; and in that most difficult case of warfare, the formulation of the conditions which justify entering into and waging a war can only be based on probable opinions.

Thus the church indicates that where there is a doubt of law involving human life or human rights, probable opinions will often offer the only possible guidelines. Such a situation differs from that in which there is a *certain* law or obligation which involves definite rights on the part of others. A probable invasion of these rights, based on a doubt of fact, would be morally wrong.

Deviation from the Tradition in the Congregation's Argument

Thus the two proposed ways for resolving what appears to be a deviation from the tradition in the *Declaration on Abortion* do not succeed. In the context of the moral tradition for handling doubts of fact, only empirically verifiable uncertainties are cited as examples. This is particularly clear in the situations where human life is at risk and probabilistic methods may not be used. On the other hand, it cannot be true that one must have a comparable certainty regarding doubts of law when basic human rights are at stake; for the magisterium has consistently allowed and utilized probabilistic methods for handling such doubts.

Therefore it appears that the Congregation is not true to its own moral tradition in teaching in the *Declaration* "This is certain: even if a doubt existed . . ., it is objectively a grave sin to dare to risk murder," and to conclude that interruption of prenatal life at any time after fertilization, and for any reason, is morally prohibited.[101]

CAN A DOUBT OF THEORY
BE A DOUBT OF LAW?

The doubt about the time of ensoulment of the embryo is of a theoretical nature; so it does not seem to fit either category of doubt proposed by the moral theologians. It is not a fact in the sense in which these moralists use that term, and yet it is not directly a doubt about a law. I shall argue, however, that it is related to doubts of law in such a way that it is most appropriately handled within that category in the tradition of systems for resolving doubts. Three arguments support this conclusion.

Relationship of Law and Theory

The first argument is based on an analysis of sentence types. A moral law, such as "Thou shalt not kill," is an imperative which does not have any truth value; one simply states it. A doubt of law is really a doubt as to whether a formulated law actually is part of the body of natural and/or divine law. Thus the doubt might be about statements like "God has commanded that thou shalt not kill," or "God has commanded that thou shalt not kill human beings except in self-defense," or "God has commanded that thou shalt not kill early human embryos." But these statements, which do have truth value, are theoretical statements. They express a state of affairs which is not empirically verifiable. As such, they have the same epistemological status as "From conception the human embryo has a rational soul." So any doubt of law is actually doubt about the truth of a theoretical proposition concerning what God commands or the moral law demands, and such theoretical propositions have never been considered to be factual in nature.

A second argument is related to the first. While every doubt of law may be a theoretical doubt, it is of course not true that every theoretical doubt is a doubt of law. For example, doubts about assertions describing the nature and life of angelic beings do not seem to translate even remotely into doubts of law. However, in the case we are considering, the theoretical doubt about the time of ensoulment is discussed precisely because of the significance it has for the application of the law "Thou shalt not kill" and other laws protecting basic human rights. The question of ensoulment is morally relevant only because it is part of an attempt to specify the scope of the law "Thou shalt not kill." Since the Congregation is presenting a moral position, which it explicitly recognizes in saying "From the moral point of view this is certain," then in this context the theoretical question about the ensoulment of the embryo is equivalent to a moral question about the scope of the law forbidding killing. The doubt which exists is therefore a doubt of law, an uncertainty about the scope of the natural and divine law against killing. And as we have seen, the church has traditionally used probabilistic methods in determining the scope and application of that law.

Uncertainly Existing Subjects and Doubtful Rights

The third argument is a response to the objection that the law against killing has already been interpreted by the magisterium in a way that is certain. A simple formulation of the interpreted law is "Thou shalt not kill directly an innocent human being." There is no doubt about this law. Rather, the doubt we are considering occurs because of uncertainty as to whether a particular living being belongs in the category of human being, and this uncertainty is not a doubt about the law.

In his study "The Removal of a Fetus Probably Dead to Save the Life of the Mother," McCormick examines an analogous situation.[102] In the case he considers, the death of an intrauterine fetus is probable but cannot be ascertained with certainty. This situation is clearly factual in nature, even though the factual doubt is unresolvable with currently available medical and scientific techniques. McCormick states the standard position, that the fetus' right to life, which is a certain right, may not be endangered by acting on a probable opinion regarding a matter of fact. According to the certain law which applies, a direct attack may not be made to remove the fetus, even though the mother's life may be at stake.

However, McCormick then reviews the opinion of L. Rodrigo, a moralist who is an authority on probabilistic methods. The criterion Rodrigo appeals to is: "Rights of an uncertain subject (uncertain by uncertainty of the subject's existence) are automatically uncertain rights."[103] (A comparable case in law might be that of a person who vanished some years ago. Because of uncertainty that this subject still exists, the law declares that his or her rights are now uncertain, and for many practical purposes no longer exist.[104]) Rodrigo argues that such uncertain rights may be "violated" for a sufficient reason.

Here a situation which is undeniably factual, i.e., whether a fetus is still alive, is transformed by the nature of the case to one where rights, or the application of a law, are in doubt. Thus a doubt of fact is practically equivalent to a doubt of law, and acting on the basis of a probable opinion may be justifiable.

The situation of a zygote or early embryo is one where the existence of a human subject is even more clearly and irresolvably in doubt. This doubt cannot be resolved even in principle, and there is solid positive evidence that a subject does not exist. If the rights of a probably (but not certainly) dead fetus are uncertain, then how much more so are the rights of a fertilized egg, a cell mass, a blastocyst? The theoretical doubt about the existence of a subject translates into uncertainty about rights, and hence into a doubt of law, even more clearly than the factual doubt about the death of McCormick's fetus.

Rahner has invoked this principle in his writings on genetic and reproductive research, arguing: "The reasons in favour of experimenting might carry more weight, considered rationally, than the uncertain rights of a human being whose very existence is in doubt."[105] And McCormick, in the position he took as a member of the Ethics Advisory Board of DHEW, appeared to be applying similar reasoning. Holding that early human embryos are "nascent" human beings but most likely not actual human beings, he apparently concluded that the rights of these beings were uncertain enough to justify not granting them full moral and legal protection. McCormick was thus able to join other members of the Ethics Advisory Board in approving certain types of research involving *in vitro* fertilization of human zygotes.[106]

These three arguments indicate that the theoretical doubt about the time of ensoulment of the human embryo is, in this context, equivalent to a doubt of law. The doubt is not one which endangers rights which are certain; rather, the existence of rights, or the scope of a law, is what is uncertain.

PROBABILITY OF OPINION ALLOWING SOME LIBERTY IN TREATMENT OF ZYGOTES AND EARLY EMBRYOS

If the doubts which exist in this situation are doubts about the scope of the law "Thou shalt not kill," then probabilistic methods are applicable to the moral question of the treatment of early embryos. While the system of probabilism appears to be acceptable in Catholic theology, a more cautious approach would suggest using equiprobabilism. Recall that an opinion is termed "probable" if there are "good and solid reasons" for holding it. According to equiprobabilism, one may act with impunity if the opinion favoring liberty is at least as probable as the restrictive opinion—in other words, if the reasons are at least as solid.[107]

Reasons for Holding That Ensoulment Does Not Occur at Fertilization

Although the Sacred Congregation claims that the presence of the soul is always probable (i.e., from fertilization on), contemporary biological data indicate that it is actually highly improbable that the zygote and early cell mass are ensouled. The phenomenon of twinning and especially that of recombination offer strong positive evidence that the human soul is not yet present in the early embryo; for, in the traditional Catholic understanding, the soul is indivisible and indestructible, and souls cannot split, fuse, or disappear. The soul is the principle of selfhood, which, like it, is a unique and indivisible marker.[108]

Additional biological evidence cited above adds substantial support to the opinions of Catholic theologians who argue that the zygote and early embryo are not human beings and are not yet ensouled. The biological data are interpreted within a variety of philosophical theories, but perhaps the most convincing arguments are those made in terms of the philosophy of Aquinas, since his anthropology has been given official sanction by the church.[109]

Theologians like Donceel and Wassmer utilize a traditional form of the Thomistic anthropology, while Rahner expresses its insights in more contemporary language.[110] It is the antidualistic orientation of the Thomistic theory which is most significant for our purposes. In this theory the human being is regarded as a body-soul composite wherein the human soul acts as the life principle of the body, or as the form which makes the being what it is. A human soul or form can only be joined to matter (or a body) which is human, because it cannot provide human life or humanness to a lower level of material life. Thus, for the soul to be present, the matter must have achieved a suitably advanced level of development. Since the human soul is characteristically rational, it appears necessary that the physical structures be developed to the level where there is some capability for supporting minimal rational activity.

Philosophers and theologians who are committed to this nondualist anthropology thus find "good and solid reasons" for not attributing ensoulment to the early embryo. In fact, it seems extremely improbable that matter which is not yet even formed into an organic human body could be united to a human soul. Through the centuries there is testimony of theologians and also of the magisterium which supports their view. For example, St. Alphonsus said: "Some are mistaken who say that the fetus is ensouled from the first moment of its conception, since the fetus is certainly not animated before it is formed. . . ."[111] The Catechism of the Council of Trent, published in 1566 and reprinted as recently as 1923, stated:

> As soon as the Blessed Virgin gave her consent to the Angel's words . . . at once the most holy body of Christ was formed and a rational soul was joined to it. . . . Nobody can doubt that this was something new and an admirable work of the Holy Spirit, since, in the natural order, no body can be informed by a human soul except after the prescribed space of time.[112]

And in a decree of the Holy Office dating from 1713 we find: "If there is a reasonable foundation for admitting that the fetus is animated by a rational soul, then it may and must be baptized conditionally. If, however, there is *no reasonable foundation*, it may *by no means* be baptized. . . ."[113] Thus both theological and magisterial opinion, up until the nineteenth century, were open to the view that the ensoulment of the early embryo is highly improbable, if not impossible. In the latter part of the nineteenth century the magisterium and most theologians came to accept the notion of immediate ensoulment, and Häring remarked in 1966 that this situation still obtained.[114] But a detailed survey of the literature conducted by H. M. Hering in 1951 showed this assessment to be wrong. Hering found that the theory of delayed animation had strong defenders, "especially among the philosophers, who are wont to investigate the matter more profoundly than the moralists and the canonists."[115]

If those who investigate the matter "more profoundly" find reasons to hold that ensoulment is not immediate, if this belief has been widespread and taught by the church through many centuries, and if the arguments currently presented are highly convincing, then we surely have a body of good and solid reasons which appear to be at least as sound as those supporting a contrary position. Donceel finds the evidence so overwhelming as to say:

> We do not know exactly when man first appeared on earth, at what stage of the evolutionary process hominization occurred. But we know that Dryopithecus and Propliopithecus were not yet human beings. . . . I do not know when the human soul is infused into the body, but I, for one, am certain that there is no human soul, hence no human person, the first few weeks of pregnancy.[116]

Weight of the Congregation's Mandate of the Safer Course

The Sacred Congregation appears to rest its case on what is called a negative doubt,[117] for it claims that immediate ensoulment is probable because "one can never prove the contrary."[118] But the questions raised about immediate ensoulment are not based on a merely negative doubt, namely, that it is impossible to prove that the soul *is* present. As shown above, the doubt is a positive doubt, one based on positive reasons which indicate that immediate ensoulment is truly improbable.

The Congregation does not recognize the use of probabilistic methods to determine the scope of the law "Thou shalt not kill" when applied to prenatal human life. In the way it presents its position, the Congregation appears to be saying that if there is the slightest chance that some type of being falls under the law, then we may not kill it. But such a position becomes ludicrous if one considers all the sorts of beings that have been proposed as coming under the law. At the present time, there are reputable ethicists who argue that dolphins, chimpanzees, wild game, and endangered species are included within the scope of the law against killing. Many vegetarians claim that it is wrong to kill animals for use as food, unless one were in a situation where no other means of sustenance was available.[119] In his essay "Animals and the Value of Life," Peter Singer actually makes an argument which resembles that of the Sacred Congregation:

> I am not certain that it would be wrong in itself to kill the pig; but nor am I certain that it would be right to do so. Since there is no pressing moral reason for

the killing—the fact that one might prefer a dish containing pork to a vegetarian meal is hardly a matter of great moral significance—it would seem better to give the pig the benefit of the doubt.[120]

Thus Singer also recommends taking the safer course where there is a doubt about a matter of life and death.

These arguments may well have merit, but I do not know of any Catholic moralist who demands that we refrain from killing every being which is presented to us as possibly falling within the scope of the law. A small probability that it may be wrong to kill beings of type X does not put us under a strict obligation not to kill them. Yet the Sacred Congregation seems to be positing that sort of obligation towards human zygotes and embryos; for the Congregation supports its assertion that the presence of the soul is probable only by saying that "one can never prove the contrary." Such an argument would involve the fallacy of argument from ignorance if it were not seen as an application of traditional methods for resolving "factual" doubts. It applies equally well to many forms of animal life. In fact, if one relies on empirical data which support the possible presence of a rational soul, there is better positive argument available for animals like mature dolphins than there is for human zygotes, morulae, and blastocysts.

Summary: Acceptability of Probable Opinions on Treatment of Early Prenatal Life

I have argued that the doubt about the time of ensoulment of the human embryo is not a doubt of fact in the context of the Catholic moral tradition on resolving doubts of fact, and that within the Catholic tradition, doubts of law, even those which impinge on human life and other basic rights, have been and often must be resolved by probabilistic methods. I have further argued that the theoretical doubt as to the time of ensoulment of the human embryo is here equivalent to a doubt of law, since the theoretical issue is debated precisely in order to determine the scope of the natural and divine law against killing. Thus, in the *Declaration on Abortion,* the Sacred Congregation was actually considering the scope of the law "Thou shalt not kill"; and its argument, which rejects consideration of even the most probable opinion favoring liberty, is inconsistent with the Catholic moral tradition. I have shown that there are "good and solid reasons," which appear to be at least as strong as those supporting the contrary position, for not including early human embryos under the full weight of the law against killing. Especially when there are compelling, or even adequate, reasons for terminating an embryonic life, the application of probabilistic methods would permit some early abortions. The reasoning of the Congregation in forbidding all abortions, including the destruction of zygotes, is linked to the stringency of the moral tradition regarding factual doubts in relation to human life. But the thesis that ensoulment is a matter of fact within this context cannot be substantiated.

NOTES

1. Richard A. McCormick, S.J., "Notes on Moral Theology: 1978," *Theological Studies* (hereafter *TS*) 40 (1979) 108–9; and transcript of meeting of Ethics Advisory Board, Department of Health, Education, and Welfare, Oct. 9–11, 1978 (Springfield, Va.: National Technical Information Service, 1978) 425.

2. Charles Curran, "*In Vitro* Fertilization and Embryo Transfer," no. 4 in *Appendix: HEW Support of Research Involving Human In Vitro Fertilization and Embryo Transfer* (Washington, D.C.: U.S. Government Printing Office, 1979) 15–16.

3. Albert Di Ianni, "Is the Fetus a Person?" *American Ecclesiastical Review* 168 (1974) 323–24.

4. Karl Rahner, S.J., "The Problem of Genetic Manipulation," *Theological Investigations* 9 (New York: Seabury, 1972) 236.

5. Sacred Congregation for the Doctrine of the Faith, *Declaration on Abortion* (Washington, D.C.: U.S. Catholic Conference, 1975).

6. Ibid.

7. James J. Diamond, M.D., "Abortion, Animation, and Biological Hominization," *TS* 36 (1975) 305–24.

8. Ibid. 316.

9. Ibid. 312.

10. André Hellegers, M.D., "Fetal Development," *TS* 31 (1970) 5.

11. Charles Curran, "Abortion: Law and Morality in Contemporary Catholic Theology," *Jurist* 33 (1973) 180.

12. Philip Devine, *The Ethics of Homicide* (Ithaca: Cornell University, 1978) 83.

13. Diamond, "Abortion" 321.

14. Di Ianni, "Is the Fetus a Person?" 324.

15. Devine, *Ethics of Homicide* 83.

16. Ibid.

17. McCormick, "Notes 1978" 109.

18. Bernard Häring, "New Dimensions of Responsible Parenthood," *TS* 37 (1976) 127–28.

19. Cf. Henri Leridon, *Human Fertility: The Basic Components* (Chicago: University of Chicago, 1977) 81.

20. Rahner, "Problem of Genetic Manipulation" 226, n. 2.

21. Joseph Donceel, S.J., "Immediate Animation and Delayed Hominization," *TS* 31 (1970) 79–80.

22. Ibid. 82.

23. The *Didache* (A.D. 100 or earlier) stated (2,2): "You shall not slay a child by abortion. You shall not kill what is generated." Cf. John T. Noonan, Jr., "An Almost Absolute Value in History;" in *The Morality of Abortion, ed.* Noonan (Cambridge: Harvard University, 1970) 9.

24. For a discussion of the implications of the Septuagint versus the Palestinian translation, see David M. Feldman, *Marital Relations, Birth Control, and Abortion in Jewish Law* (New York: Schocken, 1975) 254–59.

25. Noonan, "An Almost Absolute Value" 15.

26. George Huntston Williams, "Religious Residues and Presuppositions in the American Debate on Abortion," *TS* 31 (1970) 15.

27. Noonan, "An Almost Absolute Value" 38–39.

28. *Summa theologiae* 1, q. 76, a. 3, and q. 118, a. 2.

29. Donceel, "Immediate Animation" 89.

30. Denzinger-Schonmetzer (ed. 32) 2327 (3896); cited in Rahner, *Hominization: The Evolutionary Origin of Man as a Theological Problem* (New York: Herder and Herder, 1965) 94.

31. Cf., e.g., *A Catechism of Christian Doctrine, Baltimore Catechism Revised, No. 3* (Paterson, N.J.: St. Anthony Guild, 1941) 41.

32. Noonan, "An Almost Absolute Value" 20–23.

33. Pastoral Constitution on the Church in the Modern World, no. 51 (*The Documents of Vatican II*, ed. Walter M. Abbott [New York: Guild, 1966] 256).

34. U.S. Catholic Conference, *Ethical and Religious Directives for Catholic Health Facilities* (Washington, D.C.: U.S. Catholic Conference, 1977) 4.

35. *Expensio modorum*, Partis secundae, Resp. 101; cited in Häring, *Medical Ethics* (Notre Dame: Fides, 1973) 76.

36. *Declaration on Abortion* (n. 5 above) 13, n. 19.

37. Ibid. 6 (emphasis added).

38. Häring, "New Dimensions" 127–28.

39. Diamond, "Abortion" 321.

40. Donceel, "Immediate Animation" 105.

41. Thomas Wassmer, S.J., "Questions about Questions," *Commonweal* 86 (1967) 418.

42. Curran, "*In Vitro* Fertilization" 26.

43. Department of Health, Education, and Welfare, "Protection of Human Subjects; HEW Support of Human *In Vitro* Fertilization and Embryo Transfer: Report of the Ethics Advisory Board," *Federal Register* 44 (June 18, 1979) 35055–58.

44. Rahner, "Problem of Genetic Manipulation" 236.

45. Di Ianni, "Is the Fetus a Person?" 324.

46. Dogmatic Constitution on the Church, no. 25 (*Documents of Vatican II* 48).

47. Rahner, "Theologie und Lehramt," *Stimmen der Zeit* 198 (1980) 353–75.

48. Ibid. 373.

49. Häring, *Free and Faithful in Christ 1: General Moral Theology* (New York: Seabury, 1978) 280–81.

50. McCormick, "Notes on Moral Theology: 1980," *TS* 42 (1981) 74–121.

51. André Naud, "Les voix de l'église dans les questions morales," *Science et esprit* 32 (1980) 167.

52. McCormick, "Notes 1980" 119.

53. Pope Paul VI, *Humanae vitae* (Washington, D.C.: U.S. Catholic Conference, 1968) 17–18.

54. McCormick, "Theology as a Dangerous Discipline," *Georgetown Graduate Review* 1, no. 4 (Apr./May 1981) 2.

55. Curran, "Abortion" 173.

56. Gerard J. Hughes, "Infallibility in Morals," *TS* 34 (1973) 418 (emphasis added).

57. Ibid. 426.

58. *Declaration on Abortion* 13, n. 19.

59. Ibid. 6.

60. Häring, *The Law of Christ 1: General Moral Theology* (Westminster, Md.: Newman, 1963) 170–71.

61. Ibid. 171. In his more recent work on moral theology, *Free and Faithful in Christ*, Häring is somewhat critical of this position, and thus moves away from the traditional view (1:290).

62. Henry Davis, *Moral and Pastoral Theology* 2 (New York: Sheed and Ward, 1943) 78.

63. *Declaration on Abortion* 13, n. 19.

64. Davis, *Moral* 82, 86, and 91.

65. Ibid. 79.

66. Philip S. Kaufman, O.S.B., "An Immoral Morality? Probabilism and the Right to Know of Moral Options," *Commonweal* 107 (1980) 494.

67. Häring, *Law of Christ* 1:187; and *Free and Faithful in Christ* 1:287–90.

68. Kaufman, "An Immoral Morality?" 494.

69. Häring, *Law of Christ* 1:187–88.

70. F. J. Connell, "Morality, Systems of," *New Catholic Encyclopedia* 9 (New York: McGraw-Hill, 1967) 1133.

71. Cited in Häring, *Law of Christ* 1:186.

72. Connell, "Doubt, Moral," *New Catholic Encyclopedia* 4:1024.

73. Cf. McCormick, "The Removal of a Fetus Probably Dead to Save the Life of the Mother" (Ph.D. dissertation, Gregorian University, Rome, 1957) 200, n. 5.

74. Ibid. 200–202, n. 5.

75. Cf. Wassmer, "Questions" 417; Connell, "Morality, Systems of" 1132–33; Häring, *Law of Christ* 1:183; McCormick, "Removal of a Fetus" 327–50.

76. Davis, *Moral* 2:99.

77. Connell, "Morality, Systems of" 1133; McCormick, "Removal of a Fetus" 351.

78. *Declaration on Abortion* 6.

79. Cf. McCormick, "Personal Conscience," *Chicago Studies* 13 (1974) 241–52; Curran, "Abortion" 180; McCormick, "Notes on Moral Theology 1977: The Church in Dispute," *TS* 39 (1978) 126–28.

80. Häring, *Medical Ethics* 37, 84–85, 93, and 101.

81. Häring, "New Dimensions" 125–29.

82. Häring, *Law of Christ* 1:185; quoted in Kaufman, "An Immoral Morality?" 494.

83. Kaufman, "An Immoral Morality?" 494.

84. Wassmer, "Questions" 416–18.

85. Ibid. 417–18.

86. Ibid. 418.

87. Ibid. 416–18.

88. It could, of course, still be promulgated by church authority. But that mode of presenting moral positions is ineffective and self-defeating in the contemporary world. Note Häring, *Medical Ethics:* "In moral matters not predicated by divine revelation but resulting from shared experience and co-reflection, the magisterium (especially in our critical times) cannot speak without giving its reasons and the pastoral meaning of its position. In the realm of purely natural morality, that is, natural law, the believer is bound to the extent that the directives manifest rational insights and reflect man's shared experience and co-reflection" (37). Also see Hughes, "Infallibility" 427–28.

89. Frederick Suppe, "Facts and Empirical Truth," *Canadian Journal of Philosophy* 3 (1973) 201.

90. Raphael Demos, "Are Religious Dogmas Cognitive and Meaningful?" in *Religious Language and the Problem of Religious Knowledge,* ed. Ronald E. Santoni (Bloomington: Indiana University, 1968) 271.

91. John Hick, "Theology and Verification," in Santoni, ed., *Religious Language* 367–71.

92. Di Ianni, "Is the Fetus a Person?" 312.

93. Ibid. 316–17.

94. Cf., e.g., Marx W. Wartofsky, "The Mind's Eye and the Hand's Brain: Toward an Historical Epistemology of Medicine," in *Science, Ethics and Medicine,* ed. H. Tristram Engelhardt, Jr., and Daniel Callahan (Hastings-on-Hudson: Hastings Center, 1976) 183–84; and Peter Achinstein, *Concepts of Science* (Baltimore: Johns Hopkins, 1968) 121–29.

95. *Declaration on Abortion* 6.

96. Ibid. (emphasis added).

97. Cf. Connell, "Morality, Systems of" 1132–33; Edwin Healy, S.J., *Moral Guidance* (Chicago: Loyola University, 1943) 33–34; McCormick, "Removal of a Fetus" 327–95; Häring, *Law of Christ* 1:180–85; Davis, *Moral* 2:99; and Wassmer, "Questions" 417–18.

98. Bruno Schuller, S.J., "Remarks on the Authentic Teaching of the Magisterium of the Church," in *Readings in Moral Theology No. 3: The Magisterium and Morality,* ed. Curran and McCormick (New York: Paulist, 1982) 26–27.

99. Kaufman, "An Immoral Morality?" 495–96.

100. Healy, *Moral Guidance* 31.

101. *Declaration on Abortion* 6.

102. McCormick, "Removal of a Fetus" (see n. 73 above).

103. Ibid. 395–97.

104. Cf., e.g., Minnesota statutes 567.142, 576.143, 576.144, and 576.15, in *Minnesota Statutes Annotated 37; Cumulative Annual Pocket Part* (St. Paul: West Publ. Co., 1982) 106–7.

105. Rahner, "Problem of Genetic Manipulation" 236.

106. Cf. McCormick, "Notes 1978" 108–9; and DHEW, "Protection of Human Subjects: Report of the Ethics Advisory Board" 35055–58.

107. Cf. Davis, *Moral* 78 and 86.

108. See discussion and citations earlier in this article.

109. Cf. Pope Leo XIII, "The Study of Scholastic Philosophy," in *The Great Encyclical Letters of Pope Leo XIII* (New York: Benziger, 1903) 34–57.

110. Donceel, "Immediate Animation"; Wassmer, "Questions"; Rahner, *Hominization.*

111. Quoted in Donceel, "Immediate Animation" 91.

112. Ibid. 89.

113. Ibid. 90 (emphasis added).

114. Häring, *Law of Christ 3: Special Moral Theology* (Westminster, Md.: Newman, 1966) 205.

115. H. M. Hering, O.P., "De tempore animationis foetus humani," *Angelicum* 28 (1951) 92.

116. Donceel, "Immediate Animation" 101.

117. Cf. Häring, *Law of Christ* 1:170–71.

118. *Declaration on Abortion* 13, n. 19.

119. Cf., e.g., Charles Hartshorne, "The Rights of the Subhuman World," *Environmental Ethics* 1 (1979) 49–60; Tom Regan, "Do Animals Have a Right to Life?" in *Animal Rights and Human Obligations*, ed. Tom Regan and Peter Singer (Englewood Cliffs, N.J.: Prentice-Hall, 1976) 197–204; Peter Singer, "Equality for Animals?", chap. 3 of *Practical Ethics* (Cambridge: Cambridge University, 1979) 48–71; David Paterson and Richard D. Ryder, eds., *Animal Rights: A Symposium* (London: Centaur, 1979); and Tom Regan, "The Moral Basis of Vegetarianism," *Canadian Journal of Philosophy* 5 (1975) 181–214.

120. Peter Singer, "Animals and the Value of Life," in *Matters of Life and Death*, ed. Tom Regan (New York: Random House, 1980) 252.

Abortion, Autonomy, and Community

Lisa Sowle Cahill

Within the circle of Christian theological ethicists who converse in "the academy," as I do, it is definitely not in vogue to voice opposition to the prochoice position. This position is often believed to be entailed in a serious commitment to sexual autonomy, to feminism, and to enlightened, humanistic causes in general. To some extent, my contribution to this project is a reaction against that assumption.

In formulating my position, and in evaluating the relation of positions on abortion generally to the values affirmed and denied in contemporary North American culture, I have drawn on resources both theological and philosophical. The relevant religious resources are those biblical stories, symbols, and thematic patterns that support a willingness to sacrifice personal interests in order to protect the weakest or the "neighbor" most in need. (The latter category includes both women, who suffer the effects of injustices in the spheres of sexuality, domesticity, and reproduction, and fetuses, as dependent and unable effectively to assert claims.) Also central are the resources of the Roman Catholic tradition in social ethics, which has been considerably more "progressive" than the tradition in personal ethics, medical and sexual.[1] However, I dissent from the proposition that abortion is a narrowly religious issue. Both biblical themes and Catholic natural-law social analysis are presented here in terms congruent with many secular or humanistic perspectives on the relations of persons in community (though not all, e.g., utilitarianism). The possibility of assuming in principle an alliance between religious and rational ethics is itself a fruit of the Catholic, Thomistic, natural-law tradition of moral insight.

The principal value at stake in this essay is the existence of the fetus itself, for it must be established *who* are considered members of the "human community" before the moral relationships among these members can be addressed. The question of the status of fetal life in the human community is the most divisive and the least easy to resolve in the entire abortion debate; it is also the most fundamental. Although it is not my purpose here to defend a certain view of the fetus, of its rights, or of the rights of its mother, I have yet to be persuaded that these issues can be avoided successfully. For this reason, I feel a need to briefly indicate my own evaluation of fetal life, fully realizing that any position on the status of the fetus is vulnerable. I then proceed to my major task of broader reflections on abortion and the culture, where assumptions about the fetus also influence social attitudes and policies.

I am convinced that the fetus is from conception a member of the human species (having an identifiably human genotype, and being of human parentage), and, as such, is an entity to which at least some protection is due, even though its status may not at every phase be equivalent to that of postnatal life. (See the following section on "Dualism and Corporeality" for a further discussion of the relation between biological facts and moral value.) Further, I believe that there exists, even in our pluralist culture, a relatively broad consensus that the fetus does have some value and status in the human community, even among those who maintain that "hard choices" about sustaining its life must be left finally to the woman who bears it. My position on fetal status might be characterized as "developmentalist"[2] insofar as I view its value as incremental throughout gestation. The fact that few, if any, give absolutely equal value to the mother and the fetus is attested to by the fact that all are willing to prefer the mother in at least some "life-against-life" cases, and by the fact that virtually no one perceives the abortion of a seven-month-old fetus as the moral equivalent of the use of an abortifacient method of birth control, such as the IUD (even though both may be viewed as wrong). Nonetheless, I see the fetus as having a value at conception that is quite significant and that quickly increases; but it never overrides the right of the mother to preserve her own life. Even relatively early in pregnancy (for example, in the first trimester), I think serious considerations must be present to justify abortion. Threat to life is the classic case, although I would not exclude the possibility that other threats might justify abortion, particularly when the interest that the mother has at stake is equal to or greater than her interest in her life. (To specify such interests and to stipulate circumstances in which they might be threatened remains a perplexing task.) In summary, I endorse a strong bias in favor of the fetus and rest a heavy burden of proof on those who would choose abortion. This endorsement will in obvious ways influence my assessment of the values that form the backdrop for our culture's permissive policies regarding abortion. At the same time, I trust that much of what I have to say about such things as community, corporeality, suffering, physical or mental disabilities, and family will find agreement among many who do not share my evaluation of fetal life or my grounding in Catholic Christianity.

LIBERALISM AND THE COMMON GOOD

A central focus of my analysis of abortion and the culture is the relations between individuals and the communities in which they associate. Often, these relations are articulated in terms of "rights" and "duties." It has been observed, however, that these terms encourage moral individualism and isolation of the moral agent(s) from the social relationships in which decision making occurs.[3]

I continue to think it legitimate to use "rights" language to discuss abortion, but I want to remove that language from the context of moral and political liberalism. To shift attention away from the rights of the fetus or the woman understood individualistically does not mean that the value and rights of either thereby become irrelevant. It means, rather, that their respective rights must be defined in relation to one another (and, in a less immediate sense, to the rights of others, for example, family members). Where those rights can conflict, neither can be absolute. The rights of both are *limited*, but still significant.

Fundamentally, then, I want to speak of rights in the context of sociality and of community. Of particular relevance to the abortion dilemma is the fact that duties or obligations can bind humans to their fellows in ways to which they have not explicitly consented. Such obligations originate simply in the sorts of reciprocal relatedness that constitute being a human. The mother-fetus relation is characterized by obligations of this sort, as are all parent-child relations.

Abortion represents a conflict between, most directly, the rights of the mother and the rights of the fetus. In contemporary American culture, this conflict is settled in favor of the pregnant woman's right to dispose of the fetus as she deems necessary to protect her own rights or interests. A warrant often adduced in support of such an adjudication of claims is the woman's right to autonomous self-determination, particularly regarding her body and its reproductive capacities. Thus, a restriction of the right to choose abortion is perceived as an infringement of personal liberty in a most intimate and private sphere.

The present dominance of the prochoice position on abortion (that is, every woman has a right to decide for herself, and on the basis of her own religious and moral convictions, whether or not to have an abortion) represents *positively* the view that women must be taken seriously as autonomous moral agents. Societal and legal protection of the freedom to control childbearing, through abortion if necessary, represents a challenge to those dimensions of marriage, family, and employment that continue to oppress and subordinate the female sex. In addition, to leave abortion decisions to the discretion of the agent most directly involved is to acknowledge the individuality that attends every moral decision, especially decisions that are complex, filled with conflict, and even tragic.

However, I believe that our culture's general willingness to grant to women the exclusive power to terminate their pregnancies has other, too frequently unexamined, implications that can be described *negatively*. First, and perhaps most fundamentally, the single-minded affirmation of the rights of the pregnant woman (e.g., her "right to privacy" or "right to reproductive freedom") virtually circumvents the equally important but incorrigibly difficult problem of the status of fetal life. What sort of being is it that threatens the welfare of the pregnant woman? Does it in turn have rights? And if so, how do they weigh in the balance

against those of the woman? Furthermore, the subordination in the legal and
practical spheres of any right to life of the fetus (at least, if previable) to a whole
spectrum of rights, needs, or interests of the mother manifests a widespread and
often uncritical cultural acceptance of political and moral liberalism.

By *liberalism,* I mean a family of views concerning the person and the society
resembling or rooted in the social contract theories of John Locke, Thomas Hobbes,
and Jean Jacques Rousseau, who have influenced, at least indirectly, Western
democracy and the American constitutional tradition. In such views, persons are
seen essentially as free and autonomous agents who come into society to protect
self-interest by a series of mutually advantageous agreements. Society or community is thus secondary to the existence of the individual; persons are not social
by nature and have no natural obligations antecedent to their free consent.[4] A
woman, for example, has no *prima facie* moral obligation to sustain a pregnancy
that she has not undertaken voluntarily; to do so would constitute a supererogatory
act (Judith Jarvis Thomson[5]).

Other competing theories—for example, some Marxist and feminist social theories, or the Thomistic notion of the "common good" as reinterpreted by the
modern papal social encyclicals—begin from the contrary premise. That is, persons
are by definition interrelated in a social whole whose fabric of reciprocal rights
and duties constitutes the very condition of their individual and communal fulfillment. The concept of the *common good* envisions society in a way that is neither
liberal nor utilitarian. The community is understood as prior to the individual;
however, each individual is equally entitled to share in the benefits that inhere
in the community. The common good is not identified with the interests of any
particular group. Rather, it is a normative standard or ideal by which to criticize
and reform any existing social order. Undeniably associated with this notion are
some intransigent problems of definition shared with other attempts to elucidate
"normative" or "essential" humanity or human community. Still, fidelity to the
common good as the primary framework for social analysis guarantees, at least,
that *individual* and *community,* as well as *rights* and *duties,* will be taken as a pair
of complementary terms. Above all, it suggests that human society is characterized
by an intrinsic interdependence or cohesiveness for which paradigms that construe
society as voluntary affiliations of individuals whose mutual obligations are purely
contractual do not adequately account.[6]

From the viewpoint of the common good, understood in these terms, one
indeed has a duty, premised on the mutual interdependence and obligations implied by common humanity, to help another person when to do so involves relatively little self-sacrifice and a proportionate gain for the other. Because gestation
is a primordial, prototypical, and physically concrete form of sociality and interdependence, some obligations to the fetus may exist even when they have not
been undertaken deliberately. One consequence of the individualistic liberal view
of the pregnant woman as moral agent, besides the obvious one of minimizing

restraints on her free power of self-determination, is that it reduces the obligations of other individuals or of the community to offer support during and after a burdensome pregnancy. Moral and social dilemmas are regarded as the business and the burden of individuals, to be resolved or borne alone.[7]

DUALISM AND CORPOREALITY

Twentieth-century philosophy and theology have been accustomed to repudiating the "dualism" of ancient Greece and its remnants in Christianity or its facsimile in René Descartes. In sexual ethics, for example, we resist any attempts to define the body as "bad" and the spirit as resistant to it, and instead, we insist on attention to bodily experience in definitions of moral obligation.[8] The unity of body and spirit in human experience should also be taken into account seriously in discussions of pregnancy. The facts that a fetus is ineluctably dependent for its very existence on the body of another, and that this relation of dependence is not *prima facie* pathological or unjust, but physiologically normal and natural for a human being in its earliest stages of existence, should count as *one* factor in a moral evaluation of pregnancy and abortion. The morality of abortion is not reducible to the issue of "free consent" to pregnancy. This is not to say that abortion can never be justified (given the presence of countervailing factors), but only that we have not grasped the reality of the moral situation when we define freedom only as "freedom over" the body and not also as "freedom in" or "freedom through" the body. The body makes peculiar demands, creates peculiar relationships, and grounds peculiar obligations.

The Catholic moral theologian Louis Janssens has reformulated the notion of a normative human nature in a way that affirms the historicity, equality, sociality, and corporeality of all persons:

> That we are corporeal means in the first place that our body forms a part of the integrated subject that we are; corporeal and spiritual, nonetheless a singular being. What concerns the human body, therefore, also affects the person himself.
>
> That we are a subjectivity, or a conscious interiority, in corporeality . . . is the basis for a number of moral demands.[9]

Conversely, our culture as liberal denies both determinations of "freedom" by our concrete embodied nature and obligation without consent (as a contradiction in terms). The former denial is related to the latter as partial cause. Examples of the tendency to ignore, repress, or negate the demands of corporeality can be seen at many levels: in the rapid increase in medical litigation over the past two decades, which seems to represent the unrealistic demand that the physician free us from the vulnerability of the human body and the fallibility of the medical arts; in the denial in popular mores and in sexual ethics that there is any morally significant connection whatsoever between sex and procreation; and in the recalcitrant refusal of denizens of the developed nations to curtail their supposed right to pursue life, liberty, and happiness at the expense of the material needs of Third World citizens.

At the same time that we avoid the exaltation of autonomy to the detriment of corporeality, it is important to avoid biologism, another form of dualism, in which freedom is completely constrained by physiological functions or conditions. Examples of the latter can be found in traditional Roman Catholic analyses of sexual and medical ethics. Since the negative response of the Holy Office of the Vatican in 1869 to the inquiry whether craniotomy is licit, magisterial teaching regarding abortion has been that a fetus may be sacrificed to preserve its mother's life only when the procedure that destroys it is aimed *physically* at some other objective. Thus, the removal of the cancerous uterus of a pregnant woman would be allowed, insofar as the physically indirect method of killing the fetus (though a surgical procedure related directly to a condition other than pregnancy) "guarantees" that the intention of the agents involved is not primarily to bring about the death of the fetus, but to protect the woman. By the same token, it would be permissible to remove the entire fallopian tube in a case of ectopic pregnancy; but it would not be permissible to remove the embryo from the tube, leaving intact the tube and the woman's potential to conceive again. Much less would it be justified to remove a potentially viable fetus directly from the womb to curtail the potentially fatal strain of pregnancy on a woman suffering from renal or coronary disease. The crucial question in such dilemmas is whether the moral key ought to be the indirectness of the physical procedure of resolution or the simple fact of two lives in conflict.[10]

Another nexus of dualistic arguments about abortion is the problematic relationship of the biological development of the fetus (for example, its appearance) to its status in the human community. Equally prone to oversimplification are those who claim that a recognizably human genotype or human form is of no relevance at all to the respect accorded some particular being and those who assume that a demonstration of the membership of the fetus in the species *Homo sapiens*, or its resemblance to a baby, settles the issue of full "humanity" or "personhood," and thus of abortion. Few are unfamiliar with the attempts of some prolife advocates to substitute enlarged photographs of aborted fetuses for rational argument. More subtle are the efforts of prochoice proponents to eliminate critical recognition of the matter–spirit link in abortion. Michael Tooley and Laura Purdy asked rhetorically, "If pig fetuses resembled adult humans, would it be seriously wrong to kill pig fetuses?"[11] Dualism is the premise that allows such a question to be posed at all, as it requires us to dissociate from our notion of "humanity" what it means to exist materially and corporeally in a human (or porcine) manner. The reader is induced to answer, "No," and thus to agree with the proabortion argument framing the question, because the hypothetical situation is nonsensical.

A more thoughtful treatment of the problem is presented by Joseph Donceel's revival of the Aristotelian-Thomistic notion of "hylomorphism."[12] Donceel suggested that the material aspect of any being is naturally appropriate to its "form" or spirit. Thus, the increasingly human appearance of human offspring during gestation may be relevant to their developing status within the community of persons. Donceel suggested that the possibility of the "delayed hominization" of the fetus is not inconsistent with the acceptance by some traditional Christian authors (such as Anselm, Aquinas, and Alphonsus Liguori) of the idea that "ensoulment" takes place at some point subsequent to conception, for example, at "quickening." Abortion, although always sinful, becomes the sin of homicide only after that point.

The merit of a position such as Donceel's lies in its recognition that scientific or empirical evidence (e.g., about genotype or appearance) can be relevant to moral decisions, even if it is not in itself decisive. An integral view of the person urges recognition that neither human spirit, freedom, and valuing, on the one hand, nor the material conditions, realizations, and manifestations of same, on the other, ought to be taken alone as definitive of moral obligation. Normative ethics is dependent on the empirical sciences and other "descriptive" (as distinct from "normative") accounts of the human situation for two reasons at least: (1) the ethicist must have a realistic appreciation of the act or the relation that he or she proposes to evaluate; and (2) the fact that an entity or relation is "normal" or "abnormal" in, for example, a sociological, physiological, or psychological sense will count for or against the conclusion that its existence ought or ought not to be chosen or encouraged. (However, to determine the precise weight that empirical or statistical normality or abnormality ought to have in normative ethics is not a simple matter. It joins the ranks of the highly debated questions in ethics.) Donceel's point is not only that the entity to be evaluated, the fetus, has a corporeal dimension, but also that what is known about normal fetal development should be correlated with any normative account of fetal status.

SUFFERING

The liberal ethos discourages making personal sacrifices and encourages at best a minimal appreciation of the virtue and even the necessity of constructive suffering. Our culture has a low tolerance of the burdens and failures of life and tends to deny that life has value when conducted in irremediably painful conditions. There is an expectation of ready resort to the "technological fix" and an inability to appropriate suffering in meaningful ways.[13] To these sorts of attitudes might be contrasted the Christian ideals of reconciliation or redemption of the conditions of brokenness and evil in which we consistently find ourselves.

The notion of ability and responsibility to constructively redeem tragedy under circumstances of difficulty is not incompatible with the feminist concern that women be regarded as and regard themselves as mature moral agents who do not need protection from and do not avoid the exigencies of adulthood in the human community. I do not recommend masochism, nor the martyrdom of women who sacrifice themselves out of unwillingness or inability to assert their legitimate claims; rather, I recommend a recognition that some human situations have unavoidably tragic elements and that to be human is to bear these burdens. We cannot be freed from all infringements on our self-fulfillment, and to persistently demand that is to avoid moral agency in the complete sense. The decision to continue a pregnancy might be construed as a decision by the stronger to assume burdens that would otherwise fall on the most defenseless. However, "the stronger" includes not only the woman, who is also a victim, but the larger community of which she and the fetus are a part. (This is not to deny that the tragic elements of conflictual pregnancies may justify some decisions to abort.) As a final note, an important element in constructively assimilating suffering, and also in alleviating suffering to the extent possible, is communal support, both of the difficult pregnancy and of the abnormal fetus, child, or adult. In another context, Daniel Callahan (himself a prochoice advocate) has perceptively commented on the kind of community needed to successfully weather moral conflicts for which there appears to be a dearth of satisfactory resolutions:

> Hard times require self-sacrifice and altruism—but there is nothing in an ethic of moral autonomy to sustain or nourish those values. Hard times necessitate a sense of community and the common good—but the putative virtues of autonomy are primarily directed toward the cultivation of independent selfhood. . . . Hard times need a broad sense of duty toward others, especially those out of sight—but an ethic of autonomy stresses responsibility only for one's freely chosen, consenting-adult relationships.
>
> Whether suffering brings out the best or the worst in people is an old question, and the historical evidence is mixed. Yet a people's capacity to endure suffering without turning on each other is closely linked to the way they have envisioned, and earlier embodied, their relationship to each other. [14]

STANDARDS OF HUMAN EXISTENCE

Our culture tends to estimate the value of human life in direct proportion to its level of physical and intellectual perfection or achievement. This attitude leads to the inability of parents and others to envision creatively or positively the task of raising an abnormal child, and it creates widespread support of abortion for so-called fetal indications. A question that often could be pressed more critically is whether the abortion is intended primarily to serve the interests of the family (in its "freedom") or of the fetus (in a "happy" life), and in either case, what criteria of evaluation are used.[15]

The liberal individualistic theory of moral responsibility comes into play not only in the moral weight usually given to freedom, but also because society often seems to see parents as responsible for avoiding the births of defective (and hence burdensome) children; social willingness to provide structures of assistance for severely handicapped individuals and their families decreases correspondingly.[16]

One Christian ethicist, Stanley Hauerwas, has developed a critique of the further implications of liberalism for the nature of the family.[17] Hauerwas, who is noted for his emphasis on the narrative qualities of religion and theology, on the centrality of character in morality and ethics, and on the importance of community in embodying religious and moral commitment in life and action, observed that the modern nuclear family is perceived as a complex of intimate relationships whose purpose is the personal fulfillment of its members. Such an account of family life has lost both the connection of the "self-sufficient" family with the larger community and its institutions and any resources for understanding the purposes of family life, including having children, beyond the gratification of the couple. Hauerwas proposed that the family ought not to be understood as "a contractual social unit"[18] and that "marriage is not sustained by being a fulfilling experience for all involved, but by embodying moral and social purposes that give it a basis in the wider community."[19]

The language of rights is criticized by Hauerwas because it seems to represent the liberal commitment to the autonomy of the individual and his or her freedom to enter into moral obligations electively via contracts.[20] He also seems to detect a liberal agenda hidden behind attempts to hinge the abortion discussion on whether the fetus has or has not a "right to life." Hauerwas suggested that the precise status of the fetus as a "human being" may not be crucial as long as it is agreed that it is a "child." (These terms are not clarified precisely, but by *human being* I take Hauerwas to mean a member of the human community with full status and by *child* to mean human offspring.)

> Thus the preliminary question must be inverted: "What kind of people should we be to welcome children into the world?" Note that the question is *not* "Is the fetus a human being with a right to life?" but "How should a Christian regard and care for the fetus as a child?"[21]

I concur with Hauerwas that our evaluations of the morality of abortion, and particularly a commitment to its avoidance, cannot be understood apart from communal values and commitments. My discussion, too, concerns essentially the kinds of community (the kinds of values, attitudes, and virtues that community encourages) that will support or not support nascent life in difficult circumstances.

However, I am not convinced of the wisdom or even the possibility of setting aside the question of the status of the unborn offspring, because the presupposition that we *should* support it (even as a sign of hope in the future) seems to involve a certain understanding of its value. Our protectiveness and hope do not include in the same way other forms of sentient and nonsentient life. The point is well taken, however, that the virtue of hope embodied in inauspicious situations enables the perception of at least a *prima facie* obligation to sustain fetal life, even if that life is not clearly of equal value to postnatal human life. Indeed, this takes us far from the position that it must be demonstrated beyond a reasonable doubt that the fetus is a "person" in the full sense of the word as a precondition for according it protection. If relatedness to and concern for others and for the sort of community in which we all associate is more important to us than "defending our own territory" (by defining the precise limits of our minimal obligations not to prevent other equal beings from promoting their own self-interested welfare), then it becomes less important to show whether or not the fetus is a human with exactly the same right to consideration as our own. If we are able to foster a sense of duty to others and to our common society, a duty that precedes and grounds our own rights as individuals, then it also becomes possible to envision a moral obligation to support the cohesion in the human community of even its weakest members, those with the least forceful claim to consideration, whether they be the unborn, the sick, the poor, or the socially powerless.[22]

CONCLUSIONS

The precise value and rights of human fetal life remain questions awaiting resolution, perhaps indefinitely. However, without at least a provisional answer, the abortion discussion cannot proceed coherently, for the participants will not avoid hidden presuppositions about the consideration due the fetus as such. My own conviction that the fetus deserves considerable respect from conception may not represent a common denominator in the abortion debate. Nevertheless, I believe that there is now more of a consensus in our culture than is usually recognized that a policy on abortion attributing to the fetus no value that can ever outweigh its mother's choice to terminate pregnancy is not consonant with its membership in the human community, disputed though the exact nature of that membership may be. Failing agreement on the precise status of the fetus, we may hope still for concurrence in a generally protective attitude toward the fetus, a bias in its favor, and an expectation that those seeking to kill it will be able to claim reasonably that its continued existence imposes on others unjust and intolerable burdens. For such an attitude to be genuinely life-enhancing, rather than simply restrictive and destructive of the lives of pregnant women and their families, will require a move beyond the liberal ethos. It will require nourishment by a renewed and even redirected sense of community, one in which not only the fetus is protected, but also all who suffer disadvantage at the hands of fellow humans, nature, or chance. "Human 'flourishing' " is a phrase invented by G. E. M. Anscombe to describe what grounds, defines, and constitutes the virtues that human beings ought to cultivate.[23] A community in which the "right to abort" could be overshadowed by rather than entailed in the "duty to encourage human well-being" would be one in which human interdependence in the spheres not only of personal freedoms and civil liberties, but also of physical prosperity and amelioration of suffering, corporal and spiritual, is recognized as the very condition of human flourishing, and so as bounty, not burden.

NOTES

1. The twentieth-century popes have taken a persistent and sometimes prophetic interest in redressing imbalances in the social and economic orders, whether precipitated by socialism or by capitalism. Examples are Leo XIII's *Rerum novarum* (1891), Pius XI's *Quadragesimo anno* (1931), John XXIII's *Mater et magistra* (1961) and *Pacem in terris* (1963), Paul VI's *Populorum progressio* (1967) and *Octogesima adveniens* (1971), and John Paul II's *Laborem exercens* (1982).

2. Daniel Callahan, *Abortion: Law, Choice, and Morality* (New York: Macmillan, 1970) 381–90.

3. See, for example, Larry R. Churchill and José Jorge Siman, "Abortion and the Rhetoric of Individual Rights," *Hastings Center Report* 12 (Feb. 1982) 9–12; and Sandra Harding, "Beneath the Surface of the Abortion Dispute," in *Abortion: Understanding Differences*, ed. Sidney and Daniel Callahan (New York: Plenum Press, 1984).

4. See the critiques of liberalism by Sandra G. Harding, "Beneath the Surface of the Abortion Debate," and Jean Bethke Elshtain, "Reflections on Abortion, Values, and the Family," both in *Abortion: Understanding Differences*.

5. Judith Jarvis Thomson, "A Defense of Abortion," *Philosophy and Public Affairs* 1 (Fall 1972) 47–66.

6. The papal social encyclicals have been largely *ad hoc* in nature, addressing themselves in the name of the common good to actual abuses and imbalances of rights and duties, rather than attempting to articulate any exhaustive list of rights and duties or to formulate precisely enduring relationships among them. For instance, in *Rerum novarum* Leo XIII addressed, against socialism, the right of the worker to own private property; in *Quadragesimo anno* Pius XI asserted the rights of the worker against capitalistic property owners who neglected duties to others and to the community as a whole. Among the best concise definitions of "common good" in the encyclicals is that offered by John XXIII in *Pacem in terris* (paras. 55–58). I have further developed this analysis of common good, rights, and duties in "Toward a Christian Theory of Human Rights," *Journal of Religious Ethics* 8 (Fall 1980) 277–301.

In a recent essay ("Abortion and the Pursuit of Happiness," *Logos* 3 [1982] 61–77),

Philip Rossi, S.J., similarly asserted the connection between human freedom and inter-dependence and linked it with Kant's characterization of moral agency in accord with membership in a "kingdom of ends." Rossi argued effectively that "rights in conflict" language is insufficient to handle the morality of abortion in the absence of a unified view of happiness or the human good.

7. In *The Heretical Imperative* (Garden City, N.Y.: Doubleday, 1979), Peter Berger dubbed the "modern consciousness" a phenomenon akin to the liberal ethos. The modern man or woman is under the necessity of making choices rather than of acquiescing to fate. However, he or she also is confronted with a plurality of world views, rather than with a cohesive tradition that shapes social roles and gives them significance. A crisis of belief results because beliefs about reality, including religious and moral beliefs, require social confirmation, and that is widely unavailable in modern society. As a result, morality and religion become subjectivized and contingent on the sheer choice or "preference" of the individual (chap. 1, "Modernity as the Universalization of Heresy," pp. 1–31).

8. See, for example, James B. Nelson, *Embodiment: An Approach to Sexuality and Christian Theology* (Minneapolis: Augsburg, 1978), and Robert Baker and Frederick Elliston, eds., *Philosophy and Sex* (Buffalo, N.Y.: Prometheus Books, 1975).

9. Louis Janssens, "Artificial Insemination: Ethical Considerations," *Louvain Studies* 8 (Spring 1980) 5–6.

10. More complete discussions of the evolution of the Catholic position on abortion are offered in John T. Noonan, Jr., "An Almost Absolute Value in History," in *The Morality of Abortion*, ed. Noonan (Cambridge: Harvard University Press, 1970); and John Connery, S.J., *Abortion: The Development of the Roman Catholic Perspective* (Chicago: Loyola University Press, 1977). Critiques have been developed by Bernard Häring, "A Theological Evaluation"; James M. Gustafson, "A Protestant Ethical Approach; and Paul Ramsey, "Reference Points in Deciding about Abortion," in *The Morality of Abortion*. Charles Curran examined the problem of "physicalism" in Roman Catholic ethics generally in "Natural Law and Contemporary Moral Theology," *Contemporary Problems in Moral Theology* (Notre Dame, Ind.: Fides, 1970). Several discussions of the "principle of double effect" operative in the Catholic analysis of abortion appear in Charles E. Curran and Richard A. McCormick, S.J., eds., *Readings in Moral Theology No. 1: Moral Norms and Catholic Tradition* (New York: Paulist, 1979). Unfortunately, to cite these resources is only to skim the surface of those available.

11. Michael Tooley and Laura Purdy, "Is Abortion Murder?" in *Abortion: Pro and Con*, ed. Robert Perkins (Cambridge, Mass.: 1974) 134.

12. Joseph Donceel, S.J., "Animation and Hominization," *Theological Studies* 31 (Mar. 1970) 76–105.

13. I perceive a concern similar to mine in David Peretz's "The Illusion of 'Rational' Suicide," *Hastings Center Report* 11 (Dec. 1981) 40–42. Peretz sees planned suicide as an attempt to gain control over feelings of pain and helplessness by idealizing the freedom and autonomy of the "self as agent."

14. Daniel Callahan, "Minimalist Ethics," *Hastings Center Report* 11 (Oct. 1981) 19–20. Callahan addressed the question of whether a morality that stresses the autonomy of the individual is a "good-time philosophy," able to sustain a society in times of affluence but not in times of economic and political stress.

15. A provocative example of a criterion of the life worth preserving has been offered

by Richard McCormick in a discussion of whether and when to treat infants suffering from serious congenital anomalies. McCormick suggested that physical life can be a worthwhile good for the person living it if it offers at least "relational potential," that is, the capacity to give and receive love, and even if it does not offer "normal" intelligence or physical competence ("To Save or Let Die," *Journal of the American Medical Association* 229 [July 1974] 172–76).

16. Those who have counseled or interviewed parents of abnormal infants have commented that the availability of amniocentesis and abortion in cases of genetic defect has altered the nature of the parent-child relationship after such a birth occurs. John Fletcher commented, "If an infant is born with a severe genetic defect which might have been diagnosed pre-natally, will it not occur to the physicians and parents, that this infant might have been tested and aborted? Such thoughts will, presumably, intensify the rejection of the infant" ("Moral and Ethical Problems of Pre-Natal Diagnosis," *Clinical Genetics* 9 [October 1975] 25). See also John Fletcher, "The Brink: The Parent-Child Bond in the Genetic Revolution," *Theological Studies* 33 (Sept. 1972) 457–85; and Raymond S. Duff and A. G. M. Campbell, "Moral and Ethical Dilemmas in the Special-Care Nursery," *New England Journal of Medicine* 289 (Oct. 1973) 890–94.

17. This is accomplished most extensively in Stanley Hauerwas, *A Community of Character* (Notre Dame, Ind.: University of Notre Dame Press, 1981), especially part 3, "The Church and Social Policy: The Family, Sex, and Abortion."

18. Ibid. 171.

19. Ibid. 191.

20. Ibid. 198–99.

21. Ibid. 198.

22. In an essay entitled "The Christian, Society, and the Weak: A Meditation on the Care of the Retarded," in *Vision and Virtue* (Notre Dame, Ind.: Fides, 1974) 187–94, Hauerwas argued that the Christian's task of caring for the weak exemplifies the obligation to live the love revealed in the cross, rather than either to try to eradicate all suffering or to attribute the existence of suffering to God's hidden purposes.

23. G. E. M. Anscombe, "Modern Moral Philosophy," *Philosophy* 33 (Jan. 1958) 18.

Chapter 2

Feminist Approaches

Feminist perspectives on and concerns about abortion comprise the rubric around which the second chapter is organized. Maguire's essay offers a relational approach to the question of what constitutes personhood. She argues that covenantal love, or at least the consent of the pregnant woman, is a decisive factor in what she calls "the personing process." In her article, Kolbenschlag highlights some of the instances of "bad faith" on both sides of the debate that keep us as a community from achieving a moral consensus on abortion. Callahan identifies and then argues against four tenets that are foundational to prochoice feminism. Interestingly, she develops her prolife argument from a feminist perspective. By attending to the many similarities between childbearing and organ donation, Jung argues in her essay that abortion ought to be treated like other refusals to engage in bodily life support. She then assesses the gift-giving ethos in light of the feminist suspicion of any moral outlook that would call for the self-sacrifice of women and/or sacralize their victimization. The concluding essay explores, again from a feminist perspective, some of the religious symbols and metaphors that shape the Catholic moral imagination. Patrick's article provides Catholic feminists on both sides of the issue some insight into the deeper, perhaps unconscious, dimensions of their arguments.

Personhood, Covenant, and Abortion

Marjorie Reiley Maguire

Abortion continues to be one of the most difficult moral problems of the day for ethicists, particularly Christian ethicists. The moral debate concerns the questions of whether persons have an inviolable right to life which should always be protected by both ethics and law, and whether every act of abortion can be described as the sin of killing and a violation of a person's right to life. Behind the debates on this topic frequently lie contradictory or, more often, unexamined understandings of the meaning of person and when personhood begins.

What I intend to do here is to explore the frequently overlooked questions, "What is a human person?" "When does personhood begin?" and "Who or what is the agent or efficient cause of personhood?" I strongly disagree with Richard McCormick, who says that the word person "only muddies the moral discussion."[1] What muddies the discussion is to avoid the word person. The ontological reality of what is being aborted profoundly affects the moral evaluation of the act of abortion. The only reasons to resist questions about personhood are to avoid subjecting unexamined presuppositions about the nature of fetal life to critical analysis and to avoid threatening a preestablished agenda to either prohibit or allow all abortions.

My primary intention in this presentation is not a matter of ethics *per se*. It is a metaphysical task that might be described as preethical. But from the proposed answers to the metaphysical questions ethical conclusions concerning abortion will follow.

By way of introduction, I begin this paper with the epistemological recognition that both good ethics and objective thought occur not when one lacks any presuppositions or emotions on a subject, since that is humanly impossible, but when one recognizes the assumptions, biases, and feelings that are part of one's life, and considers how they may have influenced one's thought. In an effort to be objective on this important subject, especially since I will attempt to put forth a new understanding of the beginning of personhood that is compatible with a prochoice and a feminist point of view, I wish to share briefly with you five aspects of my individual experience and my beliefs which I acknowledge have influenced my pursuit of the questions here.

First is the experience of having been pregnant, which has served to convince me that it is romantic to speak of a human life in its early stage of development as a person. I realize that the experience of pregnancy is not unique to me, and that other women who have shared this experience may or do not share this conclusion. I hope that the definition of personhood and the description of its beginnings I will give will allow for that difference. The experience of pregnancy has also convinced me, however, that the fetus becomes a person before birth.

Second is the experience of having had a child with a genetic disorder that causes progressive degeneration of the brain and central nervous system and brings about an early death. From this child I learned in an immediate way that personhood and the value it connotes are not simply a function of a capacity for intelligent activity or an ability to perform useful tasks for society.

Third is the experience of having to face the possibility of abortion myself. We learned that our first child had his genetic disorder, and that I am a carrier of it, when I was three months pregnant with our second child. We were fortunate that amniocentesis revealed that our second child is free of this disorder, and that I did not have to have the abortion I was sure I would have had if the diagnosis had been different. However, I then had to ask the question whether it was moral to try to have any other children, if a future pregnancy would carry with it the possibility of abortion, especially since such an abortion would have to be performed relatively late in the pregnancy after amniocentesis. My decision was that it is moral to try to become pregnant under these circumstances. (Mother Nature has kept me from having to face the moral problem beyond this theoretical level.)

My fourth "bias" is a strong identification with feminism that has taken root in me in recent years. Feminism does not mean that one automatically approves of abortion, but it does mean that one looks at the reality of pregnancy from the woman's point of view. As a feminist then, one is forced at least to ask whether the availability of abortion as a legal choice represents a loss of respect for life, or whether it actually represents an increase of respect for the life of the woman, and a conviction that she can be trusted to make a responsible moral choice in an area that so intimately affects her and the life she bears within her. A feminist viewpoint would help one understand the woman who recently said to me, "The antiabortion movement presents itself as only trying to value prenatal life as much as it values my life, but what it says to me is that I am no more valuable than a fertilized egg." I might add that many Jews and blacks have the same problem as this woman when antiabortionists compare abortion to the lives taken in Nazi death camps or degraded by slavery. Finally, feminism makes one realize that any right a woman may have to choose an abortion derives ultimately not from individualistic principles of liberation that simply give persons unlimited rights over their bodies; it derives rather from the realization that self-determination is inextricably linked to embodiment. As Beverly Harrison has written, "In any social relation, body-space must be respected or nothing deeply human or moral can be created."[2]

My fifth and final presupposition, or, more correctly, creedal assumption, is the belief that persons are immortal, and that Christian ethics and any discussion about abortion is meaningless without the conviction that persons transcend death.[3] This conviction does not mean that abortion is an easier thing to justify on the grounds that the fetus, if a person, will be with God anyway. Rather, it means that abortion is harder to justify, if the fetus is a person, because there are eternal repercussions to one's act of abortion. These eternal repercussions do not involve damnation for the woman who has an abortion, but aborted connections with earthly life for the fetus who is aborted. If an afterlife has any connections with life in this world, then the quality of a person's life at the time earthly life is ended affects the quality of life in the next world. This makes voluntary and premature termination of personal life a more serious act than it would be without belief in an afterlife.

These are the elements which have influenced the questions of this paper and which have undoubtedly influenced the conclusions. I trust the conclusions reached are no less objective or true for all of that.

THE LEGALITY OF ABORTION

While this presentation will touch on the moral question surrounding abortion, it will not address the legal question of abortion. As I have argued briefly elsewhere,[4] even if prenatal human life at every stage of its development—from the first moment of fertilization to birth—is considered a person, the life of such a "person" is not entitled to protection from the law until it is viable. (Viability, of course, is a somewhat fluid category.) In other words, I would have agreed with McCormick if he had said that the word "person" muddies the *legal* discussion rather than the *moral* discussion. The reason I hold this is that previable "persons" are unlike any other persons in our experience, because they alone are absolutely dependent upon the body of another human being for their physical life-support systems. The law would have to violate its obligations to a woman, who is an independent life and a citizen, in order to protect any purported "rights" of nonviable, prenatal life. I believe that no one has a "right" to life, deserving of full protection of the law, when that life is totally dependent on the body of another human being for its life support.[5] Moreover, the legitimate rights of all citizens under the law would be undermined if the law required all persons to give bodily life support to those who needed it in the form of blood transfusions and organ or bone-marrow transplants, and even made it a criminal offense to refuse to give such support,[6] or if the law limited this obligation to only one class of citizens, i.e., pregnant women. A history of the law limiting this obligation to one class of citizens does not give warrant for the law to continue to do this, any more than it would be appropriate for the law to reinstitute slavery just because it was on the books for so many years. Thus, clarifying whether or not the fetus is a person will not solve problems of law. But it can help to solve moral problems, or at least to delineate them.

WHAT IS A PERSON?

The most influential definition of *person* in Christian theology was the one given by Boethius near the end of the fifth century: "an individual substance of a rational nature." The problem with this definition is that "rational nature" for Boethius included the notion of the presence of a spiritual soul in a being. For him and his followers, like Aquinas, the problem was not so much deciding what constituted a person, since the formal cause of human personhood was considered to be the rational soul; the problem was deciding when the soul, which could only be created by God, was infused into the body. Today we are less inclined to speak in the language of body and soul. It is too heavily tainted with dualism. So we face not only the problem of the beginning of personhood but also a decision about the precise formal element that constitutes personhood.

For the Christian, modern definitions of person are not very helpful. They usually center on the ability of a being to perform self-conscious acts. However, the Christian believes that all persons are of equal worth and equally loved by God even when it is obvious that not all persons possess an equal capacity for self-conscious activity. Infants, brain-damaged persons, and perhaps even some or all fetuses are valued by God in the Christian perspective. Yet they are not capable of the kind of conscious activity that is associated with the notion of "person" in the modern mind.

Perhaps the meaning of personhood can best be approached by examining what can be said of persons in both common parlance and in the Christian tradition. Persons are beings that have embodied existence.[7] What this means is both that persons are determined by their bodies and that they transcend their bodies. In addition to believing that persons can transcend the limitations of their bodies in the ordinary experiences of life in which they are able to think thoughts and/or perform acts which exceed the limitations of their bodies to one time, place, and condition, most Christians also believe that persons transcend the death that strikes down the life of the body. In Christian theology, a person is a being who is so valued and loved by God that God would be willing to die for this being— symbolized by Jesus' death on the Cross. In addition, God loves this being even into eternity. Furthermore, a person is a being who should be loved and valued by all other persons in the same way that God loves and values persons. A person is one who should be treated as sacred by the human community. In fact, without even appealing to Christian belief in God, it can be argued that the foundation of morality is the experience of the sacred value of persons.[8]

The important point in all of this is that for a Christian a person is a being who is called into community with God and with other human persons. So valued and sacred are persons in the Christian tradition that the language of "person" has itself been used in this tradition for the communitarian aspects of God's own existence.

Because the notion of persons' sacredness is so central in Christian theology, it is common to find attempts in philosophical and theological literature to state this insight through different language. The most common language used is the expression "the sanctity of life." Some persons, however, prefer the expression "the right to life," while others use language that implies an exact equivalence between person and human being.

The expression "the sanctity of life" is not only an erroneous expression, since life has not been treated as sacred in Christian theory or practice, but it is also most unhelpful and misleading when used to capture the idea of the sanctity of persons. The first reason it is misleading is scriptural. There is no place in Scripture where it is asserted that life is sacred.[9] Second, life ends. What ends and is conquered by death is threatened in its claim to sacredness and inviolability. In Christian theology, persons do not end. Persons are sacred, life is not. Third, life is a word that is too broad to describe what is sacred, even when the adjective "human" is attached to it. Life is a continuum that has been in existence for billions of years. Not every being on that continuum is considered as sacred as persons by the Christian tradition. Life on this continuum that is in and of a human being is human life, but all separable human life does not constitute an individual person. Human life covers everything from the separate genetic material of sperm and ovum to the developing fetus, the newborn infant, the cells that are presently taken from human beings and grown in laboratories and may even outlive the individuals from whom they were taken. In summary, for much of the Eastern religious tradition and for vegetarian pacifists, the "sanctity of life" is a basic moral principle; for Western religious thought, it is simply not a basic moral principle, no matter how often such a claim is asserted.

Another expression like the "sanctity of life" that I would also characterize as a false truism or an aphoristic fallacy is the expression "right to life." Rights inhere primarily in persons. Rights that inhere in nonpersons never take precedence over rights that inhere in persons. For this reason, it is important to decide whether the fetus is a person to determine just what rights it has. One cannot say that life has a "right" to produce new persons—unless perhaps the species were threatened with extinction on the planet or in the universe. If one really wants to say that life has such a "right" then one might have to outlaw celibacy and any other voluntary activity that limited all potential reproduction.

Others feel that "human being" is an expression that could be considered the equivalent of the word "person." In some contexts it could be equivalent. However, human being could also be considered simply the equivalent of "human life," the only difference being that it is a narrower term than human life and only applies to an individuated human life, including a prenatal individuated human life. Thus, it is not a helpful expression for deciding when personhood begins, that is, for deciding when a human life becomes sacred, valued by God, and an equal part of the human community. Another reason for using the word "person," rather than the expression "human being," is that the word "person" is applied even to God. It therefore better captures the sense of sacredness of persons, whose beginnings we want to chart.

THE INDIVIDUAL-BIOLOGICAL
APPROACH TO PERSONHOOD

Various approaches have been taken to determine criteria for the beginning of personhood, although the expressions "life" or "human life" are often mistakenly used in place of personhood in the discussion of this question, and in fact prejudice the outcome. Charles Curran outlines four of the approaches taken: an individual-biological approach, a relational approach, a multiple approach, and a societal approach.[10] My presentation will adopt a relational approach to discuss the beginning of personhood, but hopefully I will overcome the objection of Curran and others to that approach by allowing some validity to the individual-biological approach to save the relational approach from complete subjectivity. Before presenting my own approach to the beginning of personhood, however, I will consider the shortcomings of the individual-biological approach, both in the arguments of those who appeal solely to biology, as well as in the arguments of those who couple their appeal to biology with an appeal to God.

The appeal to biology[11] that is most basic is to argue that the person begins at the moment of conception, because at this moment a unique genetic code comes into being. Followers of this approach would say that any human termination of a pregnancy after this point—whether by an intrauterine device, drugs, or surgery—involves the killing of a person. Sometimes the fertilized ovum in its early stages of development is called a "potential person" rather than a "person," but there is no comparable modification of the language of killing applied to the termination of this life. If potentiality is the touchstone of sacredness, then adherents of this rigorous view of abortion should logically follow the position of recent Catholic popes who condemn contraception as evil. However, no one, including recent Catholic popes, speaks of contraception as the "killing" of a "potential person." Even farther back in the Catholic tradition, as Susan Nicholson has shown so well,[12] when words such as "homicide," "parricide" and "murder" were used in conjunction with contraception (or homosexuality), the intent was to show the evil of nonprocreative sex, rather than to make a statement that a "person" had been killed.

There are variations on the biological-approach theme among those who would locate the beginning of personhood at a biological moment later than fertilization. Some locate the earliest beginning of personhood at the moment of individuation, since twinning can no longer occur after that. Others will locate it at the first heartbeat. Others, following a more modern criterion for determining significant life, and looking for consistency with criteria for terminating life at the other end of the life spectrum, will locate the beginning of personhood at the first discernible brain wave. Still others will look to a more complex development of the brain. Some of these adherents of a later biological moment signaling the beginning of personhood would allow for some moral freedom in the area of abortion.

The problem with the biological approach, at any point on its spectrum, is that it treats personhood as if it were a purely biological reality. Yet personhood signifies a spiritual, transcendent reality, which is the basis of the sacredness of persons. The appeal to biology, furthermore, makes no real distinction between full personhood and potential personhood. It never clearly shows why the newly conceived or developing prenatal life should be considered the moral and legal peer of a newborn baby rather than ontologically closer to a separate sperm and egg.

Another more "spiritual" way that the individual-biological approach is presented is with an appeal to God as the Creator and Lord of life.[13] In this perspective God creates personhood, or "infuses a soul" into the material reality of the fertilized ovum, either at the first moment of conception or at one of the later moments of biological development. It is the special creation of every person by God that makes persons the "image of God" and makes them sacred. For persons who take this approach, the merest presence of life is the sign that God has "breathed" into the material reality, giving it a spiritual life, just as God did in the Book of Genesis for the creation of Adam and Eve. There is a fivefold problem with this approach.

First, it can appeal only to the confessional believer. Second, it fails to recognize that life is a continuum. God's breath of life touched creation at its beginning, which caused creation to be. Since then creation has continued from this original impetus. New individual lives have appeared from the life that surrounds all of us. Life comes from life, not from nothingness. Thus, the appearance of a fertilized ovum does not signal that God has visited creation with a new breath of life. From the biological point of view it is a continuation of life.

Third, and related to the second objection, is that it is circular reasoning to argue that the fertilized ovum is a person because God is the Creator and Lord of life. We cannot know God except through human reality. Therefore, it is impossible to argue that a new act of God proves that a certain material reality constitutes a new person in our midst. God has never decreed what biological moment of human reality is a new sign of the divine presence.

Fourth, if the presence of a fertilized ovum is the signal that God has created a new person, then God does not consider persons to be sacred, and so we might well ask why we should. If God creates a person every time there is the fertilization of an ovum by a sperm, then persons must be cheap and disposable, since approximately 58 percent of fertilized ova spontaneously abort prior to implantation.[14]

Fifth and finally, the creation of much human life is not very godly. This view would have God approving life begun anew in the ugly acts of rape and incest as much as in the union of two persons who have joined their lives together to become as one flesh. It would have God approving new life begun in the bodies of women who are too frail to sustain even their own life, let alone the life of another person. It would have God creating persons by whimsy, in order to surprise with contraceptive failure women who wanted no children, either because they were unmarried, or because they were at the stage in their life when they were sending the last child of a large family off to college, or because they were just catching their breath after several toddlers a year apart, or because they did not have sufficient material advantages to welcome a new child. We would find it hard to love and admire a human being who played such tricks on other humans. How can we attribute to God such a cruel or arbitrary attitude toward existing persons or new persons?

The lure of the appeal to biology for the beginning of personhood is the apparent objectivity and simplicity of this approach. But persons are not simple objects. This approach is reductionistic. It fails to establish a base for personhood that accounts for the spiritual, transcendent, sacred reality of personhood that is recognized even by those who do not believe in God. The lure of the appeal to God is its apparent spirituality and piety. However, this approach is extrinsicist and tendentially nominalistic. It states that persons are sacred but does not show what personhood is or when personhood begins.

A RELATIONAL APPROACH TO THE
BEGINNING OF PERSONHOOD

What is needed is a way of defining the beginning of personhood that takes into account the objective individual aspect of human personhood that the biological approach recognizes, as well as the spiritual, transcendent, and sacred aspect of personhood that the appeal to God attempts to convey. It must bear some relationship to the bodily existence that characterizes human beings, but it has to allow room for personhood to transcend bodily limitations. It has to be an approach aware of the processual nature of personhood, but one that can also describe the formal reality which begins this process. It must be an approach that unites the human and divine moments of a person's creation in a nonartificial or dualistic way, and it must be an approach which frees God from the limitations of biology. I believe such a way can be found in a variation of the relational approach to this question.[15]

In Christian theology it has been common to move from the seen to the unseen, to move from what we know about human beings to predicating statements about God based on the likeness of God to human persons. A movement in the other direction might offer some help in solving the question of when human personhood begins. Christian theology has hypothesized that there are three persons in God and that these persons are constituted by relations within the godhead (*S.T.* I, 29,4). In the spirit of this theology, it might be suggested that if divine persons are constituted by relations, perhaps human persons are also constituted by relations.

In looking for analogues other than in the godhead for the constitution of personhood through relationship, one might, with admitted literary freedom, look to the covenant symbolism and to the constitution of Israel as a people in the Exodus account. Here we have the beginning of the collective personhood of Israel, or the creation of a new ontological reality, through a willed relation on the part of Yahweh that is characterized as covenant love, or *hesed*. This new identity for the people of Israel calls them into a community of persons, a community which involved their relationship with God and the relationship of each member of the community with each other. This new identity was a completely free and gracious gift on the part of Yahweh, in no way predetermined or forced by the fact that Yahweh had already had a relationship to them as the Creator of their separate existences as individuals, or even that Yahweh had already entered into a voluntary relationship with them through their forefathers, Abraham, Isaac, and Jacob. Israel's creation as the People of God, a spiritual, transcendent, sacred reality beyond the fact of their material existence, can be instructive for our attempt to locate the beginning of human personhood.

From trinitarian theology we can take the insight that persons are constituted by relations. From Exodus peoplehood theology we can take the suggestion that personhood is constituted by a free and gracious act of love that establishes a covenant with the new reality that is being personed, calling that person into community that creates a covenantal relationship with God and all other persons. The problem is to determine the point at which this might be said to occur and signal a new human person in our midst.

What I am looking for is a point on the continuum of sexual union, conception, pregnancy, and birth that could be considered as producing a relationship of covenantal love marking the beginning of personhood. I am not concerned about God's part in this, since I see God as a presence along the whole continuum of life. I am concerned about the human reality that marks God's presence in a special way, a way that can be said to be ontologically new. What I am doing then is looking for the *human* agency that is responsible for the creation of personhood or "soul." We look upon each new human life as a gift of God, and yet we know that it is human agency directly and God only indirectly that is responsible for that life. Thus, I see no reason why we should not look for human agency as the direct cause of the spiritual, transcendent aspect of human life to which God then gives assent. It makes more sense to have God's personing creativity determined by a personal moment of human covenant love than simply by biology, as has often been the view in the past.

In searching for the moment of human "love making" which constitutes personhood and establishes a sacred and spiritual relationship between God and human life, I reject the time of sexual intercourse as this moment. I believe sexual intercourse is misnamed as "love making." Some, but not all sexual intercourse, not even all that between married persons, can be characterized as "making love." This was especially impressed on me once as I watched a television show on incest. I winced each time one of the young women interviewed spoke of the times her father had "made love" to her, occasions that had even included violence and threats of harm if she revealed what had happened. Nor is intercourse that *is* truly "love making" the kind of love which constitutes a person. This love is not directed to the as-yet-unconceived life that may result from the intercourse. It is directed by the spouses toward each other. Finally, there are persons who were not biologically initiated by sexual intercourse, but by artificial insemination, *in vitro* fertilization, insemination in a surrogate mother—or some day, perhaps, by cloning.

I would propose that the only person who can be the initiator of covenant love for prenatal life, bringing that life into the reality of human community and thereby making it a person, is the woman in whose womb the pregnancy exists. The personhood begins when the bearer of life, the mother, makes a covenant of love with the developing life within her to bring it to birth. Obviously the mother shows more love if she is willing to make a covenant with the fetus for more than the minimal demands of birth. However, that minimum is a gift of self which must be characterized as love. It is an act which recognizes the life within her as having a personal relationship to her. And it is an act which makes possible the introduction of the fetus into the relationship of the larger human community. The moment which begins personhood, then, is the moment when the mother accepts the pregnancy.

At the moment when the mother bonds with the fetus, the fetus becomes a Thou to her rather than an It. It is then that its potentiality for relationality and sociality is activated, because it is brought into a personal relationship with a human person, with the only human person who can actuate this potentiality while the fetus is still in the mother's body and in a previable state. The fetus cannot become related to the human social community except through the mediation of the mother. It is the mother who makes the fetus a social being by accepting its relatedness to her. Thus, it is the mother who makes the fetus a person. After that point its life is sacred because it is sacred to her.

What I am saying, in other words, is that the conception of the personhood (or "soul") of each of us was symbolically a virginal conception. Looking again to Scripture we could say that the model for the beginning of the personhood of every human being is found in Luke 1:38. Personhood is the product of the *fiat* ("Let it be done unto me . . .") of a mother. It is because of that *fiat* that all future possibilities for growth in personhood exist. It is because of that co-creative *fiat* that God can say, "Thou art my child, this day have I begotten thee" (see Psalm 2:7).

I am not proposing that a covenant made by the mother with the fetus constitutes the beginning of personhood only because abortion is now a legal option. I am proposing that it is in the nature of things as established by God that woman creates the "soul" just as much as she nourishes the body of developing human life. I am proposing that if ethics is built upon "natural law," as some ethicists hold, then this "natural law," which links the beginning of personhood to a covenant made by a woman, must affect our ethical evaluation of abortion.

If what I have proposed sounds preposterous, let us look to nature itself, and to aspects of human activity which point to the fact that the mother, the life bearer, does bear a more distinctive relationship to a person than the biological father. Dr. James Diamond, M.D., noted in an article in *Theological Studies* that the free ovum is many times larger than the free sperm, and, if fertilization occurs, the ovum supplies the energy to the nucleus of the fertilized egg. He went on to say,

> the vital activity in these early days is ordered by what is called messenger ribonucleic acid (RNA) from the mother's ovum. The sperm apparently does not enter into the ordering of this activity. The sperm resembles a man who impregnates a woman and then leaves to her all the work of raising the child. When we note of such a shiftless male "Isn't that just like a man," we may also say of the sperm, "Isn't that just like a sperm."[16]

To indulge in a mercantile image, one could say that if the biological father has a fifty-fifty share in the "corporation" that is the developing life at the first moment of conception, he quickly loses his shares, so that by the moment of birth it is difficult to say whether he holds even one share of "stock" in what has been produced and what has gone into the production, strictly from a material point of view. In other words, the relationship of the father to a new human life can simply be that of a biological donor, even if conception has taken place through sexual intercourse. The woman in whose womb the pregnancy exists can never be considered simply a donor, even if she were a surrogate mother who was pregnant as the result of *in vitro* fertilization using another woman's ovum. The continued existence of a conceptus in the womb of a woman depends not merely on biological donation but on consensual and hospitable agreement by the woman, involving a gift of self which constitutes the minimum of a personal relationship.

Further strength could be given to the theory I have proposed by a look at tradition. Quickening has been considered a significant event that signaled animation in major ethical systems through the centuries.[17] Quickening is an event that only the mother experiences. A bit of soft evidence for my theory is found by looking at the search of adoptees for their natural, biological parents. Most often the concern is to find the mother. It is not that there is a lack of interest in the biological father, or simply that he is even harder to find than the mother, but there is in most people a special attachment to the birth mother who nurtured life within her body for nine months and, according to my theory, even created the "soul."

Some may object to using the word "covenant" to describe the relationship between the mother and the intrauterine person. Does not a covenant involve an agreement between two persons? Since this unborn person cannot respond to the mother's act of self-giving love, is it proper to describe their relationship by the name covenant?

Perhaps this objection can best be addressed by looking at the Christian theology of baptism. Many Christian churches practicing infant baptism speak of this sacrament as a covenant, and many even see it as a covenant which constitutes the infant as an ontologically new being, a "new creature." (Moreover, in the Catholic tradition it is Holy *Mother* Church who makes possible this covenant.) Yet an infant can in no way actively respond to the baptismal covenant in a personal way at the moment of baptism. It can simply continue to exist and grow, until its growth in personhood through community enables it to respond.

The expressions "covenant" and "covenant love" in this discussion have the advantage of continuity with the religious tradition. Moreover, they convey the serious obligation that falls upon the mother who creates a person from the life that is growing within her body. Her decision to bring the fetus to birth constitutes it as a person, but her obligations do not end with her decision or with its birth. For her part, her decision to enter into this covenant involves the obligation either to continue her self-giving love to bring the newborn to fuller personhood or else a willingness to give the child up for adoption to someone who can assume the continuing obligations of the personing covenant. In spite of these advantages, however, the expressions "covenant" and "covenant love" could be considered too poetic or too religious to describe the relationship that constitutes human personhood. A more universally acceptable and secular expression might be "consent of the mother." The moment which begins personhood, then, could be described for the rest of the discussion of this paper as the moment when the mother *consents* to the pregnancy.

THE BIOLOGICAL OR OBJECTIVE
ASPECT OF PERSONHOOD

If the consent of the mother to the pregnancy marks the formal moment when personhood begins, does that mean that personhood is a very fluid concept and that it could even be denied to a newborn infant if the mother had not consented to the pregnancy? Does biological reality count as nothing in the personing of beings with an *embodied* existence? What I have done in placing the beginning of personhood at the moment of maternal consent is to try to pinpoint the formal constitutive element for the beginning of personhood, a moment that could not be captured by television. This might be termed the spiritual side of personhood, or even the subjective side of personhood. However, I would argue that there is, as well, a biological or objective side to personhood for embodied individuals. There is a point in the pregnancy when the biological development of the fetus is such that the consent of the mother to the pregnancy is implicit, and therefore the fetus should be considered a person, even though consent has not consciously and actively been given by the mother. I would still argue that the formal constitutive element of personhood is the mother's consent and not the stage of biological development of the fetus, but sufficient biological development can create a presumption of consent.[18] In other words, if the woman allows a pregnancy to continue long enough she has implicitly consented to the pregnancy even if she has not consciously accepted it. This would also apply to a woman who fell into a coma after a sufficiently advanced stage of pregnancy and was delivered of a baby without her explicit consent. The use of expressions such as "covenant" or "covenant love" to describe presumed consent, is, of course, completely inappropriate and illustrates the need for this legalistic expression.

To the question of what stage of biological development is a reasonable point to mark presumed consent, I believe there is room for disagreement among ethicists and theologians. However, making presumed consent the formal element in constituting personhood does change the terms of the moral debate.

In looking for the *minimum* of biological reality that would have to exist for presumed consent, I would at least have to listen to those who would argue that this minimum exists at the first moment of fertilization. However, I could only *presume* the consent of the mother at this stage *if* she had directly sought and willed the pregnancy. Willingness to engage in sexual intercourse is not sufficient to create a presumption of consent to a pregnancy.

A more reasonable but not completely acceptable biological development for marking presumed consent is the point about two to three weeks after conception when implantation has occurred—and so there is less chance for a miscarriage—when individuation has occurred, and when the mother becomes aware that she might be pregnant. If the mother consents to the pregnancy at that point, I am willing to call the developing embryo a person which is sacred to God, which should be sacred to humanity, and which will share eternal life with all other persons, even if its life should be subsequently terminated by a miscarriage. However, I am not willing to *presume* consent at this early stage of pregnancy. If a woman does not consent to the pregnancy at this time, and aborts the developing life within her, I do not believe she has killed a person who will then point a condemnatory finger at the mother as she enters eternal life. The person-making relationship had not yet occurred. This, of course, means that in one case I find it acceptable to call a three-week-old embryo a person, while in another case I do not find it acceptable. In other words, I am willing to employ only a relational criterion for determining personhood at this stage of embryonic development.

For my own part I would demand significant development of the brain and central nervous system before I would say that a biological reality existed which presumed consent of the mother to the pregnancy. It is only when the brain and central nervous system are sufficiently developed that the fetus reaches the threshold of viability. And it is only when the fetus is viable that it is no longer dependent on its mother to actuate its potentiality for relatedness and sociality. Only after viability can it be in a personal relationship with members of the human social community other than its mother. Viability, of course, is not marked by a single moment in the pregnancy that turns on like a light. It is a shifting area and, in fact, is not even purely biological but is itself dependent on society's standards as technology allows society to take over biology.

The difficult area for determining presumed consent and for ethical evaluation of abortion is the second trimester of pregnancy, when viability looms on the horizon. This is the difficult area not only for philosophers and theologians, who deal with the issue abstractly, but also for the providers of abortion services,[19] and, most especially, for the woman herself, for whom the methods of abortion at this stage are a difficult experience and, in some cases, even like vaginal or caesarean delivery of a full-term baby. I will return to an ethical consideration of second trimester abortions at the end of this paper.

If I were to end my examination of personhood here my paper would probably be criticized for exhibiting the ultimate in female chauvinism, because of its seeming suggestion that men are only useful for producing sperm in the process that we call person making. If past patriarchal scholarship's favorable treatment of male chauvinists were taken as a model, then, of course, I should expect no criticism for centuries. After all, Augustine got away with teaching that women were only useful for generating and would be no help to man apart from that.[20]

And then there was Luther, who taught that the father's semen was the source of the human soul and the mother provided only nourishment for the life.[21] However, having the advantage of better knowledge (and perhaps greater wisdom and insight!) than either Augustine or Luther on this point, I cannot end this paper leaving the impression that I am wallowing in female chauvinism. Men, and particularly the father, do have a part to play in the personing process.

PERSONS AND THE IMAGE OF GOD

Personing is not a moment. It is not a once-and-forever event. It is a process. It is a process that is begun in a moment and by a person, and it is that moment and that causality that I have thus far investigated. However, personing can only come to full flower if it continues beyond that moment and if it involves other persons. When we looked to the covenant symbolism of Exodus to locate the kind of action that begins personhood, we saw that covenant love introduced the newly created reality of Israel into community. It created a people. Peoplehood requires community but personhood also requires community. Persons cannot be persons alone. No person is an island. Sociality is the touchstone of personhood. That is why the biological side of personhood is not sufficient of itself to constitute the formal element of the beginning of personhood.

Recourse to another passage of Scripture will help to shed light on the essential link between community and personhood, between individuality and sociality. In Genesis 1:27 we read "In the image of God they were created, male and female God created them." This passage has been wrongly interpreted over the centuries to indicate that each individual in his or her own individuality is the image of God. It has been further distorted to mean that each individual is the image of God only in his or her spiritual faculties, in his or her soul. What I think this passage is really saying, however, is that the image of God is found only in community, and it is only found in community that can accept diversity, especially the most basic diversity of male and female.

A woman is the initial creator of personhood in the view that I have proposed. However, she can create personhood only because she herself is a social being. Further personing involves other persons working with or in place of the mother. Even during the pregnancy this can involve the father, insofar as he takes an interest in the personing process that is occurring, but which he cannot see and which is being mediated to him by the mother. If he has entered into a marriage covenant with the mother, he is more one with her in the personing process she is effecting than if he is not willing to become spiritually one flesh with her. After birth, during what I would call the postnatal pregnancy, an even larger social community than the mother and father is involved in the personing process.

The "soul" is conceived during the prenatal pregnancy, but it is formed during the postnatal pregnancy. Thus, while the mother begins the process, the father, if possible, and many others too, are needed to make the child a full human person and the image of God. Furthermore, it is when the father primarily but also the rest of society fail in their obligations of community toward the woman that she most often resorts to abortion, out of an implicit realization that she cannot make a covenant with the fetus.

Finally, if there is a time in the future when a pregnancy can take place completely in an artificial environment, in a "test tube" or artificial womb, then men themselves or society as a whole would have to be considered the initial creators of personhood rather than the mother. While liberating woman from the cares of pregnancy, such technology would actually usurp a spiritual power that is now uniquely hers. While this could represent the ultimate sharing and community between male and female, it could also lead to the final invasion of woman's dignity.[22]

ETHICAL CONCLUSIONS

Briefly and obviously, a number of ethical conclusions could be drawn from the position I have proposed. First, prior to actual or presumed consent to the pregnancy the mother ultimately has the moral right to make the decision to terminate the pregnancy. After consent she should still have the legal right to terminate the pregnancy, but in this view her moral right is limited.

Prior to the beginning of personhood, abortion does not require moral justifications similar to those that would be needed for the killing of persons. This does not mean that abortion needs no moral evaluation or is just another form of contraception. However, any moral evil attached to abortion, prior to the beginning of personhood, would derive from the two facts that abortion is the snuffing out of life and that it requires an invasion of the woman's body. All life should be revered and should not be arbitrarily created and then arbitrarily taken, whether it is the life of a flower, a baby seal, or a human embryo. When life is irresponsibly taken there is moral evil. When medical procedures that invade the human body are made necessary through careless human actions, there is moral evil. Neither of these evils, however, can be called murder.

The difficult area for ethical evaluation of abortion is the second trimester of pregnancy, as viability nears. Perhaps the philosophical and theological problems are solved by the fact that during the second trimester there are usually only four reasons why a woman terminates a pregnancy: to preserve her life, for fetal indications following amniocentesis or disease, when social and economic barriers prevent a woman from completing a pregnancy she wanted and had previously accepted, or finally, because of the woman's prior ignorance of her pregnancy.

There are two ways to handle these problem areas of abortion. One is a legalistic solution that accepts these abortions and justifies them by philosophical considerations revolving around individualistic and contractual interpretations of actual or presumed consent. The other is an activist solution which seeks to eliminate the conditions which create a need for second trimester abortions. Both solutions could appeal to ethicists.

The legalistic solution could accept the notion that it is the consent of the mother that is formally constitutive of personhood, and that sufficient biological development can create a presumption of consent. This solution could then offer the following distinctions: (1) presumed consent would never take away a woman's moral right to abort to save her life; (2) the notion of conditional consent could be employed morally to justify an abortion for fetal indications or for radically changed economic conditions after the stage of biological development signaling presumed consent had been reached; and (3) the notion of consent marred by ignorance could be used to justify a second trimester abortion for a woman who did not know she was pregnant before that. There are, of course, other abstract ethical principles which can be used to justify abortion of a fetus that is considered a person. Susan Nicholson ably and thoroughly presents many of these in her book *Abortion and the Roman Catholic Church.*[23]

What is really needed, however, is a more revolutionary approach to the ethical problem of second trimester abortions. If those persons and churches who are avowedly antiabortion really made an effort, they could eliminate the need for most second trimester abortions except those necessary to save the life of the mother. If society made it a priority and committed sufficient research funds to the effort, the time for fetal diagnosis by amniocentesis or other yet-to-be-discovered methods could be pushed back earlier than the sixteenth week of pregnancy. Then there would be no need to have a late abortion for fetal indications. Similarly, society could set its priorities so that no woman ever had to consider an abortion of a fetus she wanted because she discovered that she could not afford to have a child. Finally, vigorous and aggressive sex education and contraceptive information programs could help to insure that no woman would reach the second trimester of a pregnancy without knowledge of her condition or with the hope that her problem would just go away by itself if she waited that long.

Aside from influencing ethical conclusions concerning first and second trimester abortions, the position on the beginning of personhood that I have proposed also affects the evaluation of such issues as artificial insemination, *in vitro* fertilization, and "surrogate mothers." Since sexual intercourse is not a sacred moment of human community marking the beginning of personhood, conception can take place in an artificial way. Fertilization of ova outside a woman's body, the discarding of some of those fertilized ova, and even experimentation on them are not necessarily immoral if there are no persons floating on petri dishes. Finally, all of these techniques enable sterile women to fulfill a role that, with the limitations of our present technology, is unique to womankind—that is, creating a person, a "soul."

It is the relationship between maternal acceptance of a pregnancy and fetal sacredness that makes understandable the disjunctions in life that Richard McCormick has wrongly called "cultural schizophrenia."[24] Many of the same persons who approve the abortion of an unwanted fetus would advocate laws protecting the life and health of an accepted fetus. Medical personnel who countenance or even perform abortions of unwanted fetuses are some of the same persons who perform fetal surgery to save an accepted fetus or practice *in vitro* fertilization to help a woman become pregnant. A mother who loves, cherishes, and cares for a retarded or handicapped child who is already a member of her family might abort her fetus that is diagnosed as being similarly damaged. A woman who could never give her newborn up for adoption can abort the fetus she bears so intimately within her body.

In the popular children's book *Horton Hears a Who*[25] there is the constant refrain, "A person's a person, no matter how small." This could be the slogan of some ethicists in the abortion debate, who seem to make biological smallness the touchstone of personhood. What I have tried to show in this presentation is that a person's a person when personally related to other persons. (Even Horton's Who was a part of Whoville.) The fetus cannot become related to other persons except through the womb-mother. Once brought into sociality by its mother, the unborn person must be treated as sacred by other persons. No one has a right to violate her decision to bring this intrauterine person to birth. After its birth, when the mother has brought it into the fabric of the larger social whole, its rejection by its mother does not take away its right to life. It then holds it independently, although still in virtue of its reality as a social being.[26]

Early in this presentation I stated that Scripture nowhere asserts that life is sacred. What Scripture does assert, however, is that the People of God are sacred.[27] It is covenant love calling people into community which makes life sacred. In the view I have proposed, God has made woman the human co-creator who has the privilege of bringing new persons into this covenant. This privilege, however, is also a source of responsibility. But that responsibility cannot be defined as simply the obligation to bring to birth every pregnancy that takes root in her body. Rather, it is the obligation to bring to birth only those fetuses for whom she is physically, emotionally, psychologically, and economically prepared either to carry out the demands of covenant after birth, or to give the child to someone who can. She has an obligation not to make a personing covenant with a fetus if the personing covenant will not or cannot be continued with the infant after birth. When the human personing covenant is broken by the mother or by society in the postnatal pregnancy, it can critically harm a person's appreciation of God's creation covenant with humanity, which is the condition of the possibility for all covenants and for the existence of all persons.

NOTES

1. Richard A. McCormick, S.J., *How Brave a New World? Dilemmas in Bioethics* (New York: Doubleday, 1981) 194.

2. Beverly Wildung Harrison, "Theology of Pro-Choice: A Feminist Perspective," in *Abortion: The Moral Issues,* ed. Edward Batchelor, Jr. (New York: Pilgrim Press, 1982) 222. For one of the most important contributions to the abortion discussion, see Beverly Harrison's *Our Right to Choose: Toward a New Ethic of Abortion* (Boston: Beacon Press, 1983).

3. At the 1978 meeting of the Society of Christian Ethics, I presented a paper arguing that there is an essential link between Christian ethics and belief in immortality. Marjorie Reiley Maguire, "Ethics and Immortality," in *Proceedings of the American Society of Christian Ethics Annual Meeting* (Waterloo, Ont.: Wilfrid Laurier University Press, 1978).

4. Marjorie Reiley Maguire, "Can Technology Solve the Abortion Dilemma," *Christian Century* 93, no. 34 (1976) 918–19.

5. Judith Jarvis Thompson was the first to use the image of pregnancy as a state in which one person is connected to another for life support, although I must mention that I was not aware of Thompson's position when I developed a similar image for the article cited above in the *Christian Century.* See Judith Jarvis Thompson, "A Defense of Abortion," *Philosophy and Public Affairs* 1 (1971) 47–66. The implications of Thompson's position have been systematically examined by Susan Teft Nicholson, *Abortion and the Roman Catholic Church* (Notre Dame, Ind.: University of Notre Dame Press, 1978) 49–62.

6. In August 1978, Judge Flaherty of Pittsburgh ruled that the law could not require David Shimp to donate bone marrow to his dying cousin, Robert McFall, even though Flaherty indicated that he thought Shimp's refusal was morally revolting. It is my opinion that even if some people consider a woman's decision for abortion to be "morally revolting" the law should not give less protection to a pregnant woman than it gave to David Shimp. See Alan Meisel and Loren H. Roth, "Must a Man Be His Cousin's Keeper," in *Hastings Center Report* 8, no. 5 (Oct. 1978) 5–6.

7. For a history and development of the idea of embodiment as well as further bibliography, see Richard N. Zaner, "Embodiment," in *Encyclopedia of Bioethics* I, ed. Warren T. Reich (New York: Free Press, 1978) 361–65.

8. This has been argued by Daniel C. Maguire, *The Moral Choice* (New York: Doubleday, 1978).

9. This is the finding of Richard Lux in an unpublished paper entitled "What Do We Mean When We Say That Life Is Sacred?," which was presented at a dialogue between representatives of the U.S. Catholic Conference and the Synagogue Council of America on Nov. 8–10, 1982.

10. Charles Curran, "Abortion: V: Contemporary Debate in Philosophical and Religious

Ethics," in *Encyclopedia of Bioethics* I:17–26. See also Charles Curran, "Abortion: Its Moral Aspects," in *Abortion: The Moral Issues* 115–28. For other divisions and other treatments of the various abortion positions, see Daniel Callahan's classic study, *Abortion: Law, Choice and Morality* (New York: Macmillan, 1970).

11. Some examples of this approach are: John T. Noonan, Jr., ed., *The Morality of Abortion: Legal and Historical Perspectives* (Cambridge: Harvard University Press, 1970); and Germain G. Grisez, *Abortion: The Myths, the Realities, and the Arguments* (New York: Corpus Books, 1970). Two more liberal examples of the biological approach are Charles Curran and Richard McCormick. See their works cited in these notes. They both see personhood as beginning only after individuation has occurred.

12. Nicholson, *Abortion and the Roman Catholic Church* 6–7. Beverly Harrison disputes Nicholson's conclusions on this point. She says, "This carefully crafted study assumes that there has been a clear 'anti-killing' ethic separable from any antisexual ethic in Christianity. This is an assumption that my historical research does not sustain." Harrison, "Theology of Pro-Choice: A Feminist Perspective" 240–41, n. 11.

13. Two examples of this approach are Paul Ramsey, "The Morality of Abortion," in *Abortion: The Moral Issues* 73–91; and Edward Shils, "The Sanctity of Life," in *Life or Death, Ethics and Options*, ed. Daniel H. Labby (Portland, Oreg.: Reed College Press, 1968) 2–39.

14. James J. Diamond, M.D., "Abortion, Animation, Hominization," *Theological Studies* 36, no. 2 (June 1975) 311, n. 12. Another 12 percent of fertilized ova spontaneously abort after implantation so that only about 30 percent survive to birth.

15. The relational approach is found chiefly among some French Catholic moral theologians: Bruno Ribes, Bernard Quelquejeu, Jacques-Marie Pohier, and Louis Beinart. Their positions can be found in *Études* (1970), *Lumière et Vie* (1972), and in *Avortement et respect de la vie humaine*, Colloque du Centre catholique des médecins français (commission conjugale), (Paris: Editions du Seuil, 1972). Excellent summaries of the positions of these men can be found in Curran, "Abortion: Its Moral Aspects" 120–22; Curran, "Abortion: V: Contemporary Debate in Philosophical and Religious Ethics" 20; McCormick, *How Brave a New World?* 141–49. An American, H. Tristram Englehardt, Jr., also takes a relational approach to the beginning of personhood. His, like the one I will propose, also emphasizes the mother-child relationship. However, he only sees this relationship as having a personing function after the birth of the child, when he sees their relationship as a social one. He sees the mother-fetus relationship as only biological. Englehardt, "The Ontology of Abortion," *Ethics* 84, no. 3 (Apr. 1974) 217–23.

16. Diamond, "Abortion, Animation, Hominization" 310.

17. See John R. Connery, *Abortion: The Development of the Roman Catholic Perspective* (Chicago: Loyola University Press, 1977). For an excellent examination of the theory of delayed animation see Joseph T. Donceel, "Abortion: Mediate vs. Immediate Animation," in *Abortion: The Moral Issues* 110–14.

18. I am indebted to James Bresnahan, S.J., who was the commentator for a slightly abridged version of this paper presented at the 1983 meeting of the Society of Christian Ethics, for pointing out that "presumed consent" is a very legalistic concept and perhaps works against the kind of personalism I am trying to introduce into this debate. The legalistic implications of this will be brought out more clearly later in this paper and, I hope, sufficiently counterbalanced with other considerations.

19. At the Seventh Annual Conference of the National Abortion Federation held Apr. 10–13, 1983, there was a session on personhood. Two of the panelists responding to the keynote speaker were Ruth Hoesen, a nurse at an Atlanta abortion clinic, and Naim Kassar, a physician at a Kansas abortion clinic. Both spoke of the psychological and emotional problems for staff members attendant upon participating in second trimester abortions, especially ones using the technique of D & E (Dilation and Evacuation). Their remarks were not to deny the need for or legality of second trimester abortions but to face them as a human problem. Audiocassette tapes of the Proceedings of this meeting are available from the American Audio Association, Box 511, Floral Park, N.Y. 11002.

20. Nicholson, *Abortion and the Roman Catholic Church* 6.

21. James B. Nelson, "Abortion: IV: Protestant Perspectives," in *Encyclopedia of Bioethics* I:14.

22. For an article presenting "a not-so-far-out fantasy of reproductive tyranny," see Diane Sauter and Steven Feinberg, "Prima Gravids," *Ms* 11, no. 4 (Oct. 1982) 45.

23. Nicholson, *Abortion and the Roman Catholic Church.*

24. McCormick, *How Brave a New World?* 189.

25. Dr. Seuss, *Horton Hears a Who* (New York: Random House, 1954).

26. This does not mean that extraordinary efforts must be taken to save the life of an infant, or other person, whose ability to further enter into the personing process has been severely physically impaired. Just as the mother cannot initiate the personing process without a biological base, so the personing process cannot continue if the biological base is severely damaged.

27. Lux, "What Do We Mean When We Say That Life Is Sacred?" See n. 9 above.

Abortion and Moral Consensus: Beyond Solomon's Choice

Madonna Kolbenschlag

The 1984 presidential election campaign demonstrated two complementary truths: that, by and large, the American electorate is concerned about the economy and about national virility; and that a significant number of the Catholic hierarchy, as well as fundamentalists of all faiths, are concerned about female autonomy.

Indeed, Geraldine Ferraro's candidacy as the first woman running for vice-president on a major party ticket flushed out the power issues that divide the American public: to use George Bush's elegant phrase, we are preoccupied with "kicking ass," whether it is in domestic relations or in Central America; we resist the demands of the exploited for power sharing and comparable pay, whether in the global economy or in the male establishment at home; above all, we are divided over the issue of whether women are to be granted reproductive autonomy.

The smog generated by the debate over "religion and politics" obscured the fundamental anxiety that lay beneath all the sniping, posturing, and manipulating: anxiety over patriarchal power's waning influence in our national life, whether as U.S. hegemony abroad, or as family "headship" and male entitlement in our domestic institutions. In this collective smog the abortion issue acts as a kind of *volatile precipitant*, causing all the various elements of angst in church, state, and society to condense and focus themselves with a terrible intensity. Geraldine Ferraro caught a good deal of the fallout. More recently, twenty-four nuns have been threatened with dismissal from their religious orders if they do not retract their support for a statement on "Pluralism and Abortion" that appeared during the election campaign.

The persistence and coherence of this angst and its potential for divisiveness and violence have been demonstrated by the recent wave of attacks on abortion clinics; as well as by the waning prospects for passage of the Equal Rights Amendment (ERA). Those who are most opposed to the prochoice position and to the ERA seem to be those who have the most to lose from the empowerment of women, either psychologically and politically, or in terms of authority or financial resources. Thus, for many men there is a consistency between their privileged position in the family and society and the value placed on fetal life, over which they have no intrinsic control. This may help to explain the curious contradiction in the views expressed by some churchmen and politicians who are so intransigent on the issue of abortion, over which men have no physical control, and so tolerant of killing in war, over which men have always had control.

Many women who espouse the prolife position do so, at least in part, because they have internalized patriarchal values and depend on the sense of identity and worth that comes from having accepted "woman's place" in society. Thus, the polarization between the prolife and prochoice groups results in different value languages that allow no compromise. Because the two positions are so invested with the strong emotions aroused by power relations, there is little likelihood that rational argument can change them.

Carol Gilligan's study of the differences in the ways whereby men and women reach moral decisions suggests another reason for intransigence on this issue.[1] Typically but not exclusively, for men the frame of reference of moral decision-making lies in the primacy of principle, in the values of truth and fairness— inevitably a perspective that focuses on people's rights. For women, the frame of reference is decidedly relational, lying in the primacy of the values of caring for and of not hurting others—a perspective rooted in particularity and contextuality.

Thus, the matrices in which moral and political attitudes are embedded tend to be skewed by gender-related values. Our public discourse is dominated by a male-enculturated point of view that is characteristically abstract or morally solipsistic. Gilligan suggests that women, far more than men, invest ethical decisions with more particularity and with a better sense of their effects and consequences.

The male perspective, based on principles and rights, informs both the dominant prolife and prochoice views, both of which protect male hegemony, but in different ways. As a result, it is likely that the two sides on the abortion issue will remain intransigent and deadlocked indefinitely, like two bucks with their antlers intertwined. And in the impasse, other issues—child care, research on contraception, sex education, and, increasingly, the specter of reproductive technology—are neglected or distorted. The prospect of what some have called "the colonization of the womb" and the enormity of the problems looming on the horizon should stir us all to outrage at the concentration of so much energy and so many resources, so much sound and fury, on the abortion issue. It reminds one of those who, after World War II and Hiroshima and Nagasaki, were still arguing over whether or not submarine warfare was moral.

These developments are precipitating a new moment in the politics of reproductive ethics and issuing a challenge to patriarchal politics in church and state. The new technologies may accomplish what neither the right-to-life movement nor the feminist cause could bring about independently: a new basis for moral judgment on the abortion issue. Just as the missiles poised in our silos have pushed out the boundaries of moral discourse on war and peace, so the potential waiting in the petri dish is forcing us to seek higher ground in achieving an ethical perspective on human reproduction and public-policy alternatives.

Ten years ago Margaret Fraley, an ethicist at Yale Divinity School, attempted to inject some clarity into the escalating polarization in political discourse on the abortion issue when she called attention to the "bad faith" evidenced on both sides. I would like to expand her application of that notion—limited as it was by the 1974 social context—and apply it to the present moment and to the factions now arrayed in opposite camps. By "bad faith" I mean that Sartrean sense of self-righteousness, self-projection, and nonengagement which promotes exclusivism and intransigence. All manifestations of bad faith are alike in that they are characterized by absolutism. This is not to question the "good faith" that also exists on both sides: the sincerity of their claims and the validity of their issues.

Several ethical norms are currently shaping our attitudes toward abortion. One might be called the *individualistic* norm, a view that is typical of early liberal and radical feminism. It is fundamentally prochoice. Until now this perspective has treated women's autonomy as an absolute value. Political hard-liners still use the prochoice position as a litmus test for judging political candidates. The bad faith that can infest holders of this position becomes apparent when feminist cries of "femicide" and "previctimization" over the selective destruction of female embryos curiously lapse into silence at the random destruction of embryos (abortion on demand) or at multiple abortions (abortion as a contraceptive).

This rights-based ethic is being challenged by the growing recognition among feminists that the notion of "choice" may be a myth; that not only social attitudes but public policies that promote so-called "free choice" can be subtly coercive. For example, does Medicaid funding give some women only one option? Has the easy access to abortion clinics compromised conscience formation? Similarly, to the extent that the idea of choice promotes unrestricted experimentation on genetic material and on fertility mechanisms, it may actually work against the good of women and of future generations. Reproductive freedom must increasingly be considered from the perspective of the long-term consequences of uncontrolled medical experimentation.

Ironically, much of this rethinking has been precipitated by recent expositions of the prochoice argument coming in the wake of mature feminist scholarship. Beverly Harrison's *Our Right to Choose*,[2] for example, is an excellent defense of the position that people have an inalienable right to make intentional choices concerning their reproductive lives. The right to choose abortion is grounded in claims to moral agency and bodily and psychic integrity. Harrison's view assumes a world of rational choice and volitional privilege.

The flaw in her argument is perhaps more one of bad anthropology or psychology than of bad faith. It leaves no room for the unexpected, for serendipity, for mystery, ambivalence, or transformation. Some women do change their minds about whether or not they wish to carry a pregnancy to full term. Many "unwanted" children do become "wanted." If for women reproductive behavior is, finally, an issue of control and intentional management, then we would seem to be mimicking the male culture's instrumental relationship to nature. Furthermore, Harrison's perspective seems to skirt consideration of the legitimate interests and claims of the body politic. It is an elitist argument, one that ignores people's limitations and the complexity of their lives. Nevertheless, her ethic is the best current defense of each woman's intrinsic right to moral agency in her reproductive life and, especially, in the process of forming intimate attachments and relationships—since a woman's willingness and ability to nurture a child is the ultimate issue in the decision about whether or not to have one.

Another ethical perspective on abortion might be described as the *altruistic* norm, clearly represented on the political spectrum by the prolife contingent. The most visible and articulate proponents of this view are the Catholic Church's magisterium and the religious New Right. They treat all fetal life—early and late—as possessing absolute value and full human rights. The bad faith that has come to characterize this perspective is clearly evident in the role that many prolife advocates have played in a confrontational, often obstructionist, single-issue politics, often bordering on fanaticism and ignoring the wider spectrum of prolife issues.

Although the Catholic hierarchy has attempted to redress this imbalance, bad faith also plagues its position. The church's stand on abortion is a "moral teaching"—it is not a doctrine of faith. The church has at times changed its moral teachings—for example, it condemned slavery after having accepted it for centuries. Its traditional teaching on abortion and contraception has by no means been marked by consistency.

Nevertheless, the church currently persists in treating the prohibition of abortion as if it were a fundamental Christian doctrine. It places an absolute value on fetal life as full human life from the moment of conception. Yet in its own definitive formulation of the issue in the 1974 declaration by the Sacred Congregation, it acknowledged the impossibility of determining the precise moment of "ensoulment." The declaration states that while there is no certainty, the possibility that the fetus might be ensouled precludes risking an act that might be homicide.

Carol Tauer, a philosopher at Minnesota's St. Catherine's College, has recently challenged the moral logic of this declaration, as well as of the current pastoral teachings on abortion, in an incisive and thorough analysis of the tradition of probabilism—a theory of practical decision-making that is accepted in Catholic moral teaching.[3] She points out that the church is at odds with its traditional way of making moral determinations, whether in questions of fact or of law.

That the embryo does not progress to individuation before the fourth week, as embryological research on twinning and recombination has proven, is crucial to determining whether or not it should be treated as a person. Similarly, our knowledge of cortical development provides sound biological as well as philosophical reasons for treating hominization as delayed. (Some opinions mark the tenth week as the onset of true hominization.) Tauer notes that in the earliest tradition of the church, abortion was not considered homicide until the fetus was "formed." She concludes by invoking the probabilistic criterion that the "rights of an uncertain subject are automatically uncertain rights," and, therefore, for all practical purposes do not exist—or at least do not have the same status as the rights of those unequivocally recognized as persons. In any case, current embryological research now allows us to draw moral hypotheses with much more precision than we could in 1974.

Why is the Catholic Church so reluctant to follow its own tradition of moral logic and allow the benefit of a doubt in early abortions? As Lisa Cahill, Joan Timmerman, and other theologians suggest, its position may have as much to do with mistaken analogies as with logic. For example, the church's teachings on abortion and on sexual morality in general seem to have been contaminated by the mythology of the "sacredness of sperm," which dates back at least as far as Aristotle and is known to have persisted through the nineteenth century in the United States.

Theologians also point out that, in contrast to the church's teachings on social ethics and justice, its stands on sexual morality have been governed more by absolute abstract norms than by references to the human condition and experience. Here again, one notes the absence of woman's moral perspective, with its sensitivity and proximity to contextuality and consequences. Another evidence of bad faith has been the Catholic hierarchy's failure to emphasize contraceptive options and education. Their lingering proscription of contraception inevitably trivializes abortion.

Thus, bad faith mutes and pollutes both the prolife and the prochoice positions on abortion and polarizes our political discourse between the individualistic and altruistic options. Both sides have failed to consider adequately the social consequences of the legislative remedies they prefer: the prolifers have ignored the implications of recriminalizing abortion, while prochoice advocates have glossed over the social consequences of allowing abortion on demand.

In the absence of any consensus about abortion, a third ethical norm may prevail by default: the *therapeutic/technological* norm. This inexorable force, driven by the desire for profit and control, could result in the medicalization and commercialization of human reproduction. Paradoxically, the new technology makes women vulnerable to exploitation at the same time that it promises them the illusion of choice. Sperm banks, frozen embryos, artificial placentas, and surrogate mothers are opening a breach between women and their reproductive processes— a breach that makes women extremely vulnerable to exploitation. Lawyers, physicians, legislators, counselors, consultants, matchmakers, middlemen, marketing strategists, entrepreneurs, and opportunists are already rushing in. One manager of a "bionetics" company in California has suggested that Mexican and Central American women would be ideal, low-cost "host mothers." In some Third World countries, sex-selection techniques already are resulting in the mass destruction of female embryos. Elsewhere, drug companies and genetic engineering firms are engaged in "ova snatching," embryo transfer techniques, transnucleation, and ectogenesis. The potential for the exploitation of such technologies begins to acquire almost surreal proportions.

Another new medical development may provide an ambiguous solution to the abortion dilemma: home health-care kits for diagnosing and treating oneself have been welcomed as an antidote to "medicalization." It is anticipated that a low-priced suppository or pill that can induce abortion in the early weeks of pregnancy will soon be available. If such a product is marketed, it is likely to become a popular form of contraceptive—not only discouraging research on other contraceptives, but making abortion a completely privatized and commercialized act.

Neither a narrowly conceived prochoice nor a prolife agenda can provide an adequate standard for the future. Neither the imperial self nor the imperialism of dogma and sanction (law) can solve the abortion dilemma. A responsible new ethic must certainly take into account the primacy of personal conscience and of women's experience, as well as the effects and consequences of reproductive choices on the common good. Perhaps, for want of a better term, it might be described as an "ethic of *cocreation.*" Such an ethic would assume that we exist as individuals only within larger life systems. These constitute concentric envelopes of responsibility. Our relationships to the earth, to our culture, and to our families of origin are not intentional—we did not choose our planet, our civilization, or our ancestry. But this absence of choice does not excuse us from taking responsibility for all that these areas encompass. An ethic of cocreation would counterbalance our tendency to a rationalistic and individualistic bias. It would make us more open to exigency and to the unpredictable—to creation as surprise. It would also help us to regard death, imperfection, and dissolution as normal phenomena in the continuum of life. At the same time, it must be based on the moral agency and autonomy of women, the primary guardians of life for the species. For too long we have had to make either-or choices about whether to regard the fetus as a person or as a nonperson. Could we not assign, instead, a unique value to this nascent human life, without criminalizing and traumatizing those who, caught in overwhelming predicaments, choose not to carry it to term?

Marking the boundaries of the onset of personhood in fetal life is, in a sense, a superficial aspect of the abortion debate. What is at stake is a post-Enlightenment, rights-based ethic that tends to objectify fetal life at a very early stage, reducing the abortion dilemma to a conflict of rights—some favoring those of the fetus, some favoring those of the woman. A truly Catholic ethic might show more respect for the symbiotic nature of very early uterine life by regarding a woman and her fetus as a single organism, with one informing consciousness—

that of the woman. Our tolerance for such ambiguity seems to diminish as our culture's tendency to objectify everything accelerates.

A truly Catholic ethos emphasizes the sacrality of matter and substance; it nuances everything, from our understanding of the Eucharist to sexual experience. As Americans in a pluralistic society, however, we must create a milieu for moral decision-making that is somewhere between value conferred by intention or relation alone, and the abstract mystical fetishism that deifies the substance of human life in and of itself. This is not to understate in any way the dignity and value of human life, indeed of all life forms.

For women making decisions about having abortions, moral agency is often a luxury canceled out by social, economic, and psychological suffering. Clearly, assuring women's moral freedom and establishing a social policy that provides them with *real* options so that they can take responsibility for life and make authentic decisions of conscience ought to be the priority for both the prolife and the prochoice groups.

We should be grateful that the Catholic Church, among others, continues to preach the protection of innocent and defenseless life. On the other hand, we should be outraged that some of the Catholic hierarchy are so recalcitrant that they continue to harass conscientious men and women who support prochoice public policies, and so squinting in their vision that they may oppose the ERA simply because the amendment might allow women the right to choose abortions. It is too bad that so much of the energy of one of the greatest engines of conscientization the world has ever known—the Catholic Church—should be spent on regulating women's anatomy instead of promoting their autonomy and empowerment as moral persons.

Ironically, it is the Catholic tradition that today proclaims so forcefully the epistemological privilege of the poor. In the many senses in which the Gospel speaks of the poor—materially deprived, disempowered, marginated, overburdened, helpless—women often have been the poorest of all. Their experiences and perspectives, therefore, have a special claim on our attention. Women's experience will be the hermeneutic of the future. Solomon's wisdom is worth remembering: let those who are most intimately affected by the consequences of a decision make that decision.

NOTES

1. *In a Different Voice* (Cambridge: Harvard University Press, 1982).
2. Boston: Beacon, 1983.
3. "The Tradition of Probabilism and the Moral Status of the Early Embryo," *Theological Studies* 45 (March 1984) 3–33. Reprinted in this volume, pp. 54–84.

Abortion and the Sexual Agenda:
A Case for Prolife Feminism

Sidney Callahan

The abortion debate continues. In the latest and perhaps most crucial development, prolife feminists are contesting prochoice feminist claims that abortion rights are prerequisites for women's full development and social equality. The outcome of this debate may be decisive for the culture as a whole. Prolife feminists, like myself, argue on good feminist principles that women can never achieve the fulfillment of feminist goals in a society permissive toward abortion.

These new arguments over abortion take place within liberal political circles. This round of intense intra-feminist conflict has spiraled beyond earlier right-versus-left abortion debates, which focused on "tragic choices," medical judgments, and legal compromises. Feminist theorists of the prochoice position now put forth the demand for unrestricted abortion rights as a *moral imperative* and insist upon women's right to complete reproductive freedom. They morally justify the present situation and current abortion practices. Thus it is all the more important that prolife feminists articulate their different feminist perspective.

These opposing arguments can best be seen when presented in turn. Perhaps the most highly developed feminist arguments for the morality and legality of abortion can be found in Beverly Wildung Harrison's *Our Right to Choose* (Beacon Press, 1983) and Rosalind Pollack Petchesky's *Abortion and Woman's Choice* (Longman, 1984). Obviously it is difficult to do justice to these complex arguments, which draw on diverse strands of philosophy and social theory and are often interwoven in prochoice feminists' own version of a "seamless garment." Yet the fundamental feminist case for the morality of abortion, encompassing the views of Harrison and Petchesky, can be analyzed in terms of four central moral claims: (1) the moral right to control one's own body; (2) the moral necessity of autonomy and choice in personal responsibility; (3) the moral claim for the contingent value of fetal life; (4) the moral right of women to true social equality.

1. **The moral right to control one's own body.** Prochoice feminism argues that a woman choosing an abortion is exercising a basic right of bodily integrity granted in our common law tradition. If she does not choose to be physically involved in the demands of a pregnancy and birth, she should not be compelled

to be so against her will. Just because it is *her* body which is involved, a woman should have the right to terminate any pregnancy, which at this point in medical history is tantamount to terminating fetal life. No one can be forced to donate an organ or submit to other invasive physical procedures for however good a cause. Thus no woman should be subjected to "compulsory pregnancy." And it should be noted that in pregnancy much more than a passive biological process is at stake.

From one perspective, the fetus is, as Petchesky says, a "biological parasite" taking resources from the woman's body. During pregnancy, a woman's whole life and energies will be actively involved in the nine-month process. Gestation and childbirth involve physical and psychological risks. After childbirth a woman will either be a mother who must undertake a twenty-year responsibility for child rearing, or face giving up her child for adoption or institutionalization. Since hers is the body, hers the risk, hers the burden, it is only just that she alone should be free to decide on pregnancy or abortion.

This moral claim to abortion, according to the prochoice feminists, is especially valid in an individualistic society in which women cannot count on medical care or social support in pregnancy, childbirth, or child rearing. A moral abortion decision is never made in a social vacuum, but in the real life society which exists here and now.

2. **The moral necessity of autonomy and choice in personal responsibility.** Beyond the claim for individual *bodily* integrity, the prochoice feminists claim that to be a full adult *morally,* a woman must be able to make responsible life commitments. To plan, choose, and exercise personal responsibility, one must have control of reproduction. A woman must be able to make yes-or-no decisions about a specific pregnancy, according to her present situation, resources, prior commitments, and life plan. Only with such reproductive freedom can a woman have the moral autonomy necessary to make mature commitments, in the area of family, work, or education.

Contraception provides a measure of personal control, but contraceptive failure or other chance events can too easily result in involuntary pregnancy. Only free access to abortion can provide the necessary guarantee. The chance biological process of an involuntary pregnancy should not be allowed to override all the other personal commitments and responsibilities a woman has: to others, to family, to work, to education, to her future development, health, or well-being. Without reproductive freedom, women's personal moral agency and human consciousness are subjected to biology and chance.

3. **The moral claim for the contingent value of fetal life.** Prochoice feminist exponents like Harrison and Petchesky claim that the value of fetal life is contingent upon the woman's free consent and subjective acceptance. The fetus must be invested with maternal valuing in order to become human. This process of "humanization" through personal consciousness and "sociality" can only be be-

stowed by the woman in whose body and psychosocial system a new life must mature. The meaning and value of fetal life are constructed by the woman; without this personal conferral there only exists a biological, physiological process. Thus fetal interests or fetal rights can never outweigh the woman's prior interest and rights. If a woman does not consent to invest her pregnancy with meaning or value, then the merely biological process can be freely terminated. Prior to her own free choice and conscious investment, a woman cannot be described as a "mother" nor can a "child" be said to exist.

Moreover, in cases of voluntary pregnancy, a woman can withdraw consent if fetal genetic defects or some other problem emerges at any time before birth. Late abortion should thus be granted without legal restrictions. Even the minimal qualifications and limitations on women embedded in *Roe v. Wade* are unacceptable—repressive remnants of patriarchal unwillingness to give power to women.

4. **The moral right of women to full social equality.** Women have a moral right to full social equality. They should not be restricted or subordinated because of their sex. But this morally required equality cannot be realized without abortion's certain control of reproduction. Female social equality depends upon being able to compete and participate as freely as males can in the structures of educational and economic life. If a woman cannot control when and how she will be pregnant or rear children, she is at a distinct disadvantage, especially in our male-dominated world.

Psychological equality and well-being is also at stake. Women must enjoy the basic right of a person to the free exercise of heterosexual intercourse and full sexual expression, separated from procreation. No less than males, women should be able to be sexually active without the constantly inhibiting fear of pregnancy. Abortion is necessary for women's sexual fulfillment and the growth of uninhibited feminine self-confidence and ownership of their sexual powers.

But true sexual and reproductive freedom means freedom to procreate as well as to inhibit fertility. Prochoice feminists are also worried that women's freedom to reproduce will be curtailed through the abuse of sterilization and needless hysterectomies. Besides the punitive tendencies of a male-dominated health-care system, especially in response to repeated abortions or welfare pregnancies, there are other economic and social pressures inhibiting reproduction. Genuine reproductive freedom implies that day care, medical care, and financial support would be provided mothers, while fathers would take their full share in the burdens and delights of raising children.

Many prochoice feminists identify feminist ideals with communitarian, ecologically sensitive approaches to reshaping society. Following theorists like Sara Ruddick and Carol Gilligan, they link abortion rights with the growth of "maternal thinking" in our heretofore patriarchal society. Maternal thinking is loosely defined as a responsible commitment to the loving nurture of specific human beings as they actually exist in socially embedded interpersonal contexts. It is a moral perspective very different from the abstract, competitive, isolated, and principled rigidity so characteristic of patriarchy.

How does a prolife feminist respond to these arguments? Prolife feminists grant the good intentions of their prochoice counterparts but protest that the prochoice position is flawed, morally inadequate, and inconsistent with feminism's basic demands for justice. Prolife feminists champion a more encompassing moral ideal. They recognize the claims of fetal life and offer a different perspective on what is good for women. The feminist vision is expanded and refocused.

1. **From the moral right to control one's own body to a more inclusive ideal of justice.** The moral right to control one's own body does apply to cases of organ transplants, mastectomies, contraception, and sterilization; but it is not a conceptualization adequate for abortion. The abortion dilemma is caused by the fact that 266 days following a conception in one body, another body will emerge. One's own body no longer exists as a single unit but is engendering another organism's life. This dynamic passage from conception to birth is genetically ordered and universally found in the human species. Pregnancy is not like the growth of cancer or infestation by a biological parasite; it is the way every human being enters the world. Strained philosophical analogies fail to apply: having a baby is not like rescuing a drowning person, being hooked up to a famous violinist's artificial life-support system, donating organs for transplant— or anything else.

As embryology and fetology advance, it becomes clear that human development is a continuum. Just as astronomers are studying the first three minutes in the genesis of the universe, so the first moments, days, and weeks at the beginning of human life are the subject of increasing scientific attention. While neonatology pushes the definition of viability ever earlier, ultrasound and fetology expand the concept of the patient *in utero*. Within such a continuous growth process, it is hard to defend logically any demarcation point after conception as the point at which an immature form of human life is so different from the day before or the day after, that it can be morally or legally discounted as a nonperson. Even the moment of birth can hardly differentiate a nine-month fetus from a newborn. It is not surprising that those who countenance late abortions are logically led to endorse selective infanticide.

The same legal tradition which in our society guarantees the right to control one's own body firmly recognizes the wrongfulness of harming other bodies, however immature, dependent, different looking, or powerless. The handicapped, the retarded, and newborns are legally protected from deliberate harm. Prolife feminists reject the suppositions that would except the unborn from this protection.

After all, debates similar to those about the fetus were once conducted about feminine personhood. Just as women, or blacks, were considered too different, too underdeveloped, too "biological," to have souls or to possess legal rights, so the fetus is now seen as "merely" biological life, subsidiary to a person. A woman was once viewed as incorporated into the "one flesh" of her husband's person; she too was a form of bodily property. In all patriarchal unjust systems, lesser orders of human life are granted rights only when wanted, chosen, or invested with value by the powerful.

Fortunately, in the course of civilization there has been a gradual realization that justice demands the powerless and dependent be protected against the uses of power wielded unilaterally. No human can be treated as a means to an end without consent. The fetus is an immature, dependent form of human life which only needs time and protection to develop. Surely, immaturity and dependence are not crimes.

In an effort to think about the essential requirements of a just society, philosophers like John Rawls recommend imagining yourself in an "original position," in which your position in the society to be created is hidden by a "veil of ignorance." You will have to weigh the possibility that any inequalities inherent in that society's practices may rebound upon you in the worst, as well as in the best, conceivable way. This thought experiment helps ensure justice for all.

Beverly Harrison argues that in such an envisioning of society everyone would institute abortion rights in order to guarantee that if one turned out to be a woman one would have reproductive freedom. But surely in the original position and behind the "veil of ignorance," you would have to contemplate the possibility of being the particular fetus to be aborted. Since everyone has passed through the fetal stage of development, it is false to refuse to imagine oneself in this state when thinking about a potential world in which justice would govern. Would it be just that an embryonic life—in half the cases, of course, a female life—be sacrificed to the right of a woman's control over her own body? A woman may be pregnant without consent and experience a great many penalties, but a fetus killed without consent pays the ultimate penalty.

It does not matter (*The Silent Scream* notwithstanding) whether the fetus being killed is fully conscious or feels pain. We do not sanction killing the innocent if it can be done painlessly or without the victim's awareness. Consciousness becomes important to the abortion debate because it is used as a criterion for the "personhood" so often seen as the prerequisite for legal protection. Yet certain philosophers set the standard of personhood so high that half the human race could not meet the criteria during most of their waking hours (let alone their sleeping ones). Sentience, self-consciousness, rational decision-making, social participation? Surely no infant, or child under two, could qualify. Either our idea of person must be expanded or another criterion, such as human life itself, be employed to protect the weak in a just society. Prolife feminists who defend the fetus empathetically identify with an immature state of growth passed through by themselves, their children, and everyone now alive.

It also seems a travesty of just procedures that a pregnant woman now, in effect, acts as sole judge of her own case, under the most stressful conditions. Yes, one can acknowledge that the pregnant woman will be subject to the potential burdens arising from a pregnancy, but it has never been thought right to have an interested party, especially the more powerful party, decide his or her own case when there may be a conflict of interest. If one considers the matter as a case of a powerful versus a powerless, silenced claimant, the prochoice feminist argument can rightly be inverted: since hers is the body, hers the risk, and hers the greater burden, then how in fairness can a woman be the sole judge of the fetal right to life?

Human ambivalence, a bias toward self-interest, and emotional stress have always been recognized as endangering judgment. Freud declared that love and hate are so entwined that if instant thoughts could kill, we would all be dead in the bosom of our families. In the case of a woman's involuntary pregnancy, a complex, long-term solution requiring effort and energy has to compete with the immediate solution offered by a morning's visit to an abortion clinic. On the simple, perceptual plane, with imagination and thinking curtailed, the speed, ease, and privacy of abortion, combined with the small size of the embryo, tend to make early abortions seem less morally serious—even though speed, size, technical ease, and the private nature of an act have no moral standing.

As the most recent immigrants from nonpersonhood, feminists have traditionally fought for justice for themselves and the world. Women rally to feminism as a new and better way to live. Rejecting male aggression and destruction, feminists seek alternative, peaceful, ecologically sensitive means to resolve conflicts while respecting human potentiality. It is a chilling inconsistency to see prochoice feminists demanding continued access to assembly-line, technological methods of fetal killing—the vacuum aspirator, prostaglandins, and dilation and evacuation. It is a betrayal of feminism, which has built the struggle for justice on the bedrock of women's empathy. After all, "maternal thinking" receives its name from a mother's unconditional acceptance and nurture of dependent, immature life. It is difficult to develop concern for women, children, the poor and the dispossessed— and to care about peace—and at the same time ignore fetal life.

2. From the necessity of autonomy and choice in personal responsibility to an expanded sense of responsibility. A distorted idea of morality over-emphasizes individual autonomy and active choice. Morality has often been viewed too exclusively as a matter of human agency and decisive action. In moral behavior persons must explicitly choose and aggressively exert their wills to intervene in the natural and social environments. The human will dominates the body, over-comes the given, breaks out of the material limits of nature. Thus if one does not choose to be pregnant or cannot rear a child, who must be given up for adoption, then better to abort the pregnancy. Willing, planning, choosing one's moral commitments through the contracting of one's individual resources becomes the premier model of moral responsibility.

But morality also consists of the good and worthy acceptance of the unexpected events that life presents. Responsiveness and response-ability to things unchosen are also instances of the highest human moral capacity. Morality is not confined to contracted agreements of isolated individuals. Yes, one is obligated by explicit contracts freely initiated, but human beings are also obligated by implicit compacts and involuntary relationships in which persons simply find themselves. To be embedded in a family, a neighborhood, a social system, brings moral obligations which were never entered into with informed consent.

Parent-child relationships are one instance of implicit moral obligations arising by virtue of our being part of the interdependent human community. A woman, involuntarily pregnant, has a moral obligation to the now-existing dependent fetus whether she explicitly consented to its existence or not. No prolife feminist would dispute the forceful observations of prochoice feminists about the extreme difficulties that bearing an unwanted child in our society can entail. But the stronger force of the fetal claim presses a woman to accept these burdens; the fetus possesses rights arising from its extreme need and the interdependency and unity of humankind. The woman's moral obligation arises both from her status as a human being embedded in the interdependent human community and her unique lifegiving female reproductive power. To follow the prochoice feminist ideology of insistent individualistic autonomy and control is to betray a fundamental basis of the moral life.

3. From the moral claim of the contingent value of fetal life to the moral claim for the intrinsic value of human life. The feminist prochoice position which claims that the value of the fetus is contingent upon the pregnant woman's bestowal—or willed, conscious "construction"—of humanhood is seriously flawed. The inadequacies of this position flow from the erroneous premises (1) that human value and rights can be granted by individual will; (2) that the individual woman's consciousness can exist and operate in an *a priori* isolated fashion; and (3) that "mere" biological, genetic human life has little meaning. Prolife feminism takes a very different stance toward life and nature.

Human life from the beginning to the end of development *has* intrinsic value, which does not depend on meeting the selective criteria or tests set up by powerful others. A fundamental humanist assumption is at stake here. Either we are going to value embodied human life and humanity as a good thing, or take some variant of the nihilist position that assumes human life is just one more random occurrence in the universe such that each instance of human life must explicitly be justified to prove itself worthy to continue. When faced with a new life, or an involuntary pregnancy, there is a world of difference in whether one first asks, "Why continue?" or "Why not?" Where is the burden of proof going to rest? The concept of "compulsory pregnancy" is as distorted as labeling life "compulsory aging."

In a sound moral tradition, human rights arise from human needs, and it is the very nature of a right, or valid claim upon another, that it cannot be denied, conditionally delayed, or rescinded by more powerful others at their behest. It seems fallacious to hold that in the case of the fetus it is the pregnant woman alone who gives or removes its right to life and human status solely through her subjective conscious investment or "humanization." Surely no pregnant woman (or any other individual member of the species) has created her own human nature by an individually willed act of consciousness, nor for that matter been able to guarantee her own human rights. An individual woman and the unique individual embryonic life within her can only exist because of their participation in the genetic inheritance of the human species as a whole. Biological life should never be discounted. Membership in the species, or collective human family, is the basis for human solidarity, equality, and natural human rights.

4. **The moral right of women to full social equality from a prolife feminist perspective.** Prolife feminists and prochoice feminists are totally agreed on the moral right of women to the full social equality so far denied them. The disagreement between them concerns the definition of the desired goal and the best means to get there. Permissive abortion laws do not bring women reproductive freedom, social equality, sexual fulfillment, or full personal development.

Pragmatic failures of a prochoice feminist position combined with a lack of moral vision are, in fact, causing disaffection among young women. Middle-aged prochoice feminists blamed the "big chill" on the general conservative backlash. But they should look rather to their own elitist acceptance of male models of sex and to the sad picture they present of women's lives. Pitting women against their own offspring is not only morally offensive, it is psychologically and politically destructive. Women will never climb to equality and social empowerment over mounds of dead fetuses, numbering now in the millions. As long as most women choose to bear children, they stand to gain from the same constellation of attitudes and institutions that will also protect the fetus in the woman's womb—and they stand to lose from the cultural assumptions that support permissive abortion. Despite temporary conflicts of interest, feminine and fetal liberation are ultimately one and the same cause.

Women's rights and liberation are pragmatically linked to fetal rights because to obtain true equality, women need (1) more social support and changes in the structure of society, and (2) increased self-confidence, self-expectations, and self-esteem. Society in general, and men in particular, have to provide women more support in rearing the next generation, or our devastating feminization of poverty will continue. But if a woman claims the right to decide by herself whether the fetus becomes a child or not, what does this do to paternal and communal responsibility? Why should men share responsibility for child support or child rearing if they cannot share in what is asserted to be the woman's sole decision? Furthermore, if explicit intentions and consciously accepted contracts are necessary for moral obligations, why should men be held responsible for what *they* do not voluntarily choose to happen? By prochoice reasoning, a man who does not want to have a child, or whose contraceptive fails, can be exempted from the responsibilities of fatherhood and child support. Traditionally, many men have been laggards in assuming parental responsibility and support for their children; iron- ically, ready abortion, often advocated as a response to male dereliction, legitimizes male irresponsibility and paves the way for even more male detachment and lack of commitment.

For that matter, why should the state provide a system of day care or child support, or require workplaces to accommodate women's maternity and the needs of child rearing? Permissive abortion, granted in the name of women's privacy and reproductive freedom, ratifies the view that pregnancies and children are a woman's private individual responsibility. More and more frequently, we hear some version of this old rationalization: if she refuses to get rid of it, it's her problem. A child becomes a product of the individual woman's freely chosen investment, a form of private property resulting from her own cost-benefit cal- culation. The larger community is relieved of moral responsibility.

With legal abortion freely available, a clear cultural message is given: conception and pregnancy are no longer serious moral matters. With abortion as an acceptable alternative, contraception is not as responsibly used; women take risks, often at the urging of male sexual partners. Repeat abortions increase, with all their psy- chological and medical repercussions. With more abortion there is more abortion. Behavior shapes thought as well as the other way round. One tends to justify morally what one has done; what becomes commonplace and institutionalized seems harmless. Habituation is a powerful psychological force. Psychologically it is also true that whatever is avoided becomes more threatening; in phobias it is the retreat from anxiety-producing events which reinforces future avoidance. Women begin to see themselves as too weak to cope with involuntary pregnancies. Finally, through the potency of social pressure and the force of inertia, it becomes more and more difficult, in fact almost unthinkable, *not* to use abortion to solve problem pregnancies. Abortion becomes no longer a choice but a "necessity."

But "necessity," beyond the organic failure and death of the body, is a dynamic social construction open to interpretation. The thrust of present feminist prochoice arguments can only increase the justifiable indications for "necessary" abortion; every unwanted fetal handicap becomes more and more unacceptable. Repeatedly assured that in the name of reproductive freedom, women have a right to specify which pregnancies and which children they will accept, women justify sex se- lection, and abort unwanted females. Female infanticide, after all, is probably as old a custom as the human species possesses. Indeed, all kinds of selection of the fit and the favored for the good of the family and the tribe have always existed. Selective extinction is no new program.

There are far better goals for feminists to pursue. Prolife feminists seek to expand and deepen the more communitarian, maternal elements of feminism— and move society from its male-dominated course. First and foremost, women have to insist upon a different, woman-centered approach to sex and reproduction.

While Margaret Mead stressed the "womb envy" of males in other societies, it has been more or less repressed in our own. In our male-dominated world, what men don't do, doesn't count. Pregnancy, childbirth, and nursing have been characterized as passive, debilitating, animallike. The disease model of pregnancy and birth has been entrenched. This female disease or impairment, with its attendant "female troubles," naturally handicaps women in the "real" world of hunting, war, and the corporate fast track. Many prochoice feminists, deliberately childless, adopt the male perspective when they cite the "basic injustice that women have to bear the babies," instead of seeing the injustice in the fact that men cannot. Women's biologically unique capacity and privilege has been denied, despised, and suppressed under male domination; unfortunately, many women have fallen for the phallic fallacy.

Childbirth often appears in prochoice literature as a painful, traumatic, life-threatening experience. Yet giving birth is accurately seen as an arduous but normal exercise of life-giving power, a violent and ecstatic peak experience, which men can never know. Ironically, some prochoice men and women think and talk of pregnancy and childbirth with the same repugnance that ancient ascetics displayed toward orgasms and sexual intercourse. The similarity may not be accidental. The obstetrician Niles Newton, herself a mother, has written of the extended threefold sexuality of women, who can experience orgasm, birth, and nursing as passionate pleasure-giving experiences. All of these are involuntary processes of the female body. Only orgasm, which males share, has been glorified as an involuntary function that is nature's great gift; the involuntary feminine processes of childbirth and nursing have been seen as bondage to biology.

Fully accepting our bodies as ourselves, what should women want? I think women will only flourish when there is a feminization of sexuality, very different from the current cultural trend toward masculinizing female sexuality. Women can never have the self-confidence and self-esteem they need to achieve feminist goals in society until a more holistic, feminine model of sexuality becomes the dominant cultural ethos. To say this affirms the view that men and women differ in the domain of sexual functioning, although they are more alike than different in other personality characteristics and competencies. For those of us committed to achieving sexual equality in the culture, it may be hard to accept the fact that sexual differences make it imperative to talk of distinct male and female models of sexuality. But if one wants to change sexual roles, one has to recognize preexisting conditions. A great deal of evidence is accumulating which points to biological pressures for different male and female sexual functioning.

Males always and everywhere have been more physically aggressive and more likely to fuse sexuality with aggression and dominance. Females may be more variable in their sexuality, but since Masters and Johnson, we know that women have a greater capacity than men for repeated orgasm and a more tenuous path to arousal and orgasmic release. Most obviously, women also have a far greater sociobiological investment in the act of human reproduction. On the whole, women as compared to men possess a sexuality which is more complex, more intense, more extended in time, involving higher investment, risks, and psychosocial involvement.

Considering the differences in sexual functioning, it is not surprising that men and women in the same culture have often constructed different sexual ideals. In Western culture, since the nineteenth century at least, most women have espoused a version of sexual functioning in which sex acts are embedded within deep emotional bonds and secure long-term commitments. Within these committed "pair bonds" males assume parental obligations. In the idealized Victorian version of the Christian sexual ethic, culturally endorsed and maintained by women, the double standard was not countenanced. Men and women did not need to marry to be whole persons, but if they did engage in sexual functioning, they were to be equally chaste, faithful, responsible, loving, and parentally concerned. Many of the most influential women in the nineteenth-century women's movement preached and lived this sexual ethic, often by the side of exemplary feminist men. While the ideal has never been universally obtained, a culturally dominant demand for monogamy, self-control, and emotionally bonded and committed sex works well for women in every stage of their sexual life cycles. When love, chastity, fidelity, and commitment for better or worse are the ascendant cultural prerequisites for sexual functioning, young girls and women expect protection from rape and seduction, adult women justifiably demand male support in child rearing, and older women are more protected from abandonment as their biological attractions wane.

Of course, these feminine sexual ideals always coexisted in competition with another view. A more male-oriented model of erotic or amative sexuality endorses sexual permissiveness without long-term commitment or reproductive focus. Erotic sexuality emphasizes pleasure, play, passion, individual self-expression, and romantic games of courtship and conquest. It is assumed that a variety of partners and sexual experiences are necessary to stimulate romantic passion. This erotic model of the sexual life has often worked satisfactorily for men, both heterosexual and gay, and for certain cultural elites. But for the average woman, it is quite destructive. Women can only play the erotic game successfully when, like the "*Cosmopolitan* woman," they are young, physically attractive, economically powerful, and fulfilled enough in a career to be willing to sacrifice family life. Abortion is also required. As our society increasingly endorses this male-oriented, permissive view of sexuality, it is all too ready to give women abortion on demand. Abortion helps a woman's body be more like a man's. It has been observed that *Roe v. Wade* removed the last defense women possessed against male sexual demands.

Unfortunately, the modern feminist movement made a mistaken move at a critical juncture. Rightly rebelling against patriarchy, unequal education, restricted work opportunities, and women's downtrodden political status, feminists also rejected the nineteenth-century feminine sexual ethic. Amative, erotic, permissive sexuality (along with abortion rights) became symbolically identified with other struggles for social equality in education, work, and politics. This feminist mistake also turned off many potential recruits among women who could not deny the positive dimensions of their own traditional feminine roles, nor their allegiance to the older feminine sexual ethic of love and fidelity.

An ironic situation then arose in which many prochoice feminists preach their own double standard. In the world of work and career, women are urged to grow up, to display mature self-discipline and self-control; they are told to persevere in long-term commitments, to cope with unexpected obstacles by learning to tough out the inevitable sufferings and setbacks entailed in life and work. But this mature ethic of commitment and self-discipline, recommended as the only way to progress in the world of work and personal achievement, is discounted in the domain of sexuality.

In prochoice feminism, a permissive, erotic view of sexuality is assumed to be the only option. Sexual intercourse with a variety of partners is seen as "inevitable" from a young age and as a positive growth experience to be managed by access to contraception and abortion. Unfortunately, the pervasive cultural conviction that adolescents, or their elders, cannot exercise sexual self-control undermines the responsible use of contraception. When a pregnancy occurs, the first abortion is viewed in some prochoice circles as a *rite de passage.* Responsibly choosing an abortion supposedly ensures that a young woman will take charge of her own life, make her own decisions, and carefully practice contraception. But the social dynamics of a permissive, erotic model of sexuality, coupled with permissive laws, work toward repeat abortions. Instead of being empowered by their abortion choices, young women having abortions are confronting the debilitating reality of *not* bringing a baby into the world; *not* being able to count on a committed male partner; *not* accounting oneself strong enough, or the master of enough resources, to avoid killing the fetus. Young women are hardly going to develop the self-esteem, self-discipline, and self-confidence necessary to confront a male-dominated society through abortion.

The male-oriented sexual orientation has been harmful to women and children. It has helped bring us epidemics of venereal disease, infertility, pornography, sexual abuse, adolescent pregnancy, divorce, displaced older women, and abortion. Will these signals of something amiss stimulate prochoice feminists to rethink what kind of sex ideal really serves women's best interests? While the erotic model cannot encompass commitment, the committed model can—happily—encompass and encourage romance, passion, and playfulness. In fact, within the security of long-term commitments, women may be more likely to experience sexual pleasure and fulfillment.

***

The prolife feminist position is not a return to the old feminine mystique. That espousal of "the eternal feminine" erred by viewing sexuality as so sacred that it cannot be humanly shaped at all. Woman's *whole* nature was supposed to be opposite to man's, necessitating complementary and radically different social roles. Followed to its logical conclusion, such a view presumes that reproductive and sexual experience is necessary for human fulfillment. But as the early feminists insisted, no woman has to marry or engage in sexual intercourse to be fulfilled, nor does a woman have to give birth and raise children to be complete, nor must she stay home and function as an earth mother. But female sexuality does need to be deeply respected as a unique potential and trust. Since most contraceptives and sterilization procedures really do involve only the woman's body rather than destroying new life, they can be an acceptable and responsible moral option.

With sterilization available to accelerate the inevitable natural ending of fertility and childbearing, a woman confronts only a limited number of years in which she exercises her reproductive trust and may have to respond to an unplanned pregnancy. Responsible use of contraception can lower the probabilities even more. Yet abortion is not decreasing. The reason is the current permissive attitude embodied in the law, not the "hard cases" which constitute 3 percent of today's abortions. Since attitudes, the law, and behavior interact, prolife feminists conclude that unless there is an enforced limitation of abortion, which currently confirms the sexual and social status quo, alternatives will never be developed. For women to get what they need in order to combine childbearing, education, and careers, society has to recognize that female bodies come with wombs. Women and their reproductive power, and the children women have, must be supported in new ways. Another and different round of feminist consciousness raising is needed in which all of women's potential is accorded respect. This time, instead of humbly buying entrée by conforming to male lifestyles, women will demand that society accommodate itself to them.

New feminist efforts to rethink the meaning of sexuality, femininity, and reproduction are all the more vital as new techniques for artificial reproduction, surrogate motherhood, and the like present a whole new set of dilemmas. In the long run, the very long run, the abortion debate may be merely the opening round in a series of far-reaching struggles over the role of human sexuality and the ethics of reproduction. Significant changes in the culture, both positive and negative in outcome, may begin as local storms of controversy. We may be at one of those vaguely realized thresholds when we had best come to full attention. What kind of people are we going to be? Prolife feminists pursue a vision for their sisters, daughters, and granddaughters. Will their great-granddaughters be grateful?

Abortion and Organ Donation: Christian Reflections on Bodily Life Support

Patricia Beattie Jung

In this essay I intend to explore two interrelated topics: first, I will delimit the responsibility to give bodily life support; second, I will analyze Christian justifications for both the giving and refusing of bodily life support. Both of these topics have been neglected in much of the literature dealing with bodily life support. Many, including most recently the Iowa State Supreme Court, have asserted that such a gift cannot be legally required and therefore its giving ought not be coerced.[1] But few have defended that assertion, beyond claiming as the courts have that compulsory bodily life support would violate an individual's right to privacy. However, one may ask: why is this particular invasion of privacy intolerable, whereas others are legally sanctioned, if not enjoined?[2]

In her book *Abortion and the Roman Catholic Church,* Susan T. Nicholson argues that the teachings of the Roman Catholic Church on bodily life support are inconsistent. Abortion following rape is forbidden, while the responsibility to offer other forms of bodily life support, she thinks, is quite limited. She quotes Gerald F. Kelly in this regard: "One must help a needy neighbor only when it can be done *without proportionate inconvenience* and with a reasonable assurance of success" (1951:553–54) (emphasis hers). Obviously, Nicholson believes that the rape victim has no special parental responsibilities toward the fetus, and is only a neighbor to it. She concludes, with only passing attention to what she calls the "special nature of bodily life support," that the Roman Catholic proscription of abortion following rape is wrong.

There are a number of difficulties with her argument. First, it is not at all clear that rape victims have no parental responsibilities (this is discussed in more detail in note 7). However, the charge of inconsistency still stands of course because the Roman Catholic Church (and common law) has never demanded of parents that they offer other forms of bodily life support to their children except under the circumstances detailed by Kelly. The law has never mandated organ donation by parents to children even when Kelly's conditions are fulfilled.

Second, it is not clear that Kelly's statement of the principle of beneficence is all that limited. It is not evident that in all *imaginable* cases of problem pregnancies the "inconvenience" of the pregnancy would be out of proportion with the good that could predictably ensue from a decision to sustain the life support. Indeed, one could imagine a utopian situation of optimal medical, financial, and emotional support where it would be clearly disproportional to abort on the basis of a cost-benefit analysis. Beverly Wildung Harrison, in her book *Our Right to Choose*, recognizes this as a logical (though not at present a historical) possibility.

> In such a utopian world, where women's lives were really valued (a world, let us insist, quite unlike the one we know!), it probably would be possible to adhere to an ethic which affirmed that abortions should be resorted to only *in extremis*, to save a mother's life. (1983:18)

The same argument could be developed in regard to other forms of bodily life support, including bone marrow and organ donations, etc. In this essay, however I will argue that bodily life support cannot be morally required of persons. It is my contention that no person can demand access to another person's body—to their blood, for example—and that abortion, along with other refusals to give bodily life support, ought not be forbidden.

Second, let us assume for the sake of argument that traditional Roman Catholic teachings as epitomized in Kelly's maxim are indeed quite limited and hence contradict the Roman Catholic prohibition of abortion following rape. Why conclude that the injunction against abortion should be dropped? Indeed, perhaps the moral error in the tradition lies on the other side of the polarity, in its minimalism. Why not argue that persons are absolutely required to give assistance to others, including all forms of bodily life support? Nicholson did not demonstrate, but instead merely asserted, that the gift ethos which currently informs transplantations is ethically fitting or appropriate. I intend to *demonstrate* that there are good reasons for interpreting *both* organ donation and childbearing as gift relations.

In this essay, I will articulate some of the reasons why a Christian ought to initiate and/or sustain the giving of bodily life support; I will also examine the feminist suspicion of the gift ethos. While the giving of bodily life support has traditionally been exhorted and almost always respected and admired, its intelligibility and meaningfulness for Christian feminists is problematic. In light of their deconstruction of traditional rationales for such sacrificial giving, I will describe in the final section of this essay what the gift of bodily life support and its refusal might mean. This will be discussed in terms of both childbearing and organ donation.

REFRAMING THE ACTIVITY:
A DEFENSE OF THE ANALOGY

First, it is necessary to define bodily life support. By this term, I mean to designate any form of assistance that entails an invasion of the giver's body to sustain another's life. This activity arises with particular frequency in two biomedical contexts: obstetrics and transplantation. Indeed, it is my contention that childbearing and various kinds of live organ donation are morally analogous activities.[3]

Donations from living persons, whether of (1) a renewable part of the body, such as skin, blood, and bone marrow, (2) a paired organ, such as an eye or a kidney, or (3) (for the sake of argument) unpaired vital organs, such as the heart or liver, are forms of bodily life support. Similarly, pregnancy is a form of bodily life support. An optimal pregnancy involves the massive (though temporary) physical modification and the minor (permanent) bodily transformation of the mother—all for the sake of and in support of fetal life. At worst it may involve mutilation (caesarean section or hysterectomy) done solely for the benefit of the fetus, though at present such procedures frequently benefit both mother and child. Pregnancy like organ donation is a form of bodily life support that can gravely threaten the life of the donor.

When women's experience of pregnancy is taken seriously, the invasive element in the experience is quite prominent in the reframing of the activity. In an essay aptly entitled "The Moral Implications of Regarding Women as People: New Perspectives on Pregnancy and Personhood," Caroline Whitbeck makes the following claim.

> Possession and inspiration provide the closest analogy to the ultimately unique experience of pregnancy. The difference in the experience of a wanted pregnancy and that of an unwanted pregnancy is as different as the two experiences of inspiration and possession. (Perhaps all or most experiences of inspiration have some element of possession in them and vice versa, and similarly with wanted and unwanted pregnancies.) (1983:264)

One obvious strength of my proposed analogy is that it takes seriously not only women's life-supporting role *in* pregnancy, but also their experience *of* it.

Analogies in moral argument are usually not proposed without a purpose. My intent in highlighting the similarities between these various activities is to allow the moral tradition behind organ donation to inform the arguments about abortion, and *vice versa*. The ethos that pervades the medical literature dealing with organ and tissue transplants is that of gift giving.[4] Indeed the gift metaphor so pervades the discussion of informed consent in such matters that motives of duty or guilt are judged suspect because, it is argued, they reflect the donor's misunderstanding of the discretionary nature of the act or a less than voluntary "consent" to it. The ethos that pervades the medical and traditional Christian literature dealing with abortion is that of the duty of nonmaleficence, and the legitimate violations thereof.

By drawing an analogy between these forms of bodily life support,[5] I hope to increase our understanding of both the limits of and the reasons for the responsibility one person may have to give bodily life support to another. If a moral analogy between childbearing and organ donation can be established, then perhaps it will yield clues as to why abortion ought not be prohibited. Perhaps it will also yield clues as to why the giving of bodily life support through either organ donation or childbearing ought to be encouraged. It should, in addition, be noted that the analogy will enable this argument to be developed in a context free of sexist biases. As a feminist, I believe it is altogether appropriate to apply a "hermeneutics of suspicion" to the moral tradition surrounding the current abortion debate. Upon comparison, it is hard to miss the disparity between what "conservatives" have demanded of women who are pregnant and what those same persons view as obligatory in regards to other forms of bodily life support, which not incidentally can be offered by men.[6]

It is also the case that most moral analogies are not self-evident. Given the controversial implications of this analogy, a defense of it is clearly in order. One may object to the claim that these activities are morally analogous on at least the following five grounds. With the exception of the second and final objections, each criticism of the proposed analogy can be interpreted as an argument for the claim that there is a *stricter* responsibility to bear children than to donate organs, and that while the former is a duty, the latter is supererogatory.

1. First, it can be argued that it is not possible to compare organ donation with pregnancy because by definition pregnancy entails *special* (parental) obligations not necessarily entailed in organ transplants. The analogy (so the objection goes) obscures a distinctive feature of pregnancy that is morally significant, if not decisive, insofar as this *special* obligation creates a *stricter* obligation to sustain a pregnancy than to donate organs. One could argue, as Nicholson has, that since a rape victim does not participate voluntarily in the sexual act that produces fetal life, she has no *parental* obligation to the fetus, and therefore "the moral problem of abortion following rape" ought to be "conceptualized as that of the bodily life support *one human being owes another*" (1978:80) (emphasis mine). This rebuttal, however, does not withstand careful scrutiny.[7]

In cases of transplants or pregnancy, contractual responsibilities can come into play and donors may have various degrees of parental and other special obligations. The point is, however, that critics of this analogy assume that parental duties require one to give bodily life support. Yet, what strikes them as obvious in regard to pregnancy and motherhood is somehow obscured when they consider what ought to be required of histocompatible donor fathers (and mothers). Consistency requires that childbearing and paternal (parental) organ donation *both* be viewed as either obligatory or discretionary.

2. It may also be objected that fetal life is not morally convertible with other forms of human life.[8] This is indeed a hotly debated equation. However, it is not my intention to defend this key assumption, but to adopt it for the sake of the argument that follows. Therefore, this essay is addressed to three different audiences: (1) those who hold this assumption about fetal life to be true; (2) those who wish to examine this issue exclusively as it relates to organ donations (and hence will ignore portions of this argument); and (3) those who wish to explore the moral ramifications of this reconceptualization of pregnancy, even though they don't hold this presumption about fetal life. I hope to make it evident that, while the status of fetal life is clearly an important question, it is not *the* decisive issue in the abortion debate, even from within the most conservative framework. Much can be gained by exploring other frequently overlooked issues which profoundly affect bodily life support.

3. A third objection to this analogy can be made on the basis of the so-called passive-active distinction. In the case of transplants, bodily life support involves the question of our responsibility to *give* and our right to *withhold* support. However, in the case of pregnancy, bodily life support is a "given" (except perhaps in cases involving surrogate motherhood or the use of the "morning after" pill) and the central issue is the question of the *withdrawal* of bodily life support. Refusal in the former case is a passive instance of "allowing to die," whereas in the latter it is an active instance of "killing." Within the framework of this objection, the duty not to kill is viewed as stricter than the responsibility to save and so the responsibility to continue pregnancy is stricter than the responsibility to supply organs.

In responding to this objection, I must begin by explaining that throughout this essay I will assume that abortion implies primarily the severing of the host or donative relation. It does not necessarily imply either the death or killing of the fetus.[9] It is of course true that at present the withdrawal of maternal support early (before the twenty-week mark) in the gestation process invariably results in fetal death. It is also true that some abortion techniques (the D & C/aspiration and the saline-injection methods, for example) kill the fetus. Thus, as it is commonly practiced, abortion also implies killing the fetus, though sometimes "only" allowing it to die.

Proponents of this objection recognize that not all imaginable instances of "allowing to die" are justifiable. Likewise, they recognize that not all imaginable instances of "killing" are unjustifiable. They claim, however, that, all other morally relevant factors being equal, one must have more reason to kill than to decline to save primarily because, it is argued, such a practice would erode the trust essential to the health-care partnership. (Interestingly, in other contexts of death and dying, the duty not to withhold life support is generally viewed as stricter than the obligation not to withdraw life support because of the time required for diagnostic and prognostic judgments.) At any rate, the validity of this premise is the topic of much debate among many ethicists both within and without the biomedical context. Once again for the sake of argument, let us take up the most conservative perspective and assume that this premise is true. What would its implications be for the topics under consideration?

It would follow that allowing a person to die, say, of renal failure by refusing to donate a kidney takes less justification than killing the potential recipient, all other morally relevant factors being equal. Similarly, it would follow that abortion techniques which merely terminate the host relation, even though they might invariably result in fetal death, would be preferable to those methods that entail the killing of the fetus, all other morally relevant factors being equal. On the basis of these implications proponents of this objection conclude that since abortion frequently implies killing the fetus, it requires more justification than the refusal to donate organs. Indeed, they frequently jump to the further conclusion that pregnancy can therefore be required, but organ donation is discretionary.

My response is twofold. First, as I understand current abortion practices, the methods employed to terminate pregnancy vary because as a matter of fact all other morally relevant factors are not equal—specifically, the techniques which best ensure maternal well-being can vary considerably at different stages in the gestation process. Second, it does not necessarily follow that pregnancy can be mandated. It may simply be the case that organ donation is more discretionary than childbearing.

4. Fourth, this analogy may be objected to on the grounds that the physical relationship of pregnancy is natural and normal, whereas the nurturance and dependency associated with organ donation is pathological or biologically non-normative. Both are instances of "giving life," which is good. However, Lisa Sowle Cahill suggests that, "all other things being equal," pregnancy constitutes an *intrinsic* good to be preserved, whereas the donative relation is to be avoided when possible. Childbearing is a premoral good toward which human communities are naturally inclined. Thus she concludes a more serious or weightier set of reasons is necessary "to justify the destruction of such a 'positive' relation of dependency (physical or otherwise)" than of an intrinsically "negative" one (1981:14).

This is a formidable objection to the proposed analogy, particularly since Cahill is careful not to interpret this argument as supportive of an absolute prescription for procreation. Indeed, she suggests that contemporary moral theology is right in its efforts to avoid the dangers of physicalism. However, totally ignoring the moral significance of corporeality is equally problematic for her. Hence, the analogy I propose obscures according to Cahill the nonpathological character of the bodily life support constitutive of pregnancy.

It is certainly true that the gestation process is normal, in that the fetal need for dependency is neither caused by a disease nor does it originate from some sort of trauma. [10] Furthermore, one would be foolish to argue with Cahill when she suggests that the donative relationship, unlike pregnancy, ought to be avoided when possible through the prevention and/or curing of various diseases and injuries. Indeed I will even grant that pregnancy constitutes an *intrinsic* good to be preserved. Consequently, because there is *some* kind of responsibility to maintain all intrinsically good states of affairs, there is *some* kind of responsibility to continue pregnancy in every case and this is not true in regard to organ donation.

However, Cahill jumps from these premises to the conclusion that childbearing (unlike organ donation) is a *prima facie* duty or obligation mandated by the natural requirements of justice. I reject her conclusion for the following two reasons. First, neither childbearing (unlike child rearing) nor organ donation are responsibilities which can be equitably distributed among all members of the human community. Second, they are both *bodily* forms of life support. Therefore they are highly discretionary gifts, and ought to be encouraged but not required.

In summary, Cahill's argument reveals a significant point of disanalogy. However, this difference is only relevant to an evaluation of these activities insofar as they ought to be enjoined. One cannot conclude, as does Cahill, that this difference renders one activity (pregnancy) obligatory, while the other is merely supererogatory. The reframing I propose reveals that *neither* form of bodily life support can be legitimately required.

5. Finally, some feminists might object to the proposed analogy on the grounds that childbearing (unlike organ donation) is an activity that only women can do. Furthermore, they argue, it is a responsibility shouldered at present in a world which is largely hostile to both women and children. Thus, they argue, the responsibility to donate organs is stricter than that which can be ascribed to childbearing, all other factors being equal.

Clearly, because of its requirements for histocompatibility, the responsibility for most types of organ donation cannot be equally allocated. Nevertheless, this natural lottery is not influenced by gender factors, which are of particular significance given the reality of most women's lives within patriarchy. Here again we are confronted with a formidable objection. This is clearly a morally significant point of disanalogy. However, I believe it is relevant only to a comparison of pregnancy and organ donation as acts of supererogation. Because both forms of life support are (1) bodily and (2) incapable of equal allocation, *neither* can be viewed as a duty or obligation. It is this insight which I believe the proposed analogy makes clear, and which I will defend at length later in this essay.

In summary, despite notable differences these activities—organ donation and pregnancy—are morally analogous in significant ways. I intend to argue that the moral traditions behind these instances of bodily life support will fruitfully illumine one another. Indeed it is my contention that this mutual reframing of the activities will yield insights crucial to the development of cogent arguments regarding both the grounds for and the limits of our responsibility to give bodily life support. Before proceeding to these tasks, it is necessary to clarify what it means to say an activity ought to be done if it is not thereby morally required.

REFRAMING THE NOTION OF OUGHT

In his pamphlet *Supererogation: An Analysis and a Bibliography,* Willard Schumaker suggests that there is more to morality than what is minimally required of us.

> Supererogation is possible because while we always have a right to our fair share of benefits and can always rightly be forced to accept our fair share of burdens, it is sometimes morally preferable for us to take less than our fair share of the benefits of our common life or to voluntarily accept more than our fair share of burdens; and whenever we do so for altruistic reasons, we are acting supererogatorily. (1977:33)

For example, simply because it is morally permissible in some situations not to forgive does not mean that one ought not forgive or that such praiseworthy forgiveness is of only marginal significance to moral life.

As Schumaker points out, Kant is correct in his claim that if persons were just, then there would be no dire need for charity. However, it is equally true and significant that as a matter of fact persons are not always just (1977:42). Indeed, Kant's program, even when interpreted as entailing a form of moral community, establishes only those principles and rules necessary for a barely human social existence. There is no need, I would argue, for either philosophical or theological ethicists to restrict themselves to such a truncated conception of their reflective tasks. There is a need, even if not a Hobbesian one, to establish the necessary conditions of morality. It is an appropriate and important task. However, the content of the moral life is not exhausted by such work.

Since it is my aim in this essay to explore some of the reasons why Christians ought and ought not to offer the gift of bodily life support, I must sketch something of the framework through which I interpret and evaluate this activity. Thus, this essay will be explicitly both theological and political. It will criticize a modern liberal theory of community in light of an explicitly Christian vision.[11] In summary, there are at least two broad levels of responsibility. First, there are those "oughts" which are requisite for a barely human social existence. These minimal obligations are duties, the fulfillment of which is appropriately required by all moral communities. Second, there are those "oughts" which stem from other visions of communal life which exceed or go beyond that of a barely human existence. The "oughts" are best thought of as self-imposed—and in that sense, discretionary—responsibilities which stem from an agent's commitment to a particular vision of life. They are imposed by the self's desire to be in its fullness a certain kind of person and to create a certain kind of community.

It is my intention in this essay to examine the limits of and grounds for the responsibility to give bodily life support. In the next section of this essay, I will analyze what it is about this kind of *gift*—this gift of one's *bodily* self, as distinguished from a gift of one's property—that makes it a choice to be encouraged and commended but not required by either church discipline or civil law. In the final part of the essay, I will explore why, in light of the Christian vision of life, a believer "ought" or "ought not" to give bodily life support.

BODILY LIFE SUPPORT SHOULD NOT BE REQUIRED BY CANON OR CIVIL LAW

All human beings have an obligation or duty to give some minimal degree of assistance to others in life-threatening situations. Conversely, by virtue of a person's humanity, he or she may lay claim to or have a moral right to minimal assistance from others in perpetuating his or her own life. This thesis is put forward in order to distinguish my position from others. It is at least intelligible (though I believe erroneous) to delimit the responsibility to give bodily life support by attempting to demonstrate that there is no general positive duty to give assistance to others and hence no specific duty to offer bodily life support.[12] I intend to clarify the "special nature" of bodily life support by explaining its immunity from what I regard as the legitimate general requirements of both social justice and beneficence.

MINIMAL ASSISTANCE OUGHT TO BE REQUIRED BY LAW

The obligation to assist others has roots in both justice and beneficence. The obligation to give assistance to another can be derived from two very different conceptions of justice. On the one hand, it can spring from a reciprocal theory of justice. Minimal assistance is required because all persons have received and continue to expect to receive such "mutual aid" from others. On the other hand, it can be argued that there are certain primary goods—like self-preservation, health maintenance, and procreation—toward which human communities are naturally inclined, and therefore justice requires *prima facie* that all persons pursue these communal goods.

Each theory, albeit in a very different manner, helps illumine the moral intuition that a starving "thief" can have a right to or can legitimately claim the "stolen" bread. To the degree that an agent is responsible for his or her neighbor's "need"—that is, has profited in some fashion from the exploitation which produced and sustains it—to that same degree, he or she is required by justice to go beyond this minimal level of assistance. In some cases then, the starving "thief" may be said to have a right to this "donor's" bread.

However, no single donor can be justly required to carry a genuinely communal burden. It is not always the case that *this* starving thief has a right to *this* donor's bread. For these reasons the tradition has rooted the general obligation to give assistance in beneficence as well as justice. Charity is possible for three reasons: (1) not all persons carry their fair share of social burdens; (2) some communal responsibilities cannot be fairly distributed, but rather fall by virtue of the natural and/or historical lottery on the shoulders of single individuals or institutions; (3) persons can voluntarily give up their fair share of social benefits.

What has all this to do with bodily life support, specifically with childbearing and organ donation? First, it establishes that nonbodily life support can be required by the demands of justice of both individuals and communities. However, it also establishes that such life support can sometimes be at least in part a matter of charity. Why? Because for a variety of reasons, single individuals are asked to shoulder a burden, the responsibility for which is not theirs alone. It is important to understand that *both* organ donation and childbearing are always in part (if not largely) acts of charity.

This has been clearly recognized in regard to organ donation and is expressed well in the gift ethos which illumines that activity. Even though in theory the responsibility for some types of organ donation (for example, blood) could be fairly distributed, in fact many people cannot (say, for health reasons) or do not carry their fair share of this communal burden. Thus most blood donors give more than might be theoretically required of them by justice. Indeed many give who will never use their fair share of the communal blood supply. The beneficent character of organ donation is vividly dramatized when the requirements for histocompatibility become more complex, as in bone-marrow transplants. In such a case a donor is asked to carry alone a burden for which their responsibility (as that, say, of a distant cousin) may be minuscule.

Likewise, childbearing is always in part (if not largely) an act of charity. This however has not been widely understood nor is it reflected in the traditional ethos surrounding abortion. The life support of children is a *joint* parental responsibility as well as a communal one. Yet during the gestation period this burden cannot be equitably distributed even in theory. Mothers alone carry children to term. The fact that *every* pregnant woman carries far more than her fair share of this responsibility is simply and vividly dramatized when pregnancy results from rape or the failure of contraceptive measures, and when it threatens the mother's life or is accompanied by total paternal or social abandonment.

However, simply because both organ donation and childbearing are acts (at least in part) of charity does not automatically mean they ought not be required. Because justice cannot always enjoin this "donor" to give his or her loaf of bread to the starving "thief" does not mean that such a gift is purely discretionary. As David Little points out in "Moral Discretion and the Universalizability Thesis," beneficence can give rise to obligations. The robust passerby can be blamed if he or she fails to save the drowning child by rolling him or her out of the puddle. The donor can be blamed for failing to feed the starving thief, even if the thief has no right to this donor's bread. Thus I must show what is it about the gift of a womb or other bodily organ that makes it discretionary? Why should *bodily* life support not be required?

BODILY LIFE SUPPORT IS A GIFT

In struggling to identify the logic of beneficent acts, Little identifies some of the criteria for determining the extent to which assistance is discretionary. In my opinion one factor influencing the determination of the discretionary quality of a beneficent act is the extent to which the "gift" in question is truly a gift. Some gifts are more genuinely gifts than others. Compare a gift of money to the gift of a friendship. The latter is more truly a gift, and thus more discretionary (other relevant factors being equal), because friendship belongs more to and is more expressive of the giver than is money.

The giving of bread to the starving thief is only minimally discretionary because the bread belongs to the donor only in a minimal way. Even if one assumes on a penultimate level, as did Thomas Aquinas, that the notion of private property best serves communal needs and responsibilities vis-à-vis the goods of the earth, it does not follow that one can ultimately possess or own wealth or property. One is finally only a steward over such goods. The saving of the drowning child is more discretionary than the giving of the bread because an agent's actions, labor, skills, etc., belong more to him or her—are more personal—than property. Hence, they are more of a gift. (In the *particular* case cited by Little, the rescue is still required because the costs and risks of the saving activity are so minimal. Even though the "gift" is more purely a gift, its giving remains obligatory.)

What is the extent of the discretionary nature of bodily life support? Can it ever be said that a needy "thief" has a right to this "donor's" blood, bone marrow, or womb? What kind of gift is this? Is the giving of such assistance through organ donation or pregnancy ever obligatory? If persons have a general obligation to assist others based on the demands of both justice and beneficence, may this not include bodily forms of life support? If not, why not? Persons do not have a duty to give bodily life support to others. Nobody, simply as a human being in need, has a claim to the use of another's body. Charles Fried, in his discussion of "bodily integrity" as a negative right in his book *Right and Wrong*, offers a fruitful explanation of the "special nature" of bodily life support. While he admits that agents have a general obligation to assist minimally persons in urgent need, this moral requirement does not include bodily life support. So, for example, blood donations are in his judgment purely "discretionary" options. This is so because when the demands of justice or beneficence conflict with those of autonomy, the latter generally take precedence over the former. (There are, of course, exceptions for Fried. Some demands of justice—for example, the duty to contribute a fair share—override some conceivable preferences.) However, bodily integrity for Fried is essential to "the sense of possession of oneself" and hence an agent cannot use another person's body against his or her will without violating the more primary obligation to respect that person as a person (1978:154).

This is quite correct. In accord with James M. Gustafson, I would argue that "man's 'sovereignty over himself,' to use Kierkegaard's phrase, is fundamental to any serious moral view of life" (1968:112). Bodily integrity is viewed descriptively as a foundation of agency or condition necessary for human action. In Alan Donagan's *The Theory of Morality* (1979), such a condition becomes the basis for a normative judgment. In order for a person to act morally, his or her bodily integrity must be respected by others. (Indeed, we do not hold persons accountable for choices made under undue duress or coercion.) Therefore the agent must respect these same features of agency in others.[13]

But why draw the line at *bodily* life support? Why not view an agent's body regardless of gender as one of life's goods (like food, property, etc.) which can like other objects be possessed, exchanged, confiscated, and/or rightly claimed by another? Why is bodily integrity a condition necessary for agency? Bodily life support cannot be required precisely because the human body is not like the other goods of creation which an agent can objectify without distortion. The body is not like other possessions. One does not have a body—one is embodied.

Granted, there are many lived experiences of the body which tempt persons to objectify the body, and stoically to treat it like a stranger. For example, agents are often affectively besieged by their physical needs and must occasionally fight them off, as if they were foreign invaders. Or again, several medical techniques have at their foundation an analogy between the body and a machine in need of upkeep or repair. According to Paul Ricoeur, "here lies the temptation of naturalism, the invitation to deprive the experience of the body of its personal traits and to treat it as any other object" (1966:87).

If so much of our experience of the body tempts us to treat it like an object, then why not accept the invitation? Why view such an invitation as treasonous? Primarily it is because such objectifications break down, according to Ricoeur. Upon close inspection they do not fit our *personal* experience of the body, *le corp propre*. "I do not know need from the outside, as a natural event, but from within as a lived need . . ." (1966:87). In *Freedom and Nature*, Ricoeur adopts Gabriel

Marcel's basic intuition about the ultimate unity of the subject and object. This is for Ricoeur the real meaning and mystery of incarnation. This primordial link, "this inherence of a personal body in the Cognito" (1966:88), is most evident when the experience of embodiment is analyzed on the *prereflective* level. In his philosophy of the will, Ricoeur uses the phenomenological method to unravel Marcel's enigmatic insight and to elaborate systematically the meaning of incarnate agency. In his analysis this elusive unifying link between consciousness and body which is incarnation is disclosed to be "already functioning" prior to reflection at the core of the decision-making process.

For example, Ricoeur analyzes muscular effort, a typical experience of the body as object. By attending to the prereflective level of this experience, he is able to demonstrate that the body can be experienced not only as recalcitrantly alien but also, and primarily, as an available servant to the will. The prereflective experience of bodily docility is difficult to capture because it shrinks away from attention. However, as Ricoeur notes, "only willing which is already effectively deployed can encounter limitations. External resistance presupposes the docility of the body" (1966:310).

Persons do not have a right to or a claim upon parts or the use of another's body because living bodies are primordially personal. All objectifications of the body are abstractions from this lived unity. Therefore, while the needy "thief" may have a just right to another's property or wealth, such claims may not be extended to another's body without direct violation of the obligation to respect persons as persons. While beneficence may impose upon all agents a requirement to give certain kinds of "gifts"—gifts which are only marginally gifts—it can never require of agents so pure and personal a gift as the gift of one's body. This is a claim for the most part accepted but inconsistently applied by traditional bioethicists.

For example, in their now famous debates about experiments on children, *both* Paul Ramsey and Richard A. McCormick (albeit to a lesser extent) recognize the moral significance of this axiom. For Ramsey, it grounds his absolute prohibition of any nontherapeutic experiments on children. For McCormick, it grounds his prohibition of any nontherapeutic experiments on children which (1) are more than minimally invasive, or (2) carry any significant risk. Even for McCormick, *only* routine weighings and blood workups can be tolerated. Both men (although again to varying degrees) recognize the moral significance of bodily integrity when analyzing the ethics of organ donation. However, neither Ramsey nor McCormick (like many moral theologians) recognize as significant the claim to bodily integrity made by women in regard to their reproductive capacity in general, and both tend to deny its significance in the abortion debate.

In a recent essay entitled "Abortion and the Sexual Agenda: A Case for Pro-Life Feminism," Sidney Callahan reinforces this position. Therein she notes that no one ought to "be forced to donate an organ or submit to other invasive physical

procedures for however good a cause" (1986a:232). But this right to bodily integrity does not apply to childbearing, according to Callahan, because when
pregnant "one's own body no longer exists as a single unit but is engendering
another organism's life" (1986a:234). I would concur with Callahan when she
claims that a woman's right to control her own body does apply to self-regarding
choices about mastectomies, contraception, and sterilization, and I have taken
as axiomatic her premise that the fetus is not like a cancerous tumor or subhuman
parasite. Further, I agree that childbearing is clearly an other-regarding activity
and that this other can be intelligibly regarded as a person, whose very life is
dependent upon maternal bodily support. Yet isn't such also the nature of organ
donation: that is, isn't the "good cause" the preservation of another person's life?
It strikes me as blatantly inconsistent to grant potential donors the right to refuse
to participate in transplant procedures, yet view childbearing as required.

The analogy I have proposed illumines the fact that a woman denied access to
either birth control or abortion is forced into childbearing—a highly invasive
experience with significant risks—against her will. Ramsey, McCormick, and
Callahan would never tolerate such abuse of either children or reluctant organ
donors.[14] Were they consistent, they would not be able to tolerate this abuse of
pregnant women. As it stands, they contribute to and endorse that long tradition
which regards women's bodies as objects to be controlled by others, if not by
their fathers or husbands, then by the state.

Like McCormick, I believe agents ought to give minimal bodily assistance
even to strangers. Indeed, in the concluding portion of this essay I will outline
some of the distinctively Christian reasons for such gift giving. However,
McCormick errs when he argues this can be *required* of agents by the demands
of justice. He moves in this direction in order to emphasize (in contrast to Ramsey
and others) the essentially communal nature of justice. Corporate obligations are
constitutive of the moral life. He is correct when he argues that persons are not
properly construed as autonomous, if that translates into an atomistic form of
individualism. It is counterintuitive to deny that there are certain communal
goods—including health maintenance and disease control—toward which human
communities are inclined and that agents are required to pursue these goals.

While I am most sympathetic with McCormick's emphasis on the communal
character of persons and with his wariness of the current surge of liberal interest
in "autonomy," I believe he is mistaken in his attempt to link the responsibility
to give *bodily* life support with the requirements of justice. The communal character
of human agency can be accurately portrayed only when it is recognized that
persons are not parts of but rather "wholes within a whole" (Ramsey, 1970).

One final comment about bodily integrity seems in order. Many prolifers,
especially Roman Catholic, view antiabortion legislation as analogous to antislavery
and feminist "equal rights" legislation. From within this perspective the anti-
abortionist, abolitionist, and feminist are all viewed as seeking legal recognition

of and protection for groups whose full humanity has not been generally respected. Sidney Callahan, in a joint interview with her husband on their book *Abortion: Understanding Differences,* represents this perspective well.

> Just as women and blacks were considered too different, too undeveloped, too biological to have souls or rights as persons, so the fetus is now seen as mere biological life. (1986b:4)

Women who "want" abortions are viewed, like slaveowners and slave dealers, as coerced into forfeiting their "rights" by prolife legislation.

But are these really analogous types of legislation? The alleged conflict of rights in the national debate over slavery appears in retrospect to be obviously bogus, once slaves are recognized as persons and not merely property. At most, there was conflict between human rights and individual (as well as regional) financial interests. However, as my argument displays, even when fetuses are recognized as persons, an authentic conflict of rights can remain. The right jeopardized by antiabortion legislation is not the right to dispose of fetal "property" as one sees fit, but rather the right to have control over one's own body. This basic right to bodily integrity can and sometimes does stand in direct conflict with the other's basic right to life.[15]

None of the ethicists who, like McCormick, would argue that some measure of bodily life support via participation in routine studies can be required of persons contend *on the grounds of justice* that organ transplants can be required or that abortion following rape can be prohibited. This would demand that a single individual carry an unjust share of the social burden. While the rape victim as a member of society shares partial responsibility for this fetal life (in addition to her portion of parental responsibility), it is blatantly unfair to ask her to carry the full burden of life support. I would only reiterate here that this is true (though to a lesser degree) of *every* pregnant woman.

In summary, one may wish to argue that beneficence may legitimately require of all persons the giving of certain kinds of "gifts"—particularly of objectifiable possessions. Nevertheless, the more personal the gift, the more "gifty" and discretionary it becomes. I can think of no more personal and intimate type of gift than the gift of one's bodily self—whether given sexually, in pregnancy, through various forms of organ donation, or as sacrificed for another. The more a gift belongs to, indeed *is,* another, the more truly it is a gift. In his discussion of *Sacraments as God's Self-Giving,* James F. White meditates at length on the nature of gift giving:

> When we give a gift we do not ordinarily say, "This is my body," or "This is me," but this is what we mean. And the receiver understands the gift this way, and not merely as an anonymous object. (1983:20)

One can only give in the purest sense of gift giving what one is. Thus, communal responsibility ought not be conceptualized in such a way as to distort the bodily integrity of persons. Likewise, it should not place unfair burdens on individuals. Furthermore, not even minor forms of bodily life support which theoretically could be fairly distributed (like blood donations) can be required of persons because of the special nature of embodiment. [16]

The ethos of gift giving that currently pervades the practice of organ transplantation is the only ethos appropriate to the "special nature" of *all* forms of bodily life support. This ethos should be extended to our moral understanding of both pregnancy and abortion. Health-care professionals (and, I would add, moral theologians) are appropriately described by Fox and Swazey (1978) as "keepers of the gates," that is, as agents who facilitate gift giving and who guard against the theft or confiscation of what by its very nature can only be freely given. In her discussion of the wider moral framework of abortion, Beverly Wildung Harrison in *Our Right to Choose* makes the following assertion.

> We need also to acknowledge the bodily integrity of any moral agent as a foundational condition of human well-being and dignity. Freedom from bodily invasion . . . is no minor or marginal issue morally; rather, it is central to our conception of the dignity of the person. (1985:196)

My purpose in this section has been to explain and justify this axiom. The conclusion that neither pregnancy nor organ donation should be mandatory does not imply that all or even most refusals to offer bodily life support (through organ donations or childbearing) can be morally justified. Bodily integrity is a necessary but not self-evidently sufficient condition of morality.

BODILY LIFE SUPPORT:
A CHRISTIAN FEMINIST ASSESSMENT
OF ITS MEANINGS

The overarching purpose of this section of my essay is to assess the gift ethos in light of the feminist suspicion of any moral framework that might call for the self-sacrifice of women. Though I have explained why I believe bodily life support should not be mandated for any person, I have yet to examine what it might mean for a Christian to give or refuse to give such gifts either through organ donation or childbearing. [17] Clearly *ought* in this instance does not mean *required*. Furthermore, as the proposed analogy reveals, the decision to bear a child, like that to donate organs, is a complex decision through which the gift giver attempts to serve and balance a number of competing values.

Though they may be obvious, a brief rehearsal of some of these competing responsibilities is in order insofar as it will establish the context for my analysis of self-sacrifice and its refusal. Let us begin by listing some of the factors that might enter into a decision for or against donating an organ. The donor's general physical and emotional health and life-situation, the value of and likely impact of donation upon his or her life-plan (including present as well as future career considerations and family and social-life ramifications), the extent to which the community (family, church, and townspeople) will support (both financially and emotionally) the donor and his or her dependents, the value of the recipient's life as well as the recipient's best interests (which are not in all cases *obviously* served by extending that person's life), and any special responsibilities of a contractual origin that the donor may have to either the recipient or others—*all* of these factors are normally considered relevant to a decision regarding organ donation.[18] Obviously, there is considerable room for conflict among these goods and it is not always possible to balance them. In some circumstances they may be mutually exclusive; that is, sometimes morally legitimate concerns must be sacrificed for the sake of other concerns.

Decisions regarding childbearing are analogous. *All* of the factors identified above are likewise morally relevant to a woman's decision to abort or bear a child. In her essay "A Family Perspective on Abortion," Theodora Ooms notes that when one listens carefully to women who speak about their childbearing and abortion decisions, the language of "care, responsibilities and relationships" is emphasized (1986:98). Abortion is never a "simple" choice based on a single factor, such as the value of fetal life or maternal health. Pregnancies become problematic when no way of balancing the various responsibilities outlined above can be found. Whether terminated *or not*, these pregnancies never have morally "happy" endings. At best in such tragic circumstances, one aims to follow the least-evil course of action. As Whitbeck demonstrates women do not ever "want" abortions. Medea is a false image of women; it is the product of misogyny. Those who take women's experience seriously could never describe an abortion, whether spontaneous or induced, as "a matter of little consequence." Further, women ought not be deceived about or veiled from the developmental reality of aborted fetal lives. Paternalism, however beneficent in origin, robs women of the opportunity to face their situation and their decision truthfully, with integrity, courage, and self-respect. Within this wider understanding of the problem, let us first unravel and then critically assess the traditional claim that Christians ought to give bodily life support, even when this entails self-sacrifice.

From the Kantian "moral point of view," others are properly perceived as strangers and decisions about bodily life support are "purely personal" and "private." In contrast, within the Christian story a (nonpatriarchal) family model is the lens through which persons are perceived as morally linked to one another by obligations of mutual respect, service, and support. These are not merely "special relations" constituted by optional social contracts. These rights and obligations in regard to one another are not related merely to the performance or failure to perform certain acts. They are not subject only to voluntary control.

They are also "thrust on" agents who find themselves "stuck with" needy others.
   According to Hauerwas, life is out of human control, and this is not problematic
for him. Nor does it trouble him that these relations may bring neither happiness
nor self-fulfillment on a penultimate level to agents. That is not what the moral
life is chiefly all about, given this vision. The moral life is more contingent than
social-contract theorists would have us believe.

> It is the Christian belief, nurtured by the command of Jesus, that we must learn
> to love one another, that we become more nearly what we were meant to be through
> the recognition and love of those we did not "choose" to love. (1981:227)

Therefore, simply because there is no voluntary or contractual relation to the
needy recipient does not mean there is no responsibility to offer bodily life support.
(This does not, however, mean one cannot distinguish between varying degrees
of responsibility inherent in varying forms of relationships.)
   Persons find themselves linked—by virtue of blood or tissue type, or by virtue
of their sexual or social nature—to other persons in need of bodily life support.
These needy others are experienced as unalterable "givens" in an agent's life.
Their burdensome and difficult presence is experienced as totally beyond voluntary
control. It is not now, even if it might be in the future, humanly possible to
reverse in all cases the process of renal failure or prevent in all cases the rape-
induced or otherwise unwelcome conception (unless it is verified that this is in
fact what the "morning after" pill does). These are part of the radically involuntary
necessities which ground and limit human freedom. Though such givens are
unalterable they need not crush human freedom because, like other brute facts
of life, they are not only unalterable but also received. Agents have a choice
about how they are going to respond to such burdens and difficulties. This choice
informs and is informed by the dispositional stance the agent has assumed in
relation to the finitude and frailty of human existence in general.
   Such a faith stance is not mere intellectual assent to dogmas, but entails a
commitment to see and relate to "reality" through a certain lens or canonical set
of presumptions. We can only know what it means to give bodily life support
to those whose need crashes into our lives within the context of a particular faith
framework. For example, one can interpret and evaluate the decision of a rape
victim to bear the fetus to term only in light of a particular vision of reality.

TRADITIONAL CHRISTIAN FAITH PRESUMPTIONS

   As Hauerwas notes, "the Christian respect for life is first of all a statement,
not about life, but about God" (1981:226). Indeed, in the first instance it is a
statement about God's ultimate sovereignty over all of life. A voluntarist com-

mitment to or love of the potential recipient is not the necessary moral precondition for the giving of bodily life support. On the contrary, such bearing of the other is the condition for the understanding of what love is in a world where God, not humankind, is in ultimate control.

Before God humans stand in radical poverty, their life and value hang, as it were, by a providential thread. From this perspective, human existence and worth come as a gift from God. Apart from this presumption of nakedness, any human activity—including the giving of bodily life support—will become a form of idolatrous self-aggrandizement. Thus, for the Christian to offer bodily life support is to convict oneself to a life of radical poverty in a world where God is sovereign.

Implicit in such an adoption of the other is a latent valuation. It is a sign of the ultimate trustworthiness of life. It is also a symbol of hope, for the world provides little objective evidence that such confidence is justified. Presuming that life is a gracious gift from God does not entail being deceived about the frailty and faultedness of human existence. Like the presumption of a person's innocence, this belief is indefeasible. While it readily admits the existence of counterexamples (like guilty persons), they do not undermine the presumption itself. It is for Christians a faith claim made from under the shadow of the Cross. For example, it is not to assert that objectively renal failure or fetal deformations are gracious gifts. Rather it is to assert that the lives of those who suffer from such evils, despite their costly and burdensome features, remain gracious gifts. It is to consent to one's own frail and faulted life as gracious gift. It is not to seek or to yield passively to suffering, but rather to adopt it when unavoidable.

THE MORAL IMPLICATIONS OF THE TRADITIONAL VIEW

Furthermore, the faithful agent is one whose particular responses to others and whose life as a whole is characterized by these presumptions. The Christian not only comes to perceive life as gracious gift but becomes a gift giver, extending favors and mercy to others. To see faithfully one's life as graced is, in a word, to live graciously. In *Sharing Possessions,* Luke T. Johnson concluded that "the mandate of faith in God is clear: we must, in some fashion, share that which has been given to us by God as a gift" (1981:108). To grasp, hoard, or hold on to the world's goods, including ourselves, is not a proper thanksgiving. As Johnson notes in his exegesis of Sirach, "it is not enough to keep from oppression and injustice; covenant with God demands that we deliver the oppressed" (1981:99). Or again, as Hauerwas points out, to believe in the parenthood of God is to learn to see others, including strangers and even enemies, as siblings. "We must be a people who stand ready to receive and care for any child, not just as if it were one of our own but because, in fact, each is one of ours" (1981:229).[19]

Thus, sharing the gift of life seems to be a consequence of accepting the cosmology of Christian faith. Monika K. Hellwig writes of this dominical calling.

> In a wide sense we are all called to be parents to one another, to bestow on others the life and blessing with which we have been blessed, that is, to bless others with the substance of our own lives. (1976:44)

This leads to at least one other kind of reason Christians may offer for such self-giving. This latter reason focuses not so much on what Christians are called to do, but rather on who they are called to be.

Christians are called to be images of God in the world. The paradigmatic example of such an image is the kenotic Christ (Phil. 2:5–8), whose outpouring is celebrated in the Eucharist. For Christians the death of Jesus is *not* adequately portrayed as the surrogate sacrifice of the perfect scapegoat, the merits from which they passively profit. Instead the death of Jesus is seen as foundational to a covenant community in which Christians are active participants. That is why the central action of the Eucharist is not the passive, individual reception or eating of food, but the communal sharing of it, according to Hellwig. Christians are to be living incarnate signs to the world of that divine self-giving. This explains why the primitive church told the tale of her early martyrs in eucharistic terms. Those early Christians who witnessed the sacrifice of the martyrs were clearly conscious of the prototypical character of their gift. From this point of view, it seems very fitting that organ donation be described in eucharistic language—that is, as the shedding of blood and the breaking of the body given as testimony to one's experience of God.[20]

Traditionally, the church has recognized at least one woman's pregnancy as having this same prototypical character. In their perception of and devotion to Mary, the Mother of God, Christians have borne witness to certain beliefs about the purpose of human existence. In his book *The Life of the World*, the Russian Orthodox theologian Alexander Schmemann discerns in the celebration of the *Theotokos* the exclamation that "from all eternity all creation was meant and created to be the temple of the Holy Spirit, the *humanity* of God" (1963:61). In her very bearing of the Christ, Mary imaged God's self-gift. Her traditional status as the paradigmatic disciple of Christ is rooted in her willingness to give of her own flesh so that the world might see the face of God.

In her reflections on the meaning of the eucharistic claim that one person can be the bread of another, Hellwig writes:

> Literally and physically this is always true of the mother of the unborn or unweaned child, and it is not accidental that the Bible uses the image of mother to describe God's nurturing. . . . Nor is it accidental or unduly fanciful that mystics have spoken of Jesus and his relationship to the Church in terms of motherhood. (1976:27)

My purpose here has been threefold. First, I wished to give some indication of how central self-giving, indeed sacrifice, is to Christian faith and to the sacramental expressions which constitute the church. Second, I sought to highlight the explicit connection that has been made in the tradition between childbearing and God's own self-giving. Far from being owed anyone or a right, childbearing is most appropriately viewed as a gracious gift, not unlike God's own gratuitous Presence. Third, I have suggested that organ donation can be rendered intelligible and meaningful within this same vision of life.

FEMINIST REFORMATIONS OF THE TRADITION

At this point it is important to delineate and respond to the feminist critique of this view of the Christian faith experience. It might be outlined as follows. People, women especially, need to take charge of and responsibility for their lives. They need "to own," not relinquish, control over their lives. Second, for many people, women especially, sin is experienced primarily as self-negation or neglect, not as hubris or self-aggrandizement. The call to gracious living appears at best to romanticize servitude and at worst to sacralize victimization. Feminists have documented the sadomasochistic expressions such theology has given rise to in the church's history.

They have further documented that in fact Christianity has operated with a double standard: women are called to self-renunciation and submission, whereas men are empowered and given leadership positions. Harrison is well worth quoting at length on this point.

> The morally normative, *sacrificial* behavior expected from women in relation to childbearing and childrearing never applies to the public actions of men. Men's lives are to be governed by strict conformity to "duty" construed narrowly as observing established conventional behavior. Women, by contrast, are expected to achieve a "supererogatory" morality. Although women have moral obligations in relation to procreation, this sort of theology double-binds us. We are admonished to be obedient and passive but simultaneously are told that we were born to be more responsible than men for nurturing human well-being and embodying an ethic of sacrifice. We live in a world where many, perhaps most, of the voluntary sacrifices on behalf of human well-being *are* made by women, but the assumption of a special obligation to self-giving or sacrifice by virtue of being born female, replete with procreative power, is male-generated ideology. (1985:62)

In light of such discrepancies as these, it strikes me as wise to be suspicious of attempts to sanctify the "crucifixion" of women facing burdensome and unwanted pregnancies. It is equally appropriate to be wary of arguments that might force "martyrdom" on potential organ donors.

Clearly feminists are correct in asserting that God is neither a divine child abuser nor a sadist. God's self-giving in the Incarnation led to the slaughter of Calvary not by divine design but by reason of sin, as expressed in *both* the Promethean drive for power *and* self-negation, with its corresponding abrogation of personal and social responsibility. However, Christian feminists would be wise to be suspicious of other additional cultural assumptions produced by patriarchy—including the prevailing desire to avoid suffering at all costs. It is appropriate to be wary of all that results, to use Dorothee Soelle's term, in the "narcotizing of life." It is the experience of pain, she argues in *The Strength of the Weak,* that enables us to empathize on a personal level and eventually connect on a political level with others. Sidney Callahan speaks to this point directly when she notes that "the fetus is to a woman as a woman has so often been to the dominant male—in a position of weakness and vulnerability" (1986b:4).

In my own attempt to weave together these feminist and traditional Christian insights, I have reached the following tentative conclusions. First, it is important to distinguish servitude from servanthood. Though suffering accompanies both, servitude is an involuntary oppression that objectifies, subordinates, and violates persons, whereas servanthood is a voluntary vocation that seeks to break the cycle of powerlessness, domination, and violence in which we are all trapped.[21] Though within both frameworks a service may be offered unilaterally, within a system of servitude this is normative. In contrast, mutuality and solidarity characterize servanthood. The difference is *not* found in the distinction between a sadistic master (servitude) and a masochist slave (servanthood), as some would argue. On the contrary, servanthood, as I define it, breaks altogether with the master/slave paradigm, by seeking to empower and liberate all. Power in this new context stems not from dominion over and isolation from others, but is rather a strength rooted in connection and solidarity with others, *especially* the weak.

Second, the willingness to carry an unwanted child to term can be meaningfully understood as a sign of solidarity with the weak among us. And, correspondingly, a decision to abort in this context can be seen as an analgesic choice, a headlong flight from suffering. Communities that offer no web of support for persons facing such choices, who do not recognize as heroic the choice so to serve, must be held responsible for their systemic support of slavery. To offer those who suffer only opiates is in the long run to support oppression.

Many on both sides of the abortion debate continue to romanticize pregnancy and motherhood. This romantic myth blinds many to the real problems and devastating conflicts pregnant women frequently face. It blinds others to the work, delayed gratification, suffering, and sacrifice constitutive of even planned ordinary pregnancies. Romanticism about motherhood reflects a failure of persons on both sides of the abortion debate to take the experience of women seriously.

Third, the refusal to carry a burdensome child to term can be meaningfully understood as an important symbol of self-affirmation for some women. By this

I do not mean raw egoism or selfishness (though such remains a possibility). Instead I refer to that measure of self-love and self-respect which is not only the prerequisite for and enabler of other-love but also its fitting correlate. Correspondingly, a decision to continue a pregnancy could be interpreted as a blind slavery to a life the responsibility for which one has forfeited. Communities, ecclesial or civil, which seek to mandate childbearing only reinforce the powerlessness and violation many women have systematically experienced within those same communities.

In making this assertion I wish to distinguish my own position regarding suffering and self-sacrifice from that expressed by Lisa Sowle Cahill. In her essay "Abortion, Autonomy, and Community," she argues that feminists who affirm the moral maturity and adulthood of women must encourage them to "recognize that some human situations have unavoidably tragic elements and that to be human is to bear these burdens" (1986:271–72). While I concur with Cahill's rejection of the avoidance of the tragic via both romanticism and masochism, I wish to assert that elements of what is authentically human can be expressed *both* in the decision to abort and in the decision to bear the burdensome child. Self-love and other-love are both normatively human forms of love. What makes the choice tragic is precisely the fact that neither available option can express human love in its fullness.

Such a "double reading" of the choices women make about childbearing offers small comfort to those who sought in this part of my essay a "solution" to the abortion problem. It does however clarify for Christian feminists what it might mean to make such choices in a world that is truly an original blessing, however marred by original sin.

Finally, somewhat parallel judgments can be reached in regard to the practice of organ donation. As first noted by Parsons, Fox, and Lidz (1972), Christianity can frame the giving of bodily life support in such a way as to make it both intelligible and commendable. Through the donation of various types of organs, persons may enflesh certain truths about the purpose and character of all creation. Thus, the inability on the part of some (for example, Fellner and Schwartz, 1971) to understand or encourage live donation between unrelated persons may reflect not limits intrinsic to bodily life support, but rather the convictions constitutive of the modern liberal vision of life. In the future as the risks of graft-versus-host disease are minimized, unrelated live donations, at least of bone marrow, will become increasingly significant from a medical standpoint. It would seem to be a tragic form of myopia if the medical community continues to judge unrelated live donations as inappropriate, if not automatically suspect.[22] Unrelated live donation is not only intelligible but may be a sacramental act for some.

Clearly, however, health-care professionals need to remain wary of those "volunteers" manifesting masochistic tendencies. As "keepers of the gate" they ought to be especially cautious of compensation structures that might ensnare those who are economically oppressed into a personally treasonous forfeiture—into the objectification and sale of their body. This is already a reality at many inner-city blood banks. The power of biomedical commerce to erode the gift ethos which surrounds most other forms of organ donation should not be underestimated.

NOTES

1. In this case William Head, a leukemia victim, wished to participate in an experimental procedure involving bone-marrow transplants from a nonrelated donor. Because computer records indicated that Mrs. X might be a possible matching donor for Mr. Head, she was invited to participate in the research program. She refused, indicating she was unwilling to be a donor "unless it was for a relative." After being informed of her decision, Mr. Head sought a court order which would compel the researchers to reinvite Mrs. X, informing her that a specific patient might be helped by her donation. For more information about this case and Judge J. McCormick's 1983 ruling, see Cases in Bioethics, ed. Carol Levine and Robert M. Veatch (1984:83–85). For additional legal precedents against compulsory organ donation, see McFall v. Shrimp, No. 78-17711 In Equity (C.P. Allegheny County, Penn., July 26, 1978).

2. Here I have in mind such things as requests for information regarding one's sexual partners for the sake of either encouraging paternal economic support for an unwed mother and child, or containing the spread of venereal disease. Or, perhaps more relevant, if the police have reason to suspect that someone's life is in danger, they may invade one's home without a search warrant or the owner's permission.

3. This analogy has its deepest roots in the fictional case created by Judith Jarvis Thompson in her article "A Defense of Abortion," Philosophy and Public Affairs 1 (1971) 47–66. It is further developed by Susan S. Mattingly in her essay "Viewing Abortion from the Perspective of Transplantation: The Ethics of the Gift of Life," Soundings 67, no. 4 (1984) 399–410.

4. This literature would include such books as: Ray Yorke Calne, M.D., A Gift of Life (New York: Basic Books, 1970); Renee C. Fox and Judith P. Swazey, The Courage to Fail (Chicago: University of Chicago Press, 1974); J. Hamburger and J. Crosnier, "Moral and Ethical Problems in Transplantation," in Human Transplantation, ed. Felix T. Rapaport and Jean Dausset (New York: Grune and Stratton, 1968); Roberta G. Simmons et al., Gift of Life (New York: John Wiley, 1977); and such essays as: W. J. Curran, "A Problem in Consent: Kidney Transplantation in Minors," New York University Law Review 34 (1959) 891 ff.; J. Dukeminier, Jr., and D. Sanders, "Organ Transplantation: A Proposal for Routine Salvaging of Cadaver Organs," New England Journal of Medicine 279 (1968) 413–19; A. M. Sadler, Jr., and B. L. Sadler, "A Community of Givers, Not Takers," Hastings Center Report 14, no. 5 (1984) 6–9; and William F. May, "Religious Justifications for Donating Body Parts," Hastings Center Report 15, no. 1 (1985) 38–42.

5. It is mistaken to think of metaphorical comparisons as establishing a substitutionary relationship between the terms. Rather the analogical wager sets up an interaction (not

interchange) between the terms, the fruit of which is new insight into that which is compared. Though the argument that constitutes the body of this essay is not developed analogically (in the substitutionary sense rejected above), it does rest upon the insights yielded by such a reframing of the activities. In his book *Women and Equality: Changing Patterns in American Culture* (New York: Oxford University Press, 1977), William H. Chafe argues that the popular analogy between women and blacks has permitted us new understandings of "social control." At this level of generalization it is very useful. It is less (or altogether not) useful, Chafe argues, in exhibiting the material conditions which accompany either sexual or racial oppression. The analogy developed in my essay will permit us new understanding of the reasons for and limits of the obligation to give bodily life support. For a more detailed discussion of the nature and role of metaphorical thinking, see the now classic essay by Max Black entitled "Metaphor" (1954–1955).

6. This same "hermeneutics of suspicion" should be applied to the growing consideration of prophylactic (for the fetus) cesarean sections at term. For more detailed information about the current shape of this discussion, read the brief note submitted by George B. Feldman and Jennie A. Freiman on that topic to the *New England Journal of Medicine* (May 9, 1985:1264–67). Consider as well the growing discussion among both jurists and biomedical ethicists about forcing pregnant women to undergo fetal therapies. See the essay by H. Tristram Engelhardt, Jr., "Current Controversies in Obstetrics: Wrongful Life and Forced Fetal Surgical Procedures," *American Journal of Obstetrics and Gynecology* 151 (Feb. 1, 1985) 313–18.

7. In this essay the question of whether voluntary participation in sexual acts *alone*— or more pointedly, with the failure of contraceptive measures—establishes a parental relation cannot be addressed in detail. However, I wish to suggest that even if contractual considerations have a legitimate role to play in the determination of the extent of special parental obligations, they do not settle the matter. Family obligations are at least in part noncontractual in origin. Clearly a rape victim does not have as much of a *parental* obligation to her child as one who "planned" her pregnancy; nevertheless, she still has some parental obligation.

Children do not choose their parents; persons do not volunteer to be part of a family. Instead we find ourselves inescapably and inextricably "stuck with" our family and obligated to them, whether or not these parents, siblings, or children benefit us. My point is that contract theory alone cannot explain the moral significance of a person's willingness to have and care for children, particularly those who are unexpected, burdensome, or otherwise unwelcome, since these children highlight the nonvoluntary, uncontrollable, and risky nature of even "planned" parenthood.

It is simply erroneous to assume, in Lisa Sowle Cahill's words, that "only freedom creates moral obligation" (1981:15). In contrast to this liberal fallacy, Cahill accurately suggests that persons are social not only by contract but also by nature. Agents are naturally interdependent and bound by the obligations of this interdependence. Thus pregnancy and gestation can be viewed as primordial and prototypical examples of this natural social interdependence.

8. Even though this essay is deeply indebted to the work of Thompson (referred to in note 3), I agree with Witbeck when she argues that it is almost absurd to envision the fetus as a dependent "adult-stranger." Such an analogy is visualized in photographic and cinemagraphic essays when fetuses are portrayed as mini-astronauts floating about in "inner"

space connected by an umbilical life line to their "mothership." Some weaknesses in this analogy are obvious: fetuses are neither adult nor strangers; mothers are not objectifiable things like spaceships. A strength of the analogy is equally obvious: the fetus is usually dependent upon the mother for survival, though some in the third trimester may be viable.

According to Whitbeck, "a claim more worthy of examination is the claim that human fetuses are relevantly like newborn human beings" (1985:254). Some strengths of this analogy are obvious: fetuses are immature and blood relations; mothers are persons, not objects controlled by others; like neonates, fetuses have voracious appetites and place nearly constant, at times quite taxing, demands on their caretakers. Furthermore, like newborns, fetuses are speechless: they cannot articulate their needs or defend themselves. They are extremely vulnerable: this is a form of dependence quite unlike that of the astronaut. A weakness of this analogy is also obvious: though both the newborn and the fetus are dependent, the neonate's survival is not tied exclusively to the care of one particular individual.

Though neither analogy is perfect, the second one is more illuminative and less problematic. Yet, it has not informed *much* of the abortion debate. Why? Women's experience has been excluded from the pool of wisdom upon which our collective moral imagination feeds. Astronauts are apparently more familiar to those who have controlled the terms of the abortion debate than neonates.

9. Beyond the twenty-week mark, the fetal survival rate can increase if the abortion is done by hysterotomy (a technique resembling a C-section) or by the injection of prostaglandins (which simulate a normal delivery). When combined with the increased availability of neonatal intensive care nurseries, these factors generate two new moral questions. First, how should postabortion neonates be treated? Second, given a reasonable chance of fetal viability, should certain methods of abortion be legally mandated?

In his commentary on a 1976 California bill which attempted to establish guidelines on this matter, Leroy Walters reached the following conclusions. (1) All newborns should be treated equally. As "wards of the state," postabortion neonates should be given neither compensatory nor punitive treatment. (2) Women should not be required to assume higher risks for the sake of a viable fetus, "just as the law should not require parents to rescue their children from burning buildings." If, however, among abortion methods there emerges an alternative which lowers the risks for both the pregnant woman and fetus, then the state can (and I would add ought to) mandate the safer method, for the right not to offer bodily life support (to terminate pregnancy) is not identical with the right to fetal death (Levine and Veatch, eds., 1984:5–6). Furthermore, from within this perspective a woman's right to terminate pregnancy is not identical with the right to fetal experimentation. No one has ever argued that a histocompatible parent's refusal to donate a kidney to a child suffering from renal failure can be interpreted as proxy consent to nontherapeutic research on the "dying" recipient. The case, should there be one, for experimenting on abortuses rests elsewhere.

10. In one sense pregnancy may be said to result from trauma, as in the case of rape, or from a psychological disease such as immaturity among the retarded. Notice, however, that in both instances it is the "donor" who is either traumatized or diseased. The (fetal) "recipient's" dependency remains nonpathological in origin.

11. This critique will be developed along the lines proposed by Stanley Hauerwas in

his work, *A Community of Character* (1981). There he seeks to develop an ethical theory of the classical type which can account for the moral life's dependence upon a certain vision of community. Therein he engages in a polemic against modern political liberalism. As Ronald Dworkin indicated in his essay "Why Liberals Should Believe in Equality," liberalism is not a single political theory. "There are, in fact, two basic forms of liberalism and the distinction between them is of great importance" (1983:32). While both versions seek to encourage equality and legal neutrality vis-à-vis self-regarding and/or supererogatory actions, these conclusions are based on quite distinct rationales. In one form of liberalism, equality is the fundamental value and the concern for public neutrality is a derivative injunction served only to the extent made necessary by the prior commitment to egalitarianism. In the other form of liberalism, neutrality is the decisive value. It is this latter form of liberalism that Hauerwas attacks, citing as defects its basis in moral skepticism and its essentially negative political vision. Its emphasis upon individual freedom and its discrediting of dependence on and ties to others are viewed as symptomatic of this ethos for the uncommitted.

12. Within the Anglo-Saxon legal tradition, strangers have no duties to aid or rescue one another. Indeed, when it reviewed the old common-law crime of "misprision of a felony," the U.S. Supreme Court of 1822 ruled that strangers were not required even to report crimes to legitimate authorities. Lest this portion of my argument be misinterpreted, I believe a sound moral case can be made against this aspect of our legal heritage and that we ought to be expected in some minimal way to be our "sibling's keeper." Thus, I would argue that both moral and legal pressure should be brought to bear on those who can assist victims of crime, such as the witnesses of Kitty Genovese's murder in New York and the spectators of the gang rape of the woman in Big Dan's Bar in New Bedford, Massachusetts.

13. This essay diverges from the theory of Donagan in that it seeks to do more than delineate what must be protected by articulating a vision of what must be encouraged. In this sense, it has a much less restricted notion of what is properly construed as moral argument.

14. Ramsey, it should be noted, even argues against the "routine salvaging of cadaver organs" on the grounds that "a society will be a better human community in which giving and receiving is the rule, not taking for the sake of good to come." This is so even when the good at stake is life itself. "The moral sequels that might flow from education and action in line with the proposed Gift Acts may be of far more importance than prolonging lives routinely." Even corpses ought not to become involuntary "donors" (1970:210). The communal revulsion to the unauthorized harvesting of cadaver pituitary glands for humanitarian purposes in the mid-1960s was a contributing factor to the development of the Uniform Anatomical Gift Act of 1968. Prochoice groups express an analogous kind of shock in response to forced pregnancy.

15. In his essay "Abortion: A Changing Morality and Policy?" McCormick articulates a theoretical framework which seems compatible with the position I am developing, yet he fails to delineate its implications explicitly.

> For an act . . . to be the lesser evil (all things considered), there must be at stake human life or its moral equivalent, a good or value comparable to life itself. This is not what the traditional formulations say, but it is where the corpus of teachings on life taking leads. (1979:39)

For example, human freedom as expressed in political sovereignty has long been accepted as such a value within the just-war tradition. I have been arguing in regard to abortion and organ donation that human freedom expressed in bodily integrity is also such a value.

16. There is a counterexample to this argument which must be considered. Bodily life support has traditionally been *required* of soldiers during war. Further, one might imagine compulsory pregnancy and/or mandatory organ donation reasonable should the survival of the nation and/or species ever come to depend upon it. In addition, though we have awarded decorations of honor, such as the Purple Heart, to those honorably wounded in action against the enemy, strictly speaking we have not interpreted such sacrifices as above and beyond the call of civic duty. Only when a soldier takes up more than his (or her) fair share of the risk would we judge the sacrifice to be supererogatory and confer a meritorious award (such as the Bronze Star). Although there is considerable debate about the extent of one's civic responsibilities in peacetime, there is a wide consensus that military (or alternative, though still potentially life-threatening) service can legitimately be mandated during a national emergency. This practice would appear at first glance to undermine my claim that bodily life support ought not be required. However, I reject that conclusion for three interrelated reasons.

First, though this has varied throughout the history of the draft, many kinds of deferments and exemptions have been granted. Though not necessarily all legitimate, the factors considered relevant have been gender-, age-, health-, education-, career-, fortune- (a la the lottery), religious-, moral-, and family- (especially dependent) related. Therefore, society has clearly recognized the illegitimacy of making such a requirement exceptionless.

Second, while the rationale for each classification varies, several of the deferments are rooted at least in part in the conviction that this potential conscript would be asked to shoulder more than his fair share of the burden. Only if the situation worsens or as a last resort would it be appropriate to draft him, if ever.

While some are comfortable with compulsory military *service* during peacetime, most would argue that hazardous duty should remain voluntary. Bodily life support is a sacrifice that can be mandated only in a national emergency. Thus it would seem that the military "counterexample" under consideration is in fact an exception which proves the rule. As a society we have not required bodily life support for the sake of single individuals but instead mandate such sacrifice only *in extremis*.

17. My attention to the distinctively Christian rationales behind the gift ethos should not be interpreted as a claim that *only* Christians can intelligibly engage in bodily life support. There are lots of non-Christian frameworks which can render gift giving meaningful.

18. This is clearly not meant to be a comprehensive list. It is, however, a representative sample of the variety of factors relevant to such decision making.

19. Dorothee Soelle in her book *The Strength of the Weak* (1984) tells a Jewish story that makes a similar point. "An old rabbi once asked his students how one could recognize the time when night ends and day begins. 'Is it when, from a great distance, you can tell a dog from a sheep?' one student asked. 'No,' said the rabbi. 'Is it when, from a great distance, you can tell a date palm from a fig tree?' another student asked. 'No,' said the rabbi. 'Then when is it?' the students asked. 'It is when you look into the face of any human creature and see your brother or your sister there. Until then, night is still with us.' "

20. It is important to note here that such language and images are not unique to Christianity. In her recently published diaries, Etty Hillesum, a Dutch woman murdered at Auschwitz, wrote of her efforts to comfort and aid fellow Jews as follows: "I have broken my body like bread and shared it out. . . ." The unleavened bread of Passover was always understood to be not only a sign of freedom but the bread of affliction as well. See *An Interrupted Life: The Diaries of Etty Hillesum, 1941–1943*, trans. Arno Pomerans (New York: Pantheon Books, 1985), p. 195. It might also be noted that William F. May in the essay on cadaver donation cited above speaks of organ donation as a "fitting and direct sign" of the Christian's eucharistic participation (1985:42).

21. At first glance, my emphasis on the voluntary character of servanthood may appear to contradict my earlier rejection of liberalism. By voluntary I am referring not only to those burdens that may accompany contractual agreements but also to those unexpected burdens the bearing of which we may choose either to refuse or consent to.

22. At some medical schools, renal specialists automatically view unrelated donors as "crazy" and declare them to be "obviously" incompetent.

REFERENCES

Black, Max
1954–1955   "Metaphor." *Proceedings of the Aristotelian Society* 55:273–94.

Cahill, Lisa Sowle
1981   "Abortion and Argument by Analogy." Paper presented at the annual meeting of the American Academy of Religion, San Francisco.
1984   "Abortion, Autonomy, and Community." In *Abortion: Understanding Differences*, edited by Sidney and Daniel Callahan. New York: Plenum Press. Pp. 261–76. Reprinted in this volume, pp. 85–97.

Callahan, Sidney
1986a   "Abortion and the Sexual Agenda: A Case for Pro-Life Feminism." *Commonweal* 113, no. 8 (April 25) 232–38. Reprinted in this volume, pp. 128–140.
1986b   "Abortion: Understanding Our Differences," with Daniel Callahan. *Update* 2, no. 2 (March) 3–6.

Dworkin, Ronald
1983   "Why Liberals Should Believe in Equality." *New York Review of Books* 30 (Feb. 3) 32–34.

Fellner, Carl H.
1971   "Altruism in Disrepute: Medical versus Public Attitudes toward the Living Organ Donor." *New England Journal of Medicine* 284 (March 18) 582–85.

Fried, Charles
1978   *Right and Wrong.* Cambridge: Harvard University Press.

Gudorf, Christine E.
1984–1985   "To Make a Seamless Garment, Use a Single Piece of Cloth." *Cross Currents*
            34, no. 4 (Winter) 473–90. Reprinted in this volume, pp. 279–296.

Gustafson, James M.
1968   *Christ and the Moral Life.* New York: Harper and Row.

Harrison, Beverly Wildung
1983   *Our Right to Choose: Toward a New Ethic of Abortion.* Boston: Beacon Press.

Hauerwas, Stanley
1981   *A Community of Character.* Notre Dame, Ind.: University of Notre Dame
            Press.

Hellwig, Monika K.
1976   *The Eucharist and the Hunger of the World.* New York: Paulist Press.

Johnson, Luke T.
1981   *Sharing Possessions.* Philadelphia: Fortress Press.

Kelly, Gerald F.
1951   "Notes: The Duty to Preserve Life." *Theological Studies* 12 (Dec.) 550–
            56.

Levine, Carol, and Robert M. Veatch, editors
1984   *Cases in Bioethics.* Hastings-on-Hudson, N.Y.: The Hastings Center.

Little, David
            "Moral Discretion and the Universalizability Thesis." Unpublished essay.

McCormick, Richard A.
1979   "Abortion: A Changing Morality and Policy?" *Hospital Progress*, Feb.,
            36–44.

Nicholson, Susan T.
1978   *Abortion and the Roman Catholic Church.* Knoxville: Studies in Religious
            Ethics.

Ooms, Theodora
1984   "A Family Perspective on Abortion." In *Abortion: Understanding Differences,*
            edited by Sidney and Daniel Callahan. New York: Plenum Press. Pp.
            81–108.

Parsons, Talcott, Renee C. Fox, and Victor M. Lidz
1972   "The Gift of Life and Its Reciprocation." *Social Research* 39 (Autumn)
            367–415.

Ramsey, Paul
1970   *The Patient as Person.* New Haven: Yale University Press.

Ricoeur, Paul
1966   *Freedom and Nature.* Evanston: Northwestern University Press.

Schumaker, Willard
1977   *Supererogation: An Analysis and a Bibliography.* Edmonton, Alberta: St.
            Stephen's College.

Soelle, Dorothee
1984   *The Strength of the Weak.* Philadelphia: Westminster Press.

Whitbeck, Caroline
1983   "The Moral Implications of Regarding Women as People: New Per-
            spectives on Pregnancy and Parenthood." In *Abortion and the Status of the
            Fetus,* edited by William B. Bondeson et al. Dordrecht, Holland: D.
            Reidel. Pp. 247–72.

White, James F.
1983   *Sacraments as God's Self-Giving.* Nashville: Abingdon Press.

Virtue, Providence, and the Endangered Self: Some Religious Dimensions of the Abortion Debate

Anne E. Patrick

My interest in the symbolism of the abortion debate stems from a general concern for the well-being of women and girls and from a specific concern about the way Catholic energies and resources have been used in the last twenty years to fight what seems to be the wrong battle. To be more precise, I am troubled by the way Catholic voters have been manipulated into voting on a single issue—the antiabortion issue—manipulated into voting for candidates whose positions on many matters are quite opposed to Catholic principles of social justice.[1] The question I want to explore is why so many Catholics are vulnerable to this sort of manipulation. My supposition is that certain religious symbols contribute to this vulnerability and that reinterpretation of some central religious beliefs is necessary if Catholics generally are to move to a stronger, more consistent position on public policy questions related to social justice.

The adversaries in the debate that interests me are neither women-hating rightists, eager to expand the address lists of potential contributors to political action committees for neoconservative candidates, nor are they faithless, irresponsible individualists without regard for the value of life in all its stages. I have in mind opponents with much more in common than these stereotypical extremes. I am concerned with a more central debate—a debate, let's say, between a Catholic woman who no longer accepts an absolute prohibition of abortion and another Catholic woman who continues to believe that directly intended abortion is always wrong. Both consider themselves feminists. The more "liberal" woman views the procedure of abortion negatively, but believes that in certain cases abortion is justified or at least tolerable, and that where public policy is concerned it is unwise and unjust to deny this option to women who conscientiously regard abortion as less harmful than other effects that would ensue from continuing a pregnancy. Her "conservative" adversary is not without concern for girls and women with problem pregnancies. Indeed, the "conservative" I have in mind is an actual woman who has demonstrated courage and conviction in defense of women's reproductive choice, exclusive of the choice to abort. I am thinking of a maternity nurse who lost her job in a Catholic hospital because she insisted that her patients should be given contraceptive information and prescriptions. Reproductive choice for women is clearly a high value for this opponent of abortion. Why does she balk at the point where pregnancy has occurred?

I believe the reason goes deeper than ethics, and that moral arguments alone will not change her mind. The remarks that follow are part of an effort to understand her position, which may depend upon religious symbols and metaphors that operate at levels not always conscious, but nonetheless powerful and basic to the personality structure of many Catholics. Furthermore, I seek to understand how this woman's liberal opponent can also be devout, can see her "prochoice" position as consonant with her deepest religious convictions as a Catholic.

VIRTUE

In the first place, to comprehend the intra-Catholic abortion debate, it helps to realize that there is currently in progress a conflict between two different sets of ideals for character and virtue in the Catholic community. These conflicting paradigms of virtue can be termed "patriarchal" and "egalitarian," or "feminist." I believe the latter is gaining ascendancy in Catholic consciousness, and this accounts for the increasingly defensive articulations of the patriarchal paradigm by those in power who espouse it.[2]

A patriarchal model for virtue has long held sway in Roman Catholicism. Its shape has been affected by the otherworldly spirituality, the theological and social patterns of domination and subordination, the misogynism, and the body-rejecting dualism characteristic of Western culture. This model understands virtue to involve the control of passion by reason and the subordination of earthly values to "supernatural" ones. It articulates many ideals for character, but tends to assume that these are appropriately assigned greater emphasis according to one's gender and social status. All Christians should be kind, chaste, just, and humble, but women are expected to excel in charity and chastity, men are trained to think in terms of justice and rights, and subordinates of both sexes are exhorted to docility and meekness. This paradigm has come to function in a way that sees chastity as the pinnacle of perfection, absolutizing this virtue as defined by physicalist interpretations of "natural law." One of the features of this paradigm is the view that unchastity in women deserves especially severe punishment, an attitude that both expresses and nourishes misogynism, with predictable results for the abortion debate.

In contrast to the anthropological dualism of the patriarchal paradigm, the feminist paradigm understands reason itself to be embodied, and women and men to be equal partners in the human community. Instead of *control*, the notion of *respect* for all created reality is basic to this model, which values the body and the humanity of women and promotes gender-integrated ideals for character. Rather than understanding power as *control over*, this paradigm operates with a sense of power as the *energy of proper relatedness*. Ideals of love and justice are not segregated into separate spheres of personal and social ethics, with responsibility for realizing them assigned according to gender; instead, love and justice are seen to be mutually reinforcing norms that should govern both sexes equally.

Perhaps because of the exaggerated attention given by advocates of the patriarchal paradigm to sexual purity, advocates of the feminist model tend not to focus on the virtue of chastity *per se,* though a reinterpretation of this virtue may be inferred from what they have written on love and justice, and also on particular sexual questions.[3] This paradigm sees sexuality as a concern of social justice as well as of personal virtue. It recognizes that the focal sign of religious devotion cannot be the directing of one's energy to controlling bodily impulses and other people, but rather must involve a stance of ongoing commitment to the well-being of oneself and others. This entails concern for building social relations of respect, equality, and mutuality.

Presently the feminist paradigm is capturing the imaginations of many believers, but the eclipse of the patriarchal paradigm is far from complete, and understanding its residual power is crucial to following the abortion debate. We need to ask, for one thing, why the virtue of chastity has been so absolutized. One reason, I believe, is because of obvious associations between sexual activity and the origins of life. There is a negative side to this, particularly the patriarchal preoccupation with paternity and property rights, but there is also a positive side. This has to do with the fact that the origin of life is intimately tied in with fundamental Christian myths and symbols concerning providence, creation, and salvation.

PROVIDENCE AND THE ENDANGERED SELF

"Providence" is the traditional symbol for affirming God's involvement in history. This doctrine is especially important in this context because what is at issue is not abortion, but rather *induced* abortion. We are aware that a very high percentage of concepti, embryos, and fetuses are spontaneously aborted, perhaps as many as 60 percent.[4] What is happening today is that new understandings of sexuality and reproduction, new medical technologies, and new appreciation of women's humanity have combined to raise new issues concerning human responsibility and the origin of life. We are faced with basic questions: What is it proper for human agents to do? How much is our responsibility? How much is God's? How one answers depends in part on one's style of faith, on how one understands traditional religious symbols such as the doctrine of providence. Furthermore, besides the issue of what it means to affirm that a loving God is involved in human history, which entails questions concerning the scope and limits of human freedom, the abortion debate also reflects the sense of peril that is felt on behalf of those perceived to be victims of unjust social policies regarding abortion. Two such "endangered selves" are thought by one side or the other to be at risk as the debate is usually framed, but I believe that there is a third such "endangered self" involved in the controversy, and that attending to this third factor is essential if we are to reach a coherent and reasonable solution to the controversy over public policy.[5]

The first endangered self is the "responsible self" of the woman who is threatened with the lack of autonomy requisite for responsible moral agency. It is important to realize that those who oppose strict antiabortion legislation are not in most instances supporting "choice" as an absolute value nor arguing for extreme liberal individualism. They are rather insisting that an appropriate degree of freedom is needed for living responsibly as a human being in society, and pointing out that women's well-being requires the ability to make moral choices about using their reproductive powers.[6] They are aware that our culture has been biased against women for millennia, and that our legal and moral codes are only beginning to recognize women as fully human, responsible moral agents.[7] They lament the fact that women's moral wisdom has largely been discounted by patriarchal religion, and are unwilling to use coercion to add to the sufferings of existing persons for the sake of bringing new lives into a world that is not justly ordered to their nurturance. They correctly observe that it is inconsistent to allow persons to take mature human life under certain conditions while forbidding them to take fetal life under any conditions. As a minimum, they would remind fetal absolutists that their commitment to "life" is suspect if it stops at birth and is not equally and *effectively* concerned with the sufferings of adult women and children.

The second endangered self is the "possible self" of the fetus. I am convinced there is wisdom in respecting fetal life as a high value and also in recognizing the wisdom of women's experience and of liturgical and pastoral practice that senses increasing obligations of respect as fetal life develops. As I look at today's intra-Catholic abortion debate, however, I have to ask why the value of fetal life is currently being absolutized by some participants in the debate. I was astounded to read some time ago a headline over an editorial in the Jesuit weekly *America* that declared, "Life, Not Choice, Is Absolute."[8] As a Catholic, I have thought for some time that only God is absolute, and in view of the fact that our tradition esteems martyrdom and endorses a just-war theory, it cannot be the case that "life" is an absolute value. What the trend toward absolutizing the value of fetal life suggests is that the abortion debate touches a central religious nerve for many believers, and this fact invites us to probe the way in which issues about the origin of life tie in with fundamental religious symbols, and particularly with myths of creation.

This line of thought, then, leads us to recognize a third endangered self in the debate, one that is pivotal to any eventual resolution of the policy questions at issue. This is the "perplexed self" of the believer. The perplexed believer confronts a dilemma that can be put in these terms: If I tolerate human interference with the life process after conception, what will happen to my world of meaning and value?[9] A natural instinct to defend what is precious to oneself can lead to the belief that the safest policy is to be utterly passive in relation to the origins of life. But upon reflection some will acknowledge that the human task has always been to make decisions about natural processes and to accept responsibility for changing them when this seems to serve human welfare. To acknowledge this is by no means to resolve particular ethical questions, whether about *in vitro* fertilization, abortion, or other matters, but neither is it to assume that an absolute prohibition of interference is certainly God's will in every case.[10] In my view, new understandings of sexuality and reproduction and new medical technologies not only raise new ethical questions but also challenge believers to be devout in a new way, to move from uncritical ways of relating to central religious symbols (providence, creation, salvation, and church) to a postcritical style of faith, a style the philosopher Paul Ricoeur describes as one of "second naïveté," which appreciates the truth of religious symbols without taking mythic language literally.[11] And in any case, it is clear that competing ways of being religious are very important to the moral and political debates on biomedical questions.

STYLES OF FAITH

In Jewish and Christian understanding, the doctrine of creation has supported the conviction that life is good and meaningful. The myth of the origins of the earth and of life in the Book of Genesis has been a powerful feature of Western religious sensibility, serving as a basis for a way of life that respects persons as created in God's image. So too the myth of the origin of individual life as the result of special divine creation has been very powerful, particularly for Catholics whose piety was shaped from an early age by memorizing the first question and answer from the Baltimore Catechism: "Who made you?" "God made me."

This seems important in view of what the anthropologist Clifford Geertz has observed concerning the way a religious perspective functions to sustain a world of meaning and an ethical way of life for the believers of any tradition. The religious perspective, he argues, involves cultural symbols that establish and reinforce a conviction that there is an unbreakable inner connection between the way things actually are and the way one ought to live.[12] Applying Geertz's anthropological insight to the situation in contemporary America, it seems to me that for some Catholics and Protestants, their meaning system depends on a literal interpretation of symbols of creation and providence. For such Christians, life would have no meaning if it were not the result of God's direct intervention. This bedrock feature of religious sensibility cashes out in absolutist defenses of unborn life as well as in passionate espousal of creationist theories of the origin of species. We have here, in other words, another instance of the faith-versus-reason debate that has always been with us in one form or another. And from an insider's perspective, what faith provides is too valuable to be surrendered in favor of "mere reason." When the options are framed in terms of the security of fideism or literalistic, uncritical acceptance of religious myth and traditional religious authority, on the one hand, and the absurdity that results from corrosive critical reason, on the other, it is not hard to see why some people prefer the former. It is, after all, how they were brought up.

For Catholics, the myth of special individual creation ("Who made you?" "God made me") is joined with a strong doctrine of divine providence, whereby God's care is thought to involve conscious divine intervention in history: a great mystery in its workings, but one that provides meaning and support to a believer's life, particularly in times of hardship and suffering.

Furthermore, beyond doctrines of creation and providence, there is the Christian doctrine of salvation, which has been etched on the believer's consciousness through repeated hearings and visualizations of the story of Jesus. Particularly relevant to our concerns is the myth of divine incarnation in the baby Jesus, the power of which is evident annually at the Christmas season. It is perhaps to belabor the obvious to point out that Catholics have long understood that Mary's "fiat"— her acceptance of *a pregnancy she did not plan*—was essential to "the divine plan of salvation." In Mary, providence was understood to have intervened in human history through a miraculous conception and pregnancy that made possible the salvation of the world.

In reviewing these symbols of creation, providence, and incarnation, and in attesting to their mythic power in Catholic consciousness, I am using the descriptive language of religious studies as an aid to understanding the religious sensibility that influences some strains of the abortion debate. Although the issue is usually framed in moral terms, my belief is that it carries tremendous religious weight at a deep, less than fully conscious level.

But are literalistic fideism and meaningless rationalism the only alternatives? Must the myths of creation, providence, and salvation be understood in these literalistic ways? Is it necessary for God to intervene directly in the processes of nature and history for God to be present to these processes? Most contemporary theologians answer no to these questions. This leads to another question: Why hasn't this scholarship been more widely popularized? Why have so many Catholics been encouraged to continue taking religious myths and symbols literally, allowed to remain at the stage of "primitive naïveté" faith, to use Ricoeur's phrase? The answer to this question raises issues of ecclesiology and power, and would require an article of much greater length. Suffice it to say for the present that another myth of origin is relevant to this debate in addition to the myths of the origin of species and the origin of individual human life. This is the myth of the origin of the Catholic Church by biblical "blueprint," an image I borrow from New Testament scholar Raymond Brown.[13] This myth also requires critical scrutiny, though I cannot undertake this here. What I would say by way of summing up is this. If we want to mobilize Catholic energies on behalf of justice for women, then we need to be sure that believers are provided with the sort of religious education that will yield a new, more mature style of "second naïveté" faith. Such a faith will be capable of supporting a truly consistent "ethic of life," one that can be effective in a pluralistic culture because it is both realistic and willing to negotiate in the pluralism of the political realm.

One resource for such a reeducation process is a small volume by theologian John Shea, *Stories of God,* which endeavors to popularize contemporary theological views on central Christian myths and symbols. Here Shea offers a new understanding of providence that is directly relevant to the debate about human involvement in prenatal biological processes. Instead of an "interventionist" understanding of providence, which sees God as a direct agent in human history, a "disrupter of events," or "one of the cast," Shea advocates an interpretation of providence that supports a high level of human responsibility. Such a view understands God as a presence to all the cast, not a disrupter of events.[14] Building on Shea, I would add that rather than intervening directly in the workings of nature or history, this God invites us, through her Spirit of wisdom, to realize divine values of justice, truth, and love, as best we can under the conditions of finitude. Such a view of providence not only recognizes the believer's need to trust in God but also appreciates the mutuality of a divine-human relationship in which the care of creation has been *entrusted* to us, which means that we have some responsibility for processes and events once assumed to be beyond our legitimate reach. Clearly many other religious symbols and doctrines are important to Catholics on both sides of the current debates about abortion. Sorting out the differing interpretations will, as in the case of providence, illumine some of the deep-seated causes of divergent views on abortion and related social policy, helping us to understand why generous and devout believers can see the issues as differently as they do.

NOTES

1. A notable example of the problematic use of Catholic resources is a 1984 leaflet published by the U.S. Catholic Conference, which was distributed in my rural Minnesota parish (and, I presume, in other Catholic churches around the country) on "Respect Life

Sunday" in the final weeks of the presidential contest between Reagan-Bush and Mondale-Ferraro. This colorful and attractive pamphlet features a picture of a man holding an infant and displays prominently a quotation from Psalm 95, "Oh, that today you would hear his voice: harden not your hearts." The text begins as a dialogue between God and a young couple: " 'Hi,' he said. 'It's me, God. Got a minute?' 'Sure, God,' said the young couple in unison, 'for you we always have time. What's on your mind?' " The pamphlet proceeds to state that God is worried about how we are treating life and to imply that abortion is God's number one issue; indeed, it would be difficult for a reader not to draw the inference that one sure way to avoid "hardness of heart" would be to vote for a candidate who has a declared position against abortion. Such "teaching" of course fails to communicate the truth about the ambiguities of abortion politics; and, in the context of the 1984 election, its distribution came close to partisan support of Reagan, especially in view of the National Conference of Catholic Bishops' decision to withhold any publicity on the then forthcoming economics pastoral until *after* the election. Recently U.S. Senator Patrick J. Leahy, a Catholic from Vermont, has put the problem thus: "Today, the church is dangerously close to aiding single-issue groups—whether intentionally or not—in cutting down so much of what it has stood for in the past. If the right wing, through manipulation of single-issue politics, continues to defeat elected officials who support progressive steps, there will be no one left in government to shelter those broad values of compassion and justice the church has endorsed." See Leahy, "The Church We Love Is Being Used," *Conscience,* July/Aug. 1987, p. 13.

2. My discussion of these competing models for virtue is also developed in the articles "Narrative and the Social Dynamics of Virtue," in *Changing Values and Virtues,* ed. Dietmar Mieth and Jacques Pohier (Edinburgh: T. & T. Clark, 1987) 69–80, and "Character and Community: Curran and a Church Coming of Age," in *Vatican Authority and American Catholic Dissent: The Curran Case and Its Consequences,* ed. William W. May (New York: Crossroad, 1987) 127–43. The patriarchal paradigm reflects a sexist mentality and a social system that values males over females, is biased in favor of masculine authority, and is built on principles of domination and subordination. For an ethical analysis of "sexism," see Patricia Beattie Jung, "Give Her Justice," *America* 150 (April 14, 1984) 276–78. Like Jung, I understand the concepts of "sexism" and "feminism" to be dialectically related, and thus use "egalitarian" and "feminist" interchangeably in discussing the newer model for virtue. In a sexist culture, one must be feminist in order to be egalitarian. By "feminist" I mean a position that involves (1) a solid conviction of the equality of women and men, and (2) a commitment to reform society, including religious society, so that the full equality of women is respected, which requires also reforming the thought systems that legitimate the present unjust social order. Both women and men can thus be "feminist," and within this broad category there is enormous variety in levels of commitment, degrees of explicitness of commitment, and, of course, opinions regarding specific problems and their solutions.

3. Works that reflect the values of the egalitarian paradigm include Margaret A. Farley, "New Patterns of Relationship," *Theological Studies* 36 (1975) 627–46, and *Personal Commitments* (San Francisco: Harper and Row, 1986); Beverly W. Harrison, *Making the Connections,* ed. Carol S. Robb (Boston: Beacon Press, 1985); and Joan Timmerman, *The Mardi Gras Syndrome* (New York: Crossroad, 1984).

4. Carol A. Tauer gives 56 percent as a "reasonable approximation" in "The Tradition

of Probabilism and the Moral Status of the Early Embryo," *Theological Studies* 45 (1984) 6; reprinted in this volume, pp. 54–84.

5. I am basing my discussion of "endangered selves" on a social theory of the self, such as that developed by the social psychologist George Herbert Mead in *Mind, Self, and Society,* ed. Charles W. Morris (Chicago: University of Chicago Press, 1943). Such a theory recognizes that one is constituted as a self in relationships. In other words, language, social interaction, and cultural myths and symbols are all very important in shaping the self.

6. Beverly W. Harrison stresses this point in *Our Right to Choose: Toward a New Ethic of Abortion* (Boston: Beacon Press, 1983).

7. In her 1984 presidential address to the Modern Language Association, Carolyn Heilbrun effectively illustrated the difference in what it can mean to be a self as a man or woman in a sexist culture by quoting fifteen words from two American poets. The first quote included thirteen words on a man's experience of selfhood, from Walt Whitman: "I celebrate myself and sing myself, and what I assume you shall assume." That left two words from a woman, Emily Dickinson: "I'm nobody." Assuming that Heilbrun's examples say something about this culture, we must ask: How can we reverse the effects of millennia of sexism? There are ambiguities, to be sure, but I believe we must begin by recognizing the moral competence of women. See Carolyn G. Heilbrun, "Presidential Address 1984," *PMLA* 100 (1985) 281–82.

8. *America* 153 (Oct. 19, 1985) 229.

9. This is an important and deeply challenging question, and we find a parting of the ways when religious people attempt to address it. Many of the devout, whose faith often tends to be literalistic and uninfluenced by the various modern "critiques" of religion, will respond by enhancing the value of those minuscule human life forms that seem threatened by human agents to the point of absolutizing these life forms, though there is no evidence that embryos or early fetuses that spontaneously abort have become objects of parallel concern. Thus it may be that certain embryos and fetuses have come to function as symbols of the divine, besieged by modernity. What is more, they also may serve as symbols of the self—the fragile, imperiled self experiencing powerlessness in a hostile environment—and together these associations evoke the enormous energy of self-defense.

10. James E. Kraus expresses the difficulty involved in the case of abortion in the following terms: ". . . if it is a terrible thing to play God by terminating physical life, it is also a terrible thing, in another sense, to play God by imposing as a divine absolute a prohibition that may cause immense suffering both to individuals and to society." See Kraus, "Is Abortion Absolutely Prohibited?" in *Abortion: The Moral Issues,* ed. Edward Batchelor, Jr. (New York: Pilgrim Press, 1982) 109.

11. Ricoeur discusses this term in *Symbolism of Evil* (Boston: Beacon Press, 1967) 347–57.

12. See Clifford Geertz, *Islam Observed: Religious Development in Morocco and Indonesia* (Chicago: University of Chicago Press, 1971) 98.

13. See Raymond E. Brown, *Biblical Reflections on Crises Facing the Church* (New York: Paulist Press, 1975) 52–55.

14. See John Shea, *Stories of God* (Chicago: Thomas More Press, 1978) 89–116.

Part II

Abortion:
The Political Debate

Chapter 3

Religion, Morality, and Public Policy

This chapter focuses on the interplay among religion, morality, and public policy. The essay by Shannon that opens this section provides an overview of the dilemmas that emerge at this juncture. In addition to providing helpful historical and sociological information, Shannon identifies four questions that must be answered by Catholic policymakers: How adequate are the alternatives to abortion? How should abortion (and/ or its alternatives) be funded, if at all? How can religious conviction be translated into terms appropriate to the public arena? How ought the public debate about abortion be conducted?

Reflection on some of these issues by a Catholic politician follows. As the governor of New York and a practicing Catholic, Cuomo's struggle with these problems is clear. Despite his personal opposition to abortion, Cuomo argues against a constitutional ban on abortion, against legal compromises like the Hatch amendment, and against the withdrawal of Medicaid funding for abortions. He presses instead for a well-endowed campaign to eliminate the factors that create problematic pregnancies and reduce respect for life.

The Callahan essay augments the explanation offered by Cuomo for the discrepancy between his private judgment and his public policy recommendations. Callahan argues that religious reasons are insufficient as a foundation for civil law. Furthermore, she concludes that the philosophical rationale for legally prohibiting abortion is weak.

The Byrne essay evaluates the recent "speaker's ban" imposed in the Archdiocese of New York. According to this ecclesial directive, anyone who dissents from church teachings should not as a general rule be invited to speak at church meetings. Byrne identifies several problems with such a ban, highlighting in particular the punitive effect it has on candidates for political office in heavily Catholic districts. He notes the tension between such a directive and the policy of the U.S. Catholic Conference against endorsing particular candidates or political parties.

Not surprisingly, the next essay sharply contrasts with Byrne's. Though Cardinal O'Connor does not mention specifically the "speaker's ban," he develops an argument in defense of such tactics. According to O'Connor, the church must remedy four deficiencies in the conscience formation of its members if Catholics are to be effective agents in the public realm. For the most part, Catholics are ignorant of the church's social teachings and lack a clear understanding of the church's mission in the public sphere. These two educational gaps must be filled. In addition, the American Catholic "self-consciousness" and oversensitivity about engaging in partisan politics must be corrected lest they stifle efforts at social change. Finally, while some fear of dividing the church along ideological lines is justified, O'Connor believes such a division must be risked if the church wants to be politically effective.

This chapter ends with an essay by Degnan in which he defends efforts to amend the Constitution so that all abortions would be prohibited. Furthermore, he argues that politicians must be held accountable for their position on abortion. However, their performance in other respects must also be evaluated when assessing their candidacy, especially when the office in question entails broad responsibilities. One can infer from Degnan's argument that support for prolife policies does not necessarily mean support for prolife candidates.

Abortion: A Challenge for
Ethics and Public Policy

Thomas A. Shannon

The purpose of this paper is to review and analyze several issues related to the debate about public policy on abortion. What I hope to do in this article is review some of the ethical and political issues raised in abortion, describe some aspects of abortion policy in America, identify ethical problems raised by some of the policy questions, and then discuss some of the ethical issues involved in these policy debates. I will present some conclusions based on this material. What I hope to accomplish by this is to indicate some fundamental problems in the debate and hope that we as members of a professional society can return to our classrooms and communities and focus on some of the more substantive issues behind the debate.

A REVIEW OF POLICY AND INCIDENCE OF ABORTION

According to Christopher Tietze, as late as 1980 about 9 percent of the world's population lived in countries where abortion was prohibited without exception and about 19 percent of the world's population lived in countries where it was permitted only to save the life of a pregnant woman.[1] Fewer than 10 percent live in countries where statutes authorize abortions on broader medical grounds, i.e., averting a threat to a woman's health rather than only to her life, and occasionally for eugenic or fetal indications. About 24 percent of the world's population were able to take into account social factors such as income, housing, marital status in evaluating a woman's health. About 38 percent of the population live in countries which allow abortion on request without specifying a reason and this is generally limited to the first trimester of pregnancy.

These policies also have a wide range of applicability. A policy authorizing abortion to avert a threat to a pregnant woman's health could be defined narrowly or broadly. Social indications for abortion may similarly be defined. Many statutes may not be strictly enforced and, in any event, whatever statutes there are rely upon the cooperation of health-care providers and delivery systems. Consequently,

185

even though a particular country may have a liberal abortion policy which is guaranteed by statute, that does not necessarily mean that the procedure is actually available to any woman who wants an abortion.

Within the last fifteen years, many countries have liberalized their abortion laws; four countries in Eastern Europe adopted more restrictive legislation and three countries liberalized their policies and then made them more restrictive.

The reasons used by proponents of less-restrictive abortion legislation are summarized as follows: consideration of public health, especially the morbidity and mortality associated with illegal abortion; social justice, allowing poor women to have equal access to abortion; women's rights, including the right to control their own bodies. Only a few countries—Singapore, Indonesia, and China—have used the explicit motivation of curbing population growth in the interest of economic and social development as a reason for adopting nonrestrictive abortion policies. Ironically, many countries which permit abortions either at the request of the woman or on broadly interpreted social indications have low birth rates and some of these countries are now actively pursuing pronatalist population policies.[2]

Although highly speculative, the number of abortions internationally has been estimated at around fifty-five million, which would correspond to an abortion rate of around seventy per thousand women of abortion age and an abortion ratio of three hundred per thousand known pregnancies.

The differences in abortion rates in the United States between whites and blacks are interesting. Between 1963 and 1965 among whites, the abortion rate was .19 per thousand and from 1966 to 1968 it was .29 per thousand. During those same years it was .17 and .29 for blacks respectively. In 1978 the abortion rate was 22.7 for whites and 60.4 per thousand for blacks.[3]

A REVIEW OF POLICIES ON ABORTION IN THE UNITED STATES

In his book, Mohr traces the history of why in 1800 there were virtually no abortion policies and in 1900 every state had an antiabortion law. While not wanting to rehearse all of the salient elements in Mohr's book, there are a few policy issues I want to emphasize.

Mohr identifies several motives why the early abortion legislation came into being. The first motive focused on preventing the mother's death through the use of an abortifacient.[4] These laws, as Mohr notes, were primarily poison control measures focusing not so much on the fetus as on the health status of the mother and the safety of the procedure that was used. These laws also had the effect of reinforcing the traditional norm of "quickening" as the dividing line between abortions which were not governed by statutes and those which were. The other two motives Mohr says contributed to the increase in abortion laws, especially coming to a climax point at the end of the nineteenth century, have to do with changes in the perception of who was receiving an abortion and who was providing them. There was a growing fear that since first-generation American women were now receiving abortions at high rates, the WASP population might be outnumbered by the immigrants. This perception was related to the developing nativist movement and consequently statutes were enacted to restrict abortion, intending not the protection of the fetus, but the protection of the status and power of the established classes. Parallel to this was the growing professionalization of medicine. Physicians were interested both in developing and tightening their own standards of practice and in eliminating from medicine those described as quacks. Physicians lobbied against abortion to eliminate from the profession individuals who would not abide by its rules and as a means of controlling the standards of the members of the profession itself. The medical profession was also further able to control abortion by helping define medical conditions under which abortion might be appropriate and by providing competent individuals to perform the procedure. Thus, by the end of the nineteenth century, abortion legislation was present in all of the states and was contrary to the earlier experience of the country in which abortion was possible for those who wanted it. Again, the primary intent of this legislation was the protection of the mother and the enhancement of the social status of two different groups within society: the establishment and physicians.

Mohr also describes the pressures that led to the reevaluation of these anti-abortion statutes in our own time and which in turn led to the *Roe v. Wade* decision in 1972.[5] These pressures are: (1) the fear of overpopulation; (2) a growing concern for the quality of life of the fetus as opposed to the mere preservation of life; (3) the development of the women's rights movement with its emphasis on a woman's right to control her body; (4) the growing safety of abortion done under appropriate medical conditions; (5) the fact that women were getting abortions in spite of restrictive legislation. One could also add to this list the movement of several states to relax their own abortion legislation. Ultimately this led to the testing of restrictive state statutes in the Supreme Court.

What is important from this survey is that abortion legislation was developed primarily out of a variety of social issues that were not directly or quite possibly even indirectly related to concern for the fetus. The older use of the term quickening and its contemporary analogue of viability served as a touchstone for the limits of abortion. That is, in the early nineteenth century, abortion was not considered problematic morally or medically until the point of quickening. In the view of many individuals, a similar argument is being made today from at least a medical, if not a moral point of view. And, in fact, as Mohr indicates, the *Roe* decision is based somewhat upon this older traditional view within American society: abortions before quickening or viability are not problematic. But again Mohr focuses on the social context for the development of abortion legislation and its repeal. Abortion statutes—whether pro or con—were based upon neither the sanctity of life of the fetus nor disregard of it, but rather upon other social issues and concerns.

Another important review of abortion policies comes from a recent article by Tatalovich and Daynes entitled, "The Trauma of Abortion Politics."[6] These authors indicate three significant periods in the history of the policy debate. First, in the early 1960s the basic issue was the building of a consensus toward abortion reform which focused primarily on the availability of therapeutic abortion. The authors note that the proabortion advocates shared similar assumptions, made similar arguments, and held common objectives with the abortion opponents. These proponents assumed, based on the American Law Institute's recommendations, that abortion should be permitted only to a limited number of women and that it should be performed for therapeutic reasons. This position defines abortion primarily in medical terms, not moral ones. The abortion reformers were not making any radical claims. All of the abortion statutes in effect permitted therapeutic abortions when the mother's life was in danger. Some states allowed abortion when the mother's health was threatened. What the reformers were arguing for was an incremental change in the abortion laws allowing this more expanded exception. And at that point in time approximately 80 percent of the general population favored some abortion reform, and while this support came from both Catholics and Protestants, Catholics did not support the reform at the same level that the Protestants did.

A second critical period the authors identify is 1969 to 1970, shaped as it was by three interrelated developments. First, the proabortionists shifted towards repeal of all abortion laws (as opposed to therapeutic reform). Second, opposition to abortion began to focus on opposition to *any* change, thereby opposing not only the new movement towards total repeal of abortion laws, but even the incremental changes that were desired earlier. Third, the proponents of abortion began to shift their strategy to the use of the judiciary to achieve reform rather than expend their limited resources on attempts to change legislation state by state. This strategy culminated in *Roe*, which appeared to many to have a "winner-take-all" dimension. This court decision made it difficult for any compromise posture to be taken and helped change the nature of the debate. Interestingly, the authors point out that there were ample court precedents on either side of the issue and that the court was not inherently locked into a proabortion decision. But had the court come out the other way, there still would have been a public policy debate, with the sides reversed. A major problem is not so much the court's decision, as the perceived "winner-take-all" nature of the decision which has in effect polarized the debate.

The third issue concerns this polarization of perceptions on abortion, as well as strategies to achieve the ends of the antiabortion groups. One of the by-products of this polarization has been the legislative maneuverings of the antiabortion groups. Picking up their cues for strategies for reform from the proabortion groups, the antiabortion groups have gone them one better and chose to go neither the state legislative route nor the route of the judiciary but rather are attempting to circumvent the entire judicial system by having certain kinds of legislation declared judicially off limits. The antiabortion people recognize that state-by-state campaigns will be costly and time-consuming and they realize that a constitutional amendment may be very difficult to achieve. One effective strategy is to circumvent these processes by having Congress declare certain forms of legislation off limits to judicial review. They are also attempting to devise federal legislation to restrict public monies for abortion to as few cases as possible so that those who wish abortions must pay for them themselves. Two important moves here have been: first, a statute introduced to define life as beginning at conception, thus ensuring a fetus constitutional rights, making abortion illegal, and raising constitutional problems regarding certain forms of contraception; second, the Hatch amendment, recently passed by the Senate's judiciary subcommittee, which states that the right to an abortion is not guaranteed by the Constitution and that the states and Congress shall have power to restrict and prohibit abortions. This amendment also gives a state law precedence if it is more restrictive than federal legislation.

Thus the third major phase of the debate these authors identify consists of a conflict at a very high and intense level among groups who are violently prochoice or antiabortion, while simultaneously denying to legislatures the ability to make compromise moves. By focusing on an either/or position, consensus is more difficult to achieve and consequently no policy is able to gain legitimacy. Our current debate is characterized by polarization and a move from a debate of the issues to personal confrontations in which parties are perceived to be liberal or conservative with respect to this particular issue.

OPINIONS ON ABORTION

One of the issues that is important in developing a public policy is to ensure some sense of legitimacy of this policy by rooting it in the beliefs of the citizenry so that the policy at least to some degree will be acceptable and workable. I am not arguing that the morality of abortion will be settled or determined by poll taking. I do argue that we must attend to perceptions about abortion to determine if there are possible connections between the pro and con groups that can effect a compromise which enables a policy to be developed.

We need to examine first what reasons for abortion people find persuasive. One important finding is that there is an average approval of 67 percent for six specific reasons for abortion: a woman's health is seriously endangered by the pregnancy; becoming pregnant as a result of rape; a strong chance of a serious defect in the baby; the family has a low income and cannot afford more children;

the woman is pregnant and does not want to marry the man; the woman is married and does not want more children.[7] The last three reasons are known as the "soft" reasons for abortion and there is no solid social consensus on these three. The average consensus for the first three reasons, the "hard" reasons, averages about 85 percent, whereas it is about 50 percent for the soft reasons. There is clearly strong social consensus around the broadened concept of a therapeutic abortion. There is less, but slightly increasing, support for the more social or personal reasons for wanting an abortion. It is also important to note that the average approval has changed only four percentage points since 1972. There was a jump of twenty-two points between 1965 and 1972. But there has been a remarkable stability in the approval rate since 1972.[8]

With respect to the profiles of those engaged in the debate, there are some interesting correlations. First, two relevant differences are that those who are antiabortion tend to feel that obedience to authority figures is more important and that curiosity during child development is less important than do those who are in favor of abortion. Second—a finding which should surprise no one—the higher a person's social status, the greater is their tendency to approve abortion. In fact one study indicated that a formal education is the best predictor of abortion attitudes. Third, the more one disapproves of activities such as premarital sex, extramarital sex, and homosexuality, the less one favors abortion. Fourth, differences between Protestants and Catholics with respect to favoring or not favoring abortion increase in proportion to the degree of education that the individual has had. Finally, for both Protestants and Catholics approval of abortion decreases as religiosity increases, with the notable exception of Episcopalians who are more likely to approve of abortion the more religious they are. What is significantly interesting and important in one study was the allegation that the Protestant-Catholic difference accounts for only about 1 percent of the variation in abortion attitudes over the years. This leads to the interesting hypothesis that the religious differences are not the critical differences in the abortion debate and that to cast the debate in terms of religious preference is both mistaken and particularly counterproductive for policy debates. These studies would indicate that the critical variables are those beyond religion and having to do with feelings about child rearing, social practices, education, and class.[9]

A study of differences between members of the National Abortion Rights Action League (NARAL) and the National Right to Life Committee (NRLC) showed some interesting differences with respect to what the membership of each organization felt about abortion.[10] These findings are of particular importance for policy making. More than 95 percent of NARAL members and fewer than 5 percent of NRLC members approve of legal abortion when there is a strong chance of a serious defect in the baby, when the woman is married and wants no more children, when a woman's husband will not consent to an abortion, when the family is too poor to afford more children, when parents will not consent to a teenager's abortion, and when an unmarried woman wants to have an abortion. These data are not surprising, especially insofar as they refer to the soft reasons for abortion. However, it is interesting that 73 percent of NRLC members favor making abortion available to women whose life is endangered by continuation of the pregnancy. Also 15 percent of NRLC members approve of abortion if the pregnant woman's physical health is seriously endangered by carrying the pregnancy to term and 7 percent to 8 percent favor legal abortion if pregnancy is the result of rape or incest. These data indicate that members of the NRLC do not present as monolithic and absolutistic position on abortion as might be assumed. While the policy that could be based on such feelings may not be acceptable to all, nonetheless it does indicate that there are possibilities for some movement. Compromise, of course, will be called for.

Another relevant factor revealed by this survey indicates that NRLC activists are not only generally more conservative on moral issues but are also likely to describe themselves as conservatives or Republicans, and to oppose government action to reduce income differences between rich and poor. As important as those differences are, the NRLC members are much more likely than NARAL members to give priority to their views on abortion over their views on social issues. Eighty-four percent of NRLC members as opposed to 47 percent of NARAL members say that abortion is so important that they would refuse to support a candidate whose position on abortion was unacceptable. This may mean that in elections or in debates of public policy, all other things being equal, there may be a strategic advantage to having a group which has the higher percentage of single-issue voters on its side.

Kelly identified some general reasons why they were concerned for only one issue.[11] First, abortion stops a human life and is, therefore, a unique issue. Second, a single-issue focus protects the right-to-life movement from being absorbed or manipulated by any political party. Third, the passage of a human-life amendment to the Constitution requires a political coalition of people with different ideologies and, therefore, strategically they wish to avoid being perceived as members of any other group. There seems to be a recognition that the alliance present in the prolife movement is very tenuous and that it might not be able to stand the strain of having to deal with social problems that may not be perceived as having the same importance or solution, e.g., nuclear war or social-welfare programs.

It would be interesting to know how the structure and impact of the prolife movement will be affected by the interior tensions that are present, at least with respect to differences in the kinds of approvals of abortion that are tolerated by some members. The monolithic unity of the prolife movement may be a perception, not a reality. One could assume that much of the energy of the prolife movement needs to be spent in making sure that potentially disruptive issues do not enter into the dialogue and that no relationship between the ethical values surrounding the evaluation of abortion and other social issues be made, i.e., extending a prolife stance to evaluate nuclear war. One could make a reasonable case that such a position will continue to become more and more difficult as time goes by and that members of prolife groups will have to make more and more difficult choices with respect to the supporting of political candidates, especially when these candidates present viewpoints on a variety of issues that may, in fact, appeal to different populations within the prolife movement.

ETHICAL DILEMMAS AND PROBLEMS
IN THE PUBLIC POLICY DEBATE

In this section I will indicate some problems that are critical in the ethical dimensions of the public policy debate. These issues clearly relate to and occasionally emerge from the problems that I have already addressed. But they also go beyond these problems and form a critical context in which the issues are debated or, more realistically stated, argued.

Lack of Alternatives

There are few, if any, good alternatives to abortion. Adoption clearly is an alternative to abortion, but choosing adoption requires that the woman still carry the child to term and deal with the reality of separation from the newborn, a painful experience even if the woman is highly motivated. Even in the best of circumstances such a separation will not easily be made and when there is the suggestion of coercion or significant familial or other pressure to carry the child to term rather than abort, the separation will be much more problematic. Even for women who choose to carry a child to term in the expectation of allowing the child to be adopted, there may be lack of good or even adequate social, physical, and economic support to make such a process easier to accomplish and to ensure the health of the mother and the newborn. Thus as much as a woman may desire to have the child adopted, she may not have either the physical or social support to do so.

Also we need to keep in mind the other alternative to abortion, carrying the child to term and keeping the child. An increasing number of women, especially among the teenage population, are choosing to keep their babies. Among the issues here are the ability and appropriateness of such young mothers to care for their child, as well as problems related to adequate financial and psychological resources to provide an appropriate setting for the rearing of the child. Often teenage mothers need to interrupt their high school education. They frequently live at home with their parents. These individuals are often already on welfare or will need such assistance. In the light of economic philosophy of the Reagan administration, that particular means of provision will either be inadequate or unavailable.[12]

Thus even though many see adoption or the keeping of the child by the mother as preferable to abortion, there are many problems involved in doing this, especially in light of the unavailability of social programs to provide a context which would facilitate these kinds of decisions. Although a variety of both counseling and economic assistance programs have been made available on a private basis, these programs are simply inadequate to deal with the needs presented by those individuals who might wish to carry a child to term and then either allow the child to be adopted or keep the child.

Health-Care Policies: Neutrality or Discrimination?

The perception, if not the reality, of the discriminatory treatment of women who choose abortion is another major problem.[13] The question is: If the federal government funds both pre- and postnatal services under Medicaid, should it also fund services for abortion? This position has been argued before the Supreme Court and the decision was that the government does not discriminate by refusing to provide funds for abortion under Title 19 of the Social Security program. Such a requirement, however, means only that such funds cannot come out of the federal budget. It is possible to continue, and in fact many states have continued, to support such abortion programs out of state funds. Nonetheless Medicaid-funded abortions dropped from 295,000 in fiscal year 1977 to about 2,000 in 1978.

Another problem that raises the issue of discrimination is the fact that those most affected by cuts in programs will be the poor. Those individuals able to afford abortions will continue to be able to afford them, whereas individuals who either cannot afford to have an abortion or who live in states which do not provide funds for abortion may not be able to obtain them. However, one study suggested that the majority of women desiring an abortion and previously qualified for Medicaid assistance still obtained one. The economic, physical, and psychological costs of doing this are not known. Also, approximately one-fifth of Medicaid-eligible women were not able to receive abortions because of funding restrictions. Thus the issue is: Will a particular group in our society have to bear a disproportionate share of the burden of such funding policies? The consequence of such a policy is that the government's position is seen not as neutral but as an aggressive policy designed to decrease the number of abortions. And since it can only do that in cases where it provides the funding, of necessity such restrictions have their most significant impact on the poor and the disadvantaged.

There are several subsidiary issues in this problem, among which are determining how abortion fits into the delivery of health-care services and the perception that abortion may be a cost-effective method to solve many of the budgetary

problems of welfare programs. It is more cost effective to provide abortions than
to provide continuing welfare payments. This observation does not begin to touch
or even analyze the structural arrangements of our society which ensure that a
certain number of individuals will always be disenfranchised both politically and
economically. We also need to determine what government neutrality with respect
to abortion might mean. Does this mean that the government should provide
nothing in the way of funds for abortion, that the government should not interfere
with anyone who wishes to obtain an abortion, or that government should help
fund any health-related service a person may want, including abortion?

Religion-Government Relations

One of the major claims of the proabortion groups is that those involved in
the antiabortion movement are trying to impose a religious solution to the problem
of abortion on those who do not hold that position and that this violates their
religious freedom. Daniel Callahan has made an important statement: there are
religious traditions which approve abortion and, by that standard, the current
policy of liberal abortion laws in this country is the imposition of one group's
religious value on another group of people.[14] Also, the claims of foul play do
seem to be related only to the abortion issue. No one is arguing that the religious
groups which are beginning to form coalitions and speak out on the inherent
injustice of the current Reagan economic program or the immorality of our nuclear
deterrence policy are violating anyone's religious liberty and that, therefore, they
should not engage in these activities.

There are several important issues in this debate, however. One has to do with
how religious beliefs or values are translated into language appropriate for public
debate. That is, is it possible to make insights and values that come from one's
religious tradition or experiences accessible to people who do not share those
experiences or traditions? The problem here is twofold: being able to make oneself
understandable to other individuals; and making the depth of one's convictions
accessible and intelligible to individuals who do not stand within that particular
tradition. Another issue has to do with ecclesiology. How is the role of the church
seen with respect to the larger society? Is the church to witness its values to
society or is the church to analyze and evaluate, and occasionally reject, social
values? If ecclesiology leads one in the first direction, then it will not be as
important to devise a means of translating insights so they can be understandable
in a broader arena. If one chooses the second way, it will be extremely important
to develop a widely accessible language so that one can easily and helpfully engage
in policy debates.

The Catholic Church in particular has attempted to develop a means of speaking both within and without through the philosophical tradition of the natural law. While acknowledging the many theoretical and practical problems in the use of that tradition, nonetheless I think it is important to remember that it provided a means by which the church could attempt to conduct a moral and political discourse with those who did not share the same theological perspectives of the Catholic community. Using this tradition, Catholic Christians could speak to the issues of the day in a language accessible to others while maintaining insights motivated by their own faith tradition.

We must also consider the appropriateness of a particular religious group putting itself both ideologically and financially behind a particular cause. Clearly religious groups have done this in the past and will continue to do so. Important in this consideration is the history of the religion's political actions and the manner and purpose in which it is perceived to be acting now. There is a broad and generally correct perception that the abortion issue is the first time in which the Roman Catholic Church has, to so significant a degree, become involved in lobbying for a particular public policy and provided rather large sums of money to help finance different organizations.

On the other hand, there seems to be nothing inherently inappropriate about a particular religious body supporting organizations to advocate a particular point of view. Almost all religions have a social ethic by which they evaluate public policy. The labor movement, civil rights, the Vietnam War, and nuclear war provide examples of how various religions did this. The relevant difference in this particular debate seems to be that it is being done with respect to abortion and by the Catholic Church. Few comments are raised about groups and churches that make financial and ideological contributions to the proabortion half of the debate, or to other political issues. In fact, I would be willing to argue that the support of churches, both financially and ideologically, would be welcomed if the churches supported a prochoice stance, or at least so I would infer from reading the list of sponsors of prochoice advertisements.

We need to insist upon some sense of fairness when discussing how churches take public stands on matters of significant concern either to them or to the population at large. The position of a particular church may not be a popular one, but it is the position of that church, and if there are serious reasons why a church feels it should engage in fairly direct political action then that stand should at least be respected. Often the real problem is the perennial one of whose ox is being gored. For many people, I suspect, as long as a church is sympathetic to their particular position, no cause will be taken with it. But when a church says something either unpopular or problematic, then some argue that churches should not speak. Such a position is at best inconsistent and at worst requires that a church maintain an inappropriate silence on issues of moral significance and political and social consequence.

The Public Debating of Abortion

How can the abortion debate be conducted in the public arena? This question is particularly problematic when viewed from perspectives developed by MacIntyre and Hauerwas, who argue that our culture has few common premises by which competing value claims can be evaluated and judged.

Alasdair MacIntyre, in his perceptive article "How to Identify Ethical Principles," argues several theses, one of which is extremely important for the consideration of ethical issues in the public policy debate.[15] His primary claim is that morality is at war with itself because each moral agent reaches conclusions by valid forms of inference but cannot agree about the correctness or appropriateness of the premise with which the argument begins. MacIntyre then argues that moral philosophy in general, and I would argue our culture in particular, has no procedures for weighing rival value premises.

This particular situation has two major dimensions. First, we have not inherited the social or cultural context in which we can both understand and apply a particular philosophical theory. Second, we have inherited conflicting theories of ethics or social philosophy. MacIntyre argues that the social-philosophical context out of which our country developed its political philosophy comes from Aristotle, Cicero, Locke, and Sidney. Each of these presents conflicting and even contrary claims with respect to what is good for humans and, even if one could resolve the epistemological problems, one would still have the practical problem of evaluating the various goods which they claim are in the interests of human beings and the community.

Briefly stated, MacIntyre says we have inherited two conflicting worldviews. First, the classical worldview which asks the moral question: How might humans together realize the common good? This position assumes that community is natural and normative, that there are goods that human beings can rationally identify and agree upon, and that the common pursuit of these will bring both personal and social development. The second claim focuses on the moral question: How may humans prevent each other from interfering with one another as each goes about his or her own concerns? This viewpoint assumes that the state of being autonomous is the appropriate state for human existence, that individuals may not have interests or values in common, and that liberty and the pursuit of interests will maximize individual and social goods.

Our culture and society have attempted to finesse the significant philosophical and ethical problems that come from inheriting a mixed system by developing a liberal society or a pluralistic society. This strategy attempted to take controversial issues out of the political arena and relegate them to the individual conscience. This solution has worked by and large for several generations, but primarily because there was a general acceptance of many of the norms or ideals about human behavior that came out of the classical model. That is, as long as the majority of the citizenry shared a common understanding of what was right and what was wrong and what the limits of individual behavior were, then pluralism could work. Behind pluralism stood a general understanding of the limits of behavior, even though this may not have been explicitly articulated or even socially enforced by the society.

However, we now appear to be in a situation in which people are attempting to maximize their own freedom and in which the suggestion that some values are normative appears to be restrictive, coercive, or, in an extreme form, politically repressive. Individuals are pursuing their own interests limited only by noninterference with a third party or not harming an unconsenting party. Such a position generally stands behind discussions relating to issues of homosexuality, some aspects of the women's movement, the use of technologies for fetal screening, heterosexual relationships, and abortion. Consequently, we have a type of moral schizophrenia in which there is some attempt, at least culturally, to hold on to values and norms from the classical mindset, while on the other hand having our instinctual argument arise out of a more modern viewpoint that argues for the maximization of freedom. Thus, debate about the merits of a particular action or policy becomes almost impossible because of the possibly unconscious, but clearly competing, ethical premises which stand at the heart of the debate: individual autonomy versus community standards.

Thus the political-ethical problem is how, in a culture such as ours, we can discuss substantive issues with profound social consequences. Picture our culture as a giant circuitry panel. To a certain point, the panel is capable of handling the load that is required of it. One can also assume that the panel could carry a certain amount of overload if there is a degree of creative recircuiting. The problem arises when the panel is required to carry a load greater than that for which it was designed. At that point the circuits begin to shut off and the system may eventually burn out. Until a couple of generations ago, our culture was able to bear the weight of some degree of cultural diversity because the system successfully socialized immigrants to the value system of the native population. Given the pressures engendered over the last couple of decades by the assassination of Kennedy, the civil-rights movement, the Vietnam War, the feminist movement, the gay-rights movement, the various urban riots precipitated both by structural racism and endemic poverty, the rise and popularity of various religious cults, and now the abortion question, perhaps the American social system is reaching the point of circuit overload. We have been successful to a certain degree in the creative recircuiting of some issues pressing upon us for many years. We can no longer avoid dealing with the assumptions and implications of these issues. But because we have no commonly accepted framework for analyzing them, we resolve the issues procedurally, using the judicial system as a means of protecting and promoting individual rights. Such a maneuver does not evaluate cases on their merits, but on procedural technicalities precisely as a way of avoiding the merits of the case. This is no longer adequate and consequently we are beginning to see the signs of a cultural backlash in which specific values, which many people may or may not agree with, are being suggested as a normative basis for socialization. We may be in danger of moving from a culture which has provided for a variability within certain limits to a culture in which all must subscribe to the same values and applications of them. The abortion debate may be the first in a series in which revised cultural values are negotiated. If that is the case, the abortion debate may be one of the most significant events of the decade.

CONCLUSIONS

The setting of policy on abortion will establish values, structures, and behaviors. Whose values will be so enshrined, which structures will be involved, and how behavior will be influenced have yet to be determined. The debate continues with different lobbies promoting their interests, no reduction in the public rancor, and little thought to how moderation or some workable compromise might be reached.

Peter Steinfels has recently made some very significant observations about how Catholics might think through a moderate abortion policy.[16] Steinfels suggests that there are two steps that should be taken, each of which involves a break with one or the other side of the current debate. The first step argues that psychological, social, and even religious disapproval of abortion will be insufficient to restrict effectively severe attacks on the value of fetal life. This argument suggests that some legislative restrictions are necessary to protect the value of life and that some women, though Steinfels argues not all, would have to carry their pregnancies to term. Such a position will be difficult for Catholic feminists and liberals—as well as many others. This option gives a high value to fetal life and recognizes that some social supports in the form of restrictive legislation are necessary to protect that life.

The second step requires liberal Catholics to break with the prolife movement by arguing that the ethical status of the fetus is a difficult moral problem, especially in the very early stages of the development of the embryo. While one can argue that even from the earliest moments of conception the conceptus is a member of the human species and is alive, it is difficult to prove in a convincing way that at that time the developing embryo has all of the rights to the preservation and protection of life as a newborn, as a child, or as an adult. The recognition of the moral ambiguity surrounding the status of the embryo would allow room to maneuver when developing a policy on abortion. But it would require a significant degree of ethical compromise for some, perhaps many, members of different churches.

What is important about Steinfels's argument is not whether his reading of policy on abortion is correct, but the fact that he has thought through the significant compromises that will need to be made in order to establish some kind of viable policy. One condition of viability for a particular policy is that two specific populations, pregnant women and fetuses, will have to suffer as a consequence. Members of different groups will experience moral compromise, but clearly not as much as pregnant women and fetuses. Compromise is seldom easy, and it will be far less easy when one recognizes that a policy may require that some women carry an unwanted pregnancy to term and that some fetuses will be aborted.

In addition to compromise, it is important for the churches to recognize that in many ways the tone and style of the abortion debate is being set by extremes on both ends of the spectrum. Data about perceptions on abortion in both the National Right to Life Committee and the National Abortion Rights Action League suggest there is some room for compromise with respect to public policy. Compromise suggests, of course, that neither of these two groups gets its way. Yet we must remember that even within the NRLC there are members who will allow abortion under some circumstances and in NARAL there are individuals who do not think that all reasons for abortion are morally significant. We need to disregard the rhetoric of the groups and their claims to purity of doctrine, but attend to the real beliefs of individuals in these organizations and in churches. As long as policy is defined by either extreme or some other single-interest group, no progress can be made because such policies will be so extreme that a viable coalition based on actual beliefs and practice cannot support it, nor can legislation be developed that recognizes both diversity of opinion and broad areas of consensus.

In addition to compromise and a policy based on the realistic beliefs of the population, whether political or religious, it is important for the society to begin providing structures which make it possible for individuals to act on their belief in the value of life and fetal life in particular. Such structures would require a high degree of fairness and coherence among many policies and would in effect suggest that funding be provided for both abortions and pre- and postnatal care. Minimal fairness requires that provision be made for people to act out their particular choices. This position is grounded in the libertarian part of our heritage. There is a genuine problem here and a real danger, for some other values may be neglected. For example, abortion is more cost-effective than the provision of social services. However, I argue that it is reprehensible to use abortion as a solution to social problems related to the health care of pregnant women and the ability of families to provide adequate food, shelter, and education for their children, as well as a minimal quality-of-life standard. Yet I need to remember that however optimally our social structures may be arranged, there always will be, I think, the need for abortion. My own hope is that a moderately restrictive policy on abortion, together with the availability of contraceptives and reasonable social policies to support women and couples who wish to have children, might permit a genuine moral debate over abortion.

Public policy on abortion must be seen as a part of a larger policy concerning the status of individual choice within a pluralistic community. The debate of public policy must be characterized by a respect for differing and often contradictory value systems professed by members of the large society, both as private individuals and as members of various voluntary associations, including the churches; a recognition that there is a large enough middle ground between the extremes upon which to make a reasonable appeal for a moderate policy on abortion; a respect for fetal life which also recognizes the moral problems in establishing an inviolable right to life for the fetus; and finally, a respect for the different positions of the churches, but with the recognition that their public policy recommendations be tested against their beliefs and actions.

There can be a responsible public policy debate on abortion, but only if we are willing to bear the burden of compromise and the responsibility of realizing wherever a line is drawn, that line will entail hardship. We as a community must be willing to provide as best we can for those individuals who must bear the burden of a particular public policy.[17]

NOTES

1. Christopher Tietze, *Induced Abortion: A World Review, 1981* (New York: Population Council) 1.

2. Ibid. 5.

3. Ibid. 34–35.

4. James C. Mohr, *Abortion in America* (New York: Oxford University Press, 1978) 20–45.

5. Ibid. 250–55.

6. Raymond Tatalovich and Byron W. Daynes, "The Trauma of Abortion Politics," *Commonweal* 107 (Nov. 20, 1981) 644–49.

7. Donald Granberg and Beth Wellman Granberg, "Abortion Attitudes, 1965–80: Trends and Determinants," *Family Planning Perspectives* 12 (Sept./Oct. 1980) 251–52.

8. Ibid. 252.

9. Ibid. 253–58.

10. Donald Granberg, "The Abortion Activists," *Family Planning Perspectives* 13 (July/Aug. 1981) 157–63.

11. James Kelly, "Beyond the Stereotypes," *Commonweal* 107 (Nov. 20, 1981) 654–59.

12. Perihan A. Rosenthal, "Adolescence and Pregnancy," Department of Psychiatry, University of Massachusetts Medical Center, unpublished manuscript. Richard P. Perkins

and others, "Intensive Care in Adolescent Pregnancy," *Obstetrics and Gynecology* 52 (Aug. 1978), pp. 179–88.

13. The perception certainly approaches reality when one hears Senator Hyde, who sponsored legislation to restrict abortions paid for by Medicaid to those which threatened the life of the woman, say: "I certainly would like to prevent, if I could legally, anybody having an abortion, a rich woman, a middle-class woman or a poor woman. Unfortunately, the only vehicle available is the HEW Medicaid bill. A life is a life." *The Congressional Record*, June 17, 1977, p. H 6083. Quoted from *Family Planning Perspectives* 12 (May/ June 1980) 121.

14. Daniel Callahan, "Abortion: Some Ethical Issues," in *Bioethics*, ed. T. A. Shannon, rev. ed. (New York: Paulist Press, 1981) 16.

15. Alasdair MacIntyre, "How to Identify Ethical Principles," *The Belmont Report*, Appendix, Volume I. DHEW Publication No. (OS) 78-0013. 10-1-41.

16. Peter Steinfels, "The Search for an Alternative," *Commonweal* 107 (Nov. 20, 1981) 660–64.

17. Parts of this article were originally published as "Abortion: A Review of Ethical Aspects of Public Policy," in *Abortion and the Status of the Fetus*, ed. W. B. Bondeson, H. T. Engelhardt, Jr., S. F. Spicker, and D. Winship (Boston: D. Reidel, 1982).

Religious Belief and Public Morality:
A Catholic Governor's Perspective

Mario Cuomo

I would like to begin by drawing your attention to the title of this lecture: "Religious Belief and Public Morality: A Catholic Governor's Perspective." I was not invited to speak on church and state generally. Certainly not Mondale vs. Reagan. The subject assigned is difficult enough. I will not try to do more than I've been asked.

It's not easy to stay contained. Certainly, although everybody talks about a wall of separation between church and state, I've seen religious leaders scale that wall with all the dexterity of Olympic athletes. In fact, I've seen so many candidates in churches and synagogues that I think we should change election day from Tuesdays to Saturdays and Sundays.

I am honored by this invitation, but the record shows that I am not the first governor of New York to appear at an event involving Notre Dame. One of my great predecessors, Al Smith, went to the Army–Notre Dame football game each time it was played in New York.

His fellow Catholics expected Smith to sit with Notre Dame; protocol required him to sit with Army because it was the home team. Protocol prevailed. But not without Smith noting the dual demands on his affections. "I'll take my seat with Army," he said, "but I commend my soul to Notre Dame!"

Today I'm happy to have no such problem: Both my seat and my soul are with Notre Dame. And as long as Father McBrien doesn't invite me back to sit with him at the Notre Dame–St. John's basketball game, I'm confident my loyalties will remain undivided.

In a sense, it's a question of loyalty that Father McBrien has asked me here today to discuss. Specifically, must politics and religion in America divide our loyalties? Does the "separation between church and state" imply separation between religion and politics? Between morality and government? Are these different propositions? Even more specifically, what is the relationship of my Catholicism to my politics? Where does the one end and other begin? Or are the two divided at all? And if they're not, should they be?

Hard questions.

No wonder most of us in public life—at least until recently—preferred to stay away from them, heeding the biblical advice that if "hounded and pursued in one city," we should flee to another.

Now, however, I think that it is too late to flee. The questions are all around us, and answers are coming from every quarter. Some of them have been simplistic, most of them fragmentary and a few, spoken with a purely political intent, demagogic.

There has been confusion and compounding of confusion, a blurring of the issue, entangling it in personalities and election strategies instead of clarifying it for Catholics, as well as others.

Today I would like to try to help correct that.

I can offer you no final truths, complete and unchallengeable. But it's possible this one effort will provoke other efforts—both in support and contradiction of my position—that will help all of us understand our differences and perhaps even discover some basic agreement.

In the end, I'm convinced we will all benefit if suspicion is replaced by discussion, innuendo by dialogue; if the emphasis in our debate turns from a search for talismanic criteria and neat but simplistic answers to an honest—more intelligent—attempt at describing the role religion has in our public affairs and the limits placed on that role.

And if we do it right—if we're not afraid of the truth even when the truth is complex—this debate, by clarification, can bring relief to untold numbers of confused—even anguished—Catholics, as well as to many others who want only to make our already great democracy even stronger than it is.

I believe the recent discussion in my own state has already produced some clearer definition. In early summer an impression was created in some quarters that official church spokespeople would ask Catholics to vote for or against candidates on the basis of their political position on the abortion issue. I was one of those given that impression. Thanks to the dialogue that ensued over the summer—only partially reported by the media—we learned that the impression was not accurate.

Confusion had presented an opportunity for clarification, and we seized it. Now all of us are saying one thing—in chorus—reiterating the statement of the National Conference of Catholic Bishops that they will not "take positions for or against political candidates" and that their stand on specific issues would not be perceived "as an expression of political partisanship."

Of course the bishops will teach—they must—more and more vigorously and more and more extensively. But they have said they will not use the power of their position, and the great respect it receives from all Catholics, to give an imprimatur to individual politicians or parties.

Not that they couldn't if they wished to—some religious leaders do; some are doing it at this very moment.

Not that it would be a sin if they did—God doesn't insist on political neutrality. But because it is the judgment of the bishops, and most of us Catholic lay people, that it is not wise for prelates and politicians to be tied too closely together.

I think that getting this consensus was an extraordinarily useful achievement.

Now, with some trepidation, I take up your gracious invitation to continue the dialogue in the hope that it will lead to still further clarification.

Let me begin this part of the effort by underscoring the obvious. I do not speak as a theologian; I do not have that competence. I do not speak as a philosopher; to suggest that I could would be to set a new record for false pride. I don't presume to speak as a "good" person except in the ontological sense of that word. My principal credential is that I serve in a position that forces me to wrestle with the problems you've come here to study and debate.

I am by training a lawyer and by practice a politician. Both professions make me suspect in many quarters, including among some of my own coreligionists. Maybe there's no better illustration of the public perception of how politicians unite their faith and their profession than the story they tell in New York about "Fishhooks" McCarthy, a famous Democratic leader on the Lower East Side and right-hand man to Al Smith.

"Fishhooks," the story goes, was devout. So devout that every morning on his way to Tammany Hall to do his political work, he stopped into St. James Church on Oliver Street in downtown Manhattan, fell on his knees and whispered the same simple prayer: "Oh, Lord, give me health and strength. We'll steal the rest."

"Fishhooks" notwithstanding, I speak here as a politician. And also as a Catholic, a lay person baptized and raised in the pre–Vatican II church, educated in Catholic schools, attached to the church first by birth, then by choice, now by love. An old-fashioned Catholic who sins, regrets, struggles, worries, gets confused and most of the time feels better after confession.

The Catholic Church is my spiritual home. My heart is there and my hope.

There is, of course, more to being a Catholic than a sense of spiritual and emotional resonance. Catholicism is a religion of the head as well as the heart, and to be a Catholic is to say "I believe" to the essential core of dogmas that distinguishes our faith.

The acceptance of this faith requires a lifelong struggle to understand it more fully and to live it more truly, to translate truth into experience, to practice as well as to believe.

That's not easy: Applying religious belief to everyday life often presents challenges.

It's always been that way. It certainly is today. The America of the late twentieth century is a consumer society, filled with endless distractions, where faith is more often dismissed than challenged, where the ethnic and other loyalties that once fastened us to our religion seem to be weakening.

In addition to all the weaknesses, dilemmas and temptations that impede every pilgrim's progress, the Catholic who holds political office in a pluralistic democracy—who is elected to serve Jews and Moslems, atheists and Protestants, as well as Catholics—bears special responsibility. He or she undertakes to help create conditions under which all can live with a maximum of dignity and with a reasonable degree of freedom; where everyone who chooses may hold beliefs different from specifically Catholic ones—sometimes contradictory to them; where the laws protect people's rights to divorce, to use birth control and even to choose abortion.

In fact, Catholic public officials take an oath to preserve the Constitution that guarantees this freedom. And they do so gladly. Not because they love what others do with their freedom, but because they realize that in guaranteeing freedom for all, they guarantee our right to be Catholics: our right to pray, to use the sacraments, to refuse birth control devices, to reject abortion, not to divorce and remarry if we believe it to be wrong.

The Catholic public official lives the political truth most Catholics through most of American history have accepted and insisted on: the truth that to assure our freedom we must allow others the same freedom, even if occasionally it produces conduct by them which we would hold to be sinful.

I protect my right to be a Catholic by preserving your right to believe as a Jew, a Protestant or nonbeliever, or as anything else you choose.

We know that the price of seeking to force our beliefs on others is that they might some day force theirs on us.

This freedom is the fundamental strength of our unique experiment in government. In the complex interplay of forces and considerations that go into the making of our laws and politics, its preservation must be a pervasive and dominant concern.

But insistence on freedom is easier to accept as a general proposition than in its applications to specific situations. There are other valid general principles firmly embedded in our Constitution which, operating at the same time, create interesting and occasionally troubling problems. Thus the same amendment of the Constitution that forbids the establishment of a state church affirms my legal right to argue that my religious belief would serve well as an article of our universal public morality. I may use the prescribed processes of government—the legislative and executive and judicial processes—to convince my fellow citizens—Jews and Protestants and Buddhists and nonbelievers—that what I propose is as beneficial for them as I believe it is for me; that it is not just parochial or narrowly sectarian but fulfills a human desire for order, peace, justice, kindness, love, any of the values most of us agree are desirable even apart from their specific religious base or context.

I am free to argue for a governmental policy for a nuclear freeze, not just to avoid sin but because I think my democracy should regard it as a desirable goal.

I can, if I wish, argue that the state should not fund the use of contraceptive devices, not because the pope demands it, but because I think that the whole community—for the good of the whole community—should not sever sex from an openness to the creation of life.

And surely I can, if so inclined, demand some kind of law against abortion, not because my bishops say it is wrong, but because I think that the whole community, regardless of its religious beliefs, should agree on the importance of protecting life—including life in the womb, which is at the very least potentially human and should not be extinguished casually.

No law prevents us from advocating any of these things: I am free to do so. So are the bishops. And so is Rev. Falwell.

In fact, the Constitution guarantees my right to try. And theirs. And his.

But should I? Is it helpful? Is it essential to human dignity? Does it promote harmony and understanding? Or does it divide us so fundamentally that it threatens our ability to function as a pluralistic community?

When should I argue to make my religious value your morality? My rule of conduct your limitation?

What are the rules and policies that should influence the exercise of this right to argue and promote?

I believe I have a salvific mission as a Catholic. Does that mean I am in conscience required to do everything I can as governor to translate all my religious values into the laws and regulations of the state of New York or the United States? Or be branded a hypocrite if I don't?

As a Catholic, I respect the teaching authority of the bishops.

But must I agree with everything in the bishops' pastoral letter on peace and fight to include it in party platforms?

And will I have to do the same for the forthcoming pastoral on economics even if I am an unrepentant supply-sider?

Must I, having heard the pope renew the church's ban on birth control devices, veto the funding of contraceptive programs for non-Catholics or dissenting Catholics in my state?

I accept the church's teaching on abortion. Must I insist you do? By law? By denying you Medicaid funding? By a constitutional amendment? If so, which one? Would that be the best way to avoid abortions or to prevent them?

These are only some of the questions for Catholics. People with other religious beliefs face similar problems.

Let me try some answers.

Almost all Americans accept some religious values as a part of our public life. We are a religious people, many of us descended from ancestors who came here expressly to live their religious faith free from coercion or repression. But we are also a people of many religions, with no established church, who hold different beliefs on many matters.

Our public morality, then—moral standards we maintain for everyone, not just the ones we insist on in our private lives—depends on a consensus view of right and wrong. The values derived from religious belief will not—and should not—be accepted as part of the public morality unless they are shared by the pluralistic community at large, by consensus.

That values happen to be religious values does not deny them acceptability as a part of this consensus. But it does not require their acceptability, either.

The agnostics who joined the civil rights struggle were not deterred because that crusade's values had been nurtured and sustained in black Christian churches. Those on the political left are not perturbed today by the religious bias of the clergy and lay people who join them in the protest against the arms race and hunger and exploitation.

The arguments start when religious values are used to support positions which would impose on other people restrictions they find unacceptable. Some people do object to Catholic demands for an end to abortion, seeing it as a violation of the separation of church and state. And some others, while they have no compunction about invoking the authority of the Catholic bishops in regard to birth control and abortion, might reject out of hand their teaching on war and peace and social policy.

Ultimately, therefore, the question whether or not we admit religious values into our public affairs is too broad to yield a single answer. Yes, we create our public morality through consensus, and in this country that consensus reflects to some extent religious values of a great majority of Americans. But no, all religiously based values don't have an *a priori* place in our public morality.

The community must decide if what is being proposed would be better left to private discretion than public policy; whether it restricts freedoms and if so to what end, to whose benefit; whether it will produce a good or bad result; whether overall it will help the community or merely divide it.

The right answers to these questions can be elusive. Some of the wrong answers, on the other hand, are quite clear. For example, there are those who say there is a simple answer to all these questions; they say that by history and practice of our people we were intended to be—and should be—a Christian country in law.

But where would that leave the nonbelievers? And whose Christianity would be law, yours or mine?

This "Christian-nation" argument should concern—even frighten—two groups: non-Christians and thinking Christians.

I believe it does.

I think it's already apparent that a good part of this nation understands—if only instinctively—that anything which seems to suggest that God favors a political party or the establishment of a state church is wrong and dangerous.

Way down deep the American people are afraid of an entangling relationship between formal religions—or whole bodies of religious belief—and government. Apart from constitutional law and religious doctrine, there is a sense that tells us it's wrong to presume to speak for God or to claim God's sanction of our particular legislation and his rejection of all other positions. Most of us are offended when we see religion being trivialized by its appearance in political throwaway pamphlets.

The American people need no course in philosophy or political science or church history to know that God should not be made into a celestial party chairman.

To most of us, the manipulative invoking of religion to advance a politician or a party is frightening and divisive. The American people will tolerate religious leaders taking positions for or against candidates, although I think the Catholic bishops are right in avoiding that position. But the American people are leery about large religious organizations, powerful churches or synagogue groups engaging in such activities—again, not as a matter of law or doctrine, but because our innate wisdom and democratic instinct teach us these things are dangerous.

Today there are a number of issues involving life and death that raise questions of public morality. They are also questions of concern to most religions. Pick up a newspaper and you are almost certain to find a bitter controversy over any one of them: Baby Jane Doe, the right to die, artificial insemination, embryos *in vitro,* abortion, birth control—not to mention nuclear war and the shadow it throws across all existence.

Some of these issues touch the most intimate recesses of our lives, our roles as someone's mother or child or husband; some affect women in a unique way. But they are also public questions, for all of us.

Put aside what God expects—assume if you like there is no God—then the greatest thing still left to us is life. Even a radically secular world must struggle with the questions of when life begins, under what circumstances it can be ended, when it must be protected, by what authority; it too must decide what protection to extend to the helpless and the dying, to the aged and the unborn, to life in all its phases.

As a Catholic I have accepted certain answers as the right ones for myself and my family and because I have, they have influenced me in special ways, as Matilda's husband, as a father of five children, as a son who stood next to his own father's deathbed trying to decide if the tubes and needles no longer served a purpose.

As a governor, however, I am involved in defining policies that determine other people's rights in these same areas of life and death. Abortion is one of these issues, and while it is one issue among many, it is one of the most controversial and affects me in a special way as a Catholic public official.

So let me spend some time considering it.

I should start, I believe, by noting that the Catholic Church's actions with respect to the interplay of religious values and public policy make clear that there is no inflexible moral principle which determines what our political conduct should be. For example, on divorce and birth control, without changing its moral teaching the church abides the civil law as it now stands, thereby accepting— without making much of a point of it—that in our pluralistic society we are not required to insist that all our religious values be the law of the land.

Abortion is treated differently.

Of course there are differences both in degree and quality between abortion and some of the other religious positions the church takes: Abortion is a "matter of life and death," and degree counts. But the differences in approach reveal a truth, I think, that is not well enough perceived by Catholics and therefore still further complicates the process for us. That is, while we always owe our bishops' words respectful attention and careful consideration, the question whether to engage the political system in a struggle to have it adopt certain articles of our belief as part of public morality is not a matter of doctrine: It is a matter of prudential political judgment.

Recently, Michael Novak put it succinctly: "Religious judgment and political judgment are both needed," he wrote. "But they are not identical."

My church and my conscience require me to believe certain things about divorce, birth control and abortion. My church does not order me—under pain of sin or expulsion—to pursue my salvific mission according to a precisely defined political plan.

As a Catholic I accept the church's teaching authority. While in the past some Catholic theologians may appear to have disagreed on the morality of some abortions (it wasn't, I think, until 1869 that excommunication was attached to all abortions without distinction), and while some theologians still do, I accept the bishops' position that abortion is to be avoided.

As Catholics my wife and I were enjoined never to use abortion to destroy the life we created, and we never have. We thought church doctrine was clear on this, and—more than that—both of us felt it in full agreement with what our hearts and our consciences told us. For me, life or fetal life in the womb should be protected, even if five of nine justices of the Supreme Court and my neighbor disagree with me. A fetus is different from an appendix or a set of tonsils. At the very least, even if the argument is made by some scientists or some theologians that in the early stages of fetal development we can't discern human life, the full potential of human life is indisputably there. That—to my less subtle mind— by itself should demand respect, caution, indeed—reverence.

But not everyone in our society agrees with me and Matilda.

And those who don't—those who endorse legalized abortions—aren't a ruthless, callous alliance of anti-Christians determined to overthrow our moral standards. In many cases the proponents of legal abortion are the very people who have worked with Catholics to realize the goals of social justice set out in papal encyclicals: the American Lutheran Church, the Central Conference of American Rabbis, the Presbyterian Church in the United States, B'nai B'rith Women, the

Women of the Episcopal Church. These are just a few of the religious organizations that don't share the church's position on abortion.

Certainly we should not be forced to mold Catholic morality to conform to disagreement by non-Catholics however sincere or severe their disagreement. Our bishops should be teachers, not pollsters. They should not change what we Catholics believe in order to ease our consciences or please our friends or protect the church from criticism.

But if the breadth, intensity and sincerity of opposition to church teaching shouldn't be allowed to shape our Catholic morality, it can't help but determine our ability—our realistic, political ability—to translate our Catholic morality into civil law, a law not for the believers who don't need it but for the disbelievers who reject it.

And it is here, in our attempt to find a political answer to abortion—an answer beyond our private observance of Catholic morality—that we encounter controversy within and without the church over how and in what degree to press the case that our morality should be everybody else's, and to what effect.

I repeat, there is no church teaching that mandates the best political course for making our belief everyone's rule, for spreading this part of our Catholicism. There is neither an encyclical nor a catechism that spells out a political strategy for achieving legislative goals.

And so the Catholic trying to make moral and prudent judgments in the political realm must discern which, if any, of the actions one could take would be best.

This latitude of judgment is not something new in the church, not a development that has arisen only with the abortion issue. Take, for example, the question of slavery. It has been argued that the failure to endorse a legal ban on abortions is equivalent to refusing to support the cause of abolition before the Civil War. This analogy has been advanced by the bishops of my own state.

But the truth of the matter is, few if any Catholic bishops spoke for abolition in the years before the Civil War. It wasn't, I believe, that the bishops endorsed the idea of some humans owning and exploiting other humans; Pope Gregory XVI in 1840 had condemned the slave trade. Instead it was a practical political judgment that the bishops made. They weren't hypocrites; they were realists. At the time Catholics were a small minority, mostly immigrants, despised by much of the population, often vilified and the object of sporadic violence. In the face of a public controversy that aroused tremendous passions and threatened to break the country apart, the bishops made a pragmatic decision. They believed their opinion would not change people's minds. Moreover they knew that there were Southern Catholics, even some priests, who owned slaves. They concluded that under the circumstances arguing for a constitutional amendment against slavery would do more harm than good, so they were silent. As they have been generally in recent years on the question of birth control. And as the church has been on even more controversial issues in the past, even ones that dealt with life and death.

What is relevant to this discussion is that the bishops were making judgments about translating Catholic teachings into public policy, not about the moral validity of the teachings. In so doing they grappled with the unique political complexities of their time. The decision they made to remain silent on a constitutional amendment to abolish slavery or on the repeal of the Fugitive Slave Law wasn't a mark of their moral indifference; it was a measured attempt to balance moral truths against political realities. Their decision reflected their sense of complexity, not their diffidence. As history reveals, Lincoln behaved with similar discretion.

The parallel I want to draw here is not between or among what we Catholics believe to be moral wrongs. It is in the Catholic response to those wrongs. Church teaching on slavery and abortion is clear. But in the application of those teachings—the exact way we translate them into action, the specific laws we propose, the exact legal sanctions we seek—there was and is no one, clear, absolute route that the church says, as a matter of doctrine, we must follow.

The bishops' pastoral letter "The Challenge of Peace" speaks directly to this point. "We recognize," the bishops wrote, "that the church's teaching authority does not carry the same force when it deals with technical solutions involving particular means as it does when it speaks of principles or ends. People may agree in abhorring an injustice, for instance, yet sincerely disagree as to what practical approach will achieve justice. Religious groups are as entitled as others to their opinion in such cases, but they should not claim that their opinions are the only ones that people of good will may hold."

With regard to abortion, the American bishops have had to weigh Catholic moral teaching against the fact of a pluralistic country where our view is in the minority, acknowledging that what is ideally desirable isn't always feasible, that there can be different political approaches to abortion besides unyielding adherence to an absolute prohibition.

This is in the American Catholic tradition of political realism. In supporting or opposing specific legislation the church in this country has never retreated into a moral fundamentalism that will settle for nothing less than total acceptance of its views.

Indeed, the bishops have already confronted the fact that an absolute ban on abortion doesn't have the support necessary to be placed in our Constitution. In 1981 they put aside earlier efforts to describe a law they could accept and get passed, and supported the Hatch Amendment instead.

Some Catholics felt the bishops had gone too far with that action, some not far enough. Such judgments were not a rejection of the bishops' teaching authority: The bishops even disagreed among themselves. Catholics are allowed to disagree on these technical political questions without having to confess.

Respectfully and after careful consideration of the position and arguments of the bishops, I have concluded that the approach of a constitutional amendment is not the best way for us to seek to deal with abortion.

I believe that legal interdicting of abortion by either the federal government or the individual states is not a plausible possibility and even if it could be obtained, it wouldn't work. Given present attitudes, it would be Prohibition revisited, legislating what couldn't be enforced and in the process creating a disrespect for law in general. And as much as I admire the bishops' hope that a constitutional amendment against abortion would be the basis for a full, new bill of rights for mothers and children, I disagree that this would be the result.

I believe that, more likely, a constitutional prohibition would allow people to ignore the causes of many abortions instead of addressing them, much the way the death penalty is used to escape dealing more fundamentally and more rationally with the problem of violent crime.

Other legal options that have been proposed are, in my view, equally ineffective. The Hatch Amendment, by returning the question of abortion to the states, would have given us a checkerboard of permissive and restrictive jurisdictions. In some cases people might have been forced to go elsewhere to have abortions, and that might have eased a few consciences, but it wouldn't have done what the church wants to do—it wouldn't have created a deep-seated respect for life. Abortions would have gone on, millions of them.

Nor would a denial of Medicaid funding for abortion achieve our objectives. Given *Roe v. Wade*, it would be nothing more than an attempt to do indirectly what the law says cannot be done directly; worse, it would do it in a way that would burden only the already disadvantaged. Removing funding from the Medicaid program would not prevent the rich and middle classes from having abortions. It would not even assure that the disadvantaged wouldn't have them; it would only impose financial burdens on poor women who want abortions.

Apart from that unevenness, there is a more basic question. Medicaid is designed to deal with health and medical needs. But the arguments for the cutoff of Medicaid abortion funds are not related to those needs. They are moral arguments. If we assume health and medical needs exist, our personal view of morality ought not to be considered a relevant basis for discrimination.

We must keep in mind always that we are a nation of laws—when we like those laws and when we don't.

The Supreme Court has established a woman's constitutional right to abortion. The Congress has decided the federal government should not provide federal funding in the Medicaid program for abortion. That, of course, does not bind states in the allocation of their own state funds. Under the law, the individual states need not follow the federal lead, and in New York I believe we cannot follow that lead. The equal protection clause in New York's Constitution has been interpreted by the courts as a standard of fairness that would preclude us from denying only the poor—indirectly, by a cutoff of funds—the practical use of the constitutional right given by *Roe v. Wade*.

In the end, even if after a long and divisive struggle we were able to remove all Medicaid funding for abortion and restore the law to what it was—if we could put most abortions out of our sight, return them to the backrooms where they were performed for so long—I don't believe our responsibility as Catholics would be any closer to being fulfilled than it is now, with abortion guaranteed by law as a woman's right.

The hard truth is that abortion isn't a failure of government. No agency or department of government forces women to have abortions, but abortion goes on. Catholics, the statistics show, support the right to abortion in equal proportion to the rest of the population. Despite the teaching in our homes and schools and pulpits, despite the sermons and pleadings of parents and priests and prelates, despite all the effort at defining our opposition to the sin of abortion, collectively we Catholics apparently believe—and perhaps act—little differently from those who don't share our commitment.

Are we asking government to make criminal what we believe to be sinful because we ourselves can't stop committing the sin?

The failure here is not Caesar's. This failure is our failure, the failure of the entire people of God.

Nobody has expressed this better than a bishop in my own state, Joseph Sullivan, a man who works with the poor in New York City, is resolutely opposed to abortion and argues, with his fellow bishops, for a change of law. "The major problem the church has is internal," the bishop said last month in reference to abortion. "How do we teach? As much as I think we're responsible for advocating public-policy issues, our primary responsibility is to teach our own people. We haven't done that. We're asking politicians to do what we haven't done effectively ourselves."

I agree with the bishop. I think our moral and social mission as Catholics must begin with the wisdom contained in the words "Physician, heal thyself." Unless we Catholics educate ourselves better to the values that define—and can ennoble—our lives, following those teachings better than we do now, unless we set an example that is clear and compelling, then we will never convince this society to change the civil laws to protect what we preach is precious human life.

Better than any law or rule or threat of punishment would be the moving strength of our own good example, demonstrating our lack of hypocrisy, proving the beauty and worth of our instruction.

We must work to find ways to avoid abortions without otherwise violating our faith. We should provide funds and opportunity for young women to bring their child to term, knowing both of them will be taken care of if that is necessary; we should teach our young men better than we do now their responsibilities in creating and caring for human life.

It is this duty of the church to teach through its practice of love that Pope John Paul II has proclaimed so magnificently to all peoples. "The church," he wrote in *Redemptor hominis* (1979), "which has no weapons at her disposal apart from those of the Spirit, of the word and of love, cannot renounce her proclamation of 'the word . . . in season and out of season.' For this reason she does not cease to implore . . . everybody in the name of God and in the name of man: Do not kill! Do not prepare destruction and extermination for each other! Think of your brothers and sisters who are suffering hunger and misery! Respect each one's dignity and freedom!"

The weapons of the word and of love are already available to us: We need no statute to provide them.

I am not implying that we should stand by and pretend indifference to whether a woman takes a pregnancy to its conclusion or aborts it. I believe we should in all cases try to teach a respect for life. And I believe with regard to abortion that, despite *Roe v. Wade*, we can, in practical ways. Here, in fact, it seems to me that all of us can agree.

Without lessening their insistence on a woman's right to an abortion, the people who call themselves "prochoice" can support the development of government programs that present an impoverished mother with the full range of support she needs to bear and raise her children, to have a real choice. Without dropping their campaign to ban abortion, those who gather under the banner of "prolife" can join in developing and enacting a legislative bill of rights for mothers and children, as the bishops have already proposed.

While we argue over abortion, the U.S. infant-mortality rate places us sixteenth among the nations of the world. Thousands of infants die each year because of inadequate medical care. Some are born with birth defects that, with proper treatment, could be prevented. Some are stunted in their physical and mental growth because of improper nutrition.

If we want to prove our regard for life in the womb, for the helpless infant— if we care about women having real choices in their lives and not being driven to abortions by a sense of helplessness and despair about the future of their child— then there is work enough for all of us. Lifetimes of it.

In New York, we have put in place a number of programs to begin this work, assisting women in giving birth to healthy babies. This year we doubled Medicaid funding to private-care physicians for prenatal and delivery services.

The state already spends $20 million a year for prenatal care in outpatient clinics and for inpatient hospital care.

One program in particular we believe holds a great deal of promise. It's called "New Avenues to Dignity," and it seeks to provide a teen-age mother with the special service she needs to continue with her education, to train for a job, to become capable of standing on her own, to provide for herself and the child she is bringing into the world.

My dissent, then, from the contention that we can have effective and enforceable legal prohibitions on abortion is by no means an argument for religious quietism, for accepting the world's wrongs because that is our fate as "the poor banished children of Eve."

Let me make another point.

Abortion has a unique significance but not a preemptive significance.

Apart from the question of the efficacy of using legal weapons to make people stop having abortions, we know our Christian responsibility doesn't end with any one law or amendment. That it doesn't end with abortion. Because it involves life and death, abortion will always be a central concern of Catholics. But so will nuclear weapons. And hunger and homelessness and joblessness, all the forces diminishing human life and threatening to destroy it. The "seamless garment" that Cardinal Bernardin has spoken of is a challenge to all Catholics in public office, conservatives as well as liberals.

We cannot justify our aspiration to goodness simply on the basis of the vigor of our demand for an elusive and questionable civil law declaring what we already know, that abortion is wrong.

Approval or rejection of legal restrictions on abortion should not be the exclusive litmus test of Catholic loyalty. We should understand that whether abortion is outlawed or not, our work has barely begun: the work of creating a society where the right to life doesn't end at the moment of birth; where an infant isn't helped into a world that doesn't care if it's fed properly, housed decently, educated adequately; where the blind or retarded child isn't condemned to exist rather than empowered to live.

The bishops stated this duty clearly in 1974 in their statement to the Senate subcommittee considering a proposed amendment to restrict abortions. They maintained such an amendment could not be seen as an end in itself. "We do not see a constitutional amendment as the final product of our commitment or of our legislative activity," they said. "It is instead the constitutional base on which to provide support and assistance to pregnant women and their unborn children. This would include nutritional, prenatal, childbirth and postnatal care for the mother, and also nutritional and pediatric care for the child through the first year of life. . . . We believe that all of these should be available as a matter of right to all pregnant women and their children."

The bishops reaffirmed that view in 1976, in 1980 and again this year when the U.S. Catholic Conference asked Catholics to judge candidates on a wide range of issues—on abortion, yes; but also on food policy, the arms race, human rights, education, social justice and military expenditures.

The bishops have been consistently "prolife" in the full meaning of that term, and I respect them for that.

The problems created by the matter of abortion are complex and confounding. Nothing is clearer to me than my inadequacy to find compelling solutions to all of their moral, legal and social implications. I—and many others like me—are eager for enlightenment, eager to learn new and better ways to manifest respect for the deep reverence for life that is our religion and our instinct. I hope that this public attempt to describe the problems as I understand them will give impetus to the dialogue in the Catholic community and beyond, a dialogue which could show me a better wisdom than I've been able to find so far.

It would be tragic if we let that dialogue become a prolonged, divisive argument that destroys or impairs our ability to practice any part of the morality given us in the Sermon on the Mount, to touch, heal and affirm the human life that surrounds us.

We Catholic citizens of the richest, most powerful nation that has ever exisited are like the stewards made responsible over a great household: From those to whom so much has been given, much shall be required. It is worth repeating that ours is not a faith that encourages its believers to stand apart from the world, seeking their salvation alone, separate from the salvation of those around them.

We speak of ourselves as a body. We come together in worship as companions, in the ancient sense of that word, those who break bread together and who are obliged by the commitment we share to help one another, everywhere, in all we do and in the process to help the whole human family. We see our mission to be "the completion of the work of creation."

This is difficult work today. It presents us with many hard choices.

The Catholic Church has come of age in America. The ghetto walls are gone, our religion no longer a badge of irredeemable foreignness. This new-found status is both an opportunity and a temptation. If we choose, we can give in to the temptation to become more and more assimilated into a larger, blander culture, abandoning the practice of the specific values that made us different, worshiping whatever gods the marketplace has to sell while we seek to rationalize our own laxity by urging the political system to legislate on others a morality we no longer practice ourselves.

Or we can remember where we come from, the journey of two millennia, clinging to our personal faith, to its insistence on constancy and service and on hope. We can live and practice the morality Christ gave us, maintaining his truth in this world, struggling to embody his love, practicing it especially where that love is most needed, among the poor and the weak and the dispossessed. Not just by trying to make laws for others to live by, but by living the laws already written for us by God, in our hearts and our minds.

We can be fully Catholic: proudly, totally at ease with ourselves, a people in the world, transforming it, a light to this nation. Appealing to the best in our people, not the worst. Persuading not coercing. Leading people to truth by love. And still, all the while, respecting and enjoying our unique pluralistic democracy. And we can do it even as politicians.

The Fetus and Fundamental Rights

Joan C. Callahan

THE CONSISTENCY PROBLEM

Although the 1984 presidential election is history, the campaigns raised a number of questions which have not been resolved, and which need more public discussion. Not the least among these are the questions that surrounded Geraldine Ferraro's position on abortion—a position that significantly disrupted her campaign, and which, during the early fall of 1984, put all liberal Democratic Catholic politicians into political trouble from which they have not yet escaped.[1]

The trouble was focused on the question of abortion, but the problem is deeper than any single issue. The problem is one of consistency: How can a politician believe that something is profoundly morally wrong, yet insist that he or she will not use political power to right the wrong? The reply from the Geraldine Ferraros and the Edward Kennedys was that it is not the proper business of the politician to impose his or her religious beliefs on members of a pluralistic society. Although this is surely true, it was an inadequate response. It was inadequate because it missed the point; and it missed the point because it seemed to treat matters like our public policy on abortion as if they were the same in kind as eating meat on Friday or making one's Easter Duty. The Catholic politicians may not have been making a category mistake, but they certainly sometimes sounded as if they were. Bishop James Timlin of Scranton did not have to be a bishop, a Roman Catholic, or even a Christian to say with understandable astonishment that Geraldine Ferraro's position on abortion is like saying "I'm personally opposed to slavery, but I don't care if people down the street want to own slaves."[2] The Catholic liberal Democrats thought and think this analogy fails. But *why* it fails was never made clear. In what follows, I want to address Bishop Timlin's analogy and hence, the particular question of abortion, as well as the larger question of appropriate reasons for a politician's policy choices. My purpose is to get clearer on both the morality of elective abortion and the question of moral consistency in political life.

RELIGIOUS V. PHILOSOPHICAL REASONS

Bishop Timlin's analogy is faulty in at least three ways. First, refusing to use the law to fight a practice one believes is immoral does not imply that one does not *care* if people engage in that practice. Mario Cuomo, in his thoughtful, if not wholly adequate, speech at Notre Dame made that very clear.[3] There is no doubt that Mr. Cuomo cares deeply about abortion. But we can cite any number of examples (e.g., the selfish breaking of promises, the telling of lies to friends for bad reasons, etc.) of actions we believe are morally wrong and about which we care, but which we do not (and should not) attempt to eradicate by law. Thus, it does not follow from the fact that someone is unwilling to pursue a legal prohibition on some kind of activity that the person does not care if people engage in that activity. Nor does it follow from the fact that one believes that some kind of action is morally wrong that one is morally obligated to seek a legal prohibition on that kind of action.

Bishop Timlin's analogy is also faulty because it fails to recognize that the *reasons* one has for holding something to be wrong are of the utmost importance when one is trying to decide whether to pursue a legal prohibition on individual liberty. In a pluralistic society, the fact that a religious institution, or a religious contingency (no matter how large), holds something to be wrong is simply not a good reason for setting a public policy prohibiting or requiring action on the part of all citizens. Insofar as a Catholic politician's reason for holding that abortion is wrong is that this is church doctrine, there can be no obligation to try to institute a prohibition on abortion on those who do not share the same religious affiliation. Indeed, part of the politician's obligation in a pluralistic society is to guard against just such impositions by religious groups. In the vice-presidential debate, Congresswoman Ferraro made it clear that her reason for being "personally" opposed to abortion is that her church holds this as doctrine. If this is indeed *why* she is opposed to abortion, then it ought to be clear to all of us that she has no more duty (or right) to try to capture her opposition to abortion in law than she has to try to force Americans who do not share her religious affiliation to attend Roman Catholic Mass weekly. And the same is true for any other politician who is opposed to abortion *because* this is a doctrine of his or her faith.[4]

But there are other reasons for being opposed to abortion—philosophical reasons which appeal to the laws of logic and to moral rights—which might be shared by the most ardent atheist. Many who are opposed to abortion have these kinds of reasons for holding that abortion is wrong, and so profoundly wrong that it might be rightly prohibited by law, even in a pluralistic society. We need, then, to make a distinction between those who hold that abortion is wrong simply because their religion says so, and those who think that abortion is wrong because they believe that the philosophical reasons compel us to accept that human fetuses have a right not to be killed which is comparable to your right and my right not to be killed.

Reasons of the first kind (i.e., purely religious reasons) are excellent reasons for acting or not acting in certain ways in one's own life, but they are bad reasons for imposing legal requirements or legal restraints on those who do not share the same religious commitments. We all know this. If some new, large religious contingency were to come to believe that zero population growth is the will of God, and if the government set out to capture this belief in law, Roman Catholics and other Christians would lead the ranks of civil disobedients. But reasons of the second kind (i.e., reasons appealing to the logic of human rights) are of the appropriate kind to justify or even require someone's working for legal prohibitions on certain actions or practices. The problem in the abortion debate is that there is a profound disagreement about the relative strengths of the philosophical reasons given for and against holding that elective abortion is the killing of an unconsenting innocent person for inadequate moral reasons. If an elective abortion *is* the killing of an unconsenting innocent person for reasons which would not justify killing an adult person, then it is wrongful killing, and a policy allowing elective abortion cannot be morally justified. But *are* human fetuses persons? The question is a sensible one, and there are responsible philosophical reasons for saying yes and there are responsible philosophical reasons for saying no. And that's the rub.

FETAL RIGHTS AND THE LOGICAL WEDGE

Those who oppose elective abortion often insist that human life begins at conception. But this is just wrong. Human life begins long before conception. The sperm and egg are alive, and they are not bovine or feline or canine—they are living human gametes. To couch the question in terms of the beginning of human life is to muddle the issue. It is to make the question of the morality of abortion sound like one that can be answered by a very clever biologist. But the issue is not when human life begins. Unquestionably, human fetuses are, from the earliest stages, alive. What we *really* want to know is whether the living human fetus should be recognized as a bearer of the same range of fundamental moral rights that you and I have, among them the right not to be killed without *very* good reason. And the most clever biologist in the world cannot answer this for us, since the question is simply not a biological one.

But it might be objected that although some who are opposed to abortion and who have not thought carefully enough about the issue do make the mistake of thinking that the question is when biological life begins, it is also true that not everyone who talks in terms of the beginning of human life is making this mistake.

For surely many who are opposed to elective abortion mean to contend that the life of a *unique* human being, of a distinct *person,* begins at conception, and that is why a policy allowing elective abortion is wrong.

The problem with this response, however, is that it is not a single claim. For one can grant that the life of a unique human being begins at conception, yet not grant that a distinct person emerges at conception, since the two claims are not equivalent unless one begs the question in favor of fetal personhood. That is, if we mean by "human being" "a member of the biological species, *homo sapiens,"* then (if we ignore the problem of identical twins) it is uncontroversially true that the life of a unique human being begins at conception. This is merely a scientific claim, and it is one that can be conclusively defended by scientists as such. But the claim that a distinct *person* emerges at conception is not a scientific one; for to call something "a person" is already to assert that it is a bearer of the strongest moral rights—fundamental rights comparable to yours and mine, among them the right not to be killed except for the most compelling of moral reasons. If in asserting that "a human life begins at conception" the opponent of elective abortion means to assert the biological claim, that can be granted immediately. But if he or she means to assert that "a person emerges at conception," that is a very different claim—it is a moral claim. Indeed, it is the very claim that is at issue in the abortion debate. What those who oppose retaining a policy of elective abortion need to tell us is *why* we must accept that the truth of the biological claim commits us to accepting the moral claim.

But those opposed to elective abortion might still respond that those who admit that the life of a unique human being (in the biological sense) begins at conception are indeed committed to granting that (insofar as human fetuses become distinct persons) the life of a distinct person begins here as well. For where did the life of any adult person begin but at conception?

There are, however, at least two responses to this. The first is simply to make the logical point that one can allow that the life of a person begins at conception without allowing that the (biological human) being present at conception is yet a person. That is, just as one can allow that the first tiny bud in an acorn is the beginning of the life of a (future) oak tree without being committed to saying that the bud is already an oak tree, one can allow that conception marks the beginning of the life of a (future) person without being committed to saying that the conceptus is already a person.

This logical point leads to the second, more substantive, response: namely, that we think the tiny bud in the acorn is quite clearly *not* an oak tree. And we think this because the bud does not yet have the characteristics of oak trees. Indeed, acorns with tiny buds are very *unlike* oak trees, even though every oak tree began as a bud in an acorn. In just the same way, the new conceptus is very unlike beings who have the kinds of characteristics which compel us to recognize them as persons. What kinds of characteristics are these? I cannot offer a full account here. But perhaps it will be enough to point out that if we came across a being like E.T. (who is not biologically human), we would surely think him a person—a being with fundamental moral rights comparable to yours and mine. And this would be because we would recognize that he has certain characteristics— the capacity to suffer mental and physical pain, the ability to make plans, a sense of himself as an ongoing being, and so on—which are sufficient to compel us to hold that he must (and must not) be treated in certain ways. (And, of course, the film, *E.T.*, turns on precisely this point.) A conceptus, however, has none of these characteristics. Indeed, like the mystery of the acorn and the oak, what is amazing is that such radically *different* beings emerge from such beginnings. But it needs to be clearly recognized that in the case of the acorn and in the case of the conceptus, at the end of the process, we do have beings *very* unlike those at the beginning of the process.[5]

When, then, must we say of a developing human being that we must recognize it as a person? If we are talking about when we have a being with the kinds of characteristics we take to be relevant to compelling a recognition of personhood, it seems that persons (at least human persons) are, like oak trees, emergent beings, and that deciding when to classify a developing human being as a person is like deciding when to call a shoot a tree. Young trees do not have all the characteristics of grown trees—for example, children cannot safely swing from them. But when a shoot begins to take on at least some of the characteristics of full-fledged trees, we think we are not confused in beginning to call that shoot a tree. Similarly, there is no clear distinction between where the Mississippi River ends and the Gulf of Mexico begins. But settle the issue by setting a *convention* which does not seem counterintuitive. We are faced with quite the same kind of question when it comes to the matter of persons. Since fetuses do not have the kinds of characteristics which compel us to recognize beings as persons, we must, whether we like it or not, sit down and *decide* whether fetuses are to be recognized as full-fledged persons as a matter of public policy. And we must decide the question on the basis of the appropriate kinds of reasons. That is, for the purposes of setting public policy in a religiously heterogeneous society, we must decide it on the basis of the nonreligious, philosophical arguments, some of which urge us to accept that we must recognize human fetuses as having the same range of fundamental rights that you and I have, and some of which hold that this is just not so.

One possible convention is to set the recognition of personhood at birth. Another is to set it at conception. Still others might be at various stages of prenatality or at various points after birth. Those who oppose elective abortion insist that we *must* recognize personhood at conception, and central to the position is most frequently an argument known as "the logical wedge." This argument holds that if we are going to recognize older children as having the same fundamental rights that you and I have, then logic compels us to recognize that, from the moment of conception, all human beings must have those same rights. The argument proceeds by starting with beings everyone recognizes as having the rights in question and then by pointing out that a child (say) at fifteen is not radically different from one at fourteen and a half; and a child at fourteen and a half is not radically different from one at fourteen, and so on. The argument presses us back from fourteen to thirteen to twelve—to infancy. From infancy, it is a short step to late-term fetuses, because (the argument goes) change in location (from the womb to the wider world) does not constitute an essential change in the being itself. *You* do not lose *your* right not to be killed simply by walking from one room to another. Similarly, it is argued, mere change of place is not philosophically important enough to justify such a radical difference in treatment between infants and late-term fetuses. The argument then presses us back to early-term fetuses—back to conception. Logic and fairness, then, force us to accept that even the new conceptus has the same fundamental right to life that you and I have.

But those who support retaining a policy of elective abortion often point out that this kind of argument for fetal rights is faulty, since if we accept that we can never treat beings who are not radically different from one another in radically different ways, we shall be unable to justify all sorts of public policies which we want to keep and which we all believe are fair. It is argued, for example, that this kind of argument for fetal rights entails that we cannot be justified in setting driving or voting ages, since withholding these privileges until a certain age discriminates against those close to that age: An eighteen-year-old is not radically different from a seventeen-and-a-half-year-old, and so on. Thus, the implication of this kind of argument is that setting ages for the commencement of certain important societal privileges cannot be morally justified. We must give the five-year-old the right to vote, the six-year-old the right to drink, the nine-year-old the right to drive. But these implications, it is argued, show that this kind of argument for fetal rights is unsound.[6]

The response to this criticism of the logical wedge argument, however, is that the granting of societal privileges is not a matter of arbitrariness, even if there is some arbitrariness in selecting ages for the commencement of such privileges. Proper use of these rights, it may be argued, requires a certain degree of maturity—responsibility, background knowledge, experience, independence, and, in the case of driving, a certain degree of developed physical dexterity. Thus, it is because certain changes normally occur as a child matures into an adult that it is appropriate to set policies which acknowledge those changes. But this, it may be argued, is not the case when it comes to recognizing the right to life. That is, those who oppose retaining a policy of elective abortion insist that after conception *no* changes occur that are relevant to recognizing the personhood (and thus the right to life) of a human being.

But this immediately takes us back to the acorn and the oak. The bud and the tree simply *are* significantly different kinds of beings. And you and I *are* significantly different from a conceptus, which has *none* of the characteristics which morally compel us to recognize it as a being with rights. It will not do simply to deny that there are significant changes between the time of conception and the time when we have a being which we simply *must* recognize as a bearer of rights. Thus, we are once again confronted with the question of deciding where we shall set the convention of recognizing personhood.

At this point, however, there is yet another response open to the opponent of elective abortion—namely, that the kind of reasoning used to defeat the argument for fetal rights cannot be correct, since it will not only rule out our being committed to the rights of fetuses, it also entails that we are not compelled to accept that human infants are beings of a kind which must be recognized as having the full range of fundamental moral rights, since infants are, it might be suggested, more like very young kittens in regard to the characteristics in question than they are like paradigm cases of persons.

But this objection is not devastating. For, again, the question before us is a question of deciding what convention we shall adopt. And one can allow that even if infants do not (yet) have the characteristics which compel us to accept a being as a person, there are other considerations which provide excellent reasons for taking birth as the best place to set the convention of recognizing personhood and the full range of fundamental moral rights, despite the fact that infants as such are far more like very young kittens than they are like beings whose characteristics compel us to accept them as full members of the moral community.

Chief among these considerations are the facts that persons other than an infant's biological mother are able to care for the infant and have an interest in doing so. There is no radical change in the characteristics of a human being just before birth and just after birth. But once a human being emerges from the womb and others are able to care for it, there are radical changes in what is involved in preserving its life. And the crucial change is that sustaining its life violates no right of its biological mother. Thus birth, which marks this change, is not an arbitrary point for commencing recognition of personhood.

It is important to notice here that to hold that a woman has a right to terminate a pregnancy is not to hold that she also has a right to the death of her fetus if that fetus can survive, and quite the same reasons that can justify a proscription on infanticide can justify a requirement to sustain viable fetuses that survive abortion. What we are not entitled to do, it may be argued, is force a woman to complete a pregnancy because others have an interest in having her fetus. But it does not follow from this that a woman may kill a born infant that can be cared for by others. Thus, it does not follow from the kind of reasoning I have sketched above that the defender of a policy allowing elective abortion is committed to a policy allowing infanticide. Indeed, the position is fully consistent with holding that even though infants do not yet possess the kinds of characteristics which compel recognition of a being as a person, the fact that they are now biologically independent beings that can be sustained without forcing an unwilling woman to serve as a life support provides an excellent reason for setting the convention of a right to life at birth, that is, viable emergence.[7]

Perhaps it should be pointed out here that the view I have just sketched can also allow that even kittens have *some* moral rights. I, for one, believe that as sentient beings—beings capable of suffering pain—they have a strong moral right not to be treated cruelly, that is, not to have pain wantonly imposed on them. Insofar as fetuses can suffer pain, the defender of elective abortion can quite coherently hold that any pain imposed on a fetus in abortion must be justified. To say this, however, is not to be committed to holding that fetuses must be recognized as having the same full range of fundamental rights that you and I have. It is, rather, to allow fetuses (at the very least) the moral standing of any being of comparable sentience, and, hence, to hold that there is always a moral obligation not to wantonly impose pain on fetuses. But given the exquisite intimacy of pregnancy, any woman who does not want to bring a child to term has a strong reason for seeking an abortion. Thus, if pain is imposed on the fetus in abortion, it is not wantonly imposed.[8]

But it will surely still be objected that human fetuses and human infants are beings that are potentially like paradigm cases of persons, and this makes them very *unlike* other beings of comparable sentience. Kittens, after all, will never develop the kinds of characteristics that compel us to recognize them as full-fledged members of the moral community, and because of this, we must recognize human fetuses as having a far more significant moral standing that other beings of comparable sentience. Sometimes opponents of elective abortion point this out, saying that from the moment of conception a fetus is a *potential* person, and must, therefore, be granted the right to life. But the problem here is that to say that a being is a potential person is just to say that it is a person-not-yet, which is, of course, to deny that it is now a person. And this is to give the defender of retaining choice in this area the very point that is crucial to his or her argument against the argument for fetal rights, and to thereby turn the question back to the question of deciding on a convention.

ACTUAL AND POTENTIAL PERSONS

The crucial question, then, is whether we should recognize the fetus as a person now or whether we should recognize the fetus as a potential person—as a person-not-yet. If we take the first choice, then the full range of fundamental moral rights attaches to the fetus. If we take the second choice, it remains an open question what moral duties we might have toward the fetus. Either way, our *reasons* for deciding as we do must be more than religious ones if the purpose of deciding is to set policy in a pluralistic society. Bishop Timlin's analogy to slavery fails yet a third time because there are no such open questions about involuntary slavery. Enslaving a person against his or her will is a paradigm case of injustice. But we haven't anything like the same sort of moral certainty about the injustice of abortion. And since we haven't, those who recognize the complexity of the question can hold, without being heartless or inconsistent, that *they* believe abortion is wrong, but also that they are unprepared to impose that view on those who remain reflectively unconvinced by the arguments that the human fetus must be recognized as having the full moral status of a person.

Does it follow from all this that there is some serious doubt about the personhood of fetuses—that is, that the fetus might be a person? Sometimes those who support retaining a policy of elective abortion say things like this—that the fetus *might* be a person, but that the evidence just is not conclusive. But if this is the position one holds, those who oppose allowing elective abortion have a strong response. That response is that we should give the fetus the benefit of the doubt. After all, if a hunter hears a movement in the bushes and shoots without making sure she is not shooting a person, and it turns out that she has killed or injured a person, we charge her with gross recklessness. And her saying that it was possible that what she shot at was not a person is no defense. She simply should not have shot if there were even a remote possibility that she would injure a person. In just the same way, the opponent of allowing elective abortion argues that if there is *any* possibility that the fetus is a person, we have a duty to act as if it were a person—a duty to avoid acting recklessly. And part of what *that* means is that another person may not kill it for reasons less than self-defense.

This is an interesting argument, but it misses an important point. For the real doubt is not whether a fetus is a person. Rather, if there is a doubt it is about whether we should treat something which is obviously a potential person (in the sense that it has potentially the characteristics of paradigm cases of persons) as if it were a person already. And this is not something that can be decided by going and looking at the fetus, as one might go and look in the bushes. For (again) in looking, we shall find that although fetuses are quite wonderful beings, they lack the kinds of characteristics that morally compel us to accept a being as a person. The question to be resolved, then, is whether we should accept that these beings which will emerge as persons if their lives are supported ought, at this stage of their development, be treated as if they were persons already—as beings with a moral right to life comparable to yours and mine, comparably protected by the coercive power of the law.

When we are trying to resolve the real doubt, a large part of what we need to ask is what deciding to treat fetuses as beings with the full range of fundamental moral rights would really involve in practice, and whether our shared moral views about paradigm cases of persons will allow us to accept these things. Let us, then, look for a moment at just two of the implications of deciding to admit human fetuses into the class of full-fledged persons with full-fledged fundamental rights.

SOME IMPLICATIONS OF RECOGNIZING
FETUSES AS PERSONS

If we decide to recognize fetuses as full persons, the first thing that follows (as Mr. Reagan has recognized) is that abortion in cases of rape or incest must be ruled out. Suppose that I were to discover that you are the product of rape or incest. You would not think (and none of us would think) that it followed from this that I could just kill you. Fundamental rights are not a consequence of where someone came from. If we allow that human fetuses are persons, we could not consistently allow abortion for (say) an eighteen-year-old woman who had been raped by her father. What is more, if this woman were to perform an abortion on herself and be found out, we must treat her as we treat any murderer. In some jurisdictions, this might well lead to life imprisonment or even execution. During the 1984 campaigns, President Reagan was asked in the first debate with Mr. Mondale whether he believed we should treat women who abort for reasons less than self-defense as murderers, with all that might entail. He avoided the question, saying that this would be a matter for the states to decide. But the opponent of elective abortion needs to confront this question squarely and honestly. Precisely what *are* we to do with women who abort? Could we accept that states may decide to imprison them or execute them? Just what are we to do with them? If the proponent of a prohibition on elective abortion confronts this question earnestly and *cannot* comfortably hold that jurisdictions *should* treat these women as they typically treat murderers, then he or she needs to begin to think carefully about *why*. When asked in the first debate to explain his position on abortion, Mr. Mondale (echoing Governor Cuomo) said of the prohibitive policy espoused by Mr. Reagan, "It won't work." This is a woefully inadequate response. But I suspect that what Mr. Mondale had in mind was that accepting the fetus as a full-fledged person commits us to measures in practice that even those who are deeply opposed to elective abortion cannot fully accept, among them that the eighteen-year-old who aborts a fetus resulting from rape by her father is to be treated as any murderer of a helpless, innocent person. We are not, even in this pluralistic society, free to kill others for reasons less than the immediate defense of our own lives, and if we do, we are subject to the most severe legal penalties, including possible execution. If fetuses are to be recognized as full-fledged persons, then justice requires that those who abort them for reasons less than self-defense must be recognized as full-fledged murderers and treated as such. Those who are rigorously opposed to retaining a policy of elective abortion on the ground that fetuses are persons must confront this implication sincerely and sensitively, and they must be explicit on what they are willing to accept as the practical implications of their position. If they are not willing to accept that those who abort should be subject to exactly the same treatment as others who murder innocent persons, then they do not *really* believe that the fetus has precisely the same moral status as you and I.

There is yet another potent implication of recognizing fetuses as full-fledged persons. Mr. Reagan and Mr. Bush would both allow abortion in cases of self-defense—that is, in cases where the woman's life is threatened. But there is a problem with this position that generally goes unnoticed. For if our public policy is to recognize that the fetus is genuinely an innocent person, then its threat to a woman's life is an innocent threat, and the state can have no legitimate reason for systematically preferring the life of the woman to the life of the fetus.[9] That is, the argument from self-defense simply cannot justify the state's allowing a woman the use of medical specialists who will systematically prefer her life to the life of the fetus. If the fetus is a person who has precisely the same moral status as the woman, the state must, as a matter of fairness to the fetus, do nothing that would involve it in giving the woman an unfair advantage over the fetus. And, again, this means that the state should not permit the use of technologically advanced institutions or the use of technologically advanced practitioners which give the woman an unfair advantage in this battle for life between moral equals. The argument from self-defense, then, seems to entail far greater restrictions on abortion than even the most fervent opponents of elective abortion tend to want to allow, Mr. Reagan among them. If opponents of elective abortion want to allow abortions in cases where the woman's life is at stake, then they must realize that implicit in their position is the view that the woman and the fetus are *not* of equal moral stature after all.

MORAL SENSITIVITY AND SETTING PUBLIC POLICY

My own view is that there are insurmountable difficulties to finding an argument for the recognition of fetuses as persons which is cogent and compelling enough to justify imposing on women the exquisitely intimate burden of bearing an unwanted child. But even if this view is correct, it does not follow that we can do just anything to human fetuses. Kittens are not persons, but we are not at moral liberty to wantonly impose pain on them. Natural resources are not persons, but we are not at moral liberty to wantonly destroy them. Several years ago, Patrick Buchanan wrote of an experiment on human fetuses, discussed in *The Second American Revolution*, by John Whitehead. Six months after *Roe v. Wade*, Dr. A. J. Adam of Case Western Reserve University reported to the American Pediatric Research Society that he and his associates had conducted an experiment on twelve fetuses, up to twenty weeks old, delivered alive by hysterectomy abortion. Adam and his associates cut the heads off these fetuses and cannulated the internal carotid arteries. They kept the heads alive, much as the Russians kept dogs' heads alive during the 1950s. When challenged, Dr. Adam's response was that society had decided that these fetuses would die, thus they had no rights. Said Adam, "I don't see any ethical problem." I find Dr. Adam's failure to see any ethical problem chilling and morally repugnant, even though these fetuses had no real chance of long-term survival *ex utero*. One of the legitimate worries of those who are opposed to abortion is that this kind of ghoulish insensitivity will become more and more prevalent in our society, spilling over to a cavalier attitude toward human life in general. One need not be opposed to allowing elective abortion to share that worry, and one need not think nonviable fetuses are persons to be astonished at Dr. Adam's failure to see *any* ethical problem.

When asked in the 1984 campaign debate about his position on abortion, Vice President Bush replied that he had changed his view (which previously had been more liberal) because of the number of legal abortions that have taken place in this country. But the problem with this reason for disallowing elective abortion is that it misses the very point of those who have traditionally opposed abortion; for if fetuses have the same range of moral rights that you and I have, then even one abortion for reasons less than those which would justify killing an adult person is too many. Determining moral rights is not a numbers game. We don't have laws against murder because there are too many murders—we have laws against murder because every single person has a compelling moral right not to be murdered. Because that right is so compelling, the state comes forward to protect it. When one understands that persons have a compelling moral right not to be murdered, one also understands that numbers of murders are irrelevant to the question of whether society should have laws against murder. One murder is simply one too many. Mr. Bush's position, then, misses the very strong position on fundamental fetal rights that has been the moral centerpiece of the movement against elective abortion.

Still, there is much to be said for Mr. Bush's discomfort with the use of abortion as a form of birth control. Although I believe that defenders of retaining a policy of elective abortion who have thought carefully and sensitively about the issue are more than willing to admit that abortion, however well-justified, is never a happy moral choice, some who favor elective abortion angrily talk about fetuses as being, like tumors, morally equivalent to parasites. Such talk is inexcusably cavalier; and those who believe that the human fetus is of significant moral worth are understandably infuriated when they hear it or read it. Language like that does not help get us to reasonable, sensitive discussion. And it is precisely reasonable, sensitive discussion that we now most need on this difficult question of morality and public policy.

It should go without saying that public policy should not be set by those who shout the loudest—that it should not be set by those who carry the most emotively charged posters, or by those who use the most emotively charged language. But neither should it be carelessly set by an unreflective commitment to a woman's right to self-direction which fails to take into serious account the genuine moral costs of giving absolute priority to such a right. Public policy must be set by sitting down and coming to understand the legitimate concerns on both sides of hard issues. It must be set with an eye toward what *all* morally sensitive persons in a pluralistic society can live with.

The abortion issue is one about which reasonable people can disagree. We all need to realize this, and we need to do more talking instead of shouting. Deliberation in the philosophy of moral rights involves much more than repeating bumper sticker slogans; and rational agreement in such deliberation is often hard-won, and will only succeed when each side can see clearly why the other side begins from the position it does. It will not do, then, for those who are opposed to retaining a policy of elective abortion to call themselves "prolife" and to call fetuses "babies" and take the issue to be settled. And it will not do for those who believe we must retain abortion as an option for women to call fetuses "parasites" and take the issue to be settled. Trying to decide public policy must involve refusing to use language which implies that the opposition is against something that any morally reasonable person would support or which simply begs the question against the other side. It must involve sensitive deliberation which takes carefully into account the deeply felt and morally reasonable concerns of a variety of perspectives. And the effort must lead to decisions that thoughtful persons in a pluralistic society can respect, no matter what policies they would prefer to see. Defenders and opponents of a policy of elective abortion must realize that we share a large common moral ground. We must begin to work from that common ground to come to an agreement on policies that can respectfully govern us all.

The liberal Catholic politicians are in trouble, and they will stay in trouble until they more adequately explain their reasons for not seeking a moratorium on elective abortion. Mario Cuomo began that explanation at Notre Dame. But there is much more to be said if all morally concerned Americans are to understand why politicians like Geraldine Ferraro and Mario Cuomo are neither necessarily inconsistent, nor rabid moral relativists, nor insensitive moral thugs.

NOTES

1. An edited version of this essay appeared in *Commonweal* 11 (April 1986) 203–9. I am deeply indebted to Peter Steinfels for his extensive and enormously helpful comments and questions on an earlier draft. For an expanded discussion of fetal rights, see James W. Knight and Joan C. Callahan, *Contraception: Methods and Moral Controversies* (Salt Lake City: University of Utah Press, 1988) chaps. 7 and 9.

2. *Newsweek,* Sept. 24, 1984.

3. Governor Cuomo's speech was given on Sept. 13, 1984. It has been reprinted in this volume on pp. 202–16.

4. I offer a more detailed account of what it means to be "personally" opposed to some kind of action in "Religion and Moral Consistency in Politics," in progress.

5. For a fuller discussion of the kinds of characteristics morally relevant to compelling a recognition of beings (including nonhuman beings) as persons see, e.g., Mary Anne Warren, "On the Moral and Legal Status of Abortion," in *Today's Moral Problems,* ed. Richard Wasserstrom (New York: Macmillan, 1975) 120–36. See also Jane English, "Abortion and the Concept of a Person," *Canadian Journal of Philosophy* 5, no. 2 (1975) 233–43, for an even more detailed discussion of the cluster of features that enter into our concept of a person.

6. For a more detailed treatment of this response to the logical wedge, see, e.g., Jonathan Glover, *Causing Death and Saving Lives* (New York: Penguin, 1977), chap. 12.

7. Again, see Warren for a version of this line of reasoning.

8. I deal with the question of fetal sentience (as well as several related issues) in more detail in *"The Silent Scream:* A New, Conclusive Argument Against Abortion?" *Philosophy Research Archives* 11 (1986) 181–95. On the question of fetal sentience, see also L. W. Sumner, *Abortion and Moral Theory* (Princeton: Princeton University Press, 1981) chap. 4. A revised version of that chapter appears as "A Third Way," in *The Problem of Abortion,* ed. Joel Feinberg, 2nd ed. (Belmont, CA: Wadsworth, 1984) 71–93.

9. This point is argued in detail by Nancy Davis in "Abortion and Self-Defense," *Philosophy and Public Affairs* 13, no. 3 (Summer 1984) 175–207.

Thou Shalt Not Speak

Harry J. Byrne

In 1889, Pope Leo XIII in his apostolic letter *Testem benevolentiae* warned against a "religious Americanism" by which American democratic principles of popular representation would be introduced into the structure and life of the church. Archbishop John Ireland of St. Paul, Minnesota, immediately wrote to the pope condemning the notion of introducing any such political principles into ecclesiastical polity. At the same time, he declared that to apply the term "Americanism" to errors and extravagances of this sort was an insult to the church of America. It was the considered judgment of most American bishops and writers that the condemned Americanism existed only in the minds of certain European types who, as Cardinal James Gibbons of Baltimore pointed out at the time, did not understand the American church.

The distinction between state and church forecloses any transfer of the operating principles of one to the other. They are of different orders and guided by different constitutions. Hence critics who claim that the church is inhibiting free speech when it provides guidelines or regulations regarding its teachers or teachings are guilty of improperly transferring a political principle into ecclesiastical government. A church has every right to instruct its members regarding its tenets. This is not to say that every church exercise of that right will be well-advised or not counterproductive or indeed cannot transgress the line in the opposite direction by attempting to introduce church-government principles into the secular governmental process.

That a new authoritarian mode of church governance has recently been in seems clear. The authoritarian style of today's church, both in its internal governance and in its relations to the external society, is in strong contrast with the earlier style of Pope John XXIII and the spirit of the Second Vatican Council, so well articulated in the "no condemnations" policy set for the council at its outset. In his October 11, 1962, speech opening the council, Pope John XXIII declared, "Today the Spouse of Christ prefers to use the medicine of mercy rather than severity. She considers that she meets the needs of the present age by showing the validity of her teaching rather than by condemnation." Here is clear reliance on the persuasiveness of message and example rather than on the authority of the proclaimer.

Shifts and even reversals in policies and attitudes of different popes point to the need for serious study and evaluation of those policies and attitudes. One can be loyal to the pope while differing on policy. But there is something disingenuous and possibly infantile in trying to serve as cheerleader for different and even contradictory policy programs of successive popes. For example, under Pope Paul VI priests, for reasons of conscience, were permitted to leave their ministry and marry. Under Pope John Paul II, the general policy forbids such release. One can be loyal to both popes, but one cannot uncritically applaud both papal policies so thoroughly contradictory.

The present spirit in the church is reflected in the church in the United States by involvement of some bishops in the electoral process as they instruct people with messages, variously delivered, on who not to vote for. The issue is complicated by similar tactics on the part of other groups in our society: fundamentalist Christians, with their portfolio of issues, keep scorecards on legislators, and Jewish groups—more subtly, but with equal definitiveness—convey a message of defeat at the polls for legislators who would vote against even minor pro-Israel legislation. It is a problem for the three major faith groups.

To focus in this article on the Catholic aspect is not to ignore the broader reaches of the "religion and politics" question. Nor is this present study limited to examination of just the principles that are similarly at issue relative to the other major faith groups; it extends to the practical effects of the kind of political involvement here at issue. Do these tactics produce positive results, or do they have a negative influence on the election of candidates who happen to be Catholic and thus reduce the representative nature of our legislative bodies? A clearly defined example of the political involvement at issue is contained in a directive recently promulgated and implemented in the Archdiocese of New York.

On August 18, 1986, New York's Vicar General, Bishop Joseph T. O'Keefe, issued the following directive:

> Great care and prudence must be exercised in extending invitations to individuals to speak at parish-sponsored events, e.g., Communion breakfasts, graduations, meetings of parish, etc. It is not only inappropriate, it is unacceptable and inconsistent with diocesan policy to invite those individuals to speak at such events whose public position is contrary to and in opposition to the clear, unambiguous teaching of the church. This policy applies, as well, to all Archdiocesan-owned or sponsored institutions and organizations.

Cardinal John J. O'Connor, whose archdiocese issued the directive, rightly rejected the objections that such church control violates "free speech." The church can instruct its members in matters of faith and morals according to its internal rules and judgments. But given the understanding that the political and the ecclesiastical orders are to be rigidly distinguished—although frequently applied to the same individuals and the same subjects—and that free-speech principles in a political democracy do not have comparable applicability in a church pulpit or a church classroom for religious teaching, certain questions remain. Does the archdiocesan directive pose the danger of imposing church authority on participants in the democratic political process? To ban a speaker who dissents on one issue from talking on any issue, such as local housing legislation, at his parish Communion breakfast carries serious political fallout if he is running for office. Is this simply an exercise in the teaching mission of the church?

Is the directive intended to ban non-Catholic dissenters as well as Catholic? Is it intended that "parish meetings" may not be addresses by, for example, Mayor Edward I. Koch of New York City, who, as a Congressman, was a strong advocate of governmental aid to parochial school students? Would his appearance as a speaker at a parochial school graduation somehow condition his audience to accept his unspoken-on-that-occasion views on abortion? Is it intended that he should not get his "brownie points" with our people for his political support on an important issue? Would the rabbi invited to address a parish liturgy committee regarding the Jewish Passover somehow weaken his audience's acceptance of the divinity of Jesus? Or would a Unitarian minister invited to address a parish social action committee on local housing problems somehow infect its members' belief in the Trinity? To ask the questions is to provide an answer.

Such considerations raise the question about the scope of the "teaching of the church" named in the directive. Does a Catholic who does not accept the doctrine on indulgences or who questions the sanctity of St. Pius X come under the ban? Does acceptance of civil divorce in our legal system qualify as a barring criterion? Of contraception? Of abortion? Is there a line? Where is the line? Or is any and every dissent from declared "clear, unambiguous teaching of the church" grounds for the ban?

To unburden the archdiocesan directive of the embarrassment deriving from such an overly broad prohibition, it has been pointed out that the judgment is left to the pastor. But since the directive is quite clear and unambiguous in its message to the pastors, to suggest that implementation of the directive is at the discretion of any of some four hundred pastors is to suggest selective application of a regulation, a procedure unacceptable in any jurisprudential system. The church, having rid itself of its Index of Prohibited Books, could be faced in the archdiocese with four hundred lists of prohibited speakers.

Problems with the archdiocesan speaker's ban do not stop with these grave internal problems. A policy is to be judged not by its abstract terms or the surmised intentions of its makers but, more importantly, by its actual effects. Among those immediate effects of the policy are the ban on New York State Assemblyman John Dearie from speaking at his parish and the announcement by Bishop O'Keefe that he would not invite New York's Governor Mario M. Cuomo to speak at his parish. And all this within months of an election in which both were running for reelection.

Assemblyman Dearie, prior to the formal issuance of the ban last August, was made subject to its policy in June when he was told, subsequent to his talk at a Communion breakfast at his parish of St. Raymond in the Bronx, that he would not be allowed to speak again at a parish gathering. This was his parish, where he was baptized forty-six years ago, where he attended parochial school, where his two children were baptized and where he regularly attends Sunday Mass. After four years at Manhattan Prep, Dearie graduated from Notre Dame University. For fourteen years in the state assembly he has represented what is undoubtedly the most heavily Catholic constituency of any assembly district in the state. He has been in the forefront of safeguarding the interests of tenants and owners of small homes. He has consistently sponsored and voted for legislation providing various forms of state aid to parochial school students (tuition tax credits, textbook loans, and transportation) and to the parochial schools themselves (reimbursement for state-mandated services, such as attendance and test reporting). Except for his vote favoring Medicaid funding of abortions, he has voted conservatively on abortion-related matters, as, for example, his vote favoring parental notification if a minor has an abortion.

While affirming the right of Cardinal O'Connor and the bishops to teach their position aggressively, Mr. Dearie has objected to the ban. "There are so many other issues," he has said,

> the homeless, housing, senior citizens, that to simply close the door—in effect to cut off communication and the honest evaluation of a legislator trying to make a decision on this very difficult issue—it seems to me in the long and short run is not a good policy.

How does such a policy relate to "Political Responsibility: Choices for the 80's," the March 21, 1984, statement of the U.S. Catholic Conference (USCC) administrative board? It reads:

> We specifically do not seek the formation of a religious voting block; nor do we wish to instruct persons on how they should vote by endorsing candidates . . . We hope that voters will examine the positions of candidates on the full range of issues as well as their integrity, philosophy and performance.

Is abortion the single issue that bans a specific candidate? The single issue that triggers penalties? Is it applicable only to Catholic candidates?

How does placing the archdiocesan ban solely on one candidate whose opponent may hold a similar dissenting view relate to the January 1982 statement of the

New York State bishops, which declared: "Any such [lobbying] efforts *must not* contribute support for or opposition to specific candidates for political office"? This statement was mailed in mid-October by the New York Chancery to the parishes as an obvious alert prior to the November 4 elections. Although the statement had as its primary purpose the protection of the tax exemption for churches, its wording seems contradicted by the ban placed on Assemblyman Dearie.

When Archbishop O'Connor stated during the 1984 presidential campaign, "I do not see how a Catholic in good conscience can vote for an individual expressing himself or herself as favoring abortion," vice-presidential candidate Geraldine Ferraro characterized this as "a contradiction of the longstanding policy of the National Conference of Catholic Bishops that strongly opposes the targeting of any political candidate by name." It was a point, she declared in her book on the campaign, at which "in the minds of many [Archbishop O'Connor] stepped over the line that separates church and state." The policy statements of the USCC administrative board and the New York State bishops reflect a sensitivity toward such perceptions among the voting public. It seemed to Representative Ferraro inappropriate on the additional count that her opposite number, vice-presidential candidate George Bush, shared her own position on this aspect of abortion. After a campaign speech by Mrs. Ferraro in Scranton, Pennsylvania, Bishop James C. Timlin of Scranton was asked precisely why she was being singled out and not George Bush. "Because she is Catholic and is making clear she is a Catholic and Mr. Bush is not," was the bishop's reply.

That the only two persons specifically named as subject to the New York archdiocesan ban—Governor Cuomo and Assemblyman Dearie—are Catholic could suggest an underlying rationale similar to Bishop Timlin's: Since they are Catholic, they are expected to enunciate and vote the Catholic position. Failure to do so is followed by ecclesiastical punishment. Unfortunately, such a procedure encounters two serious problems, one theological, the other pragmatically political.

In the theological area, it must be asked at what point an individual following a judgment in conscience deemed erroneous by church authorities loses the right to represent himself or herself as "Catholic" and becomes subject to a sort of partial excommunication by being declared less than Catholic and by being banned as a speaker in Catholic circles. Such a penalty can have serious political ramifications in an area with a heavy Catholic voting constituency and can constitute an extrinsic pressure on the official's conscience. Speaking of the right of religious freedom, Vatican II has declared:

> This freedom means that all men are to be immune from coercion on the part of individuals or of social groups and of any human power, in such ways that no one is to be forced to act against his conscience, nor kept from acting according to his conscience privately or publicly, whether alone or in association with others, within due limits. ("Declaration on Religious Freedom," no. 2)

In addition to the problems of the inviolability of the legislator's conscience, the ecclesiastical ban on speakers encounters a pragmatic political difficulty with potentially enormous consequences. Interestingly enough, respect for the role of conscience, already theologically validated, brings with it the solution to this dangerous threat. Back in the 1940s, Paul Blanshard, in his articles in *The Nation* and in his book *American Freedom and Catholic Power,* argued that the Catholic Church would always attempt to pressure Catholic politicians to enact Catholic positions into civil law. Accordingly, Catholics could never be trusted with public office. He was able to document his case with copious quotations from the "Syllabus of Errors" of Pope Pius IX and other then-official teachings of the church. John F. Kennedy broke the barriers raised by nativist anti-Catholicism and the outmoded church-state theology of the "Syllabus." In his famous September 1960 speech in Houston to a group of Protestant ministers he said,

> I believe in an America that is officially neither Catholic, Protestant or Jewish. . . .
> If the time should ever come . . . when my office would require me to violate my
> conscience or violate the national interest, then I would resign the office . . .

After the speech, a minister asked Kennedy about such a resignation if he found the office of president to be in conflict "with your church." Kennedy quickly shot back: "No. I said, 'with my conscience.' "

Kennedy perceived that personal conscience was the mediating link between one's church and the act of a public official. He affirmed the right of a religious body to instruct its members "in the area of faith and morals" but disavowed the propriety of a religious body trying to bind directly a public official in his public duty. John F. Kennedy's position seems to be in accord with views on conscience expressed by Pope John Paul II. In 1979, he visited Poland and on his arrival at Warsaw was met by the communist government's officials. He concluded his courteous address to them with these words:

> I add the expression of my regard for all of you, the distinguished representatives
> of the authorities . . . according to the office which you exercise and according to
> the . . . responsibility incumbent on each of you before history and *before your
> conscience.*

On his 1980 visit to Brazil, Pope John Paul II, quoting Vatican II, declared:

> As citizens, [the laity] must cooperate with other citizens, using their own particular
> skills *and acting on their own responsibility.* [The church] does not claim to take on
> political activities as part of her own function. . . . But the church does claim that
> the practice of a social pastorate is her right and duty, *not in view of a purely temporal
> project, but for the formation and orientation of consciences* for their own specific ends in
> order that society might become more just. [Emphasis mine.]

The "conscience" view of John F. Kennedy has been accepted by many, Catholics and non-Catholics alike, who think that a religious body has every right to instruct its members but does not have the right in a pluralistic democracy to bind directly a public official. It is precisely the widespread acceptance of this view that negated the fears engendered by the Paul Blanshards that Catholic elected officials would be mere agents of their church. The mediating role of a legislator's conscience seems not only theologically correct, but of enormous practical importance if Catholics are to continue to be electable to public office. To go further than efforts at "the formation and orientation of consciences" and to try to coerce a particular political position of an official who voted "the wrong way" by banning him or her from speaking on any topic at a church affair is fraught with enormous risk. The question will always arise as to Catholic candidates or officials who carefully follow a church position: Do they do this for reasons intrinsic to the issue or for fear of the ban if they do not? Just raising the question damages both a candidate and the political process.

Not only is the electability of Catholic candidates put at risk, but the risk involves the election of other individuals holding even less acceptable proabortion positions. In 1975, Daniel Patrick Moynihan was engaged in a primary battle with Bella Abzug for the New York Democratic nomination for the U.S. Senate. A local right-to-life group began an effort to defeat Mr. Moynihan, whose views were not deemed to be strongly antiabortion. But his views on abortion were at a great remove from Mrs. Abzug's; she saw abortion as a form of feminist triumph. Mr. Moynihan, before and after his election to the Senate, has been a forceful advocate for freedom of choice by parents in selecting public or parochial schools for their children. In popular and scholarly articles and in proposed legislation, he has tried to advance the cause of aid to parochial school students. Bella Abzug, prochoice for abortion and antichoice for education, has been a determined and vehement opponent of such aid. But the full spectrum of issues meant nothing to local right-to-lifers. They were quite prepared to punish Mr. Moynihan, who is Catholic, for his position on abortion even at the cost of electing a candidate with stronger proabortion views.

Inflicting punishment seems to be the dynamic at work here, regardless of counterproductive effects. Regrettably, the irrational extremism of permissive abortion generates—undoubtedly out of frustration—irrational, extremist responses. Assemblyman Dearie, the Catholic, must be punished for his one adverse vote. If the preservation of clear church teaching is the intended goal, as is claimed, simple declarative statements by church officials would suffice, or perhaps at most forbidding the dissenter to speak under Catholic auspices on the subject of his or her dissent. The totality of the ban, with its obvious political consequences, carries the unmistakable aura of punishment and penalty. If indeed the ban is a penalty and a restriction on a Catholic's right (Canon 1336, 1,2), it would seem to require application of the appropriate canons (1341 and following) regarding penalties and the "judicial or administrative procedure to impose or declare penalties."

The archdiocesan speaker's ban with its political effects has the potential of violating a candidate's conscience, of improperly intruding on the political process, and of disqualifying Catholics from public office in the minds of significant portions of the electorate. Adverse reaction to the speaker's ban was immediate among great numbers of New York priests, religious, and lay people. Such reaction was not limited to Catholics. The New York *Daily News* (September 15, 1986) editorialized that the directive is indeed a ban despite the archdiocese's denial: "New York's position . . . is confusing, unrealistic, and open to charges of political manipulation." The *New York Times*'s editorial (September 13, 1986) went directly to the heart of the matter: "Voters may well reject Catholic candidates rather than risk electing someone who puts religious conviction ahead of political tolerance. And some Catholic politicians may rebel in resentment."

Both the theology of conscience and the practical dynamics of the American political system are extremely sensitive areas. American democratic political principles are not to be imposed on church governance. But church authoritarian procedures in the name of protecting its teaching are not to be imposed on the democratic governmental process. This principle works both ways. It is a fact of life that American voters will never elect someone whom they view as politically subservient to a religious body. For churchmen to cross the line between, on the one hand, instructing and informing conscience and, on the other hand, trying to force a legislative position on an officeholder by a speaker's ban is a very dangerous political game. It can result in the nonelectability of Catholics. Paul Blanshard, buried by John F. Kennedy, can rise from the dead.

From Theory to Practice in the Public-Policy Realm

Cardinal John O'Connor

I am indebted to Father Gerald Fogarty, S.J., well-known church historian, for the story about Al Smith during that winsome gentleman's ill-fated campaign for the presidency in 1927. When an anti-Catholic opponent alleged that Smith would trample all over the Constitution of the United States in slavish obedience to papal encyclicals, especially in view of Pope Leo XIII's encyclical on church-state relations, with completely innocent perplexity Mr. Smith turned to an educated Catholic assistant and asked, "What the hell's an encyclical?"

Your esteemed president, Father Campion, and his associates have assigned me the topic "Church and Society: Issues in the Future." Since I am perceived in some quarters to be a "one-issue" man, I am complimented to be entrusted with reflecting upon issues in the plural. Yet while very reluctant to pass up an opportunity to reveal the extraordinary breadth of my concerns, I feel that I can best respond to your generosity in inviting me here by restricting myself to one issue after all. It is not the issue that some believe made me in 1984 what I understand you ladies and gentlemen of the working press call a "hot media property."

In my judgment, the primary issue for the immediate future is not one of those we commonly refer to when we speak of "issues of church and society." I doubt that many of us would disagree on such issues however we would list them in order of importance or whether some lists might be longer or shorter than others.

What, then, is what I am calling the primary issue? It's the question of how to get at these various other issues. Precisely what is the point of entry for the church into the public-policy arena? How, where, when, do we legitimately engage the debate or even generate the debate ourselves if such is required? What are the rules of engagement? What are we really about when we address ourselves to public policy?

Who or what is the church, who takes the action and on what basis, with what authority, with the support of how many others in the church, when it comes to addressing public-policy issues publicly? Who takes what initiative with whose help and when, in the rough and tumble of the marketplace, in the pulpits and in the streets, in drawing rooms and in barrooms, in classrooms and in courtrooms, in the Congress, the White House, the city hall, the precinct, the ward, in board rooms and in union halls?

Who says what to whom, on whose authority, in discreet discussions behind closed doors, in the glare of television, the whirr of tape recorders, the scribbling of journalists, when even a "No comment"—or especially a "No comment"— may be construed in a hundred ways, particularly during the heat of a political campaign.

I said we know and, for the most part, would agree on what are commonly called the "issues." For example, we know there is something wrong as we pass the bag ladies, the bag men, in the streets. We know there is something wrong about gentrification that flushes lonely, elderly people out of homes and apartments with absolutely no place to go. We know there is something wrong when drugs control and destroy our neighborhoods, when we can't build prisons fast enough to meet the demand.

We know there is something wrong when the most incredible pornography is defended as freedom of speech, when child abuse reaches horrifying proportions, when people are disenfranchised or exploited because of where they were born or their sex or the color of their skin. We know there is something wrong in the sexual exploitation and violence that various agencies deal with every day in virtually every city and in the hopelessness of the burned-out buildings in cities all over the country.

We know there is something wrong in Central America, in the Middle East, in the north of Ireland, in Cambodia and in Poland, in much of the vast continent in Africa and elsewhere in the world. We know there is something wrong, something terrifyingly wrong, about the arms race and about the horrifying potential of nuclear weapons.

We know that apartheid is a sacrilege. We know that racism is obscene. We know that there is something wrong when 1.5 million children waiting in their mothers' wombs to see the light of day are destroyed every year. We know that this magnificent country, with its incredible resources, its ability to put a person on the moon, the skill to transplant hearts, this marvelous country must surely have a better answer to the violence of poverty than to inflict the violence of death on the innocent.

We know all this and more, and as a church we feel a gnawing pain, an enduring heartache and most particularly, I suspect, the frustrating anguish of seeming to be able to do so little about so much. Yet these are all public-policy issues, and I doubt that many of us believe we have no responsibility to address them. It is the how, the when, the who, I suggest, less frequently than the whether, that perplexes or even paralyzes us. Aye, there indeed, would Hamlet tell us, is the rub. But it is this "rub," if I may call it such, that we must face in the immediate future; and we must face it in the context of the real world, rough and tumble as it is. Which is only another way of defining what I call the primary issue. Perhaps we can formulate it most simply as, How do we move from the theoretical to the practical, from anguished concern to effective action?

I don't pretend to know the answer to this key question. Indeed, as one who has blundered more frequently than most in attempting the transition from concern to action, I have demonstrated rather dramatically that I don't know the answer. But I have tried to think through the complexities of the question, tried to discern for myself the obstacles to be cleared if we are to make the transition as a church. With your indulgence, I will spin out some of my reflections on a few of the many variables which I submit must be recognized and addressed by those who would constructively influence public policy. They are legion, but time restrictions and the context of these remarks persuade me to focus on but four, the first two quite briefly, the third and fourth at a bit more length.

1. I began with Father Fogarty's anecdote about Al Smith's reported ignorance of even the word *encyclical* (although I personally doubt that Governor Smith was guilty), because I believe that ignorance of church social teaching is profound, widespread, and not limited to those who don't hold or aspire to public office. Indeed, it seems to me that it is the remarkable person in or aspiring to public office who has anything resembling in-depth understanding of church social teaching or even a working knowledge of such.

I believe this to be a very real problem in what I have called and will repeatedly call the rough-and-tumble world of politics. The problem of ignorance (to say nothing about acceptance) of Catholic social teaching is one about which we must not be naive if we expect to look to Catholics or others in, or aspiring to, public office to influence public policy in accordance with the norms of such teaching— the norms, for example, of social justice. I'm afraid that those who might have to ask what the hell an encyclical is might have something less than in-depth knowledge about pastoral letters, to say nothing of "The Church in the Modern World," *Gaudium et spes.*

2. If lay persons in public life are limited in their knowledge or understanding of Catholic social teaching, a somewhat different question must be raised, not about the knowledge of such teaching on the part of the bishops, theologians, and what I might call other ecclesial professionals, but about the role they believe the church herself should play. Father Avery Dulles, S.J., brought this question into focus in his 1985 lecture at Rockhurst College, in Kansas City, Missouri.

Father Dulles raises the question, What is the purpose, importance, and necessity of the church? on the grounds that, "unless both leaders and members are convinced that the church has an important, specific task to accomplish, they cannot be expected to devote great energies or make great sacrifices for the sake of the church. Nor will they be able to reach firm decisions about priorities and the allocation of limited resources." He goes on to assert that without a clear vision of the reason for the church's existence, it is almost impossible to discuss intelligently what the church ought to be doing in the public forum.

For example, he asks whether we should be attempting to issue pastoral guidance on economic reform, sponsor a Campaign for Human Development, permit or forbid priests and religious to engage in politics, or whatever. He takes issue with some of the interpretations of the church and her mission attributed, inappropriately in his judgment, to Vatican II and comes down heavily in favor of the church as missioned to the eternal salvation and redemption of the human race, not *per se* to what we would call public-policy issues.

I join Father Dulles in insisting that our notion of church, its purpose and mission (and I would add, our moral and doctrinal teaching), must be clear and unambiguous if we would determine what the church should do in respect to society and public policy. If this is a question ecclesiastics fail to answer clearly or at least unanimously, what is to be expected of the public officeholder or aspirant? How is he or she or the ordinary politician to discern his or her own responsibilities in trying to apply church teaching to the marketplace? What is he or she to consider important? Which aspects of church teaching must he or she consider binding in conscience?

The Vatican Council tells the lay person, in essence, to help change the world through responsible political action. In what way and to what end? In accordance with what norms? What does the church teach, and to what degree is such teaching to be applied to public policy by Catholics in public life, if at all? Such questions are crucial not only for those engaged in what Vatican II calls "the difficult yet noble art of politics." They are crucial questions for the church herself if she would attempt to affect public policy.

In this whole matter Father Dulles's interpretation of *Gaudium et spes* seems to me particularly provocative. He observes: "While the members of the church are summoned to many kinds of giving, depending on their personal talents and assets, the church itself is especially called to render the spiritual service of bringing the world into union with its Creator and Lord."

3. I turn once more to church historian Father Gerald Fogarty for a third problem we confront in respect to influencing public policy in the real world: Catholic self-consciousness. Father Fogarty considers the bishops' pastoral letter on war and peace as evidence of a newfound confidence that we are indeed first-class citizens: That is, we feel secure enough to criticize governmental policy without losing our status as loyal Americans. Yet there is unquestionably a continuing defensiveness in this regard, a tendency to think twice or three times about whether we will be attacked for "imposing Catholic morality" on the citizenry at large.

Such a charge always implies un-Americanism. I am not sure that I have ever heard the same charge against any other religious body, that is, that their efforts to affect public morality—however they might be rebuffed—were somehow un-American.

Our Catholic self-consciousness showed through, for example, during the Carter-Ford campaign a few years back. We were demonstrably shaken when a mere comparison made at a high National Conference of Catholic Bishops–U.S. Catholic Conference level between the respective abortion positions of Mr. Carter and Mr. Ford was challenged on the grounds that the bishops were supporting Mr. Ford for the presidency. So sensitive was the issue that it was felt necessary that NCCB-USCC authority declare publicly that any appearance of seeming to support Mr. Ford was totally unintentional.

Never do we indict other religious bodies, however, for openly endorsing candidates or for encouraging the use of their pulpits for explicit campaigning; nor do I believe we should.

A *New York Times* headline of June 2, 1986, for example, reads, "Religious Right Challenging GOP," and the article describes what might be a presidential bid by television evangelist the Reverend Pat Robertson, who purportedly reaches sixteen million households each month. Pat Robertson's views on a number of public-policy issues and his moral positions are well-known. He preaches them very forthrightly. I will be amazed, however, if any formal Catholic protest is raised against his candidacy, if indeed he runs—amazed and distressed. None of which is to suggest for a moment that we should endorse individuals for election. Father Coughlin should surely have taught us that.

But that we alone, the "Roman" Church, with all the sinister overtones that title conveys, should have to be excruciatingly meticulous about every word spoken, every step taken—this without question imposes on us extraordinary restrictions as we attempt to affect public policy. And the more self-conscious we ourselves are, the more trepidatious we become about what has come to be called "overstepping the line," particularly if there is even the remotest danger that to address an issue is to risk addressing a person.

Yet in regard to this very sticky matter, how realistic is it to hope that we can completely separate issues from the persons who espouse them? Is it really always possible to do so or, at least, is it really possible always and under all circumstances to avoid the appearance of doing so? Public policy does not exist in a vacuum nor does the political activity which shapes public policy; it is carried out by persons, officeholders, aspirants, politicians. There is almost always going to be a spillover to the person however objectively we try to address the issue. This, in fact, occurs all the time, both in common parlance and in formal documents such as releases from the USCC. We write to the White House or to the Congress to support or to criticize actions or proposals of a particular president. Everybody knows who he is. We address various bills, such as Gramm-Rudman-Hollings, by name.

It is, after all, an individual or a group of individuals—real live persons with names—who deliberately espouse, campaign on, or execute various public policies. It is not the church who attributes such policies to them. Are they to be exempt then from public questioning or public criticism on issues they publicly espouse? Is it even possible to exempt them?

I can't answer these questions. I sincerely feel they must be raised. While it can be understandably argued that if raised during election campaigns they can be construed as partisan, one must ask whether in our society there is ever a moment when an election campaign is not being waged overtly or at least less than covertly? Moreover, many concerns do not emerge as major public-policy issues until an election campaign begins, and the identification of particular candidates with particular issues does not come into focus until then. If we are precluded from addressing given issues because they are identified with given persons, it could happen that we never address certain issues.

I think it not out of context to look for a moment, for example, at recent events in the Philippines. The bishops of the Philippines wrote a series of pastoral letters, one to be proclaimed each Sunday, for an extended period prior to the recent election. They carefully and repeatedly disclaimed political partisanship. It would be extraordinarily naive, however, to pretend that either the downfall of President Marcos or the ascendancy of President Aquino was unrelated to the activities of the bishops and notably that of Cardinal Sin, who has been lauded throughout the free world for his courage and leadership. Could the bishops have seriously dissociated the issues from the person of President Marcos or of his wife?

Another illustration. I have met on three occasions with Bishop Tutu of Johannesburg, soon to be archbishop of Capetown. In my view, Bishop Tutu's courage and leadership, that have gone far beyond his call for divestment and disinvestment, are having a major impact on the shaping of South Africa. Yet it would again be naive to divorce Bishop Tutu's unquestionably justifiable allegations of injustice and oppression against the political system (or what is called in South Africa the current "dispensation") from allegations against Mr. Botha.

Is there some uniqueness in the American system which, unlike the Philippine or South African experience, makes it possible to divorce policy from person in the practical order? If argued, for example, that there is political or theological validity in a politics that we might call "being personally opposed but," should the argument shield an officeholder or aspirant from being questioned or criticized for a position? I am not trying to be self-serving because of my own controverted activities. I am trying to be honest about what I see to be a complex problem for the church if it wishes to engage the political system realistically and effectively, and not merely theoretically.

Intertwined among the complexities, of course, is the related reality of party loyalties and personal political patronage. If the church would influence public policy it must at least recognize, if not, indeed, confront this reality. There is little doubt that for a number of Catholics party loyalty overrides many other loyalties. More recently in American life, of course, racial and ethnic loyalties have assumed critical importance as well. It is not easy for voters whose political or ethnic loyalties run deep to be influenced by church teaching or proposals that run counter to such loyalties. Again, political activities do not occur in a vacuum. Public policy is not shaped or lived in a vacuum.

Something of the same can be said of the patronage system. In recent months in my own archdiocese we have been exposed to an extraordinary learning experience in relation to the passage of a particular piece of legislation that we believed would adversely affect both the church and the broader community. First off, it was a helpful reminder of the fact that we are not professional politicians and shouldn't try to be. Second, it was fascinating to learn who had made campaign commitments to whom and to watch the resultant dynamics at work in the legislative process.

By no means do I say this critically or to suggest dishonesty. My point is simply that, once more, public policy and the political activity that creates or influences it are carried out in the real world. Real people are involved in real-life situations at both national and local levels. What happens in wards, in precincts, in electoral districts, is what shapes a great deal of public policy over the long haul as well as what happens in the Congress and the Supreme Court. And at every level we must recognize that the question of whose ox is gored strongly influences attitudes toward the church's involvement in the public-policy arena.

What is the local issue? Is it racism, drugs, pornography, rape, nuclear war, abortion? The church or its representatives may be severely chastised for "crossing the line" into politics in one location or situation and not in another, or in respect to one or more issues and not to others in direct proportion to the locale of the issues addressed and the vested interest of those in whose political arena they are addressed. One can be criticized for "imposing" the morality of the church in one instance, lauded in another for courageous moral leadership, again in accordance with whose ox is gored. I repeat once more: For the church to influence public policy can be a rough-and-tumble business.

The *New York Times* observed this editorially when it came to the support of the NCCB-USCC in regard to certain aspects of the case instituted by abortion-rights supporters who charged that the church had violated its tax-exempt status by its efforts to influence public policy on abortion. The court, you will recall, imposed fines of one hundred thousand dollars per day on the NCCB-USCC for refusing to turn over various records. That's the real world: rough and tumble indeed, as the *Times* pointed out in asserting the right of bishops to function in that world.

The doctor in Albert Camus' *The Plague* describes his lawyer-father's hobby. He knew the schedule of every train in France: when it departed from where, when it arrived, and so on. But he never rode trains. Camus is telling us that

we only make an impact on the world when we engage it in reality, not merely
in the abstract.

We are coming closer to such engagement, in my judgment, in both the
process being used in the development of pastoral letters and the content of such
letters. This is especially true of successive drafts of the proposed pastoral letter
on Catholic social teaching and the economy. I believe that one sign that we are
entering the world of political reality is evident in the fact that the first draft
was greeted with accusations that it merely aped the 1984 Democratic Party
platform. This charge was made despite the fact that its publication was deliberately withheld so that it could not affect the 1984 elections.

Further, certain public officeholders are now using the proposed pastoral not
only to indict current administration policies, but to indict the current administration for allegedly using various of its "lackeys" to attack the pastoral. When
these kinds of things occur, we are becoming either troublesome or useful to
real-world politicians in accordance with their own respective interests, which
means to me that we have engaged not simply the issues, but the politically
sensitive people whose fortunes rise or fall on the outcome of the issues.

(Permit me to note in passing that, in my personal judgment, whatever the
perceived values or perceived defects of the proposed pastoral—and I saw the
third draft only the other day—its persistent emphasis on the question that must
be asked of every economic system will itself be an immensely valuable contribution. That tripartite question is: "What does it do for people? What does it
do to people? How do people participate in it?" This is as revolutionary and as
urgently needed a question as can be raised. Thank God for it.)

4. Among the obstacles to our moving from theory into practice, from concern
into action, is the fact that we are, most of us, rightly fearful, I believe, of
dividing members of the church, the one body of Christ, along political or ideological lines. "Liberal" and "conservative" have become glib pejoratives as have,
in some quarters, Democrat and Republican respectively. Statements of bishops,
priests, religious, or prominent lay persons are quickly categorized within those
terms, and those who have made the statements indicted or lauded accordingly.
None of this would be disturbing, perhaps, if it were not used as a religious
loyalty test. It seems to me, however, that we have so blurred distinctions between
the religious and theological and the political or ideological that this is precisely
what happens. And interestingly, no one is exempt. An impeccable record of
being ideologically a liberal or conservative since three months before birth cannot
protect one whose most recent utterance (liberal or conservative respectively) is
viewed as a religious betrayal.

If a personal reference may be permitted, I don't believe I have generally been
thought of as the preferred confessor for Americans for Democratic Action or the
ACLU. Yet when in congressional testimony I suggested that some of the monies
proposed to build more MX missiles be diverted to building homes for the poor,
it became quickly obvious that to a certain number of my erstwhile devotees I

had treacherously become a religious liberal, and my right to retain my metropolitan pallium became highly questionable. Indeed, in the same vein, I know of at least one gentleman who resolved never to darken the door of St. Patrick's Cathedral again because of my constant preachments about the poor, which he saw as political statements. The greatest volume of negative mail I have ever received, however, came not in conjunction with the issue that probably springs to your mind, but with a letter I sent to President Reagan on behalf of the Jewish communities that had appealed to me in respect to his visit to Bitberg. How you classify that one ideologically is anybody's guess, but I do know that for some I had forfeited not only my political integrity but my baptismal certificate.

Most dramatic, however, in consternation caused among Catholics of various positions was our pastoral letter on war and peace. Fuzzy-minded liberals who had lost the faith we never really possessed was one of the more common appellations we were given. Ultraconservatives in the pay of the White House was another; betrayers of our moral trust. No one in his or her right mind enjoys such allegations or escapes the fear of dividing the members of God's household into hostile camps. It's a risk I believe we must take, however, a risk that does not excuse us from the demands of charity and concern, but a risk that must be taken if public policy is to be affected.

Permit me to return for just a moment to the current proposed pastoral on Catholic social teaching and the economy as another illustration of what I am talking about. I have personally distributed ten thousand copies for study in my own archdiocese. Many responses are highly objective. Others reflect the tendency to blur distinctions and to look at bishops as political ideologues at one end of the spectrum or the other; once again, there would be little harm done except that as some church members lose political trust, there is a danger of their losing at least a degree of their religious trust. For me, this is one of the most difficult of all problems in our efforts to transition from the theoretical to the practical. It categorically must be confronted by a church that would appropriately influence public policy in the real world. Vatican II enunciates the problem and the need quite clearly in "The Church in the Modern World":

> It is of supreme importance, especially in a pluralistic society, to work out a proper vision of the relationship between the political community and the church, and to distinguish clearly between the activities of Christians, acting individually or collectively in their own name as citizens guided by the dictates of a Christian conscience and their activity acting along with their pastors in the name of the church.

> The church, by reason of her role and competence, is not identified with any political community nor bound by ties to any political system. It is at once the sign and the safeguard of the transcendental dimension of the human person. (no. 76)

I must close. There are no easy answers. It can be immensely helpful, however, to recognize that good people disagree on solutions without becoming less good as persons. Anglican Bishop Tutu would call for strong economic pressures, with special emphasis on extensive economic sanctions in South Africa, including divestment and disinvestment. The South African Roman Catholic bishops, while giving qualified support to economic pressure, have said that it is only justified if it is not applied in such a way as to destroy the economy or increase unemployment. "At the moment," they say, "we can see no justification for the sort of pressure that would leave a liberated South Africa in an economically unviable situation."

Some South African Catholics would like a bolder stand; some a weaker one. This kind of disagreement is inherent in the sincere effort of good people to "get at" the complex issues we have been discussing—which brings me full circle to the topic assigned me, "Church and Society: Issues in the Future." The primary and the most difficult issue, I repeat, is that of how we get at the issues at all. How do we, as church, go from theory to practice? How do we engage the real world? What is our point of entry into the public-policy arena, who does the entering, how and when? As the king of Siam said so quaintly and repeatedly to Anna: "It's a puzzlement."

I do believe this: that every one of us who wrestles with the questions experiences the puzzlement; and that every one of us who tries sincerely to engage the issues will make mistakes; and that every one of us who enters the fray will at times feel a sense of disorientation, even of being cut off from everything familiar and secure, and not a little bit lonely. Eli Wiesel tells a delightful Hasidic tale which I personally find helpful in coping with the experience as I see it.

Once upon a time there lived an absent-minded man. So absent-minded was he that he would forget in the morning where he put his clothes in the evening. He would spend hours looking for them, which made him late for work, late for meals, late for meetings. One day a friend gave him this excellent advice, "Why trust memory? Write down everything." That very evening he took a pen and piece of paper and jotted down, "My jacket is on the chair; my shoes, under the chair; my hat is on the table; and I—I am in my bed."

That night he slept well, peacefully. He rose early, as always, and was lucky enough to find the piece of paper. "Quick, where is the jacket? On the chair. The shoes? Under the chair." In a matter of minutes he located everything. He was happy—was he happy! He felt like screaming with joy. He wanted to let the entire world know that he had finally found a solution to all his problems. He was about to sing and dance when his eyes fell on the last lines, "and I am in my bed." He was seized with horror when he looked and found that he was not in bed, not even under the bed. In a frenzy he began searching the room, the next room. In vain. And he became sad once more, terribly sad. One heard him whisper, "And I, where am I?"

Ladies and gentlemen of the working press, if there are instances in which you are not certain of where I am, be assured there are times when I'm far less certain myself. But I'm always happy to have you tell me when you think you've found out.

Thank you very much, happy anniversary, and God bless you in your difficult work. We need you.

Prudence, Politics, and the Abortion Issue

Daniel A. Degnan

The difference between morality and prudential political action as applied to abortion is the central issue in today's debate over religion, morality, and politics.

Does prudence in politics mean that all of us, citizens and politicians alike, may simply disagree about the wisdom or practicality of legal action to prohibit or restrain abortions? If prudence means this, the moral appeals of the Catholic bishops and millions of others concerning abortion may well have force, but others may say, without moral reckoning, that the issue is better left to the private sphere. Their point would not be the specious idea that induced abortion, the direct killing of fetal life, is a personal or private matter. Rather it would be the better-grounded contention that laws prohibiting abortion would be in our society unwise, impracticable, or impossible to achieve, or perhaps all of these.

I do not think that prudence means that abortion can be shunted aside by anyone, citizen or politician. Prudential judgment in politics is not a name for caution, the modern sense of "prudence." Prudence in the classical sense concerns judgments about action. Prudence describes effective, wisely chosen action for the sake of an end or goal. Prudence is right action, not caution or timidity, not an avoiding of the great issues of the day.

In political action and law, prudential judgment is central. Political action and law aim at the common good, a general name for just relationships in society: the protection of the basic rights of all and the fair distribution of benefits and burdens. Prudential political judgment, which concerns the means for attaining this end, is an enormously difficult task. It must contend, first, with the capacity of the community to achieve justice, a question of knowledge and will, and of economics, culture, and history. Prudential action contends, second, with political organization and leadership, which range from the structure and membership of political parties and the quality and capacity of leaders to the quality of the legal system. It must contend, also, with our flawed, limited perceptions of the right and just course for society. In leading a political community toward the common good, there is, from the nature of the task, wide room for disagreement and uncertainty over the means to the end.

The paradox of political prudence is that the goal—the common good and justice—invests the task with the highest urgency and moral importance, while the complexity and difficulty of political action call for political wisdom and art in the highest degree. One thinks of Abraham Lincoln steering the nation through the crises of disunion and slavery.

How does abortion relate to justice and prudential politics? The safeguarding of human fetal life creates an urgent demand for action in the field of law and politics. Certain issues of justice relate to basic human rights, the right to life, the right to be protected against violence, the right to one's reputation, the right to be protected against theft. Thomas Aquinas called these rights "the very order of justice and virtue." More recently, John Finnis of Oxford has characterized them as "constitutive elements of the common good." Protection of these rights provides the foundation and structure of all other efforts to achieve a just society.

Abortion concerns the direct killing of the human fetus in each abortion operation. In the usual case of fundamental human rights, the question is not whether to protect such rights. Nor is the question one of disagreement on the means; laws prohibiting homicide and theft are straightforward means to the end. It would appear that abortion, a form of homicide, should yield to similar prohibition. With abortion, however, the situation is more complex.

In this country, the abortion issue is affected drastically by the Supreme Court's decision in *Roe v. Wade;* by the proabortion movement; by ambivalence about abortion on the part of many Americans, including Protestant church leaders and rabbis; and by understanding of abortion itself. The developing embryo and fetus are not visibly present to us as human infants are. Thus fetal stages of development and growth can lead to different responses, depending on the stage of pregnancy. These obstacles to moral judgment and to political and legal action must be considered in the prudential political judgments of all of us and especially of political leaders.

Ordinarily, a grave issue of public morality such as the taking of fetal life in induced abortions would be decided in the states. In our federal system, the states have the direct responsibility for public safety, education, and human welfare. It was state law that forbade or restricted abortion and that was the object of a campaign of "liberalization" in the early 1970s. The most notable change had come when New York had allowed abortion on demand up to the sixth month of pregnancy; a subsequent repeal had failed to override Governor Nelson Rockefeller's veto.

In 1973, in *Roe v. Wade,* the Supreme Court undertook to settle the controversy over abortion. By the Court's decree, all state laws prohibiting abortion were rendered impotent over the full nine months of pregnancy. In the first six months, no state law could prohibit an abortion. In the final three months, when the fetus was deemed to be viable, state laws might attempt to prohibit abortions. What the Court had given, however, it then took away. No prohibition based on the viability of the fetus could prevent an abortion when a physician found the abortion necessary for the health of the mother.

The Court's decision was predicated upon an asserted "right to privacy" of the woman, a right that overcame any rights of the human fetus and any interest of the states in protecting fetal life, even the fetus viable outside the womb. The result, as Justice White said in dissent, was to make abortions available at the convenience of the woman.

The decision was widely misstated in the *New York Times,* the Harris and Gallup polls, and elsewhere. The impression was given that the Court had allowed the protection of fetal life after the first three months, or after six months. Some of this distortion persists, although the Court had decreed abortion on demand.

The abortion decision has had two major effects. First, all legal restraints on abortion have been swept aside. Only an amendment to the Constitution or a reversal or modification of the decision itself can now permit the legal prohibition of abortions. No American needs to be told about the difficulty of amending the Constitution, a difficulty borne out by the recent failure of the proposed Equal Rights Amendment.

Second, the decision in *Roe v. Wade* has given a moral legitimacy to abortion with all the weight of the Supreme Court. The so-called right to privacy in abortion fits the current emphasis on individual rights in law and in society (although fetal rights are denied). Even among religious leaders, one finds considerable support for the decision. Reasons range from a moral agonizing over the comparative demands of the mother and fetus, as with James Gustafson, to an insouciant disregard for fetal life, as with Joseph Fletcher.

This is some of the backdrop for present efforts to stem the tide of abortions. Fifteen million abortions later, with the year 1983 showing 1.7 million abortions in the United States and 3.7 million live births, the tide may be turning.

How should the American people respond to the enshrining of abortion on demand in the Constitution? More particularly, what should citizens who oppose legalized abortion require of themselves and their political leaders? What follows is an attempt to apply principles of prudence and justice to the issue of abortion.

First, a constitutional amendment restricting abortions or an amendment returning the issue to the states is the only political means of preventing abortion on demand. In the alternative, a reversal by the Court of its own decision would permit legal restrictions on abortion. The Court's reversal would be unlikely, however, if the effort for a constitutional amendment slackened. A potent, sustained moral and legal effort to protect fetal life through a constitutional amendment can give the Court the reason and the courage to reverse its recent abortion decision.

Knowledge of the true nature of abortions may be what will lead Americans to overturn the Supreme Court. There has been a fastidious rejection, fostered by the proabortion lobby, of efforts to show what the abortion operation is. Many of us, I suspect, picture abortion as some procedure in which the fetus is "born dead."

In induced abortion, the fetus is killed. In suction curettage, the vacuum pulls apart the fetus. In operative obstetrics, the authors advise that the suction method not be used after thirteen weeks of pregnancy, since the fetal structures are well formed and the operation may result in an incomplete removal of the products of conception and injury to the uterus. In cervical dilatation and curettage (D & C), to be used up to twelve weeks, the forceps extract the "products of conception," the placenta and the fetus. The authors advise that gentle, slow extraction is more likely to remove the entire product as one specimen. Otherwise the forceps may be repeatedly introduced.

In the amniotic-fluid–saline exchange, for the sixteenth to twentieth week of pregnancy (ideally the eighteenth week), the amniotic fluid is withdrawn through a needle and a saline solution is then introduced into the womb. "Fetal demise" usually occurs within two hours. The abortion then takes place within twenty-four hours.

Why should we not know these facts? Why are we revolted by them? Americans are invited to follow the details of every kind of operation from kidney transplants to coronary bypasses to prenatal corrective surgery. We suffer revulsion because in abortion human life is killed in direct and cruel ways. The proabortion lobby would have us ignorant of what an abortion is.

I would hope that the opponents of abortion could unite to support a prolife institute that had the limited purpose of gathering and presenting the truth, medical and statistical, about the abortion operation and its methods and about the nature of the fetal life that is being killed, including the development of the fetus, its viability, its adaptability to treatment in the womb, and its susceptibility to pain. The truth, when soberly presented, should do more than anything else to convince Americans that the Supreme Court's abortion decision must be overturned. I draw this hope, in part, from the powerful insight of Thomas Aquinas that morality, at base, lies in our ability to perceive the real.

Second, what should we demand of our political leaders? Can a political leader be justifiably opposed to efforts for a constitutional amendment to overturn *Roe v. Wade* or indifferent to such efforts? If abortion on demand is an urgent question of public morality and justice, many of our leaders have failed us. Much of our leadership holds, with the Supreme Court, that abortion is a matter of private morality or of "choice." The irony is that justice in the highest sense, the protection of human rights, is the first responsibility of political leaders. The further irony, not uncommon in history, is that the people, not the political leadership, lead the fight for the rights of the human fetus, aided by a prophetic voice of religion and by a few political figures. Simply put, our political leaders must be held to account for their stands on abortion.

Yet there are prudential principles. I would advance several and a few particular applications. First, a political leader is not bound to do the impossible. This is not merely a pragmatic point; it belongs to the nature of action and of political leadership. If, for example, a constitutional amendment cannot be adopted and the Court will not reverse or modify its decision, the leaders' efforts would be symbolic at best, self-defeating at worst.

It is far from clear, however, that a constitutional amendment is impossible. Opposition to abortion has recently shown new strength and broad support. If a political leader judges the effort to limit abortions by legal means to be futile, his judgment must be weighed by those who seek to protect fetal rights. The long period of struggle often required to achieve political goals argues against any judgment of impossibility.

A second prudential principle is that legal and political goals may be reachable at other times, or by other means. As the Catholic bishops have pointed out, the impossibility of achieving an amendment at one moment does not excuse the effort to achieve it. There should also be efforts by political leaders to advance a prolife public ethic, to assist the carrying of pregnancies to term, to strengthen families, to aid unwed mothers, and to regulate abortion in the few ways still possible. At a minimum, political indifference to fetal life, as evidenced by the public funding of abortions, cannot be justified by appeals to the principle of nondiscrimination. That principle cannot be applied to unjust acts even when such acts are sanctioned legally.

A third prudential principle is the most important one, because it concerns the common good. Our responsibility and, especially, that of political leaders encompasses the common good. Issues of peace and nuclear war, of security, of a strong economy, of the fair distribution of the benefits and burdens of our society, must occupy our leadership. No one has expected President Reagan to place his primary emphasis on stemming abortions. The Catholic bishops have been deeply concerned with the prevention of nuclear war and the justice of our capitalist system, as well as with abortion.

Probably the broader and more direct a leader's political responsibilities, as with a president or governor, the less we can demand that abortion be the leader's primary effort—not because the issue is not of the gravest importance, but because so many other grave issues press for action. One could expect the president or a governor to offer leadership on the issue of abortion, but the real political work will have to be done in Congress and the state legislatures.

As a corollary of the common good, there can be no hope of prudential political action on abortion and other grave issues without responsible leadership in office. This would be a mere truism, were it not for the tenuous quality of political leadership in our society. Our leaders are not the product of long careers in strong parliamentary parties. Our national leaders govern by a shifting consensus, in a political world of weak, state-based political parties. If we demand too much of a leader on the abortion question in our society, we may destroy that leader. This is especially true in the Democratic Party, whose recent political conventions have been dominated by advocates of abortion.

In my own thinking, public morality in this country would receive a grievous blow if the Democratic Party were left in the hands of what has been called the knowledge class, the least morally responsible wing of the party, just as the Democratic Party appears to be returning, hesitantly, to basic values such as support for the family. It would be equally tragic if public morality and justice were allowed to be decided by extreme right-wing elements in the Republican Party, out of horror of abortion on demand. It was the Supreme Court, not the politicians, that created the crisis over abortion. The effort to resolve that crisis should be a national one, not identified with a political party.

The injustice of abortion, in sum, does not translate directly into a moral requirement that only prolife candidates should be supported. Many may judge that abortion in the United States is such a grave injustice and so dangerous to society that this issue should have first place in our political life. One can respect this judgment, even worry that it may be correct, while still making a different prudential judgment. One can also give great weight to abortion, while not making it the sole criterion of political action.

In prudential action, we are liable to uncertainty and mistake. The paradox is that in the area where we can be honestly mistaken we also have the gravest responsibility. A politician, for example, who opposed efforts to restrict abortions as unwise or unachievable may have blocked effective action to protect fetal life. Other Americans who leave no room for prudential, principled political leadership, or for necessary compromise, may have allowed the assault on fetal life to continue unchecked when some protection was possible and when the moral effect of restrictive laws might further stem the tide of abortions.

Part III

Abortion:
The Ecclesial Debate

Chapter 4

A Seamless Garment: The Implications of Moral Consistency

This chapter examines the "seamless garment ethic" or the "consistent ethic of life." Introduced first by Cardinal Bernardin in 1983, the method seeks to integrate Catholic moral teaching into a coherent whole. Even though criticized by both the right and the left, Bernardin has nonetheless succeeded in initiating a fruitful dialogue in moral theology. His latest contribution both reviews the theoretical foundation of the consistent ethic of life—reverence for life and the obligation to protect it at all stages— and then examines the move from moral analysis to public policy choices. The essay concludes with an evaluation of the implications of this for Catholic citizens and officeholders.

Margaret Steinfels's essay helps situate the feelings of many who have participated in past debates on moral problems within Catholicism and highlights the fact that this ethic has the possibility of expanding our moral imaginations into new and exciting possibilities. John Connery provides a very detailed analysis of how one can—and must—hold a consistent ethic of life but why that does not mean that there must be an absolute prohibition on any action resulting in the loss of life. The image that Connery suggests is a garment that is intricate in design but still seamless. Christine Gudorf provides a thorough analysis and critique of the seamless-garment ethic. Reversing Connery's analysis, Gudorf shows how the moral method used to deal with war can provide the basis for a different analysis of abortion. Taken together, the Connery and Gudorf essays raise substantive methodological and policy implications about Bernardin's proposal.

259

The Consistent Ethic:
What Sort of Framework?

Cardinal Joseph Bernardin

I am deeply grateful for the invitation to address you on a topic to which I have devoted much time and energy during the past three years: the "consistent ethic of life."

This morning I will (1) give an overview of the concept, (2) explore the movement from moral analysis to public-policy choices, and (3) identify issues needing further development: the implications of the consistent ethic for citizens, office seekers, and officeholders.

THE CONSISTENT ETHIC: AN OVERVIEW

The idea of the consistent ethic is both old and new. It is "old" in the sense that its substance has been the basis of many programs for years. For example, when the U.S. bishops inaugurated their Respect Life Program in 1972, they invited the Catholic community to focus on the "sanctity of human life and the many threats to human life in the modern world, including war, violence, hunger and poverty" (National Conference of Catholic Bishops' resolution, April 13, 1972).

Fourteen years later, the focus remains the same. As the 1986 Respect Life brochure states, "The pastoral plan is set in the context of a consistent ethic that links concern for the unborn with concern for all human life. The inviolability of innocent human life is a fundamental norm."

Moreover, the bishops' pastoral letter "The Challenge of Peace: God's Promise and Our Response" emphasized the sacredness of human life and the responsibility we have personally and as a society to protect and preserve its sanctity. In paragraph 285, it specifically linked the nuclear question with abortion and other life issues:

> When we accept violence in any form as commonplace, our sensitivities become dulled. When we accept violence, war itself can be taken for granted. Violence has many faces: oppression of the poor, deprivation of basic human rights, economic

260

exploitation, sexual exploitation and pornography, neglect or abuse of the aged and the helpless, and innumerable other acts of inhumanity. Abortion in particular blunts a sense of the sacredness of human life. In a society where the innocent unborn are killed wantonly, how can we expect people to feel righteous revulsion at the act or threat of killing noncombatants in war?

However, the pastoral letter—while giving us a starting point for developing a consistent ethic of life—does not provide a fully articulated framework.

It was precisely to provide a more comprehensive theological and ethical basis for the Respect Life Program and for the linkage of war and abortion as noted by the pastoral letter that I developed the theme of the consistent ethic. Another important circumstance which prompted me to move in this direction was that I had just been asked to serve as chairman of the bishops' Pro-Life Committee. It was October of 1983, and I knew that both abortion and defense-related issues would undoubtedly play an important role in the upcoming presidential campaign.

It was urgent, I felt, that a well-developed theological and ethical framework be provided which would link the various life issues while at the same time pointing out that the issues are not all the same. It was my fear that without such a framework or vision the U.S. bishops would be severely pressured by those who wanted to push a particular issue with little or no concern for the rest. With such a theological basis, we would be able to argue convincingly on behalf of all the issues on which we had taken a position in recent years.

I first presented the theme in a talk at Fordham University in December 1983. At that time I called for a public discussion of the concept both in Catholic circles and the broader community. In all candor I must admit that the public response greatly exceeded my hopes and expectations.

Since that time there has been a lively exchange by both those who agree and disagree with the theme and its implications. By far, the majority of the reactions have been supportive. Nonetheless, it has been used and misused by those who have tried to push their own, narrower agendas. I myself have made further contributions to the discussion through subsequent talks and articles.

The concept itself is a challenging one. It requires us to broaden, substantively and creatively, our ways of thinking, our attitudes, our pastoral response. Many are not accustomed to thinking about all the life-threatening and life-diminishing issues with such consistency. The result is that they remain somewhat selective in their response. Although some of those who oppose the concept seem not to have understood it, I sometimes suspect that many who oppose it recognize its challenge. Quite frankly, I sometimes wonder whether those who embrace it quickly and wholeheartedly truly understand its implicit challenge.

Last November, when the U.S. bishops updated and reaffirmed the Pastoral Plan for Pro-Life Activities, they explicitly adopted the consistent ethic for the first time as the theological context for the plan.

In sum, to the delight of those who agree with its theological reasoning and to the dismay of the small minority who do not, the consistent ethic has entered into our theological vocabulary.

Let me now explain in greater depth the theological basis and strategic value of the consistent ethic. Catholic teaching is based on two truths about the human person: Human life is both sacred and social. Because we esteem human life as sacred, we have a duty to protect and foster it at all stages of development from conception to natural death and in all circumstances. Because we acknowledge that human life is also social, society must protect and foster it.

Precisely because life is sacred, the taking of even one life is a momentous event. Traditional Catholic teaching has allowed the taking of human life in particular situations by way of exception—for example, in self-defense and capital punishment. In recent decades, however, the presumptions against taking human life have been strengthened and the exceptions made ever more restrictive.

Fundamental to these shifts in emphasis is a more acute perception of the many ways in which life is threatened today. Obviously, such questions as war, aggression, and capital punishment are not new; they have been with us for centuries. Life has always been threatened, but today there is a new context that shapes the content of our ethic of life.

The principal factor responsible for this new context is modern technology, which induces a sharper awareness of the fragility of human life. War, for example, has always been a threat to life, but today the threat is qualitatively different because of nuclear and other sophisticated kinds of weapons. The weapons produced by modern technology now threaten life on a scale previously unimaginable. Living as we do, therefore, in an age of extraordinary technological development means we face a qualitatively new range of moral problems.

The essential questions we face are these: In an age when we *can* do almost anything, how do we decide what we *should* do? In a time when we can do anything technologically, how do we decide morally what we should not do?

We face new technological challenges along the whole spectrum of life from conception to natural death. This creates the need for a consistent ethic, for the spectrum cuts across such issues as genetics, abortion, capital punishment, modern warfare, and the care of the terminally ill. Admittedly these are all *distinct* problems, enormously complex, and deserve individual treatment. Each requires its own moral analysis. No single answer or solution applies to all. *But they are linked!*

Given this broad range of challenging issues, we desperately need a societal attitude or climate that will sustain a consistent defense and promotion of life. When human life is considered "cheap" or easily expendable in one area, eventually nothing is held as sacred and all lives are in jeopardy. Ultimately it is society's attitude about life—whether of respect or nonrespect—that determines its policies and practices.

The theological foundation of the consistent ethic, then, is defense of the person. The ethic grows out of the very character of Catholic moral thought. I do not mean to imply, of course, that one has to be a Catholic to affirm the moral content of the consistent ethic. But I do think that this theme highlights both the systematic and analogical character of Catholic moral theology.

The systematic nature of Catholic theology means it is grounded in a set of basic principles and then articulated in a fashion which draws out the meaning of each principle and the relationships among them. Precisely because of its systematic quality, Catholic theology refuses to treat moral issues in an ad hoc fashion. There is a continual process of testing the use of a principle in one case by its use in very different circumstances. The consistent ethic seeks only to illustrate how this testing goes on when dealing with issues involving the taking of life or the enhancement of life through social policy.

The analogical character of Catholic thought offers the potential to address a spectrum of issues which are not identical but have some common characteristics. Analogical reasoning identifies the unifying elements which link two or more issues, while at the same time recognizing why similar issues cannot be reduced to a single problem.

The taking of life presents itself as a moral problem all along the spectrum of life, but there are differences between abortion and war, just as there are elements that radically differentiate war from decisions made about the care of a terminally ill patient. The differences among these cases are universally acknowledged. A consistent ethic seeks to highlight the fact that differences do not destroy the elements of a common moral challenge.

A Catholic ethic which is both systematic in its argument and analogical in its perspective stands behind the proposal that, in the face of the multiple threats to life in our time, spanning every phase of existence, it is necessary to develop a moral vision which can address these several challenges in a coherent and comprehensive fashion.

The theological assertion that the human person is made in the image and likeness of God, the philosophical affirmation of the dignity of the person, and the political principle that society and state exist to serve the person—all these themes stand behind the consistent ethic. They also sustain the positions that the U.S. Catholic bishops have taken on issues as diverse as nuclear policy, social policy, and abortion. These themes provide the basis for the moral perspective of the consistent ethic.

FROM MORAL ANALYSIS TO PUBLIC POLICY

Some commentators on the consistent ethic saw it primarily as a political policy. They missed its primary meaning: It is a moral vision and an ethical argument sustaining the vision. But the moral vision does have political consequences. The consistent ethic is meant to shape the public witness of the Catholic Church in our society.

Before exploring some of the political consequences, I would like to comment briefly on some related issues which provide a broader context for such a discussion. The movement from moral analysis to public-policy choices is a complex process in a pluralistic society like ours.

First, civil discourse in the United States is influenced, widely shaped, by religious pluralism. The condition of pluralism, wrote John Courtney Murray, is the coexistence in one society of groups holding divergent and incompatible views with regard to religious questions. The genius of American pluralism, in his view, was that it provided for the religious freedom of each citizen and every faith. However, it did not purchase tolerance at the price of expelling religious and moral values from the public life of the nation. The goal of the American system is to provide space for religious substance in society, but not a religious state.

Second, there is a legitimate secularity of the political process, just as there is a legitimate role for religious and moral discourse in our nation's life. The dialogue which keeps both alive must be a careful exchange which seeks neither to transform secularity into secularism nor to change the religious role into religiously dominated public discourse.

John Courtney Murray spent a substantial amount of time and effort defending the church's right to speak in the public arena. But he also stressed the limits of the religious role in that arena. Today religious institutions, I believe, must reaffirm their rights and recognize their limits. My intent is not, of course, to produce a passive church or a purely private vision of faith. The limits relate not to whether we enter the public debate but how we advocate a public case. This implies, for example, that religiously rooted positions somehow must be translated into language, arguments, and categories which a religiously pluralistic society can agree on as the moral foundation of key policy positions.

Third, all participants in the public discourse must face the test of complexity. From issues of defense policy through questions of medical ethics to issues of social policy, the moral dimensions of our public life are interwoven with empirical judgments where honest disagreement exists. I do not believe, however, that empirical complexity should silence or paralyze religious or moral analysis and advocacy of issues. But we owe the public a careful accounting of how we have come to our moral conclusions.

Fourth, we must keep in mind the relationship between civil law and morality. Although the premises of civil law are rooted in moral principles, the scope of law is more limited and its purpose is not the moralization of society. Moral principles govern personal and social human conduct and cover as well interior acts and motivation. Civil statutes govern public order; they address primarily external acts and values that are formally social.

Hence it is not the function of civil law to enjoin or prohibit everything that moral principles enjoin or prohibit. History has shown over and over again that people cherish freedom; they can be coerced only minimally. When we pursue a course of legal action, therefore, we must ask whether the requirements of public order are serious enough to take precedence over the claims of freedom.

Fifth, in the objective order of law and public policy, how do we determine which issues are public moral questions and which are best defined as private moral questions?

For Murray, an issue was one of public morality if it affected the public order of society. Public order, in turn, encompassed three goods: public peace, essential protection of human rights, and commonly accepted standards of moral behavior in a community. Whether a given question should be interpreted as one of public morality is not always self-evident. A rationally persuasive case has to be made that an action violates the rights of another or that the consequences of actions on a given issue are so important to society that the authority of the state and the civil law ought to be invoked to govern personal and group behavior.

Obviously, in a religiously pluralistic society, achieving consensus on what constitutes a public moral question is never easy. But we have been able to do it—by a process of debate, decision making, then review of our decisions.

Two cases exemplify how we struggled with public morality in the past. First, Prohibition was an attempt to legislate behavior in an area ultimately decided to be beyond the reach of civil law because it was not sufficiently public in nature to affect the public order. Second, civil rights, particularly in areas of housing, education, employment, voting, and access to public facilities, were determined—after momentous struggles of war, politics, and law—to be so central to public order that the state could not be neutral on the question.

Today we have a public consensus in law and policy which clearly defines civil rights as issues of public morality and the decision to drink alcoholic beverages as clearly one of private morality. But neither decision was reached without struggle. The consensus was not automatic on either question. Philosophers, activists, politicians, preachers, judges, and ordinary citizens had to state a case, shape a consensus, and then find a way to give the consensus public standing in the life of the nation.

The fact that a spontaneous public consensus is lacking at a given moment does not prohibit its being created. When he was told that the law could not legislate morality, Dr. Martin Luther King, Jr., used to say that the law could not make people love their neighbors, but it could stop their lynching them. Law and public policy can also be instruments of shaping a public consensus; they are not simply the product of consensus.

In sum, in charting the movement from moral analysis to public-policy choices, we must take into account the facts that (1) civil discourse in this nation is influenced and shaped by religious pluralism; (2) there is a legitimate secularity of the political process; (3) all participants in it must face the test of complexity;

(4) there is a distinction between civil law and morality; and (5) some issues are questions of public morality, others of private morality.

This brings us to the third part of my address.

IMPLICATIONS FOR CITIZENS, OFFICE SEEKERS, AND OFFICEHOLDERS

In light of the nearly three-year debate about the consistent ethic, questions have surfaced at the level of theological principle and ethical argument. As noted earlier, I have addressed these as they have arisen. The area that now needs attention is precisely how the framework of the consistent ethic takes shape *(a)* in the determination of public-policy positions taken by the church and *(b)* in the decisions that legislators and citizens take in light of the church's positions.

Let me hasten to acknowledge that I do not have all the answers to the next set of questions. At this point in the dialogue I have chosen simply to identify questions which need further reflection and discussion. I also acknowledge that others have raised some of the questions; they are not all mine. Although I am not prepared to give answers to these questions, I do intend to address them at a later date.

What role does consensus play in the development of public policy and civil law? Earlier I suggested that its role is essential in the long run. But what about the short term? Moreover, what are the appropriate roles of civic and religious leaders in providing moral leadership in the public-policy debate within a pluralistic community? What is the difference between a bishop's role and a politician's in the public debate about moral issues which the consistent ethic embraces? Should a politician wait until a consensus is developed before taking a stand or initiating legislation?

Must a Catholic office seeker or officeholder work for all clearly identified Catholic concerns simultaneously and with the same vigor? Is that possible? If such a person need not work for all these concerns aggressively and at the same time, on what basis does one decide what to concentrate on and what not? Does theology provide the answer, or politics, or both? What guidelines does one use to determine which issues are so central to Catholic belief that they must be pursued legislatively regardless of the practical possibilities of passage? What are the consequences if a Catholic office seeker or officeholder does not follow the church's teaching in the campaign for or exercise of public office?

What is a Catholic officeholder's responsibility, in light of the Second Vatican Council's Declaration on Religious Liberty, to protect the religious beliefs of non-Catholics? What is his or her responsibility under the Constitution? How are these responsibilities related?

How is the distinction between accepting a moral principle and making prudential judgments about applying it in particular circumstances—for example, in regard to specific legislation—worked out in the political order? What is the responsibility of a Catholic officeholder or office seeker when the bishops have made a prudential judgment regarding specific legislation? How are Catholic voters to evaluate a Catholic officeholder or office seeker who accepts a moral principle, and not only disagrees with the bishops regarding specific legislation but supports its defeat?

Until questions like these are explored and ultimately answered, using the consistent ethic of life to test public policy, party platforms and the posture of candidates for office will remain problematic and controversial. I firmly believe, however, that the consistent ethic, when pursued correctly and in depth, can make a genuine contribution. Solid, credible answers to the questions raised above will require an honest exchange of the best there is to offer in theological, political, and social thought.

I assure you that the Catholic bishops will remain in the public debate, and we need help. Public officials will remain in the line of fire, and they need help. Citizens will ultimately make the difference, and they too need help if the dialogue about how we are to respond to the broad range of contemporary issues is to proceed in a constructive fashion.

As the debate proceeds, we have a wonderful opportunity to bring together the best of our religious, political, and social traditions in the service of each other and the wider society to which we are bound in hope and love.

Consider the Seamless Garment

Margaret O'Brien Steinfels

It is 1971. I am sitting at my kitchen table reading the newspaper. The inconsistency of the Catholic Church's prolife position is about to hit me. There on the front page is a photo of Cardinal Terence Cooke complete with pilot's helmet sitting in a jet bomber in Vietnam. The massacre at Mylai and the trial of Lieutenant Calley have occurred. The war is proving devastating and unwinnable. It has violated every canon of just-war teaching.

I am appalled and outraged, the more so because the previous Sunday a letter from Cardinal Cooke was read from the pulpit. He wrote opposing New York's reform law permitting abortion on demand through the twenty-fourth week. In his letter he urged New York Catholics to work to "stop this slaughter of the innocent unborn." Where was his concern, I asked myself, for the innocent Vietnamese, born and unborn—and yes, for the American soldiers being maimed or slaughtered in an unjust and useless war?

Well, I wrote him off, and with him most of the other American bishops. Lean, mean, and twenty-nine, I dashed off a column I was then writing for the *National Catholic Reporter:*

> The day has long since passed when one expected moral leadership from one's bishop. But it is never too late for them to join their fellow Christians in deploring not only the immorality of abortion, but the immorality of Mylai and, if their vision prove large enough, the immorality of the Indochinese war.

High dudgeon that. The following November, in a disappointing statement, the bishops called for reconstruction and peace in Southeast Asia; not, I assume, in response to my column.

We Americans finally exited Vietnam. The 1970s trundled on. I didn't change my view of bishops. I vacillated about capital punishment, at first impressed by the common-sense impulse toward retribution, but finally convinced that the Gospel and Christian teaching were more compelling: We must never treat other human beings as though they were beyond repentance and reconciliation. (This does have the unfortunate effect of getting Henry Kissinger off the hook.)

My view of abortion did not change. It was immoral but not, I thought, susceptible to control by legal sanctions. So, though Justice Blackmun's reasoning

268

in *Roe v. Wade* struck me as specious, I thought the efforts of the two polarized groups, prolife and prochoice, that sprang up to do battle over the decision were equally beside the point. In their political-legal wranglings, neither paid much attention to the questions that seemed central to me: Why do women have abortions? What kind of society is it that encourages (even, sometimes, subtly forces) women to choose abortion over birth? What must be done to overcome those forces by providing the moral, cultural, economic, and social supports that would encourage them to choose birth over abortion?

LIVE AND LEARN

Time has passed. It is 1984. I am forty-two, not lean, and have learned to ration my outrage, focused at present on General Jaruzelski, Ronald Reagan, and Roberto D'Aubuisson. Terence Cooke, he of the pilot's helmet, died last fall in a manner at once inspiring and ennobling—embodying in his person the church's teaching that one need not pursue extraordinary medical treatment in the face of terminal illness (a teaching that right-to-life forces are busy obscuring in their fight against euthanasia). As I sat in church one Sunday last fall, listening to his final letter, in which he wrote of his coming death, I thought perhaps it was possible to learn something from a bishop.

Then there was the pastoral letter on war and peace, approved by the bishops last year at this time. The consultative process that produced it is a model that we'd be lucky to have those stars of democracy, our elected representatives in Congress, emulate. Not bad for bishops, I thought to myself.

Lest you are wondering why all of this has come to mind, there has been an unexpected outcome to that pastoral letter. It is the effort of several bishops, notably Cardinal Joseph Bernardin, to link opposition to abortion, war, hunger, capital punishment, and euthanasia together with support for human rights and social welfare by making a case for a consistent ethic of life, the so-called seamless garment.

Cardinal Bernardin, chair of the committee that prepared the pastoral letter and now head of the bishops' Committee for Pro-Life Activities, has argued in two recent speeches (Fordham University, December 6, 1983; St. Louis University, March 11, 1984) that there is

> the need for an attitude or atmosphere in society which is the precondition for sustaining a consistent ethic of life. . . . We intend our opposition to abortion and our opposition to nuclear war to be seen as specific applications of this broader attitude.

Are the bishops about to close the inconsistency gap that so troubled me back in 1971? Perhaps, but not necessarily in ways that will satisfy everyone.

Some right-to-life advocates have read Bernardin's argument as an effort to smother their efforts by adding nuclear war and capital punishment to the prolife agenda. Pacifists, such as Gordon Zahn and Daniel Berrigan, and such groups as the Catholic Worker, Pax Christi, and Pro-Lifers for Survival—all of whom criticized the pastoral's conditioned acceptance of nuclear deterrence—nonetheless might welcome Bernardin's support for the overall position they have long held.

The temptation to search Bernardin's speeches for a political agenda is irresistible. Right-to-life and antinuke groups nervously scan for the phrase that signals its political priorities have been displaced in favor of the other's. But my well-honed ability to read between the lines was short-circuited by Bernardin's adept hand at thwarting such efforts. Certainly there is mention of public policy, but nothing clear or decisive. Perhaps searching for a political agenda is a distraction, and expecting the bishops to develop one is an error—an error we so readily embrace because we have come to believe that the only real solutions are political solutions. Perhaps the bishops are pointing to another kind of solution.

COMPLEXITY AND CONSISTENCY

In his St. Louis speech, Bernardin said, "A consistent ethic of life should honor the complexity of the issues it must address. . . . A systematic vision of life seeks to expand the moral imagination of a society, not partition it into airtight categories."

What would expanding our moral imaginations mean?

I find it hard to imagine an answer; perhaps because my own imagining powers are in need of expansion. But if that is what the bishops are up to, it is no small task.

But what if they were to try? The Christian tradition carries rich symbols and gestures, remembers bold words and actions that could embody the claim that all life is to be valued. In a moving essay in his volume *A Community of Character*, Stanley Hauerwas develops one of the convictions that could nourish our moral imaginations.

> It is the Christian belief, nurtured by the command of Jesus, that we must learn to love one another, that we become more nearly what we were meant to be through the recognition and love of those we did not "choose" to love. Children, the weak, the ill, the dispossessed provide a particularly intense occasion for such love, as they are beings we cannot control. We must love them for what they are rather than what we want or wish them to be, and as a result we discover that we are capable of love. The existence of such love is not unique or limited to Christians. Indeed that is why we have the confidence that our Christian convictions on these matters might ring true even for those who do not share our convictions. The

difference between the Christian and the non-Christian is only that what is a possibility for the non-Christian is a duty for the Christian.

The work of moral imagination is difficult and complex; it seems to live only in short spurts and in out-of-the-way places, nourished by the courage and wit of extraordinary people. Are the bishops up to it? In 1971, I did not think so. Now, I hope so.

A Seamless Garment
in a Sinful World

John R. Connery

The term "seamless garment" was used by Cardinal Joseph L. Bernardin in his recent Gannon lecture at Fordham University in New York to symbolize the single attitude one should have toward life. The meaning of the term, if not its present application, is familiar to everyone acquainted with the Gospel of St. John. In the current context it is meant to convey the idea that one should have a consistent ethic of life. Respect for life should include all human life. Thus, one should not draw a line, or put a seam in the garment, by making an exception where respect for human life is at stake.

The issue has surfaced as the result of current movements against warfare, capital punishment, and abortion. The practical question is whether a consistent ethic of life will allow a person to favor one of these movements without favoring all of them. Or perhaps more pointedly, whether it will allow him or her to favor one of them and at the same time oppose the others? Is this putting a seam in a garment that should be seamless? Let us take a closer look at the issue.

The "seamless garment," or consistent ethic, approach certainly has some reasonably clear applications. It is inconsistent, for instance, for an antiwar group to be against the killing that takes place in warfare and proabortion at the same time. The same is true of those who are opposed to capital punishment but proabortion. But what about people who are opposed to abortion? Does a consistent ethic of life demand that they be opposed to war and to capital punishment? Superficially, this would seem to follow from what has already been conceded about consistency in the other direction. At the least, one must ask why a consistent ethic should not work both ways. If one may not be selective in one direction, how can one justify selectivity in the other direction?

Before responding, I think all would have to agree that life as such is a basic value, and that therefore the loss of any life is something that must be regretted. A consistent respect for life will not tolerate any kind of line-drawing or "seam" on this level. One must never rejoice over the loss of life as such. A consistent ethic would even call for the wish or desire that taking human life would never be acceptable.

272

But a realistic approach to the world in which we live has long taught us that it is not possible to achieve this goal. It has taught us, for instance, that we do not have the kind of control over the effects of our acts to rule out the possibility of death resulting from them. This is true of almost any human activity that comes to mind. St. Augustine said that if it was wrong to place any act from which death might result, our hands would be virtually tied. We would not be able to build a house or plant a tree, because someone might hang himself from the tree or fall off the roof of the house. In our own time, given the number of lives lost in automobile and airplane accidents, the invention, or even the use, of the automobile or the airplane could never be justified. Yet no one questions the morality of these human inventions or their use. This would indicate a consensus that a consistent ethic of life would not require that we never place an act from which a death might be the result.

Actually, in this kind of human activity the choice is not really between taking a human life or not taking one. If the act in question is performed, some lives will be lost, but others will be saved. Thus, for instance, while the automobile and the airplane may be the cause of many deaths, they are also responsible for saving many lives. Without the automobile or the airplane, while those lives that would have been lost are saved, other lives are lost. So forgoing a particular act or asset may not be any more conducive to lifesaving than placing it or using it. This fact would not, of course, justify any loss of life that would result from neglect. Neglect would clearly involve an unwarranted loss of life, and hence reveal a lack of respect for life. Neither would it justify a loss of life that would be totally disproportionate to the expected benefits of an act. But it is not realistic to expect that a consistent ethic of life will eliminate all unintentional taking of human life. Such loss of life is part of the human condition.

Any attempt to eliminate all loss of life by forgoing activity that might result in death, besides being doomed to failure, would paralyze the human enterprise. We are dealing with conflict situations that involve both saving and losing life, and these effects are inseparable. An ethic of life cannot change this and should not be expected to do so.

Long experience has also taught us that the presence of sin in the world can give rise to such conflict situations. Again, these conflicts limit our options. We are no longer facing a simple choice between taking a life and respecting life. The choice is rather between respecting one life or respecting another life. It is sin or moral evil (in the form of unjust violence) that forces this choice upon us. The issue is one of response to sin or moral evil, or of coping with sin and the effects of sin. If taking a life is the only effective means of doing this, however regrettable it may be, it will be acceptable. A consistent life-ethic will not forbid it. Since the response is dictated by respect for innocent human life, I would not really consider it a seam in the garment. But if it is, it is a seam that is shaping the garment to the sinful world in which we live will allow, or even demand.

The alternative would ordinarily be victory for sin and its gradual spread with increasing loss of life.

To be more specific, if one is the victim of unjust aggression, the choice is not between respecting human life and not respecting it. The choice is rather between one life and another, between the life of the victim and that of the unjust aggressor. Respect for life, or a consistent ethic, will not demand that one sacrifice his own life to save the life of the aggressor. And if the aggression is against those for whom one holds responsibility, for example, one's wife or children, the defender may have no moral choice. To demand the kind of respect for life that would forbid defense of self or of those who are near and dear would put a premium on violence and make sin automatically victorious. This kind of consistency would constitute a threat to innocent human life.

This is true of private self-defense. It is also true of defending one's country against unjust aggression on the part of another. Again, the option is not between showing respect for life or failing to do so. It is rather the legitimate preference of one's own country and the lives of one's countrymen over the lives of the unjust aggressors.

Coping with sin has also been the basic reason underlying capital punishment. Again, the choice is not simply between respecting the life of the criminal and not respecting it. It is more a choice between the life of the criminal and the lives of possible future victims. Today that explanation is being questioned. But the issue is not that a consistent ethic makes it wrong as such to take the life of the criminal. The question is rather whether capital punishment gives the kind of protection it should, or whether some other kind of punishment would not be just as effective. The American bishops have raised this question in two recent statements (1974, 1980).

Respect for life certainly demands that the rationale behind capital punishment be investigated, and if it becomes clear that some other kind of punishment would be just as protective of human life, respect for life would demand that it be eliminated. But a consistent ethic of life would not call for an a priori condemnation of capital punishment.

Some might wish to argue that the person who takes the life of the unjust aggressor (in private or in war) or the criminal is no better than they are, since he is doing the same thing. The argument might have a point, if it were just a question of taking a life. But as we have already pointed out, self-defense and punishment are not just taking human life. They are a response to sin and by definition the only way of coping with sin and its effects. Without such a response, sin would triumph, and even worse, it would spread.

On the other side of the coin, respect for life implies an obligation to preserve our lives and the lives of those in our care. Any neglect on our part will be inconsistent with this respect. On the other hand, it has always been recognized that there is a limit to what one must or even may do to preserve life. Although basic, life is not the greatest good, nor is the loss of life the greatest evil. For instance, it would never be permitted to do something immoral, even if conceivably it would preserve life. It has always been admitted as well that there is a limit to the obligation even to use means that would be morally permissible.

This is a large subject, and one we cannot possibly deal adequately with here. It is enough to say that a consistent ethic of life does not demand that we do everything possible to hold on to life. As the recent Declaration on Euthanasia (1980) advises, a refusal of heroic means "is not the equivalent of suicide; on the contrary, it should be considered as an acceptance of the human condition."

Finally, respect for life calls for concern for the quality of life available to people. A consistent ethic of life cannot be satisfied with a quality of life inconsistent with human dignity and should oppose such incompatibility wherever it prevails. Although human life is always a basic value, human dignity calls for a complement of other goods. Without at least a minimum of such goods human beings will not be able to function in a way consistent with their dignity as human beings, but will be reduced to the level of animal living. On the other hand, realism should make it clear that one cannot hope for perfectly equal distribution of goods and that attempts at bringing about such a distribution will be both futile and disruptive. So a consistent ethic of life will not call for full equality or efforts at achieving it.

Neither will respect for life demand that one approve of any specific or particular plan or strategy (a defense plan or a welfare program) aimed at this goal. This is a very important point, since it is very easy for all of us, especially when we are dedicated to some worthy cause, to confuse goals with means and plans. For Christians it is easy to identify such projects with moral goals, or even with the Gospel message.

Vatican II cautions us that sincere Christians may legitimately differ regarding means or strategies. It tells us:

> Very often their Christian vision will incline the faithful to favor a particular solution to a problem in some given situation. Yet others with no less sincerity may judge differently, and legitimately so, about the same problem. Now if people, even contrary to the wishes of the sponsors, too easily associate one or the other of these solutions with the Gospel message, it should be kept in mind that in such cases no one is permitted to identify the authority of the church with his own opinion. Let them, then, try to enlighten each other by sincere dialogue in a spirit of mutual charity and with genuine solicitude for the common good. (*Gaudium et spes*, no. 43)

No one should adopt the attitude that a person who does not agree with a particular defense proposal or welfare program aimed at respect for life in some problematic area is less Christian, or accuse him of not having a consistent ethic of life. A consistent ethic of life is quite compatible with disagreement about the way to achieve it. So one cannot conclude from the fact that one person or group may differ with another about a particular method or program that they do not have a consistent ethic of life, or that they are less Christian. We are in an area here of prudential judgment where the difference is not on the level of principle or goal but on the best way of applying the principle or achieving the goal in practice. Sincere differences of opinion can occur here even though there may be complete agreement on the guiding principle.

Briefly, then, a consistent ethic of life requires that one respect human life in all its forms: preborn, infant, handicapped, adolescent, adult, and aged (terminal). While it does not apply immediately to conflict situations, where the choice is not simply between respect for life and taking life, but between taking one life and losing another, it will apply indirectly. Thus, for instance, while it does not demand that we give up self-defense, whether the unjust aggression is on the part of an individual or a whole nation, it does demand that we do everything possible to make the danger of such aggression more and more remote. It will demand, therefore, that we try to prevent war, crime, and unjust aggression.

It does not, however, require that we get intimately involved in all these causes. With our human limitations we are certainly not able to devote ourselves to all of these causes without spreading ourselves too thin and weakening our efforts. A consistent ethic of life would not demand that everyone get involved in all respect-for-life causes, but would allow for a reasonable division of labor. In fact, concentration on particular causes may well be a requirement for success, whereas dissipation of effort may be self-defeating. Respect for life, however, will demand that, even when we cannot get personally involved in a particular cause, we respect those who do and avoid anything that would compromise their goals or their efforts.

Concentrating on particular prolife causes can indeed give rise to problems. Problems can arise, for instance, in regard to choosing and supporting candidates for public office. There is nothing wrong, of course, in bringing to public attention the records and positions of candidates for office on particular issues. This can be a real service to the busy voter. But it can also be misused. We are speaking of the temptation to so-called one-issue voting. Certainly, even a consistent prolife ethic would not automatically qualify a candidate for a particular office. While it should be a factor in assessing him, and an important factor, it is not the only requirement for public office. Public office is multifaceted and calls for many competences and overall moral integrity. Fulfillment of one requirement will not of itself qualify a candidate for any office. It is quite possible for a candidate to qualify in one area but be so deficient, or even so corrupt, in other areas, as to be disqualified. Even if a candidate has a consistent ethic of life, which would indeed weigh very heavily in his favor, such an imbalance is still a possibility.

But the problem of one-issue voting arises more frequently in connection with respect-for-life movements limited to one particular area. Concentration on respect for life in one area—for example, antiabortion—even though perfectly legitimate, can result in too exclusive a focus on that problem. By informing voters regarding the stance of candidates in their area of concern, these movements indeed perform a service which may not be available regarding other requirements for office. They thus make it relatively easy for voters to make a judgment about a candidate's position on abortion. It is also easier in general to assess a candidate's position on abortion than it is in other respect-for-life areas.

In line with what has been said above, the judgment about a candidate's respect for life in these areas may be very difficult to infer from positions he takes, for example, in regard to war-and-peace programs, welfare programs, and so forth. Reliable information about a candidate's other qualifications may be even less accessible. Given the dependence of the ordinary voter on the media, who are too often more interested in influencing the voter than informing him, the temptation to frustration and to shortcut the process necessary for informed voting is understandable. But the difficulty of making the voting informed will not justify neglect. Put simply, an antiabortion attitude, or even a consistent prolife attitude, will not automatically qualify a candidate for office. The final judgment must be made on the basis of all the requirements of a particular office.

To insist on this is not to diminish in any way the importance of any particular prolife issue. It is merely to point out that concentration should not be allowed to result in a loss of perspective or indifference to other life issues or other requirements for office. As long as this is guarded against, the more that people become involved in particular prolife movements like the antiabortion movement, the more sensitive will they become to the values at stake and the deeper will be their appreciation of these values. This has to have a salutary impact on a society that is already becoming largely desensitized to the value of what one author aptly calls life "at the edges." The distance between life "at the edges" and life "at the center" is not that perceptible.

We can conclude by applying what has been said to the symbolism of the seamless garment. It should be clear from the above discussion that our ethic of life should be without seam in the sense that it should be consistent. An inconsistent ethic of life could not be justified, since it would be flawed. But a consistent ethic of life need not and should not be simplistic. Thus it cannot reasonably call for an absolute prohibition of any action that would result in the loss of life. As we have already seen, it must be much more nuanced. But this does not require seams in the garment. A garment may be complex and still seamless. A garment must be woven from many threads, and if it is multicolored or even includes some pattern or design, it may become quite intricate. In the same way a consistent ethic of life may be quite complex and still remain consistent. On the other hand consistency could easily be lost by simplification. Seamlessness or consistency and complexity, at least within limits, are not incompatible whether in a garment or in an ethic of life.

To Make a Seamless Garment, Use a Single Piece of Cloth

Christine E. Gudorf

Abortion stands alone along our spectrum of moral issues. In the birth control controversy, anyone who maintained that she would never use artificial contraception, and would never encourage anyone else to do so, would be welcomed with open arms as the most loyal of Catholics. But in the abortion controversy, persons such as Geraldine Ferraro—or myself—who make such disclaimers are counted as proabortion if they do not also support legislation to make abortion illegal. Among some in the Catholic community such persons are often labeled "not really Catholic."

I resent this. I am not proabortion, and I learned this the hard way. My husband and I accepted for adoption a five-year-old with multiple birth defects which were estimated to be terminal within two to five years. I had quit work to qualify as an adoptive mother, and my husband was only halfway through law school. He supported us on a weekend night job. I was to begin graduate school six months later when our new son would enter kindergarten. In the midst of all this I discovered I was five or more months pregnant (the early symptoms having been masked by the effects of earlier gynecological surgery) and that I had rheumatic fever. My doctor advised abortion immediately.

My husband and I had thought we had no strong feelings against abortion, and had linked the church's teaching with that on artificial contraception, a teaching we had rejected in order to adopt hard-to-place children. We thought this eminently moral, and rather blithely assumed that abortion would be, also. We found out differently. This was a real crisis for us: new parents already, no money, sick, far from family, and pregnant. But within twenty-four hours it was clear there would be no abortion. How could we love the abandoned children of others if we did not love and accept our own? And yet we are called "proabortion" for believing that others should be able to decide as we did whether to have a child.

The intolerance implicit in this label disturbs me; it suggests that Catholicism is reverting to a siege mentality in which everyone who is not 100 percent with us is against us, an enemy. In this essay, I suggest that we need to keep separate the decision that abortion should be made illegal. I intend to justify that separation by examining Catholic teaching on war, especially the pastoral letter of the U.S. bishops. I believe that in Catholic teaching on abortion and war we have two significantly different methods of moral decision making despite claims of and calls for a consistent ethic of life, a "seamless garment," and that only one method is compatible with the Catholic model of the human person. The other method, I believe, is a leftover from the days when the church and the state were confederates in power, when the authority of the church was imposed by the power of the state.

This distinction between a personal moral decision against abortion and a political decision by the individual to make abortion illegal is under attack, especially in New York, where the moral integrity of such prominent Catholic politicians as Geraldine Ferraro and Mario Cuomo has been called into question by the bishops of New York, who consider the distinction illegitimate.[1] I have yet to see an intellectually satisfying analysis of the differences between the bishops and the politicians. News coverage—secular as well as religious—has delved no further than slogans and clichés, perhaps because the principals have offered little more.

One must agree with the bishops that personal moral conviction cannot be legitimately divorced from political decisions; in fact, it should not only inform but be the foundation for those decisions. Ferraro and others are at fault to the extent that they have indicated that personal and political moral decisions are not synonymous without specifying whether or how they are related. On the other hand, the bishops are remiss in writing glib statements which seem to equate moral principles with specific legal applications of those principles.

A politician should not acquiesce to the wishes of the majority when they contradict his or her conscience, as Mario Cuomo has attested in thrice vetoing capital punishment laws desired by the majority in New York State. At the same time, when fundamental moral values are in conflict, as they are in the abortion instance, and strong popular support for the conclusion reached by the legislator's conscience is absent, a strong case can be made for Catholic legislators' refusing to impose their conclusions of conscience on others. The more difficult a moral decision is to reach, the less ready we should be to choose legislation as the means to promote moral change.

I intend to show that Catholic social teaching is inconsistent in its approach to the issues of abortion and war, and that the method used to deal with the issue of war can support a different treatment of abortion.

SANCTIONS FOR KILLING INNOCENT LIFE DIRECTLY

The similarity in Catholic teaching on war and abortion derives from the principle that one may never morally kill innocent life directly.[2] Obviously, fetal life is innocent. The debates within Catholic thought about abortion have centered traditionally on whether abortion could ever be justified as indirect, as in the case of tubal pregnancy (allowed under the principle of double effect) or whether self-defense could be used to justify abortion when the fetus·constituted a threat to the life of the mother (traditionally not allowed).

At the level of moral principle, our Catholic position is consistent. It is inconsistent at the level of political application. For the direct taking of innocent life in war has always been condemned by the church. One of the *jus in bello* conditions of just-war theory is noncombatant immunity. In their pastoral letter, this is a major difficulty that the U.S. bishops have with nuclear war: it cannot be discriminate enough to preserve noncombatant immunity.

Yet, in its teaching on war and abortion, the magisterium does not apply this principle with any consistency. We do not have religious sanctions for those who destroy innocent life in war. How many soldiers, bomber pilots, or generals who order or carry out the destruction of villages, towns, and cities have ever been excommunicated, or even threatened with excommunication? Modern warfare is technological, its weapons so destructive that even what we designate "conventional war" is indiscriminate. That fact needs no elaboration here.[3]

Even when we intend to avoid making war on civilians our technological systems remain prone to human error, as we saw in our bombing of the mental hospital in Grenada. The antiguerilla warfare our government supports in El Salvador too seldom distinguishes guerillas from innocent civilians. The contra war we finance in Nicaragua is primarily a war against civilians, with hospitals, schools, factories, and day-care centers among the primary targets because of their value as symbols of the revolution.

Some will surely say that the reason the church imposes sanctions on women who kill innocent life in abortion and not on men who kill innocent life in war is that war is so complex that it is difficult to judge individual guilt. The answer is inadequate. Is it so clear that the abortion decision is never complex? That women are not facing authorities with orders: employers who will fire them, men who will leave them, parents who will eject them from their homes? Are these never situations of self-defense? Surely if the direct taking of innocent life is always immoral, and women who take one such life are subject to excommunication for mortal sin, we would expect to find at the very least a threat of such sanctions against generals and politicians who in fact bankroll a war against civilians in Nicaragua and in theory stand ready to save the world through planetary suicide. But we find no such threat.

Women are threatened with dire sanctions; men in the military are treated to an exercise in persuasion. To illustrate the difference, I have rewritten a passage from the U.S. bishops' pastoral letter on nuclear war.

311. We remind all pregnant women and all in the medical profession that medical training and manuals have long prohibited, and still do prohibit, certain actions, especially those actions which inflict harm on persons. The question is not

whether certain measures are lawful or forbidden, but which measures: to refuse to take such measures is not an act of cowardice or blind obedience, but one of courage and responsibility.

312. We address particularly those involved in pregnancy counseling and those with responsibility for health programs. We are aware of your responsibilities and impressed by the standard of personal and professional duty you uphold. We feel therefore that we can urge you to do everything you can to insure that every other alternative is exhausted before abortion is even remotely considered. In developing plans in individual cases, and in planning social policy, we urge you to try to insure that these are designed to reduce violence, suffering, and death to a minimum, remembering the innocence of the unborn.

313. Those who train medical personnel must remember that the individual does not lose his or her basic human rights either by becoming a patient or by becoming a member of a medical team. No one, for whatever reason, can justly treat a patient or a health worker with less dignity and respect than that demanded for and deserved by every human person. One of the most difficult problems with abortion involves supporting a free society wherein patients make their own choices, without endangering the right of health care workers to choose in accordance with their own values. Dehumanization of patients or health workers by removing from them decision-making responsibility, or by generating hatred toward those who oppose their stance, robs them of basic human rights and freedoms, degrading them as persons.

Have women faced with an unwanted pregnancy even heard such a pastoral message from the hierarchy? They have not.

In the pastoral, we find no judgment on persons, no condemnation of those who make the wrong choice, no list of specific circumstances under which a pilot can decide to bomb a target, or a soldier to shoot or not. Instead we read:

> Our pastoral contact with Catholics in military service, either through our direct experience, or through our priests, impresses us with the demanding moral standards we already see observed and the commitment to Catholic faith we find. We are convinced that the challenge of this letter will be faced conscientiously. [4]

Indeed, the bishops wrote the pastoral letter to provoke reflection and discussion on the issue of war and the taking of life in war in the conviction that only such reflection and discussion will lead to the end of war. [5] They chose reflection and discussion rather than coercion as the means to affect social policy not only with reference to non-Catholics, whom the bishops do not have the power to coerce, but also with reference to Catholics, whom they do not order to conscientious objection either. Even the instruction of Catholic military personnel offers moral principle rather than specific commands. Why is persuasion deemed appropriate for dealing with one kind of social policy regarding the taking of innocent life, but inappropriate for another social policy regarding the taking of innocent life?

Our church has not been pacifist since the third century; in fact as late as the 1950s—long after it was clear that modern warfare necessarily kills the innocent along with the military—we find Pius XII stating that conscientious objection is forbidden to Catholics as irresponsible.[6] Why can some things be more important than preserving innocent life in war, but not in reproduction? Why no primary emphasis on helping women themselves to choose to support life, rather than coercing them into parenthood? Have women so much worse a record at preserving life than the military whom the bishops praise?

Of course not. The historical reasons for this inconsistency lie in the separation of reality into two spheres, the public and the private, and the unconscious acceptance by the church at the end of the nineteenth century of the notion that religion's home is in the private realm, the realm of compassion, humaneness, morality, the realm of the family, of personal relationships, and faith. Only since Vatican II has the church seen the public realm as an appropriate object of full-scale mission and begun regularly to address such issues as poverty, disarmament, human rights (other than religious), capital punishment, racism, and capitalism.[7] In addressing these issues the church still sees itself as a relative newcomer who must convince the principals of its right to participate and of the worth of its contribution. The church speaks to persuade, because it cannot coerce. It uses reason and is careful to consult many other views. Before writing a word of "The Challenge to Peace," the bishops invited to their hearings almost every political name ever associated with U.S. defense policy, and most groups that deal with it. Can we assume that a letter on family policy or marriage law, or any other private-realm issue, would be preceded by hearings where half or more of the witnesses were non-Catholics, or even unchurched experts? No. In the private realm, our church feels it owns the turf, that moral principles are sufficient, that social analysis, while sometimes helpful, is not necessary because the principles are absolute and their practical applications obvious.

The Catholic Church uses proportional consequentialism in public-realm issues, and a deontological natural law approach in private-realm issues. Some bishops, it has been rumored, were upset at the consequentialism (to which they are in principle opposed) of the pastoral letter on nuclear war—and well they might be in view of the case I am attempting to make here. What is astounding is that they had not already noticed their heavy reliance on consequentialism in addressing public-realm issues, as for example, in capital punishment.[8]

The political stance of the church on public-realm issues has with seeming irrevocability been committed to working within the existing socio-political framework. As a result, the bishops could not use a deontological approach based on New Testament or early-church pacifism, or even a strict just-war application, for that would necessitate outlawing all modern weapons for war and all participation in such wars because they entail indiscriminately killing the innocent. Either approach would have resulted in a new version of the nineteenth-century clash between church and state; the church, now outside the political community, would have been seen as the political adversary of the modern nation-state. To avoid this possibility, consequentialism was necessary.

The fact that many bishops who in principle oppose consequentialism as a moral method tend to support American wars and military interventions, and to disavow pacifism, no doubt influenced the final result also. The move to consequentialism is limited to public-realm issues. The church is attempting to retain a deontological, law-centered approach to the private realm—which includes not only personal morality (especially sexual) but also intraecclesial questions. One might conjecture that consequentialism is perceived as relatively harmless in the public realm, which has already passed beyond the control of the church. Consequentialism in the private realm, one might guess, is perceived as dangerous to the power structure in the church because consequentialism, which requires rigorous contextual analysis best done by persons immersed in a specific context, would force the magisterium at the very least to share the power of moral decision making with the laity. That sharing is difficult when those immersed in the situations are men; a consequential morality of abortion cedes power to women.

When we consider the methodological inconsistency between the church's treatment of war and of abortion, it is small wonder that femjinists charge the church with misogyny because of its apparent distrust of women as moral decision makers. Women with the medical option of abortion seem, in the bishops' eyes, to be a greater danger to life than men armed with tanks, missiles, and bombs.

This is a grave matter for the future of the church. Though I do not believe that the source of the inconsistency is misogyny, I do feel that the continuation of methodological inconsistency which discriminates against women as moral persons is possible only in a climate of misogyny. In a society where many, and potentially all, women are not in control of their own bodies, but are raped, beaten, and molested by fathers, husbands, and strangers, as well as subjected to medical care which often treats care of women's bodies as if they were not women's to control[9]—in such a society we move in entirely the wrong direction when we refuse to allow women final responsibility for their bodies' reproduction.

Much present thinking among Catholics on this issue is reprehensible, especially those recent voices which maintain that since the courts might use state equal-rights amendments to support abortion funding, Catholics are morally obliged to oppose equal rights laws.[10] The argument that women should not be granted equality because it might be misused is not different from past arguments for not freeing the slaves or giving the vote to the unpropertied, because they might misuse these rights. Freedom cannot be refused whole classes of persons on the ground that some of them might, or even probably would, use that freedom to commit grievous sin.

CHURCH AND POLITICS

These reflections lead to another difference in treatment of war and abortion by the bishops, and that is the use of the political realm as an instrument of the church's moral policy. The church is involved in politics, and always has been,[11] though it has fairly consistently in this country abstained from electoral politics (supporting particular candidates and parties). Attempts by the church to safeguard religious practice have always involved the church in politics. For example, the 5D exemptions for priests, ministers, and seminarians in our World War II draft, law were the result of the lobbying efforts of the Catholic bishops of the U.S., efforts that set precedents for similar laws in subsequent wars.[12] Despite the oft-heard charge that the church should stay out of politics, or did stay out of politics until recently, we have, even here in the U.S. (the case being easier to make in Europe where the church has concordats with nations), a rather consistent record of church involvement in politics not only regarding war, but also other aspects of social policy, such as the right of labor to organize. Today the Catholic Church, like many other churches, cooperates with federal and local governments in the areas of foreign aid (especially under P.L. 480, Food for Peace) and local and regional social welfare programs.

The new element in the abortion issue is not the involvement of the church in politics. The new element is the type of political involvement: political involvement aimed at extending rights to persons unrecognized by law by limiting vital rights of others. Antiabortion legislation is aimed at protecting the right of the unborn to life through limiting the right of women to control their bodies' reproduction.

All action aimed at protecting some human lives or rights involves placing limits on the lives and rights of others. We usually understand the limits placed on us to protect others as minimally harmful: limits on our rights to pollute our common water or air, to drive as fast as we wish, to hire and fire on the basis of racial, sexual, or religious considerations, among others. Certainly in the abortion issue, for those who agree that the fetus is directly endangered human life, the need for protection is much greater than in these other cases, and the limits imposed on others to protect fetal life may be more stringent.

The dual problem with the limits proposed in antiabortion legislation is that those limits necessarily apply only to some persons (women) and consist of a denial of bodily integrity. Bodily integrity is a rather basic human right, certainly more basic than the right to pollute, speed, or hire whom we wish. Many wonder whether real personhood is possible without a sense of bodily integrity. The body constitutes in a concrete way the limit of the self; an inability to control one's body due to the power of (an)other(s) over it can easily prevent one from developing the ability to draw the boundaries of the self, to know at what point a self exists for whom the individual is responsible. Women, as remarked above, already live in a context that very unsubtly conveys the message that women's bodies are not their own, but are to be used by individual men and by advertising, that women's bodies are to some extent not personal, but public property like the flag, to be displayed and enjoyed at the will of men. Women as a group have not been taught to know and use their own bodies, but to save them for men who will bestow on women knowledge and appreciation (even if impersonal) of their female bodies. Women have been taught to see their bodies as commodities, not as intrinsic to self, not as their functioning, active self. To legally remove the ability to decide for or against nurturing another human life in one's body surely confirms the social message that women's bodies are not personal but public.

Bishops and many Catholics have not recognized that they propose any real restrictions on women in their support for antiabortion legislation. The Catholic bishops of New York wrote:

> We fail to see how officeholders can escape their responsibility in this grave matter. Particularly we fail to see the logic of those who contend "I am personally opposed to abortion, but I will not impose my personal view on others." That position is radically inconsistent because a third party's right is at stake. It is the same as a 19th century legislator saying "I am personally opposed to slavery, but I support the right of others to hold slaves if they choose." The analogy is all the more appropriate when we recall that the Supreme Court, in its Dred Scott decision, said the slaves were not citizens with rights. If people of influence had not acted on their moral conviction to oppose that decision, slavery would still be the law of the land.
> *It is no exercise of civil liberty to own a slave, nor is it an exercise of civil liberty to destroy an unborn child.*[13]

But it is an exercise of civil liberty to decide to become or not to become a parent. The bishops fail to see the serious conflict of rights involved in the abortion question. I am forced to agree with many in the women's movement that this failure results from not taking women seriously as human persons, but understanding them solely in biological terms as created for reproduction. Only if women's purpose is reproduction can one assert that forcing pregnant women into motherhood is not depriving them of liberty. Bodily integrity is recognized by the church as a basic human right in other contexts; we have condemnations of slavery, forced labor, and torture, for example. That the right of a fetal life to continue living must be defended should not, and ultimately cannot, mean that we exclude from the discussion the rights with which that right conflicts.

Some say that women themselves choose parenthood when they engage in sexual intercourse knowing that pregnancy could result. There are two difficulties with such a position to which I will turn shortly. It should be immediately clear, though, that this defense—which ignores the rights of women on the ground that the rights were voluntarily surrendered—cannot apply in rape cases. This is why some advocates of antiabortion legislation want to make exceptions for rape cases. From the bishops' perspective, this exception is not defensible, for the life to be terminated is still itself innocent, and its right to life is absolute. A similar problem exists with proposed exemptions for cases where pregnancy endangers the mother's life: Catholic teaching holds that no direct killing of innocent life is permissible. Every effort must be made to save both lives, the final decision resting in the hands of God. To agree to either of these exceptions should bring down the wrath of the bishops on the heads of Catholic antiabortion legislators—for would they not be inconsistent in voting for legislation contrary to their religious/moral stance? And yet *this* inconsistency does not seem to bother either the bishops or Catholics in the right-to-life movement. Either fetal life is real human life, above which no other life, and certainly no right less than life itself, should ever be preferred—as Catholic moral tradition has maintained— or else we turn to consequentialism and do the best we can to preserve the greatest mix of respect for human life, dignity, and responsibility. Defending a political action as required by an absolute moral principle, when that political action contains aspects which contradict the absolute principle in question, is patently dishonest.

Dismissing the right of women to bodily integrity on grounds that women surrender that right with intercourse has, as I mentioned earlier, two chief problems. The first is that the very social attitudes towards women's bodies described above have created a situation in which one must question to what extent women freely choose to engage in sexual intercourse. For many women, and at least at times for most women, intercourse is not a fully chosen moral act. Rather, women's acquiescence is taken for granted, both within and without marriage. The attitude that women's bodies are for the perusal and possession of men, where it does not lead to total disregard of the wishes of women altogether, frequently leads to the idea that once a woman has given herself to a man either in sex or in marriage vows she has surrendered her rights to her body forever. Many women do not have, even within marriage (and many would say *especially* within marriage), any control over how often, when, where, or how intercourse takes place, or whether it will be open to the possibility of pregnancy or not. This is one of the worst problems with family planning, as many poverty workers and multitudes of poor women in this country and around the world attest. It is difficult to secure the agreement of husbands to forgo intercourse in natural methods of birth control. But inconvenience to husbands is not the sole obstacle, for men discovering wives on the pill are often irate not at the decision to forgo another pregnancy, but at the audacity of a wife's presuming that she can make any decisions about sexuality at all. The simple fact is that women do not, in many, many cases, have the ability to make moral choices with regard to intercourse.

"A conservative estimate is that, under current conditions, 20 to 30 percent of girls now twelve years old will suffer a violent sexual assault during the remainder of their lives," writes Allen Griswold Johnson.[14] Some studies indicate that as many as 14 percent of women have been violently sexually assaulted by their husbands; 33 percent of women in some random studies have been the victims of completed rapes, 44 percent the victims of completed or attempted rape.[15] And the figures for such sexual crimes against women go up every year, as do the figures for wife battering, which, depending upon the study, occurs in 10 percent to 25 percent of all the families in the nation.[16]

The lack of freedom of women to control their participation in intercourse far exceeds these statistics, for the existence of the 14 percent or the 33 percent, or 44 percent, provides a climate of intimidation which affects *all* women. To say that only these women of the statistics have no control resembles demanding that a woman prove that she physically resisted a rapist in order to claim rape: vindication is achieved only at greater cost to the victim.

This lack of choice for women is not always the work of men addicted to the victimization and domination of women. Many men would like women to take initiative, to be more responsible in their sexual lives. But they do not know how to break through role conditioning to ask, just as women do not know how to break through their conditioning and fear to assert themselves and take responsibility. Nevertheless, the result is that for many women sexual intercourse is not an area of life where they are agents, capable of exercising responsible choice.

There is a second problem with maintaining that women agreed to parenthood when they agreed to intercourse: popular attitudes no longer automatically equate intercourse and procreation. The two are still related as cause and result, of course, but today pregnancy is possible without intercourse, and individual acts of intercourse rarely lead to pregnancy. This separation is not something that the church can readily deplore, for it has had a hand in this change. When the church admitted that (1) procreation is not the only or the single primary purpose of the marriage act, but shares that role with nurture of the marital relationship, and (2) that natural methods of contraception were morally acceptable, it effectively severed the equation of intercourse with procreation.

Agreeing to intercourse is not to be equated with agreement to parenthood. Methods of contraception fail, partners are sometimes dishonest about contraceptive coverage, and ignorance about procreation is still rampant, especially among the young. Less than five years ago in my parish school I conducted a sex-education program for seventh and eighth graders, some of whom were sexually active, and found that the girls were unanimous in insisting that they didn't need to worry about pregnancy because one can only get "caught" during one's period—and they didn't do it then.

In addition to the special problems of conflicts between crucial human rights in the abortion situation there are other problems with the attempt to reflect religious/moral value in civil law on abortion. Chief among these problems is, of course, that many persons do not recognize the fetus as a human person, and so understand antiabortion law as limiting the rights of women over their bodies illegitimately, with no corresponding social gain.

It is difficult to cite similar concrete examples justifying civil action in such situations. Regardless of the analogy of the New York bishops, when representatives of the church have championed in the past the rights of other groups whose humanity was not recognized, such as Native Americans, or blacks, or women, the laws which recognized their humanity and supposedly established their protection did not cut so deeply into the rights of others in the society. Slave owners lost property, slave dealers lost their livelihood, landowners lost some control over Indian peasants, men lost control over women's property and person, but no one was legally deprived of rights over their own person. For those who do not see the fetus as human life, a law with such a cost for a disputed gain is extremely coercive, even tyrannical.

What is the possibility for effectiveness of such a law? We know from secular experience and from religious reflection since the Scholastics that law, to be accepted as legitimate, must meet, among other requirements, those of clear sanctions, the possibility of compliance and enforceability, and acceptance as useful by the majority of the governed.[17] While there is little doubt that antiabortion laws would reduce the number of abortions performed in this country, these other criteria of effectiveness are problematic. Sanctions involve making women who procure, and medical personnel who provide, abortions into criminals, liable to courts and prison. At the same time that some Catholics, following the lead of our bishops, are condemning capital punishment and criticizing the inhumanity of our entire criminal-justice system, we would be committing a whole new class of citizen to that system, citizens claiming a right legally recognized in other contexts.

The enforceability of antiabortion laws is also questionable. While abortion mills can be closed down or chased underground, the abortion procedure is so simple that many relatively untrained persons will undoubtedly go into business. After all, such persons have always been in business, even before the maternal risks were so drastically lowered and the demand for abortion became so high. Relevant to enforceability is whether the law would be seen as useful to the common good. Majority acceptance is doubtful, for according to recent research while most people seem to favor many fewer abortions than go on at present, they want abortion available for rape, birth deformities, the very young, incest, and danger to the mother's life and health. On the other hand, most do not favor expensive and unwieldy systems of appeals hearings for abortion. What the majority want is for women *themselves* to choose fewer abortions.[18] What is not clear to most is how that can be done.

We have learned what happens to laws which do not have popular support; Prohibition has been our example of this. The failure of citizens to respect such laws make citizens less respectful of law in general and more cynical about the possibility of achieving the ideal the law aimed at. We do not need further disrespect for law, nor can we afford more cynicism about the human capacity to respect life.

Our church cannot merely use government to achieve its ends—however good those ends be—without taking seriously the effect such use has on the ability of government to protect the common good. Law can itself change social attitudes over time by affecting social structures, as most of us would agree has happened in this country in the area of civil rights for blacks. While minorities are not by any means treated justly or equally by all, there is virtually no social legitimacy any more for the public denial of equality—a very different situation from thirty years ago.

I do not believe abortion is an issue amenable to the same kind of treatment. We would lack a social group to represent to society those protected by the law, for when abortion is illegal what parent would admit, what child know, that the parent would have had an abortion if it had been possible? The absence of the beneficiary group will lead, I believe, to the public's understanding the law chiefly in terms of its limitations on women. We can imagine which cases would be used as illustrations of the injustice of the law: fifty-year-old welfare mothers of ten whose last five children had Down's syndrome. Furthermore, there would be 1.5 million more unwanted children every year. I am sure that many parents over time would become reconciled to these children and come to love and care for them, but it would be naive not to expect that enforcing parenthood in such numbers will swell the rates of child abuse and neglect as well as the numbers of children given up to or taken by state welfare agencies. As a twice adoptive parent I have seen some of the thousands and thousands of children shuffled from institution to foster home and back again, and have seen how few people ever consider adoption. What is to happen to those unwanted children? Many of them will inevitably end up dead from the violence of abuse, or more probably, from the violence of neglect. The nightly news will hold antiabortion forces responsible for the fate of these children; few will consider that the death toll would be even higher otherwise.

Law works best to change social attitudes when the benefits are clearly visible, represented by direct beneficiaries who exert support for the law. Law itself will not change the minds of those who do not recognize the fetus as human—but it will create other major problems.

CHURCH POLITICS AND WAR

With all these difficulties, why has the church chosen the civil law as the mechanism for creating social recognition of fetal life? Has it turned to civil law, either its passage or enforcement, in order to protect other innocent life? Certainly not to protect the innocent life in war. The church has not pressed legislation aimed at forcing government to disarm, or even to outlaw or forgo particular weapons systems which violate noncombatant immunity. The bishops backed off from explicit support of the nuclear-freeze movement in their pastoral letter, and have neither endorsed nor funded any campaign to lobby against indiscriminate weapons systems. Though the bishops have urged negotiation over military solutions to problems in Central America, there has been no mobilization of clergy and laity, no financial support for any specific program to change foreign military policy involving the killing of innocent civilians, neither in Central America, East Timor, the Philippines, nor *jus ad bellum* conditions before invading Grenada, where there was innocent life taken—though "minor" by standards of mass murder to which we have become accustomed. Concerning war, the bishops state principles and rely on persuasion, and do not mobilize the laity for political/legislative action.

Why is organization of mass lobbying on foreign and military policy political and therefore to be avoided but lobbying for an end to abortions within the legitimate mission of the church? Why does morality require outlawing clinics which provide services which result in the death of innocents, and not require the outlawing of sales of products and services which are designed to bring about the same results?

Many persons seem to assume that these deaths, this killing, is indirect, as opposed to direct killing in abortion. I disagree. The object of both abortion and military policy is territorial integrity, control of one's body or a nation's land. Action designed to produce this effect also has the effect of killing. We have in the Catholic tradition a principle for deciding the morality of action with two effects, one good, the other evil, and that is the "principle of double effect."[19] The principle of double effect states that in order for the action to be moral it must satisfy four conditions. The first is that the intention be the good effect, which both abortion and war can sometimes meet. The second is that the action itself must not be intrinsically evil. Some acts of war can meet this: attacks on military targets and personnel, for example, are allowed within *jus in bello* conditions of just-war theory provided they meet proportionality conditions.

An examination of the morality of the act of abortion requires first that we do not immediately place abortion in the category known as intrinsically evil acts. It makes no pedagogical sense on the contemporary theological scene to assert that abortion is intrinsically evil because it thwarts God's will, as expressed in human biology, that intercourse be open to procreation; too many have opted for a broader understanding of God's will than physicalism can provide. Rather than classifying abortion with artificial contraception, we should understand it as we do killing. Killing is not intrinsically evil; murder is. Abortion as an act that kills must meet the same criteria that other kinds of killing do. It must be subjected to the other three conditions of the principle of double effect to determine whether this killing can be justified.

The third condition of double effect is that there be sufficient reason for tolerating the evil effect. This is the equivalent of the principle of proportionality in just-war theory. It is questionable whether most cases of abortion, or most cases of war, meet this condition.

The only possible grounds I see for abortion to be justified killing require understanding the fetus as an aggressor, which traditionally has been rejected because of the innocence of the fetus. However, from the perspective of women, there are certainly cases where the fetus is an aggressor, a trespasser, to whom the women owes no more than any other person owes to strangers whose lives are threatened. It is certain that even if the fetus can sometimes be classified as an aggressor, this is not true in many abortions. Where the fetus is an aggressor, the proportionality condition required in just-war theory and in self-defense would further limit the number of abortions which could be justified, thus eliminating what many call abortions of convenience.

The fourth condition of the principle of double effect most directly illuminates the question of directness. It requires that the good effect cannot result from the evil effect. And here again war seems to have the same difficulty that abortion does, in that both achieve the good effect through, or at least simultaneously with, the evil effect. Can one defend one's nation's interests in war any way but through the destruction of innocent life? Perhaps in the past—but with bombers, tanks, and missiles? It would seem not. At least modern warfare theorists tell us that waging war to win (any other way being contrary to just-war theory) requires demolishing the enemy's civilian support and will to fight through mass destruction. There is consensus among military theorists that it is impossible to wage a general war without the prior knowledge of inflicting large-scale civilian casualties, and a great deal of doubt that counterinsurgency warfare can be fought any other way either. Is this not direct killing, achieving the good through the evil effect? Or is it not direct killing because it does not matter to the planners or war wagers *which* thousands of the enemy die?

Even more, when we sell, or even buy for ourselves, huge expensive weapons systems, have we not *first* chosen that the world's hungry die? It is not accidental that using over $595 billion of the world's resources on military preparation— 125 percent of the world's health budget—leaves much of the world hungry so that forty thousand children die *every day* of hunger and hunger-related causes.[20] The rise of military spending under Reagan has fed a huge national deficit which has in turn raised interest rates on the debt of developing nations, so that larger and larger proportions of their national budgets go to pay interest on external debt. Many of these nations, who have massive hunger problems, then use remaining income to purchase weapons from the U.S. and other developed nations.[21]

When the two effects—death by hunger and military arming—are linked so closely can we really maintain that the killing is not direct? If in medical ethics it is immoral to deprive the dying of food because food is accounted an "ordinary means of preserving life" (as opposed to optional "extraordinary measures of preserving life") surely such deprivation—depriving those who are not dying *except* for lack of food—in economic situations is immoral?

It is undeniably true that in abortion the good achieved—the termination of an undesired physical and emotional strain from hosting in one's body a biological parasite—is achieved at the cost of the death of an innocent life. But war also fails the principle of double effect. Why do we only see moral inadequacy in abortion?

If we cannot assume that all pregnant women have direct responsibility for the fetal life they carry due to lack of consent and control, then we must ask: What obligations do persons have toward innocent life, in general? Innocent life perishes in tremendous numbers constantly. What are we required to sacrifice to preserve innocent life? We do not require nations to sacrifice any of their national interests, neither military nor economic, to protect innocent life. What obligations does faith place on us as individuals to preserve the children dying of hunger in the world? Are we obliged to lobby for more foreign aid, to forswear unnecessary luxuries in order to share the resources of the world with the hungry? Are we obliged to house, at the risk of imprisonment, the illegal aliens fleeing death in El Salvador and Guatemala? Are we obliged to adopt the innocent homeless children of our own country and of the world, to support the thousands and millions of unwanted children who suffer from physical, emotional, and mental disability resulting from their lack of care? Are we obliged to give up parts of our bodies—a kidney, for example—to preserve the life of a dying innocent? No, we are not. These are good deeds, but they are not obligatory. Catholics are not obliged to shelter those refugees whose lives are threatened. Nor are we obliged to live as the poor to feed the dying hungry. Nor are we obliged to parent the parentless, or donate body parts even after our death, much less while we live. We are not obliged by our faith, much less by our government, to sacrifice our time, freedom, or lives to protect threatened innocent life. And we do not see any campaign in our church to change church or civil law to make such actions obligatory.

Yet women, and not only Catholic women, but all women, are to be forced to sacrifice in order to protect innocent life. And there is no question about this raised within the Catholic community. Do we really have a consistent ethic of life when we mobilize our laity, commit our economic resources, and command the obedience of our faithful with the most serious religious sanctions in support of the legal protection of only one group of threatened innocents, and at the expense of only one group in our society?

CONCLUSION

The ongoing abortion of 1.5 million children a year is morally intolerable, but it cannot be dealt with through legislation. Christians should be willing to sacrifice out of love for others, but the virtue, the beauty, of altruism lies in its voluntariness. If sacrifice is forced, it is worthless. If sacrifice is forced on only some persons, it becomes worse than useless—it becomes destructive of both moral sensitivity and community.

The 1.5 million abortions a year are not the most threatening social problem we face, but are rather a terrible symptom of the deeper problem, which is the victimization of women, a victimization that has prevented the full development of moral sensitivity in women. As a feminist, I find this humbling to admit, but, on another level, to be expected. Victimization can not only ennoble, sensitize, and give clearer perspective on the world—it also kills and maims not only the body but the soul. I suspect women might more easily admit to the moral deformation that can occur in situations of victimization if such an admission did not seem by default to imply that men are morally superior, thereby legitimizing the power differential that allows victimization in the first place. In our world over half the human beings are victims of the moral callousness of the other half, and many of those victims are now sacrificing another group of victims in their attempts at self-assertion and self-defense.

Attempts to ameliorate this cycle of victimization must be careful not to worsen the tragedy. Institutions such as the church which are implicated in the long-standing victimization of women should beware of self-serving hypocritical measures cloaked in moral rhetoric, and should deal with the root causes of the present abortion tragedy. I am wary of the attempt to sketch limit situations, situations where all would agree that abortion is illegitimate, where legal prosecution is proper. It is too easy to decide that a second, third, or fourth abortion, abortions for middle-class married couples, or abortions paid for by the tax dollars of persons opposed to abortion are always illegitimate. No matter what helpful criteria we can arrive at by examining hypothetical situations, we cannot merely insert real persons into prejudged situations and do justice to their personhood. There will always be rare cases where even in these extreme situations there are not only serious impediments to moral responsibility, but perhaps the absence of truly moral alternatives. The church needs to couple a call to more responsible decision making on the part of women with strong commitment to remove the serious long-standing social impediments to the development of free, moral personhood in women. When the church recognizes that abortion is as complex, as social, and as conflictive of rights as the issues of war or hunger, then perhaps we, the church, can address abortion with more evenhanded compassion and war and hunger with even more rigor.

I second Cardinal Bernardin's call for a consistent ethic of life, a "seamless garment." But that ethic's consistency must reach beyond the level of principle to embrace the entire area of application so as to treat persons, both the varied groups of threatened innocents and those groups who should protect the innocent, consistently. We will never convince those involved in the taking of one and a half million aborted lives a year to consider the life of the unborn reverently if we do not evince reverence for the mothers of those unborn, for the starving millions of our world, the hundreds of thousands of innocent civilians threatened by death in war. We will be accused of romanticizing the unborn out of disdain for the already born, of ignoring the personhood of women, and of passing the burdens of protecting life onto the shoulders of pregnant women rather than accepting the very real burden belonging to all of us to protect all human life.

NOTES

1. Apr. 6, 1984, statement by the Catholic bishops of New York, *Origins* 13 (Apr. 26, 1984). Bishop James W. Molone of Youngstown has also recently attacked this position (*Time,* Aug. 10, 1984, p. 26).

2. Dec. 6, 1983, address of Cardinal Joseph Bernardin, *Origins* 13 (Dec. 6, 1983) 493.

3. Richard A. Preston and Sydney F. Wise, *Men in Arms: A History of Warfare and Its Interrelationships with Western Society,* 4th ed. (New York: Holt, Rinehart and Winston, 1969) chaps. 16–18, esp. p. 330.

4. "The Challenge of Peace," no. 310.

5. Ibid., no. 4, nos. 328–29.

6. Pius XII, Christmas Message of 1956. In World War I and World War II Catholic conscientious objection was extremely rare, and not supported by bishops or clergy in any nation. This only began to change with Vietnam after 1970.

7. Christine E. Gudorf, "Renewal or Repatriarchalization: Responses of the Roman Catholic Church to the Feminization of Religion," *Horizons* 10 (Fall 1983) 231–51.

8. U.S. Catholic Bishops, "Statement on Capital Punishment," *Origins* 10 (Nov. 20, 1980) 373–77.

9. Marie Fortune, *Sexual Violence: The Unmentionable Sin* (New York: Pilgrim Press, 1983); Diane Russell, *Rape in Marriage* (New York: Macmillan, 1983); Martha Kirkpatrick, ed., *Women's Sexual Experience: Exploration of the Dark Continent* (New York: Plenum Press, 1982); and R. Emerson Dobash and Russell Dobash, *Violence vs. Wives* (New York: Free Press, 1979).

10. Douglas Johnson, "Proof of Abortion-ERA Link Massive, Compelling," *National Catholic Reporter* 20 (July 26, 1984) 27.

11. Christianity *began* with the mixture of religion and politics—that was what got Jesus crucified, and many of the apostles and disciples as well. We too often in this country confuse nonestablishment with separation of religion and politics. Nonestablishment was intended to *free* the churches, not limit them.

12. Peter Brock, *Twentieth Century Pacifism* (New York: Van Nostrand Reinhold, 1970) 175.

13. Apr. 6, 1984, statement of New York bishops. Emphasis mine.

14. Allen Griswold Johnson, "On the Prevalence of Rape in the United States," *Signs* 6 (Autumn 1980) 145.

15. Russell, *Rape in Marriage* 64, 67.

16. Del Martin, *Battered Wives* (San Francisco: Glide, 1976) 11, and Russell, *Rape in Marriage* 89.

17. Thomas Aquinas, *Summa Theologiae*, ed. Blackfriar Dominicans (New York: McGraw-Hill, 1964). Sanctions, 1a2ae. 99, 6; reasonableness and feasibility, 1a2ae. 95, 3; custom's influence on observation, 1a2ae. 97, 2. Also Timothy O'Connell, *Principles for a Catholic Morality* (New York: Seabury, 1978) 185–87.

18. Rosemary Ruether, "Abortion: Capturing the Middle Ground," a review of Kristen Luker's *Abortion and the Politics of Motherhood* (Berkeley: University of California Press, 1984) in *Christianity and Crisis* 44 (July 9, 1984) 285–86.

19. O'Connell, *Principles for a Catholic Morality* 170–72.

20. *World Military and Social Expenditures 1983* (statistics from 1981), by Ruth Leger Sivard (Leesburg, Va.: World Priorities, 1983) and *The State of the World's Children, 1982,* UNICEF.

21. Peru, for example, in 1984 is paying 39 percent of its national budget for interest on external debt, and another 23 percent for military expenditures, while new studies indicate that as many as 30 percent of children in some areas of Peru may suffer retardation from malnutrition. Report of Instituto Alternativa, on studies in San Martin de Porres district, Lima, Peru.

Chapter 5

Dissent in the Church

This chapter moves into one of the most fiercely debated topics among Catholics—the relation of the magisterium and the moral theologian. The abortion debate has served only to sharpen this debate, which was revived after Vatican II. Excerpts from an address by Cardinal Ratzinger focus on the bishop as the teacher of morality and the tasks of the moral theologian. Ratzinger notes that (1) the teaching office depends on expert knowledge but also serves to protect persons against themselves and (2) the moral theologian is to precede the magisterium into uncharted waters but is also to follow the magisterium by bring its teaching into the contemporary world.

Charles Curran, around whom much of the current discussion on dissent is centered, provides a broad analysis of the issues involved, focusing not only on the ecclesial questions, but also on their relation to academic freedom and procedural issues of justice and fairness. In addition, Curran provides an argument justifying the possibility of dissent from fallible church teachings. Rosemary Ruether examines the issue of authority and dissent in the context of the October 4, 1984, *New York Times* advertisement contending that there is more than one legitimate Catholic position on abortion. This essay specifically evaluates dissent within the context of religious communities and the university.

Bishops, Theologians, and Morality

Cardinal Joseph Ratzinger

III. APPLICATIONS

Now that we have considered all of this, we can formulate the essential tasks of both bishop and specialized theologian in moral questions and from this will automatically emerge the rules for their working together in a correct manner.

1. The Bishop as Teacher of Morality

(a) The bishop is a witness to the *mores Ecclesiae Catholicae*, to those rules of life which have grown up in the common experience of the believing conscience in the struggle with God and with historical reality. As a witness the bishop must in the first place know this tradition in its foundations, its content and its various stages. One can only bear witness to what one knows. The knowledge of the essential moral tradition of the faith is therefore a fundamental demand of the episcopal office.

(b) Since it is a question of a tradition which comes from conscience and speaks to conscience, the bishop himself must be a man of a seeing and listening conscience. He must strive, in living the *mores Ecclesiae Catholicae*, to see that his own personal conscience is sharpened. He must know morality not second-, but firsthand. He must not simply pass on a tradition, but bear witness to what has become for himself a credible and proven lifestyle.

(c) Setting out from such a personal knowledge of the moral word of the church, he must attempt to remain in discussion with those experts who seek the correct application of the simple words of faith to the complicated reality of a particular time. He must therefore be prepared to become a learner and a critical partner of the experts. He must learn to see where it is a question of the knowledge of new realities, new problems, new possibilities for understanding and so for maturing and cleansing the moral heritage. He must be critical when expert science forgets its own boundaries or reduces morality to a simple specialization.

2. The Tasks of the Moral Theologian

On the basis of our reflections so far, we might define the tasks of the moral theologian in the following manner:

(*a*) As a theologian, the moral theologian also finds his starting point in the *mores Ecclesiae Catholicae* which he researches and which, in their essential link with what is Catholic, he distinguishes. And so he also tries to recognize in the mores that which is specifically moral and constant and to understand them in a unified way in the total context of the faith. He seeks the *ratio fidei.*

(*b*) He then brings this reason of faith in a critical way into dialogue with the reason and the plausibility of the particular time. He helps toward the understanding of the moral demands of the Gospel in the particular conditions of his day and so serves the formation of conscience. In this way he serves also the development, purification and deepening of the moral message of the church.

(*c*) Above all, the moral theologian will also take up the new questions which new developments and relationships pose for the traditional norms. He will attempt to know precisely the objective components of such discussions (for example, the technology of armaments, economic problems, medical developments, etc.) in order to work out the best way to pose the questions and so to arrive at the relationship with the constants of the moral tradition of the faith.

In this sense he stands in critical dialogue with the moral evaluations of society and in all this he helps the teaching office of the church to present its moral message in the particular time.

3. The Relationship between Bishop and Theologian

From our reflections on the individual tasks it is now possible to derive the fundamental rules for the relationship between teaching office and expert.

(*a*) The teaching office depends on the specialized knowledge of the experts and must let itself be thoroughly informed by them about the content of the matter in question before making an utterance regarding new problems. The teaching office must therefore not be too hasty in taking up a position regarding questions that are not yet clarified nor must it apply its binding statements beyond what the principles of tradition permit.

On the other hand, the teaching office of the church must defend man against himself to prevent his destruction even if this means opposing the philosophy of an entire epoch. For example, in a period in which the world thinks of itself only as a product and as an end, the teaching office of the church must continually try to get nature to be recognized as creation in its defense of the unborn. There is an obligation to information, an obligation to respect the boundaries of universally binding moral statements and an obligation to witness. The moral catechesis must go beyond that which can be determined with certainty and should offer models of behavior in concrete circumstances (casuistry).

But it seems important to me clearly to distinguish between these cases and the specific moral teaching. I have the impression that the regular and unnuanced introduction of cases into the specific moral statement or likewise the failure to distinguish between them has contributed to discrediting the moral teaching of the church in our century in a substantial way.

(b) But the task of the moral theologian is not simply being in service to the teaching office. It also stands in dialogue with the ethical questions of the time and contributes, through the development of models of behavior, to the process of the formation of conscience. As regards the magisterium, his task is to precede it: He goes before it, noticing new questions, gathering knowledge of their objective content, and preparing answers. The moral theologian likewise accompanies the magisterium and follows it, bringing its pronouncements into the dialogue of his time and relating the basic lines of the discussion to concrete situations.

4. Criticism of the Magisterium: Its Rules and Limits

Today interest in the relationship between the episcopal magisterium and scientific theology is concentrated above all on the question: Can the moral theologian criticize the teaching office?

After what we have said about the structure of moral expression and about its relationship to specialized science, we must distinguish:

(a) First of all, we must apply here what the Second Vatican Council said about the steps of assent and in like manner the stages of criticism with regard to church teaching. Criticism may be framed according to the level and demands of the magisterial teaching. It will be all the more helpful when it fills in a lack of information, clarifies shortcomings of the linguistic or conceptual presentation and at the same time deepens the insight into the limits and range of the particular teaching.

(b) In the light of our reflection, on the other hand, we see that it is not for the expert himself to draw up norms or to annul the norms, perhaps by setting up factions or pressure groups. As we have seen, norms can only be witnessed to, but not produced or annulled by some calculated analysis. When this happens the peculiar nature of morality itself is misunderstood. Therefore, dissent can only have meaning in the area of casuistry, not in the specific area of norms. The most important thing in the relationship between the magisterium and moral theology appears to me, in the last analysis, to lie in what Plato recommends as the path to moral knowledge, in "regular familial discussion," a discussion in which we must all learn to become more and more hearers of the biblical word, vitally addressed and directed to the *mores Ecclesiae Catholicae.*

Public Dissent in the Church

Charles Curran

In the fall of 1985 I agreed to accept the kind invitation of our convention program committee to give this plenary session on the topic: "Authority and Structure in the Churches: Perspective of a Catholic Theologian." Since that time there has been some water over the dam. The Vatican Congregation for the Doctrine of the Faith has urged me to "reconsider and to retract those positions which violate the conditions for a professor to be called a Catholic theologian." According to Cardinal Ratzinger, the prefect of the congregation, there is an inherent contradiction if "one who is to teach in the name of the church in fact denies her teaching."

This paper will attempt to be faithful to the original topic by focusing on the pertinent issues and aspects involved in my present case. From the very beginning I am conscious of my own prejudices and biases. This paper is presented from my own perspective and therefore is bound to serve as an apologetic or defense of my position. However, at the same time I have the broader intention of using this case to raise up the important issues which the theological community, the hierarchical teaching office in the Roman Catholic Church and the total people of God need to address.

The subject of this paper will thus be specifically Roman Catholic, dealing with the role of the theologian in the Roman Catholic Church. However, the questions raised and the issues discussed have not only an indirect interest for other Christian churches and other Christian theologians, but they also deal directly with many of the same issues which arise for all Christian churches and all their theologians. Before pointing out and discussing the more specific issues involved in this case, it is important to recognize the context and presuppositions for the discussion.

CONTEXT AND PRESUPPOSITIONS

The general context for this paper and for the entire case is that of the Roman Catholic Church and Catholic theology. I have made it very clear that I am a believing Catholic and intend to do Catholic theology. Despite my intentions,

I still might be wrong; but I maintain that my positions are totally acceptable for a Catholic theologian who is a believing Roman Catholic.

The mission of the entire church is to be faithful to the word and work of Jesus. God's revelation has been handed over and entrusted to the church, which faithfully hands this down from generation to generation through the assistance of the Holy Spirit. Roman Catholicism recognizes that revelation was closed at the end of apostolic times, but revelation itself develops and is understood in the light of the different historical and cultural circumstances of the hearers and doers of the Word.

Roman Catholic faith and theology have strongly disagreed with the emphasis on the Scripture alone. The Scripture must always be understood in light of the thought patterns of our own time. The Catholic insistence on the Scripture and tradition recognized the need to develop and understand God's revelation in Jesus Christ in the light of the contemporary circumstances. The early councils of the fourth, fifth and subsequent centuries illustrate how in matters touching the very heart of faith—the understanding of God and of Jesus Christ—the living church felt the need to go beyond the words of the Scripture, to understand better and more adequately the revelation of God. Thus, the Christian church taught there are three persons in God and two natures in Jesus. Fidelity to the tradition does not mean merely repeating the very words of the Scripture or of older church teaching. The Christian tradition is a living tradition, and fidelity involves a creative fidelity which seeks to preserve in its own time and place the incarnational principle. Creative fidelity is the task of the church in bearing witness to the word and work of Jesus.

In carrying out its call to creative fidelity to the word and work of Jesus, the church is helped by the papal and episcopal roles in the church. The existence of this pastoral teaching function of pope and bishops in the church must be recognized by all. However, there has been much development in the understanding of the exact nature of that teaching office, how it is exercised and what is its relationship to the other functions connected with the office of pope and bishops in the church. Much of the following discussion will center on what is often called today the ordinary magisterium of the papal office. This term *ordinary magisterium* understood in this present sense has only been in use since the nineteenth century. A Catholic must recognize the pastoral office of teaching given to the pope and bishops, but also to realize that this teaching function has been exercised in different ways over the years.

These aspects briefly mentioned in this opening section are very important and could be developed at much greater length and depth. However, in this paper they are being recalled as the necessary context and presuppositions for the discussion of the issues raised by the case involving the Congregation for the Doctrine of the Faith and myself. I understand myself to be a Catholic theologian and a

Catholic believer who recognizes the call of the church to be faithful in a creative way to the word and work of Jesus and gratefully and loyally accepts the papal and episcopal functions in the church.

This paper will now focus on what in my judgment are the primary issues involved in my case. In the process I will state briefly my own position on these issues, but the primary purpose is to raise up for discussion the primary issues which are involved. Five issues will be considered: the role of the theologian, the possibility of public theological dissent from some noninfallible hierarchical church teachings, the possibility and right of dissent by the Christian faithful, the justice and fairness of the process, and academic freedom for theology and Catholic institutions of higher learning.

The September 17 letter from Cardinal Ratzinger calls upon me to retract my positions in the following specific areas: contraception and sterilization; abortion and euthanasia; masturbation, premarital intercourse and homosexual acts; the indissolubility of marriage. However, as Richard McCormick perceptively points out, these issues and agreement with my positions on these issues do not constitute the major points of contention in the dispute between the congregation and myself. These are important topics, but they are primarily illustrative of the more fundamental issues involved. However, it is necessary to point out that in all these issues my position is quite nuanced.

ROLE OF THE THEOLOGIAN

There has been much written on the role of the theologian and the relationship between the function of bishops and theologians in the church. It is impossible to add to this discussion in this short space, but rather the purpose is to raise up the underlying issues involved in the present controversy. Many and probably the majority of Catholic theologians writing today see the role of the Catholic theologian as somewhat independent and cooperative in relationship to the hierarchical office and not delegated or derivative from the role of pope and bishops. The theologian is a scholar who studies critically, thematically and systematically Christian faith and action. Such a scholar must theologize within the Catholic faith context and must give due importance to all the *loci theologici,* including the teaching of the hierarchical magisterium. The Catholic theologian to be such must give the required assent to official church teaching, but the theologian does not derive his or her theological office from delegation by the hierarchical officeholders. Likewise the teaching function of pope and bishops uses an entirely different methodology from the teaching function of theologians. Note that I have described this understanding of the Catholic theologian as somewhat independent and cooperative with regard to the hierarchical role in the church.

The above paragraph has tried to explain concisely in what the independence consists and how that independence is modified by the call of the theologian and all believers to give due assent to the pastoral teaching role of bishops and pope.

However, there is a very different understanding of the role of the theologian found in more recent church legislation. The new Code of Canon Law, which came into effect in the fall of 1983, and the apostolic constitution for ecclesiastical faculties and universities, *Sapientia Christiana*, understand the role of the theologian as primarily derived from the hierarchical teaching office and functioning by reason of delegation given by the hierarchical teaching office. A good illustration of this understanding of the theologian as delegate and representative of the hierarchical teaching office is found in Canon 812 of the new Code of Canon Law: "Those who teach theological subjects in any institution of higher studies must have a mandate from the competent ecclesiastical authority."

According to the code, this mandate is required for all those who teach theology in any Catholic institution of higher learning. Earlier versions of the code spoke of a "canonical mission" instead of a mandate. *Sapientia Christiana*, the apostolic constitution governing ecclesiastical faculties, requires a canonical mission from the chancellor for those teaching disciplines concerning faith or morals. The final version of the code uses the word *mandate* and not canonical mission because canonical mission appears to imply the assignment of a person to an ecclesiastical office. The implication of this new canon and of other recent legislation is that the Catholic theologian in a Catholic institution officially exercises the function of teaching in that school through a delegation from the bishop. The role of the Catholic theologian is thus derived from the hierarchical teaching function and juridically depends upon it.

It seems there has been an interesting, even contradictory, development in Catholic documents within the last few years. The more theoretical documents seem to indicate a recognition for a somewhat independent and cooperative role for theologians, whereas the legislative documents understand the theological role as derivative and delegated from the hierarchical teaching office.

There is no doubt that from the nineteenth century until recent times the role of the theologian was seen as subordinate to and derivative from the hierarchical teaching office. However, Vatican Council II in its general ecclesiology and in its understanding of theologians can be interpreted to adopt a more cooperative and somewhat independent understanding of the role of theologians vis-à-vis the hierarchical magisterium. The cooperative model does not deny the official role of the hierarchical office in protecting and proclaiming the faith, but theology is a scholarly discipline distinct from but related to the proclamation of the faith by the hierarchical teaching office.

However, canonists recognize that recent canonical legislation, including the new Code of Canon Law, understands the theological function as derivative from the hierarchical teaching function. Newer legislation and its interpretation by canonists indicate that the development has been moving very much in this direction. In the older Code of Canon Law there was no requirement for theologians in Catholic institutions to have a canonical mandate or mission to teach theology. The older code saw the role of the ordinary or diocesan bishop in terms of negative vigilance with regard to individual teachers of theology and not one of positive deputation.

There can be no doubt that present church legislation tends to see the theological function as derivative from the hierarchical teaching function. However, very many Catholic theologians today appeal to more recent developments in Catholic understanding to substantiate a somewhat cooperative and independent understanding of the theological role vis-à-vis the hierarchical role. History indicates that the derivative understanding really began only in the nineteenth century. In this section I have purposely and consciously used the expression hierarchical teaching office or function to indicate that the teaching function and role of the total church and of others in the church cannot be totally reduced to the hierarchical teaching office.

The correspondence between the Congregation for the Doctrine of the Faith and myself never explicitly goes into this question as such, but the congregation is operating out of a derivative understanding of the role of the theologian while I adopt the somewhat independent and cooperative understanding.

PUBLIC THEOLOGICAL DISSENT FROM SOME NONINFALLIBLE HIERARCHICAL CHURCH TEACHINGS

The correspondence from the congregation indicates that the problem is public dissent and not just private dissent. However, the meaning of public is never developed. The entire investigation centers on my theological writings, so the only logical conclusion is that *public* here refers to theological writings. Private dissent apparently means something that is not written and is not spoken publicly.

In 1979, after receiving the first set of observations from the congregation, I had the feeling that the investigation would soon focus clearly on the public aspect of dissent and on the manner and mode of dissent. Past experience was the basis for this judgment.

In 1968 I acted as the spokesperson for a group of theologians who ultimately numbered over six hundred and issued a public statement at a press conference which concluded that Catholic spouses may responsibly decide according to their conscience that artificial contraception in some circumstances is permissible and even necessary to preserve and foster the values and sacredness of marriage. In response to this statement, the trustees of The Catholic University of America on September 5, 1969, mandated an inquiry in accord with academic due process to determine if the Catholic University professors involved in this dissent had violated by their declarations and actions their responsibilities to the university.

A few months later the object of the inquiry had definitely changed. "Hence the focus of the present inquiry is on the style and method whereby some faculty members expressed personal dissent from papal teaching" and apparently helped organize additional public dissent to such teaching. The board of trustees did not question the right of a scholar to have or hold private dissent from noninfallible church teaching. In the context of the inquiry it became clear that public and organized dissent referred primarily to holding a press conference and to actively soliciting other theologians to sign the original statement. The primary question of public dissent thus was not regular theological publication but the use of the more popular media.

In response to this new focus of the inquiry, the subject professors at Catholic University, through their counsel, pointed out the changed focus but went on to show that such public and organized dissent in the popular media was a responsible action by Catholic theologians. The shift in the focus of the inquiry seemed to come from the fact that the trustees, including the bishops on the board of trustees, were willing to recognize the possibility of even public dissent in theological journals as being legitimate, but objected to the use of the popular media. The faculty inquiry committee fully agreed with the thrust of the argument proposed by the professors, and the professors were exonerated in this hearing.

However, to my surprise, the investigation from the congregation never moved explicitly into the direction of the manner and mode of dissent and even at times the use of popular media. The conclusion logically follows from the position taken by the congregation that the only acceptable form of dissent on these issues is that which is neither written nor spoken publicly. At most the theologian can think in a dissenting way, perhaps even discuss the matter in private and write private letters to the proper authorities explaining the reasons for one's dissent. It is safe to say that the vast majority of Catholic theologians writing today explicitly disagree with the position of the congregation. For this reason I have remained surprised even to the present day that the Congregation for the Doctrine of the Faith was proposing such a restricted notion of legitimate theological dissent from such noninfallible teaching. In principle, they seem to allow for no public theological dissent even in theological journals on noninfallible church teaching.

The central point at issue in the controversy is the possibility of public theological dissent from some noninfallible teaching. I have always pointed out in the correspondence that I have been dealing with the noninfallible hierarchical teaching office. This position was accepted by the congregation in all of the correspondence prior to the September 17, 1985, letter to me from Cardinal Ratzinger. A very few Catholic theologians have maintained that the teaching on artificial contraception is infallible from the ordinary teaching of pope and bishops throughout the world. However, this position is not held by the vast majority of theologians and has not been proposed or defended by the congregation. One could also maintain that the Catholic teaching on divorce is infallible by reason of the teaching of the Council of Trent. However, the phrasing of the canons with regard to the indissolubility of marriage, the attempt not to condemn the practice of *economia* of the Greek church and the somewhat broad understanding of *anathema sit* at that time of Trent argue against the infallible nature of the Catholic Church's teaching on the indissolubility of marriage. Accepted standard textbooks, such as that of Adnes, recognize that the teaching on absolute intrinsic indissolubility is not infallible. Thus my position all along has been that I have never denied an infallible teaching of the church.

However, in the September 17 letter Cardinal Ratzinger seems to claim that the assent of faith is somehow involved in my case. I have strenuously maintained that the assent of faith is not involved and we are dealing with the *obsequium religiosum* which is due in cases of noninfallible teaching. I assume as a result of my meeting with Cardinal Ratzinger in Rome on March 8 that we are in no way involved with the assent of faith. However, it is very clear that the congregation maintains that the *obsequium religiosum* due to noninfallible teaching does not allow the theologian to dissent publicly in these cases.

Cardinal Ratzinger himself has called the distinction between infallible and noninfallible teaching "legalistic." Only in this century have theologians made this distinction in such a sharp way. "When one affirms that noninfallible doctrines, even though they make up part of the teaching of the church, can be legitimately contested, one ends up by destroying the practice of the Christian life and reduces the faith to a collection of doctrines." Ratzinger deemphasizes the distinction between infallible and noninfallible teaching to help support his position that a theologian cannot dissent publicly from noninfallible church teaching. What is to be said about Ratzinger's understanding?

It is true that the sharp distinction between infallible and noninfallible teaching is recent, for it became prevalent only at the time of the First Vatican Council (1870), which defended the infallibility of the pope. After that time, theologians quite rightly distinguished the two levels of teaching and the two different assents which are due to such teachings. All the faithful owe the assent of faith to infallible teaching and the *obsequium religiosum* of intellect and will to authoritative or authentic, noninfallible teaching.

The distinction became well entrenched in the theology manuals of the twentieth century before Vatican II. Such a distinction helped to explain that official teaching on some issues had been wrong and had subsequently been corrected (e.g., the condemnation of interest taking, the need for the intention of procreation to justify conjugal relations). At the time of Vatican Council I and later it was also pointed out that Popes Liberius (d. 366), Vigilius (d. 555) and Honorius (d. 638) all proposed erroneous teachings which were subsequently rejected through theological dissent.

Vatican Council II changed many earlier teachings such as those on religious freedom and the relationship of the Roman Catholic Church to other Christian churches and to the true church of Jesus Christ. Scripture scholars for the last generation or so have publicly disagreed with the teachings that were proposed by the biblical commission in the first two decades of this century. The theologians thus recognized the distinction between infallible and noninfallible teaching and used it, among other purposes, to explain why certain earlier errors in church teaching did not refute the Vatican I teaching on papal infallibility. These theologians likewise recognized the possibility of dissent from such noninfallible teaching at times, but did not explicitly justify public dissent.

The theologians are not the only ones to use this distinction. *Lumen gentium*, the Constitution on the Church of the Second Vatican Council, recognizes this distinction between infallible and noninfallible teaching and the two different types of assent which are due (no. 25). The new Code of Canon Law clearly distinguishes between the assent of faith and the *obsequium religiosum* of intellect and will which is due to the authoritative teaching of the pope and college of bishops even when they do not intend to proclaim that doctrine by a definitive act (Canon 752). This distinction is thus not only accepted by theologians but also by official documents and by the new Code of Canon Law.

Some theological manuals and many contemporary theologians understand the *obsequium religiosum* owed to authoritative, noninfallible teaching to justify at times the possibility of theological dissent and, at the present time, even public dissent. Some bishops conferences explicitly recognized the legitimacy of dissent from the papal encyclical *Humanae vitae* issued in 1968. Also documents from bishops conferences have recognized the possibility of public theological dissent from some noninfallible church teaching. The U.S. bishops in their 1968 pastoral letter "Human Life in Our Day" pinpoint that in noninfallible teaching there is always a presumption in favor of the magisterium—a position held by most theologians. However, the pastoral letter also recognizes the legitimacy of public theological dissent from such teaching if the reasons are serious and well-founded, if the manner of the dissent does not question or impugn the teaching authority of the church and if the dissent is such as not to give scandal. Since I have developed at great length in my correspondence with the congregation both the arguments justifying the possibility of public dissent and the many theologians and others in the church who recognize such a possibility, there is no need to repeat this here.

One significant aspect of the question deserves mention here because of some recent developments—the understanding and translation of *obsequium religiosum*.

Obsequium has often been translated as submission or obedience. Bishop Christopher Butler was, to my knowledge, the first to translate the word *obsequium* as respect. Francis Sullivan, in his book on magisterium, rejects the translation of "due respect," but still allows the possibility of legitimate public theological dissent from noninfallible church teaching.

(Sullivan, a Jesuit professor at the Pontifical Gregorian University in Rome, in a recent interview strongly defends the distinction between infallible and non-infallible church teaching. Sullivan sees the position taken by the Vatican congregation in its correspondence with me as threatening the critical function of the theologian with regard to the nondefinitive teaching of the magisterium. "The idea that Catholic theologians, at any level of education, can only teach the official church position and present only those positions in their writings, is new and disturbing." Sullivan, who considers his approach "rather moderate" and "standard," has been teaching the possibility of public theological dissent from some noninfallible teaching at the Pontifical Gregorian University in Rome. Sullivan adds that "no one has ever questioned what I teach.")

Sullivan claims that "submission" and not "due respect" is the proper translation of *obsequium,* but the Gregorian University professor still recognizes the possibility and legitimacy of public dissent from authoritative, noninfallible teaching.

The English text of the Code of Canon Law found in the commentary commissioned by the Canon Law Society of America and authorized by the executive committee of the National Conference of Catholic Bishops in the United States translates *obsequium* as respect. Ladislas Orsy, in a recent commentary on Canon 752, recognizes difficulties in translating *obsequium* but opts for respect. Orsy also recognizes the possibility of legitimate public dissent from some authoritative, noninfallible teaching. The discussion over the proper understanding and translation of *obsequium* has been an occasion for many to recognize the possibility of legitimate public dissent from some noninfallible church teaching.

There can be no doubt that church documents, the Code of Canon Law, theologians in general and canonists in general have accepted the importance of the distinction between infallible and noninfallible hierarchical teaching. Although I believe the distinction between infallible and noninfallible teaching is very important and necessary, there is a need to say more in dealing with the possibility of public dissent. I disagree with Cardinal Ratzinger's attempt to smooth over somewhat the clear distinction between fallible and noninfallible teaching, but his remarks show the need to say something in addition to the distinction between infallible and noninfallible teaching. What about the danger of reducing the Christian faith in practice to a small, abstract core?

In my own comments about this case, I have been careful not only to use the distinction between infallible and noninfallible teaching but also to talk about what is core and central to the faith as distinguished from those things that are more removed and peripheral. Also I have consistently spoken about the right to dissent publicly from *some* noninfallible church teaching. The distinction between infallible and noninfallible church teaching is absolutely necessary, but not sufficient. The older theology tries to deal with questions of the relationship of church teaching to the core of faith through the use of theological notes. These notes and their opposites, in terms of censures, attempted to recognize the complexity by categorizing many different types of noninfallible teaching. In a true sense there is a need today to redevelop the concept of theological notes in the light of the realities of the present time.

As important as the concept of infallible teaching is, there are some very significant limitations involved in it. Infallible teaching, especially of the extraordinary type by pope or council, has usually come in response to an attack on or a denial of something central to the faith. However, some points which have never been attacked, such as the existence of God, have never been defined by the extraordinary hierarchical teaching office. On the other hand, the limits and imperfections of any infallible teaching have been rightly recognized. Infallible teaching itself is always open to development, better understanding and even purification. Thus, one must be careful when speaking about infallible teaching both because some things might pertain to the core of faith which have at least not been infallibly taught by the extraordinary teaching function of the pope and bishops, and because even infallible teaching itself is open to development and further interpretation. However, in the present discussion the distinction between infallible and noninfallible is very important. It allows me to deal with a limited area—the area of noninfallible teaching. I am in no way questioning what is an essential matter of Catholic faith.

Within this large area of what is noninfallible and not central to the Christian faith, it is necessary to recognize various degrees and levels of relationship to faith. Here an updating of the older theological notes would be very useful. I have recognized this fact by consciously referring to dissent from *some* noninfallible teachings which are somewhat removed from the core and central faith realities. It is true that I have not attempted to develop all the distinctions involved in noninfallible teaching, but in the light of the purposes of the present discussion I have tried to show that the particular issues under discussion are removed from the central realities of Christian faith.

The Catholic tradition in moral theology has insisted that its moral teaching is based primarily on natural law and not primarily on faith or the Scripture. The natural law is understood to be human reason reflecting on human nature. Even those teachings which have some basis in Scripture (e.g., the indissolubility of marriage, homosexuality) were also said to be based on natural law. This insistence on the rational nature of Catholic moral teaching recognizes such teaching can and should be shared by all human beings of all faiths and of no faith. Such teachings are thus somewhat removed from the core of Catholic faith as such. The distance of these teachings from the core of faith and the central realities of faith grounds the possibility of legitimate dissent.

In addition, the issues under discussion are specific, concrete, universal moral norms existing in the midst of complex reality. Logic demands that the more specific and complex the reality, the less is the possibility of certitude. Moral norms, in my judgment, are not the primary, or the only, or the most important concern of moral teaching and of moral theology. Moral teaching deals with general perspectives, values, attitudes and dispositions as well as norms. Values, attitudes and dispositions are much more important and far-reaching for the moral life than are norms. These values and dispositions by their very nature are somewhat more general and can be more universally accepted as necessary for Christian and human life.

Within the church all can and should agree that the disciples of Jesus are called to be loving, faithful, hopeful, caring people who strive to live out the reality of the paschal mystery. Disrespect for persons, cheating, slavery, dishonesty and injustice are always wrong. However, the universal binding force of specific concrete material norms cannot enjoy the same degree or level of certitude. Norms exist to protect and promote values, but in practice conflicts often arise in the midst of the complexity and specificity involved. Thus the issues under consideration in this case are quite far removed from the core of faith and exist at such a level of complexity and specificity that one has to recognize some possibility of dissent.

It is also necessary to recognize the necessary distinction between the possibility of dissent and the legitimacy of dissent on particular questions. Reasons must be given which are convincing in order to justify the dissent in practice. The central issue involved in the controversy between the Congregation for the Doctrine of the Faith and myself is the possibility of public theological dissent from some noninfallible teaching which is quite remote from the core of faith, heavily dependent on support from human reason, and involved in such complexity and specificity that logically one cannot claim absolute certitude.

There is a further question which has not received much discussion from the Catholic theological community but which should at least be raised. We have generally talked about the responsibilities and rights of Catholic theologians in general. Are there any distinctions that must be made concerning theologians? Are the rights and responsibilities of Catholic theologians and the particular right to dissent in these areas the same for all Catholic theologians? Is there a difference between the theologian as teacher and as researcher and writer? Is there a difference if the theologian teaches in a seminary, a college or a university? In the particular cases under discussion, I would develop the thesis that these differences do not affect the possibility and legitimacy of public theological dissent. All of us can agree on the need to explore this question in much greater depth. In addition, more attention must be given to the limits of legitimate dissent.

THE CHRISTIAN FAITHFUL AND DISSENT

There is a third aspect or issue which has not received the attention it needs— the possibility and legitimacy of dissent on the part of the members of the church. In a very true sense my present controversy involves more than just the role of theologians in the church.

There can be no doubt that much of the friction between theologians and the hierarchical magisterium has occurred on more practical questions, including moral issues touching on sexuality. The issues are not just abstract questions about which people speculate, but they involve concrete decisions about specific actions which are to be done. Problems arise in these areas precisely because they involve more than speculation. Here the position proposed by theologians might have some practical bearing on how people live. All must recognize that the distinction between the roles of bishops and theologians would be much clearer if the role of theologians were restricted to the realm of speculation, with no effect on what people do in practice. However, life is not so easily compartmentalized.

Elsewhere I have defended the fact that on some issues a loyal Catholic may disagree in theory and in practice with the church's noninfallible teaching and still consider oneself a loyal and good Roman Catholic. In a sense, under certain conditions one can speak of a right of the Catholic faithful to dissent from certain noninfallible teachings. In the aftermath of *Humanae vitae* in 1968 some bishops conferences recognized that dissent in practice from the encyclical's teaching condemning artificial contraception could be legitimate and did not cut one off from the body of the faithful. The congregation, in its correspondence with me, has not gone into this issue. Those who deny the legitimacy of such dissent in practice would seem to face a difficult ecclesiological problem when confronted with the fact that the vast majority of fertile Catholic spouses use artificial contraception. What is the relationship of these spouses to the Roman Catholic Church?

The importance of recognizing this possibility and even right on the part of the faithful greatly affects how the theologian functions. If there is such a possibility, then the individual members of the Catholic Church have a right to know about it. I hasten to add that the individual members also have a right to know what is the official teaching of the church and should be conscious of the dangers of finitude and sin that can skew any human decision. Public dissent by a Catholic theologian would then be called for not only because theologians must discuss with one another in the attempt to understand better God's word and to arrive at truth, but also because the people of God need this information to make their own moral decisions. Thus, for example, in the light of the situation present at the time of the issuance of the encyclical *Humanae vitae* in 1968, it was important for Roman Catholic spouses to know that they did not have to make a choice between using artificial contraception under some conditions and ceasing to be members of the Roman Catholic Church. The Catholic theologian, among others, had an obligation to tell this to Catholic spouses.

The possibility for legitimate dissent in practice by the faithful also affects the matter of scandal. The U.S. bishops in their 1968 letter proposed three conditions under which public theological dissent is in order. One of these conditions is that the dissent be such as not to give scandal. In my correspondence with the congregation I repeatedly asked them for criteria which should govern public dissent in the church. No developed criteria were ever forthcoming. However, in the April 1983 observations from the congregation, it was mentioned briefly that to dissent publicly and to encourage dissent in others runs the risk of causing scandal.

Scandal in the strict sense is an action or omission which provides another the occasion of sinning. In the broad sense, scandal is the wonderment and confusion which are caused by a certain action or omission. Richard McCormick has already discussed the issue of scandal understood in the strict sense. What about scandal as the wonderment and confusion caused among the faithful by public theological dissent?

There can be no doubt that in the past there has been a strong tendency on the part of the hierarchical leaders of the church to look upon the faithful as poor and ignorant sheep who had to be protected and helped. This same vision and understanding of the ordinary common people also lay behind an older Catholic justification of monarchy and government from above. Catholic social teaching itself has changed in the twentieth century and accepted the need for and importance of democratic political institutions. No longer are the citizens the poor sheep or the "ignorant multitude," to use the phrase employed by Pope Leo XIII. So too the members of the church can no longer be considered as poor sheep; but greater importance must be given to their increased education and rights in all areas, including religion.

Perhaps at times theologians, who often associate with people who are well-educated, will fail to give enough importance to the danger of disturbing some of the faithful with their teachings. However, in this day and age it seems many more Catholic lay people would be scandalized if theologians were forbidden to discuss publicly important topics of the day such as contraception, divorce, abortion, and homosexuality. These issues are being discussed at great length and in all places today, and theologians must be able to enter into the discussion even to the point of dissenting from some official Catholic teaching. In addition, if the faithful can at times dissent in practice and remain loyal Roman Catholics, then they have the right to know what theologians are discussing.

In this entire discussion it would ultimately be erroneous to confine the question just to the possibility and right of theologians to dissent publicly from some noninfallible teachings. This present discussion is complicated by the fact that the dissent is not just speculative but is also practical. There is need for further development and nuancing, but on all the moral issues under consideration I have carefully tried to indicate what the legitimate possibilities are for the faithful in practice. The right of the faithful in this matter definitely colors one's approach to public theological dissent and to the dangers of scandal brought about by such dissent or the lack of it.

JUSTICE AND FAIRNESS OF THE PROCESS

Catholic theology has always emphasized the incarnational principle with its emphasis on visible human structures. Catholic ecclesiology well illustrates this approach by insisting on the church as a visible human community—the people of God with a hierarchical office. The visible church strives to be a sacrament or sign of the presence of God in the world, in and through this visible community.

Within the community there are bound to be tensions involving the role of bishops and the role of theologians. Both strive to work for the good of the church, but there will always be tensions. To claim there is no tension would be illusionary and ultimately would deny that the church is a living, pilgrim community. The church is always striving to know and live better the word and work of Jesus in the particular historical and cultural circumstances of time and place.

The role of the theologian by definition will often be that of probing and tentatively pushing the boundaries forward. The hierarchical teaching office must promote such creative and faithful theological activity, while at the same time it must rightly wait until these newer developments emerge more clearly. The church, in justice, must find ways to deal with this tension in the relationship between theologians and the hierarchical teaching office. The good of the church, the credibility of its teaching office and the need to protect the rights of all concerned call for just ways of dealing with these inevitable tensions.

The present case raises questions of justice and of the credibility of the teaching office in the church. It is recognized by all that there are many Catholic theologians who publicly dissent from some noninfallible teachings. Likewise there are many Catholic theologians who hold similar positions and even more radical positions on the moral issues involved in the present case. However, the issues of justice and credibility go much deeper.

First, it is necessary for the congregation to state its position on public theological dissent from noninfallible teaching. Is such dissent ever allowed? If so, under what conditions or criteria? From the correspondence, it would seem that the congregation is claiming that all public theological dissent is wrong or at least public dissent on these particular issues is wrong. Does the congregation truly hold such a position?

As mentioned earlier, the U.S. bishops in 1968, in the light of the controversy engendered by *Humanae vitae*, proposed three conditions for justifying public dissent from noninfallible teaching. The three conditions are: The reasons must be serious and well-founded; the manner of the dissent must not question or impugn the teaching authority of the church; and it must not give scandal. I have consistently maintained that my dissent has been in accord with these norms. The congregation was unwilling to accept these norms. Does the congregation disagree with the U.S. bishops and with the vast majority of Catholic theologians?

Archbishop John Quinn, then of Oklahoma City, at the Synod of Bishops in 1974 pointed out the real need to arrive at some consensus and understanding about dissent and urged discussion between representatives of the Holy See and representatives of theologians to arrive at acceptable guidelines governing theological dissent in the church (*Origins* 4, 1974–5, 319–20). Archbishop Quinn brought up the same problem again at the Synod of Bishops in 1980. For the good of the church there continues to be a "real need" to arrive at some guidelines in this area.

In addition, there is need for juridical structures which better safeguard justice and the rights of all concerned. Some of the problems with the present procedures of the congregation have already been pointed out in the correspondence. The congregation, in a letter to me, has defended its procedures because the *ratio agendi* is not a trial, but rather a procedure designed to generate a careful and accurate examination of the contents of published writings by the author. However, since the process can result in severe punishment for the person involved, it seems that such a process should incorporate the contemporary standards of justice found in other juridical proceedings.

One set of problems stems from the fact that the congregation is the prosecutor, the judge and jury. Some people have objected strongly to the fact that the cardinal-prefect has commented publicly on the present case and disagreed in the public media with my position while the case has been in progress. Problems have also been raised against the existing procedures from the viewpoints of the secrecy of the first part of the process, the failure to allow the one being investigated to have counsel, the failure to disclose the accusers and the total record to the accused, and the lack of any substantive appeal process (Granfield, 131f).

There have been many suggestions made for improvements in the procedures. The German bishops have adopted procedures for use in Germany. Cardinal Ratzinger in 1984 admitted that there has been a decree of the plenary session of the congregation in favor of a revision of the current procedures of the congregation.

The proposals made by the German conference of bishops have been accepted in principle. However, because of the workload and time constraints, the decree has not been put into effect (*National Catholic Reporter*, August 12, 1984, p. 6).

In 1980 a joint committee of the Catholic Theological Society of America and the Canon Law Society of America was formed to address the question of cooperation between theologians and the hierarchical magisterium in the United States, with a view toward developing norms that could be used in settling disputes. The committee prepared a detailed set of procedures in 1983, but they are still under study by the U.S. bishops.

In the meantime there has been one case involving the investigation of a theologian's writings by the doctrinal committee of the U.S. bishops. Little is known about the process itself, but the final statement from the committee indicates that the dialogue was fruitful and that the theologian in question, Richard McBrien, had the right to call other theologians to defend and explain his positions. Perhaps the process used in this case might prove helpful in other similar cases. A detailed discussion of proposed guidelines lies beyond the scope of this present paper.

The major points made here are that justice and the credibility of the church's teaching office call for a recognition of the norms or criteria governing public dissent in the church, the equitable application of these norms and the review of existing procedures to incorporate the safeguards of contemporary justice in the process of examining theologians. The call for these changes has been repeatedly made in the past. The need is even more urgent today.

ACADEMIC FREEDOM, THEOLOGY, AND
CATHOLIC INSTITUTIONS

Catholic higher education in the United States well illustrates the tension between being Catholic and being American which has challenged Catholic life and institutions in our country. In this particular case the pertinent question was often phrased in the following terms: Is a Catholic university a contradiction in terms? Colleges and universities in the United States have stressed the importance of institutional autonomy and academic freedom as two essential characteristics of what constitutes a college or university.

Until 1960 most Catholic institutions of higher learning emphasized their uniqueness and either implicitly or explicitly denied the need for academic freedom and institutional autonomy. However, as the sixties progressed there was a growing acceptance of the need for these characteristics. By the end of the 1960s the major Catholic institutions of the United States had expressed a strong commitment to a true autonomy and academic freedom in the face of authority of whatever kind, lay or clerical, external to the academic community itself.

Many reasons help explain this change—a greater Catholic interest in higher education at that time; the influx of people from secular universities into Catholic academe; the growing recognition of the greater compatibility between Catholicism and American institutions; the recognition of the meager Catholic contribution to intellectual life in this country; a theoretical and practical appreciation of the role of the laity in higher education; a greater acceptance of professionalization in all aspects and departments of Catholic institutions of higher learning, including theology and religion departments.

Today the leaders of Catholic higher education in the United States strongly insist on the need for academic freedom and institutional autonomy. The crux of the problem is to reconcile the existence of academic freedom and institutional autonomy with the truth claims made by the Catholic Church and its hierarchical teaching office. More specifically, the question is, Can and should Catholic theology be responsibly taught and researched in the context of academic freedom and institutional autonomy?

From the viewpoint of the American academy, there is a greater awareness today of the bankruptcy of an older insistence on being value free or value neutral. Values should be very important in all the human disciplines. Thus there is in general a greater openness in American academe today to accept the academic respectability of disciplines like theology. However, the question is, Can Catholic theology accept the American concept of academic freedom? There has not been as much discussion in this area as there should be.

I will briefly describe how I think academic freedom and Catholic theology are compatible. Academic freedom and institutional autonomy mean that any decision affecting promotion, hiring, or dismissal of faculty members must be made by peers in the academy and not by outside persons or forces of any kind. Academic freedom respects the freedom of the scholar to pursue truth with no limits placed on scholarship other than honesty and competency. The accepted principles of academic freedom recognize that even tenured faculty members can be terminated if they are incompetent and the judgment of incompetency is made by academic peers.

Competency for the Catholic theologian demands that one theologize within the pale of the Roman Catholic faith. The Catholic theologian must teach Catholic theology as such; otherwise one is incompetent as a Catholic theologian. Peers in judging the competency of a Catholic theologian must give due weight to the teaching of the hierarchical magisterium. However, the ultimate decision with juridical effects must be made by peers in the academy. The hierarchical magisterium is always free if it deems it necessary to point out the errors and ambiguities in the work of a theologian, but it cannot make decisions having direct juridical effect in the academy.

There is no doubt that academic freedom gives some added protection to the rights of the Catholic theological scholar. However, in my judgment, such protection is totally compatible with the understanding of the role of the Catholic theologian as somewhat cooperative with and somewhat independent of the role of the hierarchical teaching office. Such protection is not only good for the discipline of Catholic theology, but also is good for the total church as it strives for creative fidelity to the word and work of Jesus. In this way I maintain one can do justice both to the demands of the academy and to the demands of Catholic theology and the good of the Catholic Church.

The academic freedom of Catholic institutions and of Catholic theology is an important theoretical question with many practical consequences. I think that the issue has to be settled on grounds of good theory, but one cannot ignore the practical consequences. Perhaps the most significant practical consequence at the present time concerns the financial threat to the very existence of Catholic higher education in the United States.

Catholic colleges and universities receive a large amount of financial help in different forms from the public monies of the state. In the past the Supreme Court has ruled such public funding is acceptable for Catholic higher education but not for Catholic elementary and high schools. The difference between higher and lower education is that in higher education there is no indoctrination and the principles of academic freedom are observed. Thus, if there were no academic freedom and institutional autonomy for Catholic higher education, it might very well be that the court would rule that public funding for Catholic institutions of higher learning is unconstitutional. There are many complex and intricate questions that need to be discussed, but the general outline of this possible outcome is clear. The leaders of Catholic higher education are quite aware of and worried by these implications.

If the Vatican congregation or any ecclesiastical authority can declare someone no longer a Catholic theologian and unable to teach in the name of the church, and thereby prevent that professor from continuing to teach Catholic theology in a Catholic institution, this seems to be a violation of academic freedom. However, in the present context, some maintain that this is the case only for a very few ecclesiastical faculties or universities such as The Catholic University of America, but it does not apply to the vast majority of American Catholic colleges and universities which are not chartered by the Vatican.

Yes, there is some difference between Vatican-chartered ecclesiastical faculties or institutions and the vast majority of Catholic colleges and universities in the United States. However, in the light of the new Code of Canon Law with its Canon 812, the same problems about academic freedom exist for all Catholic institutions of higher learning. According to Canon 812, teachers of theological disciplines need a mandate from a competent ecclesiastical authority. Thus the decisions of ecclesiastical authority can have a direct effect in the hiring, promotion and dismissal of faculty members.

The proposed schema for Catholic colleges and universities now being circulated by the Congregation for Catholic Education enshrines and develops the same basic structural understanding. Catholic leaders of higher education in the United States have strongly disagreed with the new Canon 812 and with the proposed new schema for Catholic higher education. Such legislation and proposed legislation are seen as threats to the academic freedom and institutional autonomy of Catholic higher education in the United States. I insist that the question of the academic freedom and institutional autonomy respecting Catholic higher education and Catholic theology should not ultimately be decided because of practical consequences for Catholic higher education; but, on the other hand, one cannot ignore these possible consequences.

In conclusion, this paper has examined what I think are the five most significant issues involved in my present dispute with the Congregation for the Doctrine of the Faith—the role of the Catholic theologian, the possibility of public theological dissent from some noninfallible hierarchical teaching, the possibility of dissent by the faithful in such cases, some practical aspects and academic freedom. In discussing all these issues I have also indicated my approach to the questions under discussion. I welcome your reactions.

Catholics and Abortion: Authority vs. Dissent

Rosemary Radford Ruether

On October 4, 1984, a paid advertisement appeared in the *New York Times* under the sponsorship of a group called Catholics for a Free Choice. The ad contended that there is more than one legitimate—i.e., theologically and ethically defensible—viewpoint on abortion within the Roman Catholic tradition. It called for a dialogue on abortion among Catholics—a dialogue that would acknowledge this situation of pluralism, not only in regard to practice (Catholics have about the same proportion of abortions as Protestants in the United States), but in regard to the ethical state of the question. This ad explicitly asked for the cessation of institutional sanctions against those with dissenting positions on abortion:

> Catholics—especially priests, religious, theologians and legislators, who publically dissent from hierarchical statements and explore areas of moral and legal freedom on the abortion question—should not be penalized by their religious superiors, church employers or bishops.

The ad was published in the specific context of the presidential campaign, in which a Catholic candidate for vice-president, Geraldine Ferraro, was being characterized by Cardinal John O'Connor of New York as a politician for whom Catholics could not vote because of her mildly prochoice position on abortion. Thus, while the ad's basic ideas had been circulating among Catholic theologians and ethicists for more than a year, those ideas were made public in this particular manner in order to defend Catholic legislators' right of public dissent on abortion.

In the months following the ad's appearance, however, its admonition that dissenters should not be penalized has not been heeded. Threats and penalties have rained thick and fast upon priests, religious, and theologians from religious superiors, church employers, and bishops. But the chief initiative in this repression has come from a source beyond that envisioned by the writers of the ad—namely, the Vatican.

In early December 1984 there arrived in the mailboxes of the religious superiors or bishops of the four priests and brothers and most of the twenty-four nuns who signed the statement a letter from Cardinal Jean Jerome Hamer, O.P., head of the Vatican's Sacred Congregation for Religious and Secular Institutes. Dated November 30, 1984, this letter stated that the position taken in the *New York Times* advertisement was "in contradiction to the teachings of the Church" and that the ad's signers were "seriously lacking in religious submission to the mind of the Magisterium." Pointing out that the revised code of canon law declares that anyone who procures an abortion incurs automatic excommunication, the letter then directed the superiors of each of the nuns, brothers, and priests to demand that the signer under their supervision make a public retraction. Any signer who declined to make such a retraction was to be warned by the superior with an explicit threat of dismissal from his or her religious community.

The two priests and the two brothers quickly made *pro forma* statements of retraction and got the Vatican "off their case." None of the nuns who signed was willing to do so since, for them, such a retraction represented a serious violation of their moral conscience. It would also have violated the basic principles of their relationship with their religious orders, which in their view are not simply a part of a military-type hierarchy that could be ordered about from the "top." Since most of the women superiors of the thirteen religious orders involved were not prepared to deal with this issue, an organizational meeting was quickly set up to allow the nun-signers, their lay fellow signers, and the religious superiors to sort out the issues together and create a collective strategy.

For a while, in the early months of 1985, it appeared that the collective strategy the women devised had thrown the Vatican off course. Vatican officials had assumed that each woman would be forced to conform or would be dismissed individually. When the nun-signers, through their religious superiors, indicated that they would not retract the *New York Times* statement nor would the superiors threaten them with dismissal, the Scared Congregation appeared to back off; it asked only that the nuns affirm their support for the "teaching authority of the Church"—a statement that might be construed in several ways. But by March it was made clear that this request meant that the twenty-four should affirm the church's teaching authority on abortion—i.e., the monolithic nature of the present official position. To date, none of the nuns has either fully complied with this request or been dismissed from her order. But the Vatican clearly is not pleased with this insubordination, and new efforts to gain compliance or dismissal will doubtless be forthcoming.

By January of 1985 it was evident that reprisals against the lay signers were beginning as well—particularly against Daniel Maguire, professor of ethics at Marquette University, the male signer most generally regarded as holding something close to official status as a Catholic theologian. Although Marquette itself refused to bow to pressure from Catholic conservatives to censure or fire Dr. Maguire, he began to receive cancellations of long-standing teaching and speaking engagements from other Catholic colleges. St. Martin's College in Lacey, Washington; St. Scholastica in Duluth, Minnesota; Villanova University in Pennsylvania; and, finally, Boston College canceled speaking or teaching contracts. Maguire had clearly become *persona non grata* on the Catholic lecture circuit. The exact source of these reprisals is unclear, but apparently they were not the result of direct orders from bishops or the Vatican; rather they came from college presidents engaging in self-censure out of fear of picketers from the "prolife" movement.

This repression of academic freedom at Catholic universities was taken seriously enough by the American Association of University Professors for it to agree to intervene in the case. The association has asked all four universities to reinvite Dr. Maguire, citing AAUP guidelines on academic freedom. At least one ad signer, well-known Catholic novelist Mary Gordon (*The Company of Women* and *Final Payments*), has declined an invitation to speak at Boston College until it complies with the AAUP request.

In addition to the reprisals against Maguire, four lay female academics at Catholic universities have been asked by their bishop to meet with him or his representative to discuss "doctrinal matters." In each case it was stated that this request originated with the Vatican. The Thomas More Society in San Diego had scheduled a speech by Jane Via, one of these academics, but later canceled—by order, she was told, of the bishop in San Diego, acting in response to instructions from Rome to silence her. Via was also told that she would not be able to speak at any public Catholic forum in the diocese until she retracted the statement.

Kathleen O'Connor, a lay signer and professor at the Maryknoll School of Theology, was asked to speak with the college's president in response to a request from New York's Cardinal O'Connor. In clarifying her position, Dr. O'Connor stated that although she personally condemns abortion, she believes the greater harm would result from its legal prohibition. So far this clarification appears to have satisfied the president and the cardinal. Mary Buckley, a tenured professor of theology at St. John's University, was asked to meet with Bishop Francis J. Mugavero of Brooklyn, along with the president of the university and the chair of the theology department. She declined to do so unless she could have a legal counsel present, and the meeting was postponed until fall. A fourth female academic, who prefers to remain anonymous, also was told to meet with her bishop. She refused to do so unless the meeting's agenda was disclosed. To date, no further action has been taken against her by the bishop or the university.

Several other scholars have received notices canceling jobs or speaking engagements under suspicious circumstances in which the signing of the *New York Times* ad was not specifically cited as the cause. But many signers, such as Elisabeth Schüssler Fiorenza, have simply experienced the "drying up" of speaking engagements from Catholic sources. Since the situation has moved quickly from one marked by cancellations to one in which no initial invitations are extended, it becomes difficult to trace the trail of reprisals against the signers.

These incidents have led the signers and their supporters to redirect their attention from the question of pluralism on abortion to the right of dissent itself. A network calling itself the Committee of Concerned Catholics is gathering signatures for a new ad which will appear in the *New York Times* sometime in October [1985] to mark the one-year anniversary of the previous ad. The new ad will repeat the first one's statement on pluralism in regard to abortion, adding to it a statement of solidarity with the original signers and a defense of the right to dissent. The statement of solidarity reads:

> Such reprisals consciously or unconsciously have a chilling effect on the right to responsible dissent within the church; on academic freedom in Catholic colleges and universities; and on the right to free speech and participation in the U.S. political process.
>
> Such reprisals cannot be condoned or tolerated in church or society.
>
> We believe that Catholics who, in good conscience, take positions on the difficult questions of legal abortion and other controversial issues that differ from the official hierarchical positions, act within their rights and responsibilities as Catholics and citizens.
>
> We, as Roman Catholics, affirm our solidarity with those who signed the Statement and agree to stand with all who face reprisals. We shall become the dismissed, the disinvited and the unwelcome. "The ties which unite the faithful are stronger than those which separate them. Let there be unity in what is necessary, freedom in what is doubtful and charity in everything" (Declaration on the Church in the Modern World, no. 92).

The solidarity statement thus takes its text from the defense of religious freedom affirmed at the Second Vatican Council. By seeking additional signers for such a statement, the "concerned Catholics" wish both to widen the support and to diffuse the targets of the Vatican and the bishops. To most Catholics it is less acceptable to censure those who defend the right to dissent than it is to censure those who appear to reject the official position on abortion. American Catholics are Americans culturally, and for them religious and academic freedom is part of the nation's constitutional tradition. With a large increase in the number of dissenters—including, doubtless, many nuns—it becomes harder for the Vatican to take action against them in a consistent fashion.

There are rumors, however, that the upcoming synod in Rome in November [1985] will be the staging ground for a broad reassertion of centralized ecclesiastical power. The synod is viewed by many as having been called by the pope in order to rescind Vatican II, while ostensibly "affirming and clarifying" its principles.

Dissent on reproductive rights will be only one of many targets in the reassertion of conservative authority. Respected Catholic journalist Peter Hebblethwaite, who regularly reports on Vatican affairs for several major magazines in both the United States and Great Britain, wrote in the August 16 [1985] issue of the *National Catholic Reporter* (p. 27) that the pope intends to declare the ban on artificial contraception, which was reaffirmed by Paul VI in 1968, to be "infallible."

Such a declaration would certainly "up the ante" on dissent; it would also make clear that the official Catholic rejection of abortion continues to be based on a rationale that rejects artificial contraception as well. Since the most effective way to avoid abortion would be to promote contraception, this double ban indicates that the real battle is not over the lives of fetuses or their mothers, but over the rights of women to be moral agents in the reproductive capacities of their own bodies. The ban on contraception means that the Catholic Church is willing, in practice, to see fetuses and their mothers die for the sake of the principle that women should submit to "nature" and "God" in matters of reproduction.

A declaration that the ban on artificial contraception is "infallible" was specifically ruled out by Paul VI when he issued *Humanae vitae.* Paul VI, it should be remembered, reasserted the ban after the Papal Commission on Birth Control had arrived at a majority position upholding the moral acceptability of artificial birth control. Thus Paul VI was aware that the ban not only did not reflect the "sense of the faithful," but also did not reflect the view of the majority of his own experts.

Catholics have not grown any more docile concerning the reasserted ban on contraception in the years since 1968. Rather, it is generally recognized that this particular law is disregarded by the vast majority of Catholics who continue to practice their faith. An effort to declare the ban on contraception "infallible" would have the immediate effect of focusing Catholic dissent on the doctrine of infallibility itself. Such an effect of the birth-control ban was anticipated by Hans Küng in his book *Infallible? An Inquiry* (original German edition, 1970), written after the publication of *Humanae vitae.* For Küng, the pope's declaration that the ban on contraception was still binding, in opposition to the majority vote of his own birth-control commission, indicated that infallibility itself was the major block to church reform. In effect, the Catholic Church could not officially admit that any teaching asserted for some period of time in the past was wrong, or in need of change, as long as it could not admit that it could err.

Hans Küng suffered the loss of his official status as a Roman Catholic theologian (his *missio canonica*) as a consequence of having raised the issue of infallibility in his 1970 book. Most Catholic theologians declined to join him in his challenge to the doctrine of infallibility, deciding that it was better to ignore infallibility than to confront it head on. But any effort to declare "infallibility" a teaching rejected by the majority of both practicing Catholics and Catholic ethicists—such as the ban on birth control—would make a confrontation inevitable.

It seems likely that the Vatican conservatives and Pope John Paul II himself are seriously out of touch with the mood of the global church on the birth-control issue, as well as on the wider question of the credibility of official church teaching authority. They do not seem to understand that a storm of dissent, and even ridicule, directed at infallibility itself would ensue from such a declaration. They seem to imagine that they face problems with a noisy handful of "insubordinates" who can be put down by methods used in earlier generations, while the "majority of the faithful" submissively look upward to the "Holy Father" for signals as to what to think and do.

Above all, John Paul II and his associates, such as Cardinal Hamer of the Sacred Congregation for Religious and Secular Institutes and Cardinal Ratzinger of the Congregation for the Doctrine of the Faith (formerly the Inquisition), seek to reassert centralized, unilateral authority, which they regard as essential to any order of authority in the church. They reject, in principle, the possibility of a pluralistic church in which the right to dissent on important matters of ethics or doctrine is respected. For them, "truth" is single, unitary, and definable. There is one teaching authority, the pope, who both originates and finalizes such "truth," without having to listen to or be corrected by other sources of insight such as the *sensus fideli* (the actual beliefs and practices of the people) and the scholarly reflections of biblical exegetes and theologians.

Church councils also are seen as rubber stamps for papal policy, not as autonomous sources of teaching authority that gather up the wisdom of the global church. This papal absolutism contradicts much in the historical Catholic tradition that defends these more pluralistic sources of truth that engage in dialogue and make official definitions only when a broad consensus has been established on a particular issue. The Second Vatican Council, simply by being a church council, represented a reassertion of this more pluralistic approach to teaching authority, over against the papal absolutism of Vatican I. Thus, if the Vatican conservatives intend to rescind Vatican II at the November synod, they will be endeavoring to bury the conciliar tradition itself once again, as an alternative source of teaching authority which can check and balance papal power.

It is almost certain, however, that the "toothpaste cannot be put back into the tube," as one nun expressed the question of getting American nuns back into habits. The same slogan can apply to the efforts to get Catholics in America, and throughout the world, back into the habit of unquestioning obedience to authority, once they have gotten used to thinking that they too are the church. Ironically, the effort to make "truth" unitary and absolute, as a way of strengthening acquiescence to church teaching authority, has exactly the opposite effect. It means that the credibility of all church teaching is made to stand or fall as a whole. If the church can be wrong on birth control, it can be wrong on anything. If uncertainty exists about something which the church has taught with its full authority, then anything it teaches with its full authority may be wrong.

Catholics are thrown willy-nilly into deciding for themselves which parts of the Christian tradition are meaningful and which are not, with little guidance from bishops, priests, and theologians. Thus Vatican absolutism promotes the very chaos which it most fears. There is no way back to the absolutism of the past. There is only a painful way forward to a church in which people try to listen to and respect differing opinions and to work, through a combination of experience and tradition, to develop teachings that have authority because they are credible to most Christians.

The United Library
Garrett-Evangelical/Seabury-Western Seminaries
2121 Sheridan Road
Evanston, IL 60201

Sources and Acknowledgments

Archbishop John R. Roach and Cardinal Terence Cooke, "Testimony in Support of the Hatch Amendment." Originally published in *Origins* 11 (November 19, 1981) 357–72. Reprinted with permission of Archbishop Roach.

Thomas J. O'Donnell, "A Traditional Catholic's View." Originally published in *Abortion in a Changing World,* edited by Robert E. Hall (New York: Columbia University Press, 1970). Copyright © 1970 Columbia University Press. Reprinted with permission of the author and the publisher.

Joseph F. Donceel, "A Liberal Catholic's View." Originally published in *Abortion in a Changing World,* edited by Robert E. Hall (New York: Columbia University Press, 1970). Copyright © 1970 Columbia University Press. Reprinted with permission of the author and the publisher.

Carol A. Tauer, "The Tradition of Probabilism and the Moral Status of the Early Embryo." Originally published in *Theological Studies* 45 (March 1984) 3–33. Reprinted with permission of the author and the publisher.

Lisa Sowle Cahill, "Abortion, Autonomy, and Community." Originally published in *Abortion: Understanding Differences,* edited by Sidney Callahan and Daniel Callahan (New York: Plenum Press, 1984). Reprinted with permission of the author and Plenum Publishing Corporation.

Marjorie Reiley Maguire, "Personhood, Covenant, and Abortion." Originally published in the 1983 volume of *The Annual of the Society of Christian Ethics.* Copyright 1983 The Society of Christian Ethics. Reprinted with permission of the author and the publisher.

Madonna Kolbenschlag, "Abortion and Moral Consensus: Beyond Solomon's Choice." Originally published in *The Christian Century* 102 (February 20, 1985) 179–83. Copyright 1985 The Christian Century Foundation. Reprinted with permission of the author and the publisher.

Sidney Callahan, "Abortion and the Sexual Agenda: A Case for Pro-Life Feminism." Originally published in *Commonweal* 123 (April 25, 1986) 232–38. Reprinted with permission of the author and the publisher.

Patricia Beattie Jung, "Abortion and Organ Donation: Christian Reflections on Bodily Life Support." Forthcoming in *The Journal of Religious Ethics*. Reprinted with permission of the author and the publisher.

Thomas A. Shannon, "Abortion: A Challenge for Ethics and Public Policy." Originally published in the 1982 volume of *The Annual of the Society of Christian Ethics*. Copyright 1982 The Society of Christian Ethics. Reprinted with permission of the author and the publisher. Parts of this work originally appeared in *Abortion and the Status of the Fetus*, edited by W. B. Bondeson and others (Boston: D. Reidel Publishing Company, 1983), and are reprinted with permission of the author and the publisher.

Mario Cuomo, "Religious Belief and Public Morality: A Catholic Governor's Perspective." Address delivered at the University of Notre Dame, September 13, 1984. Reprinted with permission of the author.

Joan C. Callahan, "The Fetus and Fundamental Rights." Originally published in *Commonweal* 123 (April 11, 1986) 203–9. Reprinted with permission of the author and the publisher.

Harry J. Byrne, "Thou Shalt Not Speak." Originally published in *America* 155 (December 6, 1986) 356–59. Reprinted with permission of the author and America Press, Inc., 106 West 56th Street, New York, NY 10019. © 1986. All rights reserved.

Cardinal John O'Connor, "From Theory to Practice in the Public-Policy Realm." Originally published in *Origins* 16 (June 19, 1986) 107–12. Reprinted with permission of the author.

Daniel A. Degnan, "Prudence, Politics, and the Abortion Issue." Originally published in *America* 152 (February 16, 1985) 121–24. Reprinted with permission of the author and America Press, Inc., 106 West 56th Street, New York, NY 10019. © 1985. All rights reserved.

Cardinal Joseph Bernardin, "The Consistent Ethic: What Sort of Framework?" Originally published in *Origins* 16 (October 30, 1986) 345, 347–50. Reprinted with permission of the author.

Margaret O'Brien Steinfels, "Consider the Seamless Garment." Originally published in *Christianity and Crisis* 43 (May 14, 1984) 172–74. Reprinted with permission. Copyright May 14, 1984, Christianity and Crisis, 537 West 121st Street, New York, NY 10027.

John R. Connery, "A Seamless Garment in a Sinful World." Originally published in *America* 153 (July 14, 1984) 5–8. Reprinted with permission of the author and America Press, Inc., 106 West 56th Street, New York, NY 10019. © 1984. All rights reserved.

Christine E. Gudorf, "To Make a Seamless Garment, Use a Single Piece of Cloth." Originally published in *Cross Currents* 34 (Winter 1984) 473–91. Reprinted with permission of the author and the publisher.

Cardinal Joseph Ratzinger, "Bishops, Theologians, and Morality." Originally published in *Origins* 13 (March 15, 1984) 665–66. Reprinted with permission of the President, University of St. Michael's College, Toronto, Ontario.

Charles Curran, "Public Dissent in the Church." Originally published in *Origins* 16 (July 31, 1986) 178–84. Reprinted with permission of the author.

Rosemary Radford Ruether, "Catholics and Abortion: Authority vs. Dissent." Originally published in *The Christian Century* 102 (October 2, 1985) 859–62. Copyright 1987 The Christian Century Foundation. Reprinted with permission of the author and the publisher.

The United Library
Garrett-Evangelical/Seabury-Western Seminaries
2121 Sheridan Road
Evanston, IL 60201

Contributors

Cardinal Joseph Bernardin is the Archbishop of the Archdiocese of Chicago.

Msgr. Harry J. Byrne, J.C.D., is pastor of Epiphany Parish in New York City.

Lisa Sowle Cahill is Associate Professor of Christian Ethics in the Department of Theology at Boston College.

Joan C. Callahan is in the Department of Philosophy at the University of Kentucky in Lexington.

Sidney Callahan is Associate Professor of Psychology at Mercy College, Dobbs Ferry, New York.

John R. Connery, S.J. was Emeritus Professor of Moral Theology at Loyola University in Chicago.

Cardinal Terence Cooke was Archbishop of the Archdiocese of New York from 1968 to 1983.

Mario Cuomo is the Governor of New York State.

Charles Curran is Professor of Moral Theology in the Department of Theology at the Catholic University of America.

Daniel A. Degnan, S.J. is at the School of Law at Seton Hall University in Newark, New Jersey.

Joseph F. Donceel, S.J. is Emeritus Professor of Philosophy at Fordham University in New York City.

Christine E. Gudorf is in the Department of Theology at Xavier University in Cincinnati, Ohio.

Patricia Beattie Jung is Visiting Assistant Professor of Social Ethics at Wartburg Theological Seminary in Dubuque, Iowa.

Madonna Kolbenschlag, from Washington, D.C., is an author and lecturer on women's development, spirituality, public policy, and religious affairs.

Marjorie Reiley Maguire has taught ethics and is currently a law student at the University of Wisconsin.

Cardinal John J. O'Connor is the Archbishop of the Archdiocese of New York.

Thomas J. O'Donnell, S.J. is rector of the Lincoln Diocesan Seminary and director of Good Counsel Retreat House in Waverly, Nebraska.

Anne E. Patrick is Chair of the Religion Department of Carleton College in Northfield, Minnesota.

Cardinal Joseph Ratzinger is the Cardinal Prefect for the Congregation for the Doctrine of the Faith.

Archbishop John R. Roach is the Archbishop of the Archdiocese of St. Paul, Minnesota.

Rosemary Radford Ruether is the Georgia Harkness Professor of Applied Theology at Garrett Evangelical Seminary in Evanston, Illinois.

Thomas A. Shannon is Professor of Religion and Social Ethics in the Department of Humanities at Worcester Polytechnic Institute, Worcester, Massachusetts.

Margaret O'Brien Steinfels is editor of *Commonweal*.

Carol A. Tauer is a Professor of Philosophy in the Department of Philosophy at St. Catherine's College in St. Paul, Minnesota.